Innovations in Social Work Research

Part of the Research Highlights in Social Work series

Innovations in
SOCIAL WORK
RESEARCH

Using Methods Creatively

Edited by
LOUISE HARDWICK,
ROGER SMITH AND
AIDAN WORSLEY

Jessica Kingsley *Publishers*
London and Philadelphia

First published in 2016
by Jessica Kingsley Publishers
73 Collier Street
London N1 9BE, UK
and
400 Market Street, Suite 400
Philadelphia, PA 19106, USA

www.jkp.com

Library of Congress Cataloging in Publication Data
Innovations in social work research / edited by Louise
Hardwick, Roger Smith and Aidan Worsley.
     pages cm
 Includes bibliographical references.
 ISBN 978-1-84905-585-7 (alk. paper)
 1. Social service--Research. I. Hardwick, Louise. II. Smith,
Roger S. (Roger Shipley), 1953- III. Worsley,
Aidan.
 HV11.I466 2016
 361.3072--dc23
                                        2015009110

British Library Cataloguing in Publication Data
A CIP catalogue record for this book is available from the British Library

ISBN 978 1 84905 585 7
eISBN 978 1 78450145 7

Printed and bound in Great Britain

MIX
Paper from
responsible sources
FSC
www.fsc.org   FSC® C013056

LC: To C, my constant

RS: To Maggie, as ever

AW: To Lesley, for her love, support and guidance

Contents

SECTION 2: INNOVATIONS IN RESEARCH METHODS

SECTION 3: INNOVATIONS IN DATA ANALYSIS

SECTION 4: INNOVATIONS IN DISSEMINATION AND IMPACT

INTRODUCTION

ROGER SMITH
Durham University

The origins of this book are twofold, really. First, it has its roots in pure
coincidence in that the editors were separately responsible for producing
two books with the same name ('Doing Social Work Research') at
almost exactly the same time. Rather than get into the same situation
again, we decided it was better to collaborate this time round!

More significantly though, our common experience in writing
those previous books led us to conclude that research in social work
is an area of activity that demonstrates much enterprise, creativity and
rigour, which is not always recognised or properly documented. We
also believe that there is much to be learnt from sharing examples of the
work going on, which in turn can inform further high-quality research
in future.

Like social work itself, research in the field has perhaps sometimes
been viewed as rather derivative, drawing extensively on the insights
and techniques of other disciplines, whilst contributing little that is
original and distinctive. And yet, just as is the case with practice, what
we have found in our own exploration of the terrain is a very different
picture. For very good reason, social work researchers almost inevitably
approach their subject matter with a particular orientation, that is based
on a commitment to understanding – and improving – what happens
in the practice setting. This in turn leads to what we see as a unique
and valuable perspective on the design and implementation of empirical
inquiry.

We would suggest that the underlying factors that inform and
inspire social work research include: a primary focus on 'problematic/
problematised' areas of human activity; the expectation of being
closely engaged with practice; a value-based concern to foreground

the perspective and interests of service users; and arising from these, a consequent need to develop original and creative investigative strategies.

It has to be acknowledged that social work research does draw extensively on more established traditions of inquiry, such as those conventionally associated with sociology and psychology; and indeed, this is entirely justified for a discipline whose sphere of interest is by definition the interface between the individual and the social, and the problems associated with it. Thus, research in and on social work relies to a great extent on well-established and predominantly qualitative techniques, in many cases relying very heavily on the (semi-structured) interview as the primary data source. In some instances, though, concerns have been expressed that social work has not always availed itself of these traditional methodologies to the extent that it might, as in the case of randomised controlled trials, for example, which have sometimes been viewed as both impractical and unethical (Dixon *et al.*, 2014). In both cases, though, the risk is that implicit assumptions, or established norms, may set unhelpful limits to what is considered appropriate and effective.

Significantly, our own previous work has identified for us a number of important additional considerations that should apply (Smith, 2009; Hardwick and Worsley, 2010). First, we need to be sure that the techniques we use are attuned to the domain in which they are applied – in other words that they are fit for purpose. Second, following on from this, it is also important to consider whether or not researchers have become unduly constrained by their reliance on established approaches. And, third, we should perhaps consider whether the field of social work itself actually necessitates creative and original approaches to the formulation and delivery of research relevant to this domain of practice (we think it does). Not least among the implications of this point is that we should not be constrained, either in our approaches to research in this area, or in our understandings of what constitutes social work practice by unduly narrow formulations, which might be based on conventional assumptions, professional boundaries or organisational prescriptions.

In drawing together the contributions that make up this book, we have tried to follow the logic suggested by these questions, and our answers to them, and we have sought to identify and 'showcase' a series of examples of creative thinking, where social work researchers have initiated or adapted modes of inquiry that are both distinctive and productive and span a wide variety of 'social work' practice settings and strategies.

We would argue that social work research is not only demonstrating a very healthy degree of originality in this respect, but that it is also taking the lead in illustrating the value and contribution of some of the methods exemplified here – in user-led participatory inquiry, in ethical approaches to experimental design and in developing effective 'practice-near' methodologies, for instance. In presenting the examples in this collection, we are hoping not just to substantiate this claim, but also to offer a series of insights for those currently engaged in, or intending to undertake, research in this particular field of inquiry, and who may therefore gain useful knowledge to support their own further social work research. This collection is, therefore, intentionally (and proudly) eclectic – our concern is to feature high-quality, value-led initiatives in social work research, rather than to engage in what is by now a rather sterile debate about which type of method stands in which place in an assumed methodological 'hierarchy'.

Turning to the substantive content of the book itself, the aim is to provide a series of informative accounts of original research, highlighting in particular the methodological strategies adopted that we believe to be of value because of their innovative qualities. In taking this approach, we have structured the book to try and capture the different phases of research, from its original planning and design, through implementation and analysis to the point that is of increasing interest, especially in an applied discipline such as social work, and that is the dissemination and 'impact' phase, where robust and high-quality research is quite properly promoted and its findings put to use.

The aim is both to capture the natural flow of the research process and to provide sufficient detail of its different aspects to inform and support those who may be intending to carry out their own investigations, at whatever stage of their research careers. So, it is both a 'look at this' and a 'how to do it' book, and we anticipate that it will be of genuine interest to those approaching its contents from either of these starting points.

The book is organised in four sections, each more or less representing a specific aspect of the research process as it progresses from conception to completion, although any claims we might make to precision of design must be modified in light of the observation that a number of chapters could legitimately appear in more than one part! And at the same time, the eclectic nature of the collection also means that it does not always 'flow' in the way that might be expected of a conventionally authored book. The first part, therefore, introduces a range of perspectives on the orientation, preparation and planning of social work research, with rather different emphases and methodological underpinnings. They do, nonetheless, share common ground to the extent that they are informed by a common concern to approach research from an explicit (social work) value base and to take this actively into consideration in approaching the task of project design and development.

The second part of the book shifts the focus to the implementation phase of research and includes a number of chapters that identify both the inherent challenges and the rich rewards available to social work researchers who adopt investigative strategies deriving from a wider array of promising and quite exciting contemporary innovations in social research methods, notably in this case including chapters on both visual and mobile methods and their particular relevance to social work practice. We can see from these chapters how these methods can potentially make a major contribution to our understanding when applied in social work settings, but also how social work research itself can rake a leading role in furthering such a process of innovation.

In the third part of the book, our interest turns to analysis, a phase of the research process that is sometimes rather overlooked, both in the concrete process of planning investigations and in the methodological literature. Here, though, our contributors explore key aspects of the analytical task, including the introduction and systematic application of theoretical frameworks, the recognition of cultural variations, not just in data generation, but also in how it is analysed and made sense of, and in the direct engagement of people who use services in the process of understanding and drawing conclusions from the evidence. At the same time, though, we are reminded here of the contemporary interest in the analysis of 'big data' and how such sources of material might themselves be a powerful source of original insights into the terrain of social work, for instance in helping us to take account of the persistent effects of poverty in the lives of those with whom social workers intervene.

And finally, and once again in line with contemporary development in the terrain of social research, we turn the spotlight on 'social work' strategies for disseminating our findings and promoting change ('impact'). In one sense, perhaps, this aspect of social work research should be comparatively unproblematic – if our underlying aim is to make a positive difference to the lives of people experiencing disadvantage and/or using caring services, then we should clearly make a priority of sharing the findings and recommendations of research inquiries and making every effort to ensure that these are used to promote wider social change and enhance well-being. These concluding chapters therefore outline some of the ways in which social work research can, should and does achieve positive influence for good.

References

Dixon, J., Biehal, N., Green J., Sinclair, I., Kay, C. and Parry, E. (2014) 'Trials and tribulations: Challenges and prospects for randomised controlled trials of social work with children.' *British Journal of Social Work 44*, 6, 1563–1581.

Hardwick, L. and Worsley, A. (2010) *Doing Social Work Research*. London: Sage.

Smith, R. (2009) *Doing Social Work Research*. Maidenhead: McGraw Hill/Open University Press.

Section 1

INNOVATIONS IN DESIGN AND PLANNING

Chapter 1

ACTION RESEARCH FOR SOCIAL JUSTICE

Researching and Organising on Issues of Household Debt

SARAH BANKS
Durham University

Introduction

This chapter discusses an action research project on debt in low-income households in the Teesside area of North East England. The project, *Debt on Teesside: Pathways to Financial Inclusion*, involved collaboration between a university, a local community organisation and a national charity. It entailed collecting detailed financial information from 24 households, a money mentoring scheme and local and national campaigning for reform of the high-cost credit sector. A distinctive feature of the project was its location within a community organising framework, with a focus on mobilising people to take action for social change. This approach is described as 'community organising-based action research'. The chapter discusses the strengths of the project as embedded, locally initiated action research with a national impact, whilst also outlining some of the practical and ethical challenges of community–university partnership working with a social justice agenda. It is written from the perspective of a female academic, who co-produced the research with many others.

Overview of the research project

Design

Debt on Teesside was a partnership between Durham University's Centre for Social Justice and Community Action, Thrive Teesside (a grassroots community organisation) and Church Action on Poverty (CAP, a national campaigning organisation). It was funded by the Northern

Rock Foundation for two years during 2011–13. The project was jointly designed by staff from the three organisations. It built on previous work by Thrive and CAP that had identified unmanageable debt as a significant problem for households in poorer neighbourhoods in Teesside and on subsequent earlier collaborations between Thrive and Durham University (Beacon NE, 2011; Friends Provident Foundation 2010; Orr *et al.*, 2006 2010). This previous research and community work had highlighted the deleterious effects of the use of high-cost credit offered by doorstep lenders, rent-to-own, payday loan and catalogue companies – with annual percentage rates ranging from 100 per cent to 3000 per cent and higher. These credit sources are often used by people who are excluded from mainstream low-cost credit due to poor credit ratings and/or lack of a bank account. People in these circumstances are often described as 'financially excluded' (Devlin, 2005; Ellison *et al.*, 2011; Flaherty and Banks, 2013; Patel, Balmer and Pleasance, 2012). Following the 2008 economic crisis, with increasing unemployment, precarious work and cutbacks in welfare benefits, it seemed likely that even more households on low incomes would become indebted, many taking out high-cost loans.

The project had three main elements:

1. **Data collection** on the financial and social circumstances, behaviours and attitudes of 24 low-income, indebted households, with the aim of enhancing knowledge of the dynamics of debt and what can be done to reduce indebtedness.

2. **A mentoring scheme**, involving trained community-based volunteers, with the aim of supporting these households to develop their skills in money management and move away from high-cost credit.

3. **Local and national campaigning** on specific issues arising from the household data and mentoring scheme, including holding local public assemblies, with the aim of contributing to changes in policy and practice.

The staff comprised a newly appointed half-time researcher employed by the University (Jan Flaherty), who focused particularly on household data collection and analysis; half of an existing community organiser post employed by CAP and based at Thrive (subsequently split into two posts – Community Organiser (Greg Brown), who focused more on campaigns, and Project Officer (Tracey Herrington), who organised the mentoring scheme); and a one-day-a-week secretary (latterly Helena Kilvington). Existing Thrive volunteers and unpaid community organisers, along with newly recruited volunteers, also contributed to the project as mentor-researchers. The project was based in the Thrive offices in Thornaby-on-Tees, supervised by Sarah Banks from Durham University and Mark Waters from CAP. Sarah Banks had overall responsibility for the project as 'principal investigator', as Durham University was the fund holder. An agreement between CAP and the University was drawn up relating to the distribution of money and responsibilities.

Approach and methods
ACTION RESEARCH

The project was designed as 'action research' – that is, it had an explicit focus on using research to empower people and bring about social change (Hart and Bond, 1995; Greenwood and Levin, 1998; Berry and Campell, 2001; Burns, 2008; Reason and Bradbury, 2008b). It also involved elements of participatory research – that is research in which people who are usually the subjects of study themselves play a role in designing and/or doing the research (Kemmis and McTaggart, 2000; Kindon, Pain and Kesby, 2007; McIntyre, 2007; Kemmis, McTaggart and Nixon, 2014). In this case, local residents were trained to act as mentor-researchers, gathered data for the project from the mentoring sessions they undertook and fed back their experiences and reflections on a continuous basis. Some members of households who participated in mentoring schemes later became involved in campaigns.

'Action research' covers a broad range of different approaches – indeed, Reason and Bradbury (2008a, p.7) suggest it is a 'family of approaches'. At one end of the spectrum it may involve professional researchers studying aspects of organisations, feeding back their findings to key stakeholders and working with them to introduce changes. Here the focus is on research, albeit action-oriented research. Alternatively, action research may entail community-based activists collecting pertinent information to prime their actions for change. Here the focus is on action, albeit 'research-informed' action. The latter was the approach adopted by Thrive, and this very much influenced the practice of the project.

COMMUNITY ORGANISING

At the time of the project, Thrive and CAP were using a 'broad-based community organising' approach in their work. The model was based on the work of Saul Alinsky, a North American activist who developed tactics for mobilising coalitions of organisations around a specific issue, organising campaigns and training local organisers (Alinsky, 1969, 1989; Beck and Purcell, 2013; Bunyan, 2010; Chambers, 2003; Pyles, 2009; Schutz and Miller, 2015; Walls, 2015). In particular, Thrive followed the approach of the Chicago-based Gamaliel Foundation,[1] which offered training in the UK through CAP for organisers and local people. The Gamaliel Foundation philosophy is:

> People have a right and a responsibility to define their own destiny, to participate in the decisions affecting their lives, and to shape the social, political, economic and physical environment to include their values (quoted in their training in Stockton-on-Tees in 2010-11).

Thrive would hold meetings and carry out direct actions and campaigns on 'issues' raised by members and participants in its community projects. The plan was for the *Debt on Teesside* research project to generate evidence on issues of concern relating to household debt to present to, and influence, politicians, financial regulators and loan companies. Household members would also be offered one-to-one financial mentoring and it was hoped that some would go on to engage in campaigns and the broader work of Thrive.

COMMUNITY ORGANISING-BASED ACTION RESEARCH

Thrive had collected household-level financial data previously, but had insufficient resources to analyse it systematically. So the partnership with the University over several years prior to the start of the *Debt on Teesside* project enabled the research element of its work to be strengthened. This fitted well with the ethos and principles of the Centre for Social Justice and Community Action – a university-based research centre with a focus on Participatory Action Research (PAR) for social justice and membership from within and outside the University (Centre for Social Justice and Community Action, 2014). The Centre is used to working on action-oriented and participatory projects that value a range of ways of knowing and different types of expertise and involve flexibility of roles and unpredictability of processes and outcomes.

---

1   www.gamaliel.org

Hence the methodology and methods of the project were a mixture of traditional social research, along with community development and community organising approaches to mobilising individuals, forming groups and supporting collective action. Table 1.1 lists different elements of the project, indicating whether the methods used were primarily those of community organising or social research. However, it is important to note that these aspects of the project were not separate in practice, and on many occasions all workers on the project and Thrive volunteers contributed (for example, in the recruitment of households and organising assemblies).

Table 1.1: Combining community organising (CO) and social research (SR)

Aspects of the *Debt on Teesside* action research process	Methodological focus
Recruiting an advisory group through Thrive networks, including representatives from local advice, community finance and housing agencies	CO
Recruiting households through targeting neighbourhoods based on local knowledge; door knocking with community volunteers	CO
Recruiting mentors through existing Thrive volunteers and other agencies	CO
Preliminary focus groups with low-income households to gauge issues and interest and inform the questionnaire design	SR
Design of questionnaire for households with input from advisory group	SR
Run mentor training, including focus on mentors' research role	CO/SR
Initial household interviews and data collection; mid-point and final interviews	SR
Mentoring sessions, including collecting data for research	CO/SR
Workshops and meetings with key agencies and individuals	CO
Work nationally with Centre for Responsible Credit on reforms to rent-to-own sector	CO
Public assemblies in Stockton and Middlesbrough	CO

Workshops for households participating in the mentoring project	CO/SR
Incentivised savings scheme for households with the local credit union	CO
Doorstep lending campaign	CO
Community organising training	CO
Making a film with some households for the affordability campaign	CO
Celebratory learning event with householders and key stakeholders	CO/SR
Contribute to national campaigns, Drowning in Debt (CAP) and Charter to Stop Payday Loan Rip Off	CO
Launch and dissemination of reports and mentoring toolkit	CO/SR
Follow-on work by Thrive with local authorities, advice agencies, etc.	CO
Follow-on work, policy and practice briefings and roundtables	CO/SR

Data analysis, reflection and action

Like most action research, this project went through an ongoing cyclical process of feeding in early research findings, considering progress on the interventions and actions and developing new strategies. Regular team meetings and quarterly advisory groups (which latterly included three mentors) discussed all aspects of the project. Preliminary findings from the initial interviews and the mentoring relationships as they progressed over time fed into the firming up of issues for campaigns and modifications to the mentoring scheme. One key issue emerging was that household participants were being offered new loans without any proper affordability checks. This was identified as a potential campaign issue and was refined and worked on by the community organiser and volunteers over several months, leading to the affordability campaign that was eventually launched at the Thrive assembly in November 2012. A problem identified by mentors early on was mentees missing and cancelling appointments; the project secretary developed systems for reminders and rescheduling, and additional support was given to the mentors by the project officer.

The university researcher took responsibility for analysing the household interview data using SPSS and NVivo. This provided an overall picture of the 24 households in the project, including their levels and sources of debt, reasons for taking on high-cost credit and attitudes towards money management, savings and debt (see Banks *et al.*, 2013a; Flaherty and Banks, 2013). Several case studies of individual households were created, as these showed details of people's life circumstances, the build-up of debt and the impact of any mentoring received. Case studies were also compiled by several household members working with the project officer for a celebratory learning event towards the end of the project (Thrive Teesside and Durham University, 2013). The process of compiling the case studies enabled participants to reflect on their lives and the impact of their involvement in the project.

Dissemination, impact and creating outputs

As action research embedded in a community organising framework, dissemination of findings, publicising issues emerging and above all creating change in people, organisations and policies was of prime importance. This was built in from the start. Advisory group members were able to feed their ongoing learning from the project into their own organisations. Indeed, two organisations represented on the advisory group offered to provide mentors from their staff when the project was short of mentors. For the local Citizens Advice Bureau (CAB), one of the motives was to get first-hand experience of the life circumstances of people in severe debt who were not accessing the CAB, and see how people fared when offered continuing support rather than one-off advice. As the project progressed, invitations were received to speak at events, especially from Teesside local authorities concerned with the impact of reforms to welfare benefits. A combination of Thrive staff, volunteers and the researcher attended these events. Workshops were also organised by the project, targeted at key stakeholders – including local authority officers and members, MPs, advice agencies, housing providers, credit unions and community organisations at various stages of the project to present initial findings, engage in dialogue and gain new insights. Two public assemblies were held by Thrive in the autumn of 2011 and 2012. These followed the community organising model of inviting key power-holders to listen and respond to the voices of people experiencing the issues being targeted. Both public assemblies were emotionally charged and involved hearing from households in the project about their experiences of indebtedness and some of the unethical practices of loan companies.

During 2011–12, members of Thrive were part of a national roundtable initiated by Thrive and CAP with the Centre for Responsible Credit, with the aim of introducing voluntary reforms to the rent-to-own sector of the high-cost credit market. Evidence from the research with Teesside households was used and a voluntary code introduced (Gibbons, 2012). The project contributed to several other national campaigns, including 'Stop the Payday Loan Ripoff' in Autumn 2013, and some of the participating households made a film linked to the Thrive affordability campaign that was used by CAP in its 'Drowning in Debt' campaign (Debt on Teesside, 2013). The film encapsulated the issue graphically (depicting a doorstep lender pushing money down the throat of a borrower) and ended with specific demands for action.

After the project ended, further work continued, with the production of a final report (Banks *et al.,* 2013a) research briefing (Banks *et al.,* 2013b) and community mentoring toolkit (Centre for Social Justice and Community Action, 2013), which were launched in October 2013. A group of stakeholders convened by Durham University and Thrive prepared and submitted evidence to a Financial Conduct Authority consultation on the regulation of short-term, high-cost credit. As a result of considerable pressure and evidence from a range of groups and organisations, to which *Debt on Teesside* contributed, the Financial Conduct Authority introduced a price cap to control high-cost, short-term credit in January 2015.[2]

As part of separately funded follow-up work in 2014, the University and Thrive, in partnership with Stockton Borough Council, held policy and practice roundtables attended by the two local MPs and a large gathering of public and third sector stakeholders from North East England (Centre for Social Justice and Community Action, Centre for Responsible Credit and Thrive Teesside, 2014b). Policy and practice briefings were also prepared for this event (Centre for Social Justice and Community Action, Centre for Responsible Credit and Thrive Teesside, 2014a; Centre for Social Justice and Community Action and Thrive Teesside, 2014b) in partnership with the Centre for Responsible Credit. As a result, Thrive undertook further work with local authorities on building financially resilient communities, gained funding to work with people experiencing welfare benefit sanctions and is regularly asked for advice on community mentoring.

---

2   www.fca.org.uk/news/ps14-16-detailed-rules-on-the-price-cap-on-high-cost-short-term-credit

The mentoring scheme had mixed outcomes. Of the 24 households in the project, 16 had mentoring sessions. Many reported improved confidence generally and more control over finances, and some had moved away from high-cost credit. Some of the participating households became active with Thrive and helped with the campaigns and filmmaking. One participant went to Manchester to undertake community organising training with CAP. However, one of the key findings of the evaluation of the mentoring scheme was that people who are struggling with their finances are often struggling in many aspects of their lives and find it very hard to commit to a process of change. Many participants faced huge daily challenges linked to poverty, unemployment, poor health and difficult family circumstances. One of the recommendations of the research, therefore, was to embed one-to-one mentoring in group-based programmes and courses to help build financial resilience at local level. This led to the production of a practice briefing and a resource pack on money mentoring (Centre for Social Justice and Community Action and Thrive Teesside, 2014b, 2014a), which are currently being used by Thrive and many other organisations locally and nationally in developing support for people in debt.

Key innovative elements

What was innovative about this project? This is a challenging question to answer in the light of the long traditions of both action research and community organising. As Wiles *et al.* (2013) point out in their critical discussion of innovations in research methodology, most methods are developments, modifications and variations on what has gone before. Arguably, what counts as innovative in one context and with one group of people, may be commonplace in another. We need to ask: innovative in what context and for whom? Indeed, it may be less arrogant to consider what was distinctive about this project than what was innovative *per se*.

Action research as embedded and emergent

Compared with other research on household debt (for example, Dearden *et al.*, 2010; Jones, 2010; Mathers and Sharma, 2011), this project was unique in its strong action-orientation, based on a community organising approach in a locality. While it involved a fairly traditional social research element of collecting quantitative and qualitative data from households via interviews based on a questionnaire survey, the integration of a mentoring scheme alongside campaigning and community action made it distinctive. The location of the project, including the University-employed researcher and secretary, in Thrive's office base ensured that it was embedded in the everyday activities and interactions of the community organisation. The researcher could not remain aloof from the action, but was also involved in the design and development of the mentoring scheme and planning and implementing the public assemblies, for example.

The project grew out of, and was designed in relation to, issues identified by the community organisation, Thrive. It was refashioned over time according to local circumstances. In other words, it was *situated* research, with research questions based on insider, local knowledge, with the aim of making life better for people experiencing indebtedness in the local area and nationally. It also involved a political analysis, locating individual debt problems in the larger context of structural inequality, consumer society and poorly regulated financial services (Flaherty and Banks, 2013; Gibbons, 2014).

While there were certain milestones for the project set in advance, these were regularly reviewed and changed. The mentoring and campaigning were planned, re-evaluated and redesigned in the light of changing circumstances, feedback from participants and ongoing research data. This unpredictability, flexibility and responsiveness is typical of action research, which works with a continuous, recursive learning cycle of action and reflection. Action research has been characterised as 'messy' (Cook, 2009). It blurs many distinctions, including those between activists and researchers, action and research, and community work and research.

Therefore, in one sense, all action research is innovative, in that the process is not defined – there are no set methods. It relies on the creativity, ingenuity and practice wisdom of the participants – a willingness to take risks and to break with the positivist paradigm of researchers as detached, impartial observers, measuring the social world through tried and tested methods regarded as valid and reliable. As Reason and Bradbury (2008a, p.5) comment:

> In action research knowledge is a living, evolving process of coming to know rooted in everyday experience; it is a verb rather than a noun. This means action research program is less defined in

terms of hard and fast methods, but is, in Lyotard's (1979) sense, a work of art emerging in the doing of it.

Community organising-based action research

I referred earlier to the *Debt on Teesside* project as 'community organising-based action research'. By this I mean: action research specifically within a community organising model. This was not a label that we used at the time, but in reflecting afterwards on the approach it seems a good shorthand description and follows in the tradition of inventing new names for different branches of the action research family. I hasten to add that while I think the name may be new – at least it does not feature in the list of over 60 named methodologies in the *Encyclopedia of Action Research* (Coghlan and Brydon-Miller, 2014) – the principles of the approach are not. Indeed, the approach taken by many of the locally based projects that were part of the British Community Development Project in the 1970s involved a radical weaving of systematic research and political action (Green and Chapman, 1992; North Tyneside CDP, 1978).

As already mentioned, community organising entails 'cutting an issue' – that is, finding a specific issue that is of concern to the people involved, where there is a clear target (person in power who can be challenged) and which is potentially winnable. To identify an issue requires a systematic, in-depth process of gathering information and views from people and organisations. It involves what Alinsky (1989, p.68) refers to as 'digesting' happenings in people's lives so they become experiences:

> Happenings become experiences when they are digested, when they are reflected on, related to general patterns, and synthesized.

Community organising also entails assessing how to frame an issue and gathering evidence against the target. Chambers (2003) identifies three phases in the organising process: research, action and evaluation. These are outlined in Beck and Purcell (2013, p.15), of which the following is a summary:

1. *Research* – this involves undertaking an internal power analysis, holding relational and small group meetings to identify winnable issues and assess whether the organisation has the internal capacity to work on an issue and whether the action will build the organisation. Then an external power analysis is conducted

- key decision makers are identified and opposition and support assessed.

2. *Action* – building from the research process, the community is mobilised to personalise and polarise the issue. People and organisations are targeted and held to account.

3. *Evaluation* – participants discuss their feelings and analyse their behaviour and the behaviour of the opposition in order to learn from the experience, ensure social knowledge is produced and create a clear rationale for future action.

Viewed in this way, community organising could be characterised as research-informed action. Indeed, for Thrive, since its core business was community organising, and the *Debt on Teesside* project was embedded in its day-to-day work, what the project contributed was a strengthening and systematising of the research element of community organising. However, arguably this entailed more than just using action research to assess and identify issues as implied, for example, by Pyles (2009, p.108), which might be described as 'research-for-action'. Rather it also involved 'research-in-action'. This includes not only putting research to use, but also the digesting of research data from happenings, leading to new happenings based on the research digestings. It entails the roles of key actors in the project comprising elements of community work and research – as researcher-community workers or community worker-researchers. On this model, it is impossible to separate research and action, and hence neither has primacy.

The defining feature of action research is its holistic and embedded nature, hence the inseparability of action and research. Action research is often depicted as a cyclical or spiral process as shown in Figure 1.1.

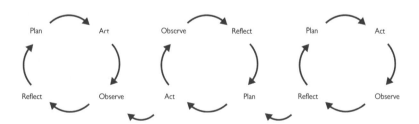

Figure 1.1: The recursive action research spiral

However, while such two-dimensional diagrams are useful, they can still be interpreted as implying distinct phases (e.g. plan, act, observe, reflect) that take place sequentially, albeit recursively. Hence it might seem as if we can abstract the observing, reflecting and planning phases as the research elements. However, once the process is in train, the micro-moments are often 'research-in-action' or 'action-in-research'. To take apart or disentangle this process can turn it into research-for-action, or action-based-on-research, and its holistic nature is lost.

The circles and spiral are, of course, simplifications – abstract conceptualisations. A more concrete, three-dimensional, textured and messy metaphor is collaborative knitting. Different people with different perspectives (academic researchers, residents, community workers) all contribute different elements of action and research. The research and action are intertwined, and the more participatory the project, the more different coloured wools are knitted into the piece by different participants, resulting in a piece of knitting with different tensions and stitches, knots, dropped stitches, unravellings and messy joins (Banks, 2013a). This metaphor suggests why it is so difficult to analyse the action research process and impossible to depict it in terms of distinct phases or step-by-step methods.

Strengths and challenges

Many of the strengths of the project also created challenges, but I will separate them out for the sake of clarity. What follows is how I assess the project from my perspective as a university academic and former community worker, who was, in university language, the principal investigator for the project.

Strengths
PARTNERSHIP
The project developed out of an existing partnership that had involved university staff and students working with Thrive on several other pieces of research and campaigning linked to high-cost credit and the practice and ethics of co-inquiry and community-based participatory research for several years (Banks *et al.*, 2013c, 2014; Beacon NE, 2011a, 2011b; Beacon NE, 2012; Durham Community Research Team, 2011). This meant that key participants had already established that they could

work together and shared some common values (social justice and campaigning on poverty-related issues). We also knew each other's strengths and weaknesses. In that sense it could be regarded as a strong community–university partnership (Hart, Maddison and Wolff, 2007).

CO-DESIGN

The design of the project was developed jointly by Thrive, CAP and the Centre for Social Justice and Community Action. It built on earlier work, so we had an idea of what might work and what we wanted to try out – especially the mentoring scheme. We had several meetings with the funder, both prior to submission and afterwards when revisions were requested before funding was finally agreed. This meant we had to justify what we planned to do to an outsider and also had to incorporate a clearer set of more traditional research aims and objectives. The advisory group, comprising a wide range of stakeholders, was involved in ongoing redesign as the project developed. This ensured that the practice wisdom of the stakeholders was incorporated into the project as it unfolded.

EMBEDDING IN THE COMMUNITY ORGANISATION

Basing the whole project in Thrive's premises meant it was an integral part of the organisation's work. Thrive volunteers could get involved and assist with recruiting households and planning events. It was also accessible to volunteer mentor-researchers. Furthermore, it meant that: the learning from the project was embedded in the organisation; the capacity and reputation of Thrive were enhanced; and ongoing action could continue to build on the learning from the original project after it ended.

READINESS OF COMMUNITY ORGANISATION TO TAKE ACTION

Members of Thrive were already well versed in using research as a basis for action and knew how to organise and mobilise people.

SCALING UP WAS FACILITATED THROUGH LINKS
TO LOCAL AND NATIONAL ORGANISATIONS

Thrive was a community organisation working under the aegis of CAP, and both organisations had links with the national Centre for Responsible Credit. This meant that the potential to scale up actions from local to national level was built in from the start.

FLEXIBILITY AND DYNAMISM OF THE PROJECT

Although there were research questions to answer and milestones set, the team had a commitment to giving room for flexibility in how the project developed and what actions were taken.

PRODUCTION OF IMPACT-FOCUSED OUTPUTS

The team produced a range of popular, useable products from the research designed to be of use in campaigning (e.g. the film) and for policy makers and politicians aiming to create financially resilient communities and local organisations setting up money mentoring schemes (e.g. the briefings and toolkit).

Challenges

CAPACITY OF THE COMMUNITY ORGANISATION

Thrive is a small community organisation with no core funding and minimal administrative infrastructure. It is entirely reliant on project grants for its survival and has to juggle pieces of work when grants are successful. At times, especially at the start of the project, Thrive found it hard to give the *Debt on Teesside* project the time allocated in the bid. This caused frustration and additional work for the University staff. Later, when the mentoring scheme was underway, the Thrive project officer contributed more than the allocated time, and the administration of the scheme with a one-day-a-week secretary proved challenging.

DIFFERING ETHICAL STANCES

Despite sharing common values, including a commitment to social justice, an issue emerged unexpectedly that brought into stark relief differing views on the rights and wrongs of taking donations. Thrive was offered, and accepted, a donation of several thousand pounds from the staff fundraising efforts of a high-cost credit company against which Thrive had previously campaigned. The company had since worked with Thrive to reform some of its practices and had been part of a roundtable group that met to introduce voluntary reforms to the rent-to-own sector. Thrive had not told the University partners about this donation. The University partners (the researcher and I) felt that Thrive should not take money from companies that were, in effect, profiting from people in poverty; that the company was gaining credibility by associating itself with Thrive; and that potentially the integrity and credibility of Thrive's work and our joint action research project could be compromised by this donation. However, we recognised that this was Thrive's decision and it was easier for us to have a 'clean hands' policy than it was for a small community organisation. Furthermore, the University donations policy had itself had recently been a subject of controversy, when it came to light that it had taken money from a tobacco company to fund postgraduate education for Afghan women.

THE UTILITARIAN APPROACH OF ALINSKY-STYLE ORGANISING

The issue of the donation highlighted the community organising philosophy of the ends justifying the means used to achieve them (Alinsky, 1989, pp.24–47). Indeed, the Thrive community organiser and a senior member of staff of CAP, both responded to the donation issue with the community organising mantra, 'No permanent friends, no permanent enemies', meaning that once the target of an action responds with some changes, they are no longer an 'enemy' and if it is useful they can become an ally. There are many other criticisms of this style of community organising that were raised by university staff and can be found in the literature (Beck and Purcell, 2013, pp.16–18), including: its polarising and conflict-focused approach to actions; its lack of attention to 'race' and gender issues, including women's ways of working; and the danger of exploiting people who are in vulnerable positions and are asked to give testimony in public. Since *Debt on Teesside* ended, Thrive has moved away from a full-blown community organising as promoted by the Gamaliel Foundation, while retaining aspects of the approach and philosophy in its work.

COMMUNITY ORGANISING AS THE
ACCEPTED FRAME OF REFERENCE

Whilst evaluation of the process and outcomes of the mentoring was part of the original brief, evaluation of the processes of organising the campaigns and actions was less prominent. This was partly because community organising was the frame into which the project fitted. While action research often entails a high degree of reflexivity and critical analysis of organisational structures and assumptions in which it is located, for the *Debt on Teesside* project this would have added an additional layer of complexity and potential controversy into an already challenging and complex project. The lack of critical reflexivity also fits with some features of Alinsky-style organising, which is task focused and outcome oriented.

ACADEMICS BECOMING ACTIVISTS

Given the inseparability of the research and the action, and my belief in the importance of tackling the high-cost credit problem, I was more engaged in the action side of the project than would have been expected in a traditional research project. However, I was aware that this was time consuming and that I needed to keep an appropriate distance in order to be able to supervise and manage the project. On several occasions a Thrive volunteer asked me if I would go on the Management Board, and I declined, as I felt it was important that I did not become part of Thrive. I also applied for several small grants from the University for additional pieces of work linked to the project, for which Thrive was paid. If I had been a member of the Board then I would have had a conflict of interest.

BALANCING ACADEMIC WITH POLICY AND PRACTICE OUTPUTS

It was a conscious decision on my part to focus on practice-relevant outputs, as this fitted the philosophy of the project. However, the time I spent working on reports, briefings and toolkits, and organising dissemination and consultation events, including radio and TV appearances, meant I had less time for 'academic' outputs in the form of journal articles. The researcher and I published one journal article based on the initial household interviews and questionnaires (Flaherty and Banks, 2013), and this book chapter explores the methodology.

THE CONSTANTLY CHANGING FIELD OF HIGH-COST CREDIT AND ALTERNATIVE LOW-COST CREDIT SOURCES

When the project started in 2011, despite clear evidence of great hardship caused by the unregulated availability of high-cost credit, the regulators were not enforcing existing rules (e.g. on affordability checks) and there was no appetite from government to regulate the sector further (e.g. by putting a cap on the interest rates charged or on total cost of credit). Government funding had been allocated to modernise credit unions (community-based, low-cost sources of credit), but change was very slow. In the meantime, the use of short-term, low-cost credit began to escalate – particularly payday loans. Payday loans enable people to borrow money easily on a short-term basis. However, if borrowers fail to repay within the specified time period, they incur rapidly escalating charges and interest. By 2013 the extortionate charges of payday loan companies were repeatedly in the news (Banks, 2013b) and the movement to regulate these companies gained momentum.

The Financial Conduct Authority finally introduced a cap on the total cost of credit in 2014. Credit unions are also merging and growing, and experimenting with more flexible online loans and products. There is a continuing need for new research and new action to keep pace with developments.

THE ACTION RESEARCH SPIRAL CONTINUES
Although the terrain has changed since the *Debt on Teesside* research report was published in 2013, the fundamental problems for families living in poverty persist and the personal debt crisis is worsening (Gibbons, 2014). While the research project and immediate follow-up work have ended, at the time of writing (January 2015) Thrive continues to work on the issue of debt. This includes revisiting the practices of the rent-to-own companies with which Thrive worked in 2011–12, as these are not covered by the cap on credit introduced for short-term high-cost loans. In January 2015, a Thrive volunteer organiser and member of staff went to London to give oral evidence at an All Party Parliamentary Group inquiry into the rent-to-own sector. In the local area, based on the policy and practice briefings produced as a result of the *Debt on Teesside* project, Thrive is working with Middlesbrough Council on building financially resilient communities, including the use of money mentoring. I am working with colleagues from Goldsmiths, University of London and local organisations to organise a workshop on alternative sources of credit.

Concluding comments

This chapter has offered a partial analysis and discussion of a complex and challenging action research project. It is partial because it is impossible to do justice in one chapter to the project as a whole and the local and national political and economic context in which it operated. It is also written from one perspective – that of a university academic. However, it has served a purpose in stimulating further critical reflection-on-action and continuing the action learning cycle. I hope that it may also provide some resonances, inspirations, insights and cautions for others engaging in, or contemplating embarking upon, community-based action research projects.

The model of community organising-based action research presented here highlights the advantages of building research into an already politically active local organisation with strong national links.

It also illustrates the emergent process of action research and the need for those involved not only to tolerate but also positively to embrace conflict, creativity, flexibility and challenge. Community organising-based action research is designed to disrupt existing power structures in the 'outside world', but it also disrupts relationships and power structures within research teams and their associated networks.

There are many approaches to community organising, ranging from utilitarian (of which the Alinsky approach is an example) to transformative models (including critical consciousness raising and Freirean approaches) (see Beck and Purcell, 2013; Pyles, 2009, pp.59–73). Regardless of the approach, one of the strengths of community organising is the concept of an 'issue', and the process of 'cutting an issue' from a broader problem, ensuring that it is deeply felt by all the people involved, suggests clear demands and is winnable and easy to understand (Bobo, Kendall and Max, 2001). This is crucial for turning research into effective action and is a key learning point for all forms of action research.

Acknowledgements

I would like to acknowledge the contribution of the households, mentors, community organisers, advisors and funders who contributed to the *Debt on Teesside* project, with particular thanks to Greg Brown, Kath Carter, Jan Flaherty, Tracey Herrington, Richard Walton and Mark Waters for their ideas and hard work.

References

Alinsky, S. (1969) *Reveille for Radicals*. New York: Vintage Books.

Alinsky, S. (1989) *Rules for Radicals*. New York: Vintage Books Edition (first published in 1971 by Random House).

Banks, S. (2013a) 'Knitting and knowledging: Between metaphor and reality', *Ways of Knowing*. Available at https://waysofknowingresearch.wordpress.com/2013/05/24/knitting-and-knowledging-between-metaphor-and-reality/, accessed on 2 April 2015.

Banks, S. (2013b) 'Payday lenders are out of time in their fight against credit cap.' *The Conversation*. London: The Conversation. Available at https://theconversation.com/payday-lenders-are-out-of-time-in-their-fight-against-credit-cap-19398, accessed on 2 April 2015.

Banks, S., Brown, G., Flaherty, J., Herrington, T. and Waters, M. (2013a) *Debt on Teesside: Pathways to Financial Inclusion, Final Report*. Durham: Centre for Social Justice and Community Action, Durham University. Available at www.dur.ac.uk/beacon/socialjustice/researchprojects/debt_on_teesside/, accessed on 2 April 2015.

Banks, S., Brown, G., Flaherty, J., Herrington, T. and Waters, M. (2013b) *Debt on Teesside: Pathways to Financial Inclusion: Research Briefing.* Durham: School of Applied Social Sciences, Durham University. Available at www.dur.ac.uk/beacon/socialjustice/researchprojects/debt_on_teesside/, accessed on 2 April 2015.

Banks, S., Armstrong, A., Carter, K., Graham, H. *et al.* (2013c) 'Everyday ethics in community-based participatory research.' *Contemporary Social Science 8,* 3, 263–277.

Banks, S., Armstrong, A., Booth, M., Brown, G. *et al.* (2014) 'Using co-inquiry to study co-inquiry: Community-university perspectives on research collaboration.' *Journal of Community Engagement and Scholarship 7,* 1, 37-47.

Beacon NE (2011a) *Case Study: Collaborating for Social Justice: A Community-university Partnership.* Durham: Durham University. Available at www.dur.ac.uk/beacon/socialjustice/toolkits/coinquirycase/, accessed on 2 April 2015.

Beacon NE (2011b) *Co-inquiry Toolkit: Community-University Participatory Research Partnerships: Co-inquiry and Related Approaches.* Newcastle: Beacon NE. Available at www.dur.ac.uk/beacon/socialjustice/toolkits/coinquiry/, accessed on 2 April 2015.

Beacon NE (2012) *Community Toolkit: A Guide to Working with Universities.* Newcastle: Beacon NE. Available at www.dur.ac.uk/beacon/socialjustice/toolkits/community/, accessed on 2 April 2015.

Beck, D. and Purcell, R. (2013) *International Community Organising: Taking Power, Making Change.* Bristol: The Policy Press.

Berry, H. and Campell, R. (2001) *Action Research Toolkit.* Edinburgh: Edinburgh Youth Inclusion Partnership.

Bobo, K., Kendall, J. and Max, S. (2001) *Organizing for Social Change: Midwest Academy Manual for Activists.* Santa Ana, CA: Steven Locks Press.

Bunyan, P. (2010) 'Broad-based organizing in the UK: Reasserting the centrality of political activity in community development.' *Community Development Journal 45,* 1, 111–127.

Burns, D. (2008) *Systemic Action Research.* Bristol: The Policy Press.

Centre for Social Justice and Community Action (2013) *Community Mentoring Toolkit: Working with Socially Excluded Households.* Durham: Centre for Social Justice and Community Action. Available at www.durham.ac.uk/beacon/socialjustice/researchprojects/debt_on_teesside, accessed on 2 April 2015.

Centre for Social Justice and Community Action (2014) *Centre for Social Justice and Community Action: The First Five Years, 2009–2014.* Durham: Centre for Social Justice and Community Action. Available at www.dur.ac.uk/beacon/socialjustice/, accessed on 2 April 2015.

Centre for Social Justice and Community Action and Thrive Teesside (2014a) *Money Mentoring: A Resource Pack.* Durham: Centre for Social Justice and Community Action. Available at www.durham.ac.uk/beacon/socialjustice/researchprojects/debt_on_teesside, accessed on 2 April 2015.

Centre for Social Justice and Community Action and Thrive Teesside (2014b) *Money Mentoring: Working with Low-income Households Experiencing Problematic Debt: Practice Briefing.* Durham: Centre for Social Justice and Community Action, Durham University. Available at www.durham.ac.uk/beacon/socialjustice/researchprojects/debt_on_teesside, accessed on 2 April 2015.

Centre for Social Justice and Community Action, Centre for Responsible Credit and Thrive Teesside (2014a) *Building Financially Resilient Communities: The Need for Local Action: Policy Briefing.* Durham: Centre for Social Justice and Community Action, Durham University. Available at www.dur.ac.uk/beacon/socialjustice/researchprojects/debt_on_teesside/, accessed on 2 April 2015.

Centre for Social Justice and Community Action, Centre for Responsible Credit and Thrive Teesside (2014b) *Tackling the Personal Debt Crisis in the NE: A Short Report of a Policy and Practice Event on 27th June, 2014.* Durham: Centre for Social Justice and Community Action, Durham University. Available at www.dur.ac.uk/beacon/socialjustice/researchprojects/debt_on_teesside/, accessed on 2 April 2015.

Chambers, E. (2003) *Roots for Radicals: Organizing for Power, Action, and Justice,* New York: Bloomsbury Academic.

Coghlan, D. and Brydon-Miller, M. (eds) (2014) *The SAGE Encyclopedia of Action Research.* London: Sage.

Cook, T. (2009) 'The purpose of mess in action research: Building rigour though a messy turn.' *Educational Action Research 17,* 2, 277–291.

Dearden, C., Goode, J., Whitfield, G. and Cox, L. (2010) *Credit and Debt in Low-income Families.* York: Joseph Rowntree Foundation.

Debt on Teesside (2013) *Loadsadebt* [film]. Manchester: Church Action on Poverty. Available at www.thrive-teesside.org.uk/index.php/clips-by-thrive/audio-video/video/loadsa-debt, accessed on 7 July 2015.

Devlin, J. (2005) 'A detailed study of financial exclusion in the UK.' *Journal of Consumer Policy 28,* 75–108.

Durham Community Research Team (2011) *Community-based Participatory Research: Ethical Challenges.* Durham: Centre for Social Justice and Community Action, Durham University. Available at www.dur.ac.uk/beacon/socialjustice/researchprojects/cbpr/, accessed on 2 April 2015.

Ellison, A., Whyley, C., Forster, R. and Jones, P. (2011) *Credit and Low-income Consumers: A Demand-side Perspective on the Issues for Consumer Protection.* Dorking: Friends Provident Foundation.

Flaherty, J. and Banks, S. (2013) 'In whose interest? The dynamics of debt in poor households.' *Journal of Poverty and Social Justice 21,* 3, 219–232.

Friends Provident Foundation (2010) *A sustainable Livelihoods Approach to Poverty and Financial Exclusion (Summary of Research Conducted by Thrive and Durham University).* Available at www.friendsprovidentfoundation.org/a-sustainable-livelihoods-approach-to-tacking-poverty-and-financial-exclusion/, accessed on 7 July 2015.

Gibbons, D. (2012) *Improving Practice in the Rent to Own Market.* London and Manchester: Centre for Responsible Credit and Church Action on Poverty. Available at www.responsible-credit.org.uk/uimages/File/Improving%20Practice%20in%20the%20Rent%20to%20Own%20Market%20final.pdf, accessed on 2 April 2015.

Gibbons, D. (2014) *Britain's Personal Debt Crisis: How We Got Here and What To Do About It.* London: Searching Finance.

Green, J. and Chapman, A. (1992) 'The British Community Development Project: Lessons for today.' *Community Development Journal 27,* 3, 247–258.

Greenwood, D. and Levin, M. (1998) *An Introduction to Action Research: Social Research for Social Change.* Thousand Oaks, CA: Sage.

Hart, E. and Bond, M. (1995) *Action Research for Health and Social Care: A Guide to Practice.* Milton Keynes: Open University Press.

Hart, A., Maddison, E. and Wolff, D. (eds) (2007) *Community-university Partnership in Practice.* London: NIACE.

Jones, P. (2010) *Access to Credit on a Low Income: A Study into How People on Low Incomes in Liverpool Access and Use Consumer Credit.* Manchester: The Cooperative Bank.

Kemmis, S. and McTaggart, R. (2000) 'Participatory Action Research.' In N. Denzin and Y. Lincoln (eds) *Handbook of Qualitative Research.* London: Sage.

Kemmis, S., McTaggart, R. and Nixon, R. (2014) *The Action Research Planner: Doing Critical Participatory Action Research.* Singapore: Springer.

Kindon, S., Pain, R. and Kesby, M. (eds) (2007) *Participatory Action Research Approaches and Methods: Connecting People, Participation and Place.* Abingdon: Routledge.

Lyotard, J.-F. (1979) *The Postmodern Condition: A Report on Knowledge* (trans. G. Bennington and B. Maasumi, English translation 1984). Manchester: Manchester University Press.

Mathers, I. and Sharma, N. (2011) *A Vicious Cycle: The Heavy Burden of Debt on Low Income Families.* Ilford: Barnardo's.

McIntyre, A. (2007) *Participatory Action Research (Qualitative Research Methods).* Thousand Oaks, CA, Sage.

North Tyneside CDP (1978) *Organising for Change in a Working Class Area: Final Report.* Newcastle: Newcastle Polytechnic.

Orr, S., Brown, G., Smith, S., May, C. and Waters, M. (2006) *When Ends Don't Meet: Assets, Vulnerabilities and Livelihoods.* Manchester/Oxford: Church Action on Poverty/Oxfam GB.

Patel, A., Balmer, N. and Pleasance, P. (2012) 'Debt and disadvantage: The experience of unmanageable debt and financial difficulty in England and Wales.' *International Journal of Consumer Studies 36*, 5, 556–565.

Pyles, L. (2009) *Progressive Community Organising: A Critical Approach for a Globalising World.* New York: Routledge.

Reason, P. and Bradbury, H. (2008a) 'Introduction.' In P. Reason and H. Bradbury (eds) *The Sage Handbook of Action Research: Participative Inquiry and Practice.* London: Sage.

Reason, P. and Bradbury, H. (eds) (2008b) *The Sage Handbook of Action Research: Participative Inquiry and Practice.* London, Sage.

Schutz, A. and Miller, M. (2015) *People Power: The Community Organizing Tradition of Saul Alinksy.* Nashville, TN: Vanderbilt University Press.

Thrive Teesside and Durham University (2013) *Debt on Teesside: Pathways to Financial Inclusion, Household Experiences.* Thornaby: Thrive Teesside and Durham University. Available at www.dur.ac.uk/beacon/socialjustice/researchprojects/debt_on_teesside/, accessed on 2 April 2015.

Walls, D. (2015) *Community Organising.* Cambridge: Polity Press.

Wiles, R., Bengry-Howell, A., Crow, G. and Nind, M. (2013) 'But is it innovation? The development of novel methodological approaches in qualitative research.' *Methodological Innovations Online 8*, 1, 18–33.

Chapter 2

A RANDOMISED CONTROLLED TRIAL OF A THERAPEUTIC INTERVENTION FOR CHILDREN AFFECTED BY SEXUAL ABUSE

TRICIA JESSIMAN, JOHN CARPENTER
AND TRISH O'DONNELL
University of Bristol and NSPCC

Introduction

Randomised controlled trials (RCTs) are the 'gold standard' in evaluating the effectiveness of interventions in medicine and health (Guyatt *et al.*, 2008). The logic behind RCTs is simple: if we want to know whether an intervention works, we need to compare its outcomes with those of a control group that receives no intervention or a different intervention. Randomly allocating participants to the different conditions effectively ensures that the intervention and control groups are as similar as possible at baseline and thus that any group differences at follow-up may be attributed to the intervention.

Given the elegance of RCTs as a research design, it is not surprising that they are very common in medicine. They are, however, quite rare in social work in the UK: why? One answer is that while RCTs of social work interventions have strong advocates (MacDonald, Sheldon and Gillespie, 1992; Newman and Roberts, 1997), there are also many opponents on principle (Trinder, 1996; Webb, 2001). In contrast, the US has a much stronger tradition of evidence-based practice and quantitative research methods, and RCTs are much more common (see as a recent example, a school-based intervention by Maynard, Kjellstrand and Thompson, 2014). The second answer is that, in spite of their simple logic, RCTs of social work interventions are generally difficult and expensive to carry out. This is often because researchers have experienced problems in recruiting a sufficient sample to satisfy the statistical 'power calculation', an essential requirement to ensure that findings are robust. Nevertheless, there are recent examples of RCTs in the UK, for example of a training intervention for foster families (Macdonald and Turner, 2005).

In this chapter, our concern is not with epistemological debates (which have been discussed at length elsewhere), but with the practical challenges in doing an RCT. We consider these in relation to a large 'pragmatic' RCT of an intervention for children affected by sexual abuse provided mainly by qualified social workers working for the NSPCC, a voluntary child protection organisation in the UK. We begin however with a summary of the challenges identified by researchers who conducted recent RCTs of social work interventions in the UK.

Rushton and Monk (2010) reflected on their RCT of a parenting programme for adopters of children with serious psychosocial difficulties. With a target of 75 participants, they identified 80 eligible adopters, but less than half (37) took part. This meant that though the results of the intervention were quite positive for those who received it, the numbers in intervention and control groups were too small to draw conclusions (statistically underpowered). Also, given the low take up, participants may not have been representative of adopters in general. Recruitment difficulties were attributed to the ethics committee's requirement that local authority social workers, not the researchers, had to engage the adopters. In spite of avowed senior management support in all participating authorities, there was considerable variation in recruitment rates. The researchers attributed this to social workers' workloads but also to their disposition towards the trial and, 'It was on the willingness of front-line workers to present the study positively to the adopters that the recruitment depended' (p.547).

Dixon and colleagues (2014) faced even greater problems in recruiting a sample of 'looked after' adolescents with challenging behaviour to receive 'treatment foster care', an intervention that includes individual therapy, social skills training and educational support, and placement with a specially trained foster carer. Only 6 out of 18 local authorities agreed to randomisation in the first place and 34 children out of a target of 130 cases were actually recruited. Their paper presents a detailed and informative discussion of the challenges and their efforts to surmount them, including: professional anxieties about randomisation; concerns about accountability; and an inadequate pool of children eligible for the intervention.

Coulter (2011) reported a trial of cognitive behaviour therapy (CBT) versus CBT plus systemic family therapy. In addition to difficulties in recruitment and gaining consent from families for the evaluation, the study experienced high drop-out rates from both interventions and, of those who did take part, a generally low number of therapy sessions received and poor adherence to the agreed study protocol for arranging appointments. In total, only 27 out of 105 eligible families took part in the trial. Like the authors of the previous studies, Coulter (2011) reiterated his commitment to RCTs in principle but concluded that, 'The key pragmatic lesson from this study is that the challenges and very real difficulties associated with RCT studies must be taken seriously' (p. 511). With these cautionary tales in mind, we turn to our own efforts to set up a large-scale RCT.

The problem: child sexual abuse

The prevalence of child sexual abuse (CSA) in the UK is unknown but there is evidence to suggest that a significant minority of children will be affected. A recent UK survey of over 6000 children, young adults and carers for the NSPCC (Radford *et al.*, 2011), found that 16.5 per cent of 11–17 year olds self-reported experiencing some form of sexual abuse (4.8% report *contact* sexual abuse); carers reported 1.2 per cent of under tens had been sexually abused (0.5% contact sexual abuse). With underreporting acknowledged as a problem in both official statistics and self-report measures, the real prevalence figure is likely to be higher (Gilbert *et al.*, 2009; MacMillan, Jamieson and Walsh, 2003; Melchert and Parker, 1997). Therapeutic services for children affected by sexual abuse are in high demand; a UK-wide mapping study estimated that 16,256 children were receiving some sort of therapeutic service in 2006–07. Using a conservative estimate that only 5 per cent of affected children will want to access a service in any given year, the authors used estimates from Radford *et al.*'s (2011) survey to calculate a shortfall of 55,794 spaces in the UK (excluding Wales) for children experiencing contact sexual abuse, and a greater shortfall again for all forms of sexual abuse (Allnock *et al.*, 2009).

The experience of child sexual abuse (CSA) is associated with a complex range of psychological and behavioural symptoms in both childhood and adulthood (Berliner and Elliott, 2002; Putnam, 2003). A meta-analysis of the published research found a substantial effect of CSA on post-traumatic stress (PTSD), depression, suicide, sexual promiscuity, sexual perpetration and academic achievement (Paolucci, Genuis and Violato, 2001). Recent work estimating the costs of child sexual abuse in the UK (Saied-Tessier, 2014) cited evidence that victims will be twice as likely as non-victims to experience depression (Diaz, Simantov and Rickert, 2002), alcohol and drug misuse (Felitti *et al.*, 1998; Kendler *et al.*, 2000), and three times more likely to experience attempts at suicide (Andrews *et al.*, 2004; Bebbington *et al.*, 2009), self-harming behaviour (Hawton *et al.*, 2002) and PTSD (Molnar, Buka and Kessler 2001; Saunders *et al.*, 1999). Additionally, the negative impact of CSA appears heightened when the child's experience of sexual abuse occurs within the context of other forms of victimisation and trauma; a concept that Finkelhor, Ormrod and Turner *et al.* (2007) termed 'polyvictimisation'. Consequently, research on the effectiveness of interventions for children affected by CSA is very important.

As discussed above, the most rigorous method for evaluating the effectiveness of an intervention is the RCT. One systematic review of RCTs of psychological treatments for CSA found 12 rigorous studies of treatment outcomes, with the largest number of research trials and evidence for best effects coming from studies of CBT (Ramchandani and Jones, 2003). The most convincing evidence of beneficial effects was on pre-school children when their carer also received CBT, though there was less strong evidence of positive outcomes for older children. Similarly, a recent Cochrane systematic review of CBT for children affected by CSA reported a modest reduction in depression, PTSD and anxiety symptoms, concluding that while CBT may be beneficial, the evidence is muted (Macdonald *et al.*, 2012). There is little or no evidence to support the use of other therapeutic approaches; the latest Cochrane review of psychoanalytic/psychodynamic psychotherapy for CSA failed to find a single study that met the inclusion criteria (Parker and Turner, 2014). The authors suggested this absence of evidence may reflect a reliance on case reports and a reluctance to subject the interventions to the rigours of empirical evaluation for fear of losing the rich complexity and individuality of cases (Midgley and Kennedy, 2011; Parker and Turner, 2014). Similar claims have been made about social work (MacDonald *et al.*, 1992; Newman and Roberts, 1997).

The NSPCC commitment to evaluation

The study under discussion in this chapter begins to address this gap in the evidence. *Letting the Future In* (LTFI) is a 'best practice guide' for a therapeutic intervention for sexually abused children and young people. The guide was developed by a practitioner group within the NSPCC, led by one of the authors of this chapter. Practitioners with a complementary range of background and experience in working with victims of CSA, primarily in social work but also in play therapy and in family and systemic therapy, developed the guide based on their own experience of treating CSA and an evidence review of existing interventions (Allnock and Hynes, 2011). The model provides individual work with the child plus support to the 'safe carer' (typically the non-abusing parent, but sometimes a grandparent or foster carer). Both the existing research and practitioner experience pointed to an approach that needed to: place emphasis on high-quality initial assessment; have a child-centred therapeutic approach that could respond to individual needs and preferences; draw on different therapeutic approaches including cognitive, play and psychodynamic therapies. Central to all of this is a strong therapeutic alliance between practitioner and child. LTFI is largely based on Anne Bannister's 'recovery and regenerative model' (Bannister, 2003), which emphasises the power of play and the importance of therapeutic relationships as central to addressing the child's experience of sexual abuse. Such an approach makes theoretical and intuitive sense in that it works to rebuild disrupted attachments, rebalance power relationships and counter the abuse of trust inherent in the abuse experience itself. However, it had not been formally evaluated.

LTFI was piloted in six teams in 2011 before being rolled out to NSPCC teams across England, Wales and Northern Ireland. It is available to children aged between 4 and 17 without a diagnosed learning difficulty who have been affected by sexual abuse. Eligibility criteria also include that the abuse should have been subject to investigation by the police and/or children's social services, and the child should be living in a safe and stable home environment with a carer able to support their recovery. The exclusion of children with learning difficulties is common in therapeutic interventions (Allington-Smith, Ball and Haytor, 2002; Peckham 2007), perhaps because of concerns about the level of cognitive function and verbal communication required (Sinason, 2002). Given the concern that children with learning difficulties may be more at risk of CSA (Spencer *et al.*, 2005; Sullivan and Knutson, 2000), the NSPCC has recently addressed this gap through the development of an adapted version of the LTFI guide for children and young people with mild, moderate, severe or profound and multiple learning difficulties, with less emphasis on CBT and more reliance on creative therapies.

This is currently being piloted and is not part of the evaluation discussed in this chapter.

Children are offered up to four therapeutic assessment sessions followed by up to 20 intervention sessions (extended to 30 if necessary) with a children's services practitioner (CSP). CSPs delivering the intervention vary in their background, training and experience but most commonly are qualified social workers with additional training in therapeutic work with children. At the same time, their safe carer is offered up to eight sessions to help them process the impact of discovering that their child was sexually abused and to support the child in their recovery.

Acknowledging the gap in evaluations of non-CBT approaches to treatment of CSA, the NSPCC was committed to evaluating the intervention from its inception, stating in the evidence-scoping study that the:

> ...existing shortage of hard evidence about the effectiveness of different therapeutic approaches underlines the importance of designing a robust evaluation methodology for the guide. This will include assessing outcomes, using matched control groups, at the completion of therapy and again at intervals thereafter (Allnock and Hynes, 2011).

An invitation to tender for the evaluation was issued in July 2011 during the initial piloting phase, outlining plans for an impact, process and economic evaluation of the guide as implemented by 18 NSPCC teams, to report in early 2015. By August 2011 the NSPCC agreed to commission a team from Bristol and Durham universities to carry out the evaluation, subject to agreeing the methodology. This was relatively straightforward for the process and economic elements of the evaluation and at the time of writing, these are well underway. Both have innovative aspects, not least ensuring that the views of service beneficiaries, often underrepresented in evaluation design, are explored through qualitative interviews with children and their carers. However, it is the outcome evaluation that is the subject of this chapter.

Designing a study

Our first dilemma in designing the outcome evaluation was the identification of a suitable comparison group. We considered children referred to children's social care but not to LTFI to determine whether outcomes under LTFI were superior to the support and protection services provided by children's social care alone. Alternatively, we could compare the outcomes with those for children referred to a different treatment condition, such as CBT or other therapeutic services offered by child and adolescent mental health services (CAMHS). Without randomisation neither of these comparisons would have told us whether differences in outcomes were due to the treatment itself or to external factors such as demographics and symptomatic variables in children that may well have influenced the decision about which service they should receive. It is highly unlikely that any outside agency would have agreed to a randomised trial. In addition there would likely be pragmatic difficulties persuading children's social care and/or CAMHS to provide access to a comparison group, which would have significant time and resource implications for them, with little benefit. Our third, and preferred, option was a comparison group who would receive 'treatment as usual' (TAU) from the NSPCC, achieved by rolling out LTFI in only half of the NSPCC delivery centres and allocating teams to condition through either a randomisation or matched-comparison approach. This would control for many confounders as well as being pragmatically easier than involving an outside agency. However, the NSPCC was committed to rolling out the intervention in all 18 teams and would not delay implementation to allow this.

Going back to the drawing board, we suggested the option of an RCT using a waiting list control. This design had been employed in 16 of 45 studies included in a meta-analysis of the outcomes of therapeutic interventions with sexually abused children and adolescents (Harvey and Taylor, 2010) and has several advantages. As noted in the introduction to this chapter, a randomised trial is the 'gold standard' in evaluation research and would provide the most persuasive evidence should a positive effect of LTFI be detected. Randomisation of children post-referral to the NSPCC would offer the most rigorous control for known and unknown confounders. And, thankfully, the difficulties in seeking a comparison group from an external agency would be avoided. We proposed that this be a 'pragmatic trial' allowing a 'real-life' evaluation of LTFI. Pragmatic trials, unlike their explanatory counterparts, do not require 'ideal' conditions but allow for the rather messier complexities of everyday life including greater variability in beneficiary type and treatment implementation by regular practitioners (Roland and Torgerson, 1998). Furthermore, in a pragmatic trial we would be analysing the outcomes of offering the service, whether or not the participating children completed the full 'dose' of 20 sessions, or even completed none at all; this, after all, is what happens in 'real life'. In other words, the primary research question was not: 'Does LTFI work (with the children who receive the full course of therapy)?' but 'What are the outcomes for children and young people affected by sexual abuse of providing a therapeutic intervention (LTFI) delivered by NSPCC teams?'

It can be seen that the answer to the second question is what service commissioners need to know, because it addresses their concern about generalisation: yes, it may work in a 'centre of excellence' with highly trained and experienced staff with highly selected clients, but will it work in 'ordinary' teams with a mix of service users with varying levels of motivation?

Developing a partnership

By the end of 2011 we had agreement in principle with the NSPCC's Head of Evaluation that this approach offered the best way forward in the evaluation of LTFI. Our dilemma of identifying a suitable comparison group and evaluation design had been resolved. And yet, the difficulties in getting the evaluation off the ground were only just beginning.

Conducting an RCT of any type of social intervention demands a healthy, working and cooperative partnership between researchers, practitioners, managers and, we would add, beneficiaries of the intervention. Without exception, all NSPCC stakeholders agreed that rigorous evidence was needed on whether LTFI 'works' for children affected by sexual abuse. However, there was almost no agreement at this time that an RCT with waiting-list control was the best approach, both pragmatically and ethically. The invitation to tender did not specify an RCT and consent to run one had to be sought at the highest levels of management and the trustees. The challenge was significant, with the Development Team often the lone advocates of this design. Even if it had been more straightforward, we could not rely simply on high-level support to implement the RCT. We needed to win the 'hearts and minds' of practitioners and managers in teams who would be involved in the study implementation, not least in explaining randomisation to potential beneficiaries of LTFI, gaining their consent to the study and data collection. At worst, the CSPs may have refused to support it or subverted the process. But importantly, we all believed this was the best way to evaluate LTFI and wanted them to support the approach. We embarked on a lengthy dialogue with the NSPCC, through regional workshops and team visits led by the research team and regular senior management meetings, encouraging CSPs and managers to voice their concerns so that we could respond with counterargument or, in some cases, adaptions to the study design. The key points raised are discussed below.

'We know that this intervention will work, so we must offer it to vulnerable children without delay'

Based on their own experience of similar work, many NSPCC staff felt strongly that LTFI 'worked'. Nevertheless, it is untested and it is possible that at best it has no effect and worse may even be harmful. We outlined the limitations of the evidence for CBT and the absence of evidence for non-cognitive approaches to CSA. We invited them to reflect on a systematic review and meta-analysis of the use of psychological debriefing after traumatic events to prevent the onset of PTSD to illustrate that 'common sense' interventions may not only be ineffective, but may actually make matters worse (Rose *et al.*, 2002); rigorous testing was essential. In addition we argued that if the evaluation found evidence of positive effect, this would give LTFI greater credibility in the eyes of referring agencies and funders.

'We cannot have practitioners doing nothing'

The prospect of randomising 50 per cent of referred children to a waiting list left staff worried that practitioner caseloads would immediately be reduced by half, leaving them with spare capacity not easily filled. We agreed that this was untenable for a busy organisation with a range of in-demand services for vulnerable children and families. In addition, it would be unethical to create a waiting list for LTFI where capacity existed. We explained that teams would only enter the RCT when they reached capacity and in normal non-trial circumstances would have closed to new referrals. (In practice, teams entered the trial when they were just beneath this level, as practitioners needed to have some capacity to accept the case should it be randomised to immediate intervention).

'Randomising children is very unfair'

Prior to the trial, teams would accept cases largely on a first-come, first-served basis. When they had a full caseload, the service would close to new referrals (the NSPCC had a no-waiting-list policy at the time) and in many cases the practitioners would have very limited (or no) contact with families denied immediate service. The trial protocol changed this and, unlike other RCTs that the NSPCC was involved with, practitioners in this trial had considerable contact with families prior to randomisation. They would meet the child and carer, usually during home visits, to carry out an eligibility assessment for the intervention as well as a research assessment prior to randomisation. Suddenly, the impact of denying an immediate service was far more apparent to practitioners, who also worried that children may begin to form an attachment to practitioners during the assessment period. In addition, this design meant that some new referrals would be offered immediate intervention while others remained on the waiting list. Understandably, this proved emotionally very difficult for practitioners motivated to bond with and support families in need. However, we argued that this approach was in fact advantageous to referred families. In this trial design, *all* eligible families would be offered a service (albeit, some after a defined waiting-list period), with none turned away because of lack of capacity.

'We cannot ask children to wait'

In reality, delays to public services of all types are increasingly common, including for vulnerable children and families. In this case, the length of the wait would be clearly defined and families would be told when their first appointment would be.

An important consideration was the length of the waiting period. This needed to give us enough time between baseline assessment (T1) and first follow-up (T2) to detect any intervention effect. The LTFI guide advises that the intervention is expected to comprise 20 to 30 sessions. With weekly sessions, this meant the intervention could last up to eight months and in practice, may go on longer. However, we were all keen to minimise the waiting list time, and this was a difficult balance. Of the studies in Harvey and Taylor's (2010) review, around 75 per cent of interventions studied comprised 20 sessions or fewer, with 60 per cent lasting 20 weeks or less. This period was evidently sufficient to demonstrate change in the outcomes measures

(Harvey and Taylor, 2010). We therefore proposed that the T2 measures be taken at six months. While some of those offered immediate intervention may finish sooner, and others would continue after T2, for those on the waiting list T2 marked the beginning of the service and the waiting-list period was fixed. We encouraged practitioners to emphasise this to families randomised to the waiting list and tell them the month in which they would be contacted to come in for reassessment and service. Meantime, because this was a pragmatic trial, children and their carers could access other services during the waiting-list period if they were available.

'Some children need the intervention now;
it is dangerous to make them wait'
NSPCC is clear that LTFI is not a crisis intervention, and children who present with very high levels of trauma, or suicide risk, should be referred elsewhere as appropriate. Serious safeguarding concerns needed immediate attention. It is possible that initial referral information and/or assessment tools used (including the Trauma Symptoms Checklist for Children (TSCC) (Briere, 1996)) may indicate that the child is in need of a further mental health assessment for possible depression or anxiety and, as such, should be referred to CAMHS. In such cases, the child would drop out of the evaluation and no further data would be collected.

However, practitioners were anxious that there may still be exceptional circumstances where the child should be seen immediately. We agreed and introduced a safeguard that team managers could decide to exempt a new referral from the trial and offer immediate service. It was very important to teams that exemption decisions remained with the team manager rather than the research team, who would have far less knowledge about the circumstances surrounding the case. The team manager was encouraged to discuss the possible opt-out with a senior regional manager or the strategic development lead. We provided guidance stating that exemptions should not be for reasons of perceived greater trauma, because the capacity to assess this during the referral assessment process was very limited, but also because removing cases with high levels of trauma from the trial would bias the trial (and likely to skew the results in a way that would make LTFI look less effective). In practice, there have been very few exemptions from the trial and in most cases, we have agreed with the reasons. Examples include a child whose sexualised behaviour was risking her own and sister's current stable placement in foster care; a child from a military family due to move overseas within the year; and children with siblings already in receipt of LTFI. There have been some we would *not* have exempted, for example a very young child exempted following pressure from the referring agency for an immediate service. However these have been few and we feel that a good balance has been struck between maintaining the integrity of the trial and team manager's autonomy in these circumstances.

'What if a child on the waiting list cannot cope?'
We believed that the fixed-term waiting period, knowing there would be a service offered at the end of it, would help children and their carers manage this period. Nevertheless, some may have found it difficult. Families were provided with the contact details of local support services (where these existed) and could contact and access these. In addition, the NSPCC set up a dedicated helpline number staffed by a counsellor who had knowledge of the trial and could contact the teams if she believed the family needed to be reassessed.

We inserted a further safeguard into the trial protocol, that if a team manager became aware that the child experienced a significant deterioration in circumstances while on the waiting list, they may be considered for immediate intervention and not wait for the remaining period. Again, such circumstances were likely to be linked to reasons other than increased trauma, which would require referral and assessment by CAMHS. Again, very few cases were removed from the waiting list.

'How do we manage a waiting list?'
Team managers were worried about the increased burden that a waiting list would place on managing staff caseloads. Within teams, the number of new referrals varies from month to month, staff can have unplanned leave or move and the length of time cases are open can sometimes be difficult to predict. We suggested that a fixed-length waiting list was the most predictable variable; managers could allocate waiting list cases to practitioners months in advance as the date of re-assessment was fixed.

There were two scenarios that emerged throughout the trial that we were not fully prepared for. The first of these was the number of siblings referred. The protocol stated that siblings would not be split across conditions so that one child received the immediate service and the others did not; this would have been unmanageable in the family. Also, the guide recommends that each child would be allocated a different practitioner; hence larger groups (in one case four siblings) would demand careful caseload management to allow simultaneous allocation regardless which condition they were randomised to. Second, the randomisation was 50:50 across all participating teams, not at individual team level. Two teams experienced runs of up to five cases allocated to the same condition, something we could do nothing about except observe in horror. In particular, consistent allocation of cases to the waiting list caused practitioners understandable distress and would at times mean they fell way under capacity. Two teams left the RCT for a period for this reason and had to allocate all new referrals immediately for a few months until they re-entered the trial.

'We are practitioners, not researchers'

As agreed with the Research Ethics Committee, the research team has no contact with children and their carers in this evaluation, with the expectation of a very small number of families who have opted in to take part in qualitative case studies. Information about the trial is provided through leaflets written by the research team and explained in person by CSPs, who are also responsible for gaining informed consent and data collection. This is primarily for ethical reasons – families retain their anonymity and do not have another professional (researcher) involved in their lives at what will already be a traumatic time. CSPs are also best placed to administer the research measures and be on hand to support respondents should they need it. There are also pragmatic reasons – we did not have capacity to undertake data collection across 18 (now 20) sites across England, Wales and Northern Ireland. This has placed a significant administrative burden on practitioners, particularly at the start of their relationship with families when information, consent and T1 data collection procedures need to be completed soon after referral. We provided support: a detailed evaluation manual outlining both the rationale for the trial design and measures used, and clarity on gaining informed consent (we had 14 iterations of this, responding to problems and issues raised by NSPCC staff); regional workshops for CSPs and managers; many individual site visits to teams; and ongoing email and telephone support. We underestimated how much support would be required over the trial period and have risked burying teams in the administration of the research. It has helped to provide regular reminders of the rationale for the RCT and the importance of empirical evidence. We also benefited greatly from the support of teams who entered the RCT quickly, and were willing to share their experience and skill in managing the RCT process with teams coming in behind them. CSPs and team managers often found their peers more reassuring, persuasive and encouraging about the trial than an external researcher could be. We also benefited hugely from the support of team administrators and the administrative leads for LTFI in managing data collection and working with CSPs and managers to keep to the research timescales.

While our dialogue with the NSPCC about the trial design was taking place, we were granted approval to begin collecting 'before and after' data from all consenting beneficiaries from November 2012, to be used in a statistical examination of the predictors of outcomes for beneficiaries of the service. By early 2013 we had enough feedback from practitioners to finalise the RCT design, an outline of which is shown in Figure 2.1. Our primary outcome is a measure of the child's trauma symptoms using the TSCC (or a proxy measure completed by carers, TSCYC) (Briere, 1996; Briere *et al.*, 2001). Secondary outcomes include parental stress (Abidin, 1995) and child polyvictimisation (Finkelhor *et al.*, 2005). These are measured on referral (T1) and at two further six-month intervals (T2 and T3). We are also using these in our predictors of outcomes analysis, alongside process measures such as the number of sessions received and a measure of therapeutic alliance (Shirk and Saiz, 1992). Data about the nature of the abuse experienced by the child is also collected.

Progress and (interim) conclusion

The RCT was finally agreed in early 2013 and two teams began randomising new referrals in May that year. In RCTs, size matters, and at the time of writing we have 243 randomised cases in the trial, which is on the way to being the largest ever RCT of any intervention for CSA (currently the largest is 229 (Cohen *et al.*, 2004)). This is largely due to the number of teams involved, who joined in as they reached RCT capacity, and by May 2014 18 teams had joined. However, some of the implementation lessons we have outlined here will be applicable to a smaller-scale study. It would be perfectly possible to run an RCT with waiting-list control across a single or smaller number of teams, providing there was sufficient demand for the service. Smaller-scale trials would limit generalisability and reduce statistical power, as well as being more vulnerable to the difficulties caused by variable referral rates and randomisation. In our study, teams that have dropped way below capacity have been able to 'opt-out' without significantly affecting the progress of the trial, and this would be harder to accommodate on a smaller scale. However, with a smaller number of teams involved, the challenges of bringing everyone on board with the study design, maintaining the integrity of the trial and supporting data collection would be reduced.

We believe several factors contributed to the success of the study. First was the commitment of senior management within the NSPCC to undertake a rigorous evaluation of an untested intervention. Furthermore, there was a shared vision across all levels of the organisation of the need to provide evidence of what works in the treatment of children affected by sexual abuse. Concerns about how best to provide this evidence were addressed through dialogue between the research team, senior management and front-line staff before the evaluation design was finalised. This required far more time and resource than we were prepared for but was crucial in achieving a workable trial design. Indeed, we know that the research protocol is all the better for it. Specific objections were addressed through counterargument or, where feasible, amendments to the trial protocol, in particular the introduction of additional safeguards for children. We have continued to provide support to CSPs responsible for managing the consent and data collection process and to team managers making decisions about how best to manage waiting lists and deal with potential exemptions to the trial. In turn, practitioners and managers have risen incredibly well to the challenges of implementing an RCT and managing the implications for children, young people and their carers. We have continually reinforced the rationale for the study and the need for a rigorous approach to evidence when this has been in danger of getting mired in research administration. And where we lacked credibility in answering practice-based questions, team managers from early-entry teams helped us manage the concerns of those teams more reluctant to enter the trial.

In this chapter we have outlined the evidence gap that exists for therapeutic interventions for CSA, and in particular the lack of RCTs of psychological approaches other than CBT. RCTs are the 'gold standard' of impact evaluations, but RCTs of social work interventions are rare in the UK and the difficulties of implementing them have been well documented by other authors. We have faced similar challenges in the evaluation of LTFI, and we hope that this account of them and our responses will be useful for those setting up similar trials in the future. The evaluation of LTFI will report in Autumn 2015 and will, importantly, begin to fill the acknowledged gap of any RCT of a non-cognitive-based intervention for CSA.

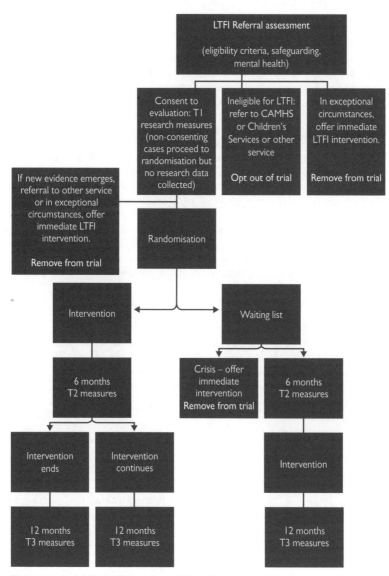

Figure 2.1: LFTI RCT with waiting list control

References

Abidin, R. R. (1995) *Parenting Stress Index (PSI) Manual* (3rd edition). Charlottesville, VA: Pediatric Psychology Press.

Allington-Smith, P., Ball, R. and Haytor, R. (2002) 'Management of sexually abused children with learning disabilities.' *Journal of Continuing Professional Development 8*, 66–72.

Allnock, D. and Hynes, P. (2011) *Therapeutic Services for Sexually Abused Children and Young People: Scoping the Evidence Base.* London: NSPCC.

Allnock, D., Bunting, L., Price, A., Morgan-Klein, N., Ellis, J., Radford, L. and Stafford, A. (2009) *Sexual Abuse and Therapeutic Services for Children and Young People.* London: NSPCC.

Andrews, A., Cory, C., Slade, T., Issakidis, C. and Swanston, H. (2004) 'Child Sexual Abuse.' In M. Ezzati, A. D. Lopez, A. Rodgers and C. Murray (eds) *Comparative Quantification of Health Risks.* Geneva: World Health Organization.

Bannister, A. (2003) *Creative Therapies with Traumatized Children.* London: Jessica Kingsley Publishers.

Bebbington, P. E., Cooper, C., Minot, S., Brugha, T. S., Jenkins, R., Meltzer, H. and Dennis, M. (2009) 'Suicide attempts, gender, and sexual abuse: Data From the 2000 British Psychiatric Morbidity Survey.' *American Journal of Psychiatry 166*, 1135–1140.

Berliner, L. and Elliott, D. (2002) 'Sexual abuse of children in the field of child maltreatment.' In J. Myers, L. Berliner, J. Briere, C. T. Hendrix, T. Reid and C. Jenny (eds) *The APSAC Handbook on Child Maltreatment* (2nd edition) London: Sage.

Briere, J. (1996) *Trauma Symptom Checklist for Children (TSCC) Professional Manual.* Odessa, FL: Psychological Assessment Resources.

Briere, J., Johnson, K., Bissadac, A., Damond, L., Crouche, J., Gilf, E., Hansong, R. and Ernsth, V. (2001) 'The Trauma Symptom Checklist for Young Children (TSCYC): Reliability and association with abuse exposure in a multi-site study.' *Child Abuse and Neglect 25*, 1001–1014.

Cohen, J. A., Deblinger, E., Mannarino, A. P. and Steer, R. A. (2004) 'A multisite, randomized controlled trial for children with sexual abuse-related PTSD symptoms.' *Journal of the American Academy of Child and Adolescent Psychiatry 43*, 393–402.

Coulter, S. (2011) 'Systemic family therapy for families who have experienced trauma: A Randomised Controlled Trial.' *British Journal of Social Work 41*, 502–519.

Diaz, A., Simantov, E. and Rickert, V. I. (2002) 'Effect of abuse on health: Results of a national survey.' *Archives of Pediatrics and Adolescent Medicine 156*, 811–817.

Dixon, J., Biehal, N., Green, J., Sinclair, I., Kay, C. and Parry, E. (2014) 'Trials and tribulations: Challenges and prospects for randomised controlled trials of social work with children.' *British Journal of Social Work 44*, 1563-1581.

Felitti, V. J., Anda, R. F., Nordenberg, D., Williamson, D. F., Spitz, A. M., Edwards, V., Koss, M. P. and Marks, J. S. (1998) 'Relationship of childhood abuse and household dysfunction to many of the leading causes of death in adults: The adverse childhood experiences (ACE) study.' *American Journal of Preventive Medicine 14*, 245–258.

Finkelhor, D., Ormond, R., Hurner, H. and Hamby, S. (2005) 'Measuring poly-victimisation using the Juvenile Victimisation Questionnaire.' *Child Abuse and Neglect 29*, 1297–1312.

Finkelhor, D., Ormrod, R. K. and Turner, H.A. (2007) 'Poly-victimization: A neglected component in child victimization.' *Child Abuse and Neglect 31*, 7–26.

Gilbert, R., Widom, C. S., Brown, K., Fergusson, D., Webb, E. and Janson, E. (2009) 'Burden and consequences of child maltreatment in high-income countries.' *The Lancet 373*, 68–81.

Guyatt, G. H., Oxman, A. D., Vist, G. E., Kunz, R., Falck-Ytter, Y., Schunemann, H. and Grp, G. W. (2008) 'GRADE: What is "quality of evidence" and why is it important to clinicians?' *British Medical Journal 336*, 995–999B.

Harvey, S. T. and Taylor, J. E. (2010) 'A meta-analysis of the effects of psychotherapy with sexually abused children and adolescents.' *Clinical Psychology Review 30*, 517–535.

Hawton, K., Rodham, K., Evans, E. and Weatherall, R. (2002) 'Deliberate self harm in adolescents: Self report survey in schools in England.' *British Medical Journal 325*, 1207–1211.

Kendler, K. S., Bulik, C. M., Silberg, J., Hettema, J. M., Myers, J. and Prescott, C. A. (2000) 'Childhood sexual abuse and adult psychiatric and substance use disorders in women: An epidemiological and Cotwin control analysis.' *Archives of General Psychiatry 57*, 953–959.

Macdonald, G. and Turner, W. (2005) 'An experiment in helping foster-carers manage challenging behaviour.' *British Journal of Social Work 35*, 1265–1282.

Macdonald, G., Higgins, J. P. T., Ramchandani, P., Valentine, J. C., Bronger, L. P., Klein, P., O'Daniel, R., Pickering, M., Rademaker, B., Richardson, G. and Taylor, M. (2012) 'Cognitive-behavioural interventions for children who have been sexually abused.' *Cochrane Database of Systematic Reviews*. London: Cochrane.

Macdonald, G., Sheldon, B. and Gillespie, J. (1992) 'Contemporary studies of the effectiveness of social work.' *British Journal of Social Work 22*, 615–643.

Macmillan, H. L., Jamieson, E. and Walsh, C. A. (2003) 'Reported contact with child protection services among those reporting child physical and sexual abuse: Results from a community survey.' *Child Abuse and Neglect 27*, 1397–1408.

Maynard, B. R., Kjellstrand, E. K. and Thompson, A. M. (2014) 'Effects of check and connect on attendance, behavior, and academics: A randomized effectiveness trial.' *Research on Social Work Practice 24*, 3, 296-309.

Melchert, T. P. and Parker, R. L. (1997) 'Different forms of childhood abuse and memory.' *Child Abuse and Neglect 21*, 125–135.

Midgley, N. and Kennedy, E. (2011) 'Psychodynamic psychotherapy for children and adolescents: A critical review of the evidence base.' *Journal of Child Psychotherapy 37*, 232–260.

Molnar, B. E., Buka, S. L. and Kessler, R. C. (2001) 'Child sexual abuse and subsequent psychopathology: Results from the National Comorbidity Survey.' *American Journal of Public Health 91*, 753–760.

Newman, T. and Roberts, H. (1997) 'Assessing social work effectiveness in child care practice: The contribution of randomized controlled trials.' *Child Care Health and Development 23*, 287–296.

Paolucci, E. O., Genuis, M. L. and Violato, C. (2001) 'A meta-analysis of the published research on the effects of child sexual abuse.' *Journal of Psychology 135*, 17–36.

Parker, B. and Turner, W. (2014) 'Psychoanalytic/psychodynamic psychotherapy for sexually abused children and adolescents: A systematic review.' *Research on Social Work Practice 24*, 389–399.

Peckham, N. G. (2007) 'Evaluating a survivors group pilot for women with significant intellectual disabilities who have been sexually abused.' *Journal of Applied Research in Intellectual Disabilities 20*, 308–322.

Putnam, F. W. (2003) 'Ten-year research update review: Child sexual abuse.' *Journal of the American Academy of Child and Adolescent Psychiatry 42*, 269–278.

Radford, L., Corral, S., Bradley, C., Fisher, H., Bassett, C., Howat, N. and Collishaw, S. (2011) *Child Abuse and Neglect in the UK Today.* London: NSPCC.

Ramchandani, P. and Jones, D. P. H. (2003) 'Treating psychological symptoms in sexually abused children: From research findings to service provision.' *British Journal of Psychiatry 183,* 484–490.

Roland, M. and Torgerson, D. J. (1998) 'Understanding controlled trials: What are pragmatic trials?' *British Medical Journal 316,* 285–285.

Rose, S., Bisson, J., Churchill, R. and Wessely, S. (2002) 'Psychological debriefing for preventing post traumatic stress disorder (PTSD).' *The Cochrane Database of Systematic Reviews* (CD000560-CD000560). London: Cochrane.

Rushton, A. and Monk, E. (2010) 'A "real-world" evaluation of an adoptive parenting programme: Reflections after conducting a randomized trial.' *Clinical Child Psychology and Psychiatry 15,* 4, 543–554.

Saied-Tessier, A. (2014) *Estimating the Costs of Child Sexual Abuse in the UK.* London: NSPCC.

Saunders, B., Kilpatrick, D., Hanson, R., Resnick, H. and Walker, M. (1999) 'Prevalence, case characteristics, and long-term psychological correlates of child rape among women: A national survey.' *Child Maltreatment 4,* 187–200.

Shirk, S. and Saiz, C. (1992) 'Clinical, empirical, and developmental perspectives on the therapeutic relationship in child psychotherapy.' *Development and Psychopathology 4,* 713–728.

Sinason, V. (2002) 'Treating people with learning difficulties after physical or sexual abuse.' *Journal of Continuing Professional Development 8,* 424–432.

Spencer, N., Devereux, E., Wallace, A., Sundrum, R., Shenoy, M., Bacchus, C. and Logan, S. (2005) 'Disabling conditions and registration for child abuse and neglect: A population-based study.' *Pediatrics 2005,* 116, 609–613.

Sullivan, P. M. and Knutson, P. M. (2000) 'Maltreatment and disabilities: A population-based epidemiological study.' *Child Abuse and Neglect 24,* 10, 1257–1273.

Trinder, L. (1996) 'Social work research: The state of the art (or science).' *Child and Family Social Work 1,* 233–242.

Webb, S. (2001) 'Some considerations on the validity of evidence-based practice in social work.' *British Journal of Social Work 31,* 57–79.

Chapter 3

FRONT ROW SEATS

Why Researchers Need to Get Closer to
Practice and How We Can Do So

DAVID WESTLAKE
University of Bedfordshire

Introduction

Social work practice is a public service that is delivered in private places. Perhaps in part as a result of this we know remarkably little about how social workers talk with parents, children and families. Direct work in social work usually involves a single social worker speaking to family members in their homes or in local authority offices. Supervisors relatively rarely observe home visits and in Children's Services (unlike schools) inspectors rely predominantly on accounts of practice in agency records rather than direct observation. Much of the face-to-face work that is central to social work therefore remains cloistered from scrutiny.

Fortunately, this is beginning to change. Alternate models of practice that encourage joint working have proliferated recently (Goodman and Trowler, 2012) and a growing interest in direct practice is gaining momentum (Trowler, 2014). Politically, this reached a milestone with the Munro Review of Child Protection. It recommended that, as part of creating 'a system that values professional expertise', practice supervisors and external inspectors should observe direct practice encounters (Munro, 2011, p.39). Of course, social workers have long recognised the value of face-to-face work, repeatedly calling for their administrative workload to be reduced so they can spend more time on home visits. This is at the very least a key part of social work – and for most involved in child and family social work it is perhaps seen as the heart of social work. Despite this, researchers have struggled to get close enough to practice often enough.

The lack of research directly observing practice was commented upon by Trevithick *et al.* (2004), and Forrester *et al.* (2008) found very few studies that had this focus. Observation has played a larger role in fields close to social work. For example, addiction researchers have more commonly observed and analysed direct practice (Allen *et al.*, 1997; UK Alcohol Treatment Trial (UKATT) Research Team, 2005). Indeed, observation and feedback have been foundational in the development of Motivational Interviewing (MI) (Miller and Rollnick, 2012). This is a therapeutic method originally developed in the alcohol field, which is the focus of one of the studies I discuss below. Through observational methods researchers here have devised a coding system that measures skills (Moyers *et al.*, 2010). However, as Ferguson states, the home visit in social work, 'has been largely ignored in analyses of practice' (Ferguson, 2010, p.1109). This is, on the face of it, an extraordinary gap in our knowledge. Why might this have happened?

Barriers to research limit the evidence base

The theoretical and practical origins of the lack of research in this area represent a cause and effect dilemma. On the one hand, face-to-face encounters can often be complex interactions and there is a lack of conceptual development within social work around what good practice entails. On the other hand, they lend themselves to observational approaches that are prone to several obstacles, including difficulties around access due to layers of gatekeeping, consent and ethical issues. These practical barriers to getting close to practice have stymied social work researchers in various ways. While these are probably most acute for research involving direct observation, they also contribute to poor response rates more generally. This is particularly true of studies that have attempted to interview parents (see, for example, Forrester and Harwin, 2011; Ward, Brown and Westlake, 2012). Key aspects of this central pillar of social work therefore remain a puzzle, for which we have a lack of theory and a lack of data.

At a prosaic level teaching and writing on effective communication in social work relies on a very limited evidence base (Forrester *et al.*, 2008; Trevithick *et al.*, 2004). The salience of this is further underlined by the negative impact it has had on policy. Critiques of recent policy failures have been traced back to weaknesses in this area, most notably in the case of the Integrated Children's System where mistakes are attributed to 'practice-distant' approaches that do not understand the nature of the work (White *et al.*, 2009). Notwithstanding the inherent challenges of getting close to practice, there are significant opportunities that can be seized with the help of innovative research methods.

An innovative approach to observing practice

In this chapter I will explore an approach to observing practice systematically on a relatively large scale. This evolved during the course of two rather different studies, but both were concerned with practice in a children and families setting. They involved an unprecedented amount of direct observation and established a unique dataset of audio-recorded practice encounters. The approach also unlocked access to a large sample of interviews with families, demonstrating its potential to address perennial challenges facing researchers at a wider level. I will focus on overcoming practical challenges in gaining access to observe direct practice encounters, setting out a methodological strategy for researching practice through such observations.

I hope this encourages other researchers to explore the world of direct practice by giving an insight into its value. Underlying my presentation of these case studies is the central argument that I have begun to set out: the paucity of research that observes direct practice is problematic. It means we have a limited understanding of how social workers help bring about change in families. For readers convinced by this, a second objective is to offer a 'how-to' style description for getting close to practice based on one approach that has proved fruitful.

A strategy for getting close to practice

Direct observation offers an approach that brings the researcher as close to practice as possible. Through research and teaching programmes undertaken at the Tilda Goldberg Centre, University of Bedfordshire, we are gathering observations and recordings of direct practice across the UK. We are using these to explore various questions, including some of those mentioned above. By 2016 this dataset will contain over 3000 such recordings.

The two studies that inform this chapter established this programme and enabled the approach to develop. Both were relatively large and complex, so detailing every aspect of the methodology here is not possible. With that in mind, I give a brief overview and go into more detail about the observation of direct practice that they both have in common in the following section. Further details about the studies themselves are available in the referenced reports.

1. **Reclaiming Social Work? An Evaluation of Systemic Units as an Approach to Delivering Children's Services** (Forrester *et al.*, 2013; hereafter referred to as 'the Reclaiming Social Work study'). This study was a comparison between three local authorities. It aimed to evaluate an innovative new approach to practice used in one authority by comparing this with practice in the other two, where there were more traditional structures. The new approach used a 'systemic unit' model often referred to as 'Reclaiming Social Work' or 'the Hackney model'. The evaluation described the context within which services are delivered in each authority. It then considered in some detail the way in which context shapes practice.

    With a focus on practice and the factors shaping it in three settings, this study required a methodology that would enable us to explore practice at the level of individual workers and also at the level of teams and broader local authority systems. A core component of this was the use of naturalistic observation, through a team of researchers shadowing workers in each setting. Researchers were embedded within each local authority for agreed periods of time. Shadowing operated on a convenience sampling basis, which was highly dependent on the working relationships individual researchers built with the teams they were assigned to. Typically, researchers would agree to shadow one worker each day and aim to spend some time with every team member (although this was not possible in all teams). Shadowing included all elements of what social workers do on a day-to-day basis, such as supervision with line managers, desk-based case recording, team meetings, decision-making panels and multiagency work. This also involved face-to-face meetings with parents and family members, sometimes in public places and often in the office and in family homes.

    The team of seven researchers shadowed workers for around 46 weeks between June 2011 and March 2012. Other data was collected from social workers and families through interviews, questionnaires and surveys. This piloted various elements of the following study, particularly the approach to embedding researchers, observing home visits and some other areas of data collection.

A key finding was that the systemic unit model appeared to be a more effective way of working for various reasons. Workers spent more time focussing on direct work, they had a shared therapeutic approach (as all were trained in systemic methods) and they shared casework, meaning debate and discussion characterised all elements of decision making.

2.   **Engaging Parents and Protecting Children? A Randomised Controlled Trial of the Impact of Training in Motivational Interviewing on the Engagement of Parents in Child and Family Social Work** (Forrester *et al.*, in preparation; hereafter referred to as 'the RCT').

Building on the Reclaiming Social Work study, this project explored the skills of social workers in communicating with parents during direct practice encounters. It was designed to interrogate links between training workers in the MI communication style, their skill levels in MI after the training and how well these skills enabled them to engage parents and improve outcomes for children and families.

The study design was a randomised controlled trial (RCT). Workers in the Children in Need (CiN) service of a London local authority were randomly assigned to either an intervention group that received an intensive programme of training in MI or a control group that did not receive training. After the training, all families referred to the service were randomly allocated between the groups for seven months, starting in December 2012. Elements of data collection that were piloted in the Reclaiming Social Work study, such as observing practice and interviewing parents, united to form the backbone of data collection in the RCT. A systematic sample of families meeting certain criteria was constructed, with families invited to take part in the study shortly after social work involvement began.

A complex set of findings emerged and analysis is ongoing at the time of writing. Some key components of MI were found to correlate with important factors, such as parental engagement, however the between group comparison resulted in a null finding. This suggests the training did not have a significant impact on practice (Forrester *et al.*, in preparation).

Common features amidst different designs

Although the two studies differed considerably in terms of design and methodology, the research questions in both shared a common curiosity about practice. In the first, we were interested in how practice varied between the organisations and the role of organisational structures in driving practice. In the second, our focus was more individualistic: did the training lead to increases in skill among workers, and what impact did this have on practice?

Observing and evaluating practice in a systematic way was therefore central to answering these questions, though this brings various challenges. Research has been described as a process of 'Getting in, getting on and getting out' (Irvine and Gaffikin, 2006), and the first of these has proved perhaps the most fundamental barrier to researchers seeking to observe social work practice. The key innovation developed in our studies therefore aimed to find a way of accessing face-to-face encounters, which are surrounded by layers of gatekeeping.

Key innovative elements

The maxim above was particularly relevant in both our studies, but the challenge of obtaining a large enough sample of participants was amplified in the RCT. The experimental design meant the study would live or die on its ability to recruit a large and systematic sample. Without this, it would lack the statistical 'power' needed for validity. Once organisational and ethical approval has been granted, recruiting participants to take part in research appears to depend on two factors. First, the individuals concerned being made aware of the opportunity to take part and, second, their agreeing to do so. The approach used to address this central challenge was therefore broken down into two parts:

1. Engaging professionals – this involved navigating layers of gatekeeping, involving local authority leaders, managers and practitioners.

2. Engaging families – this was done in collaboration with workers who approached families and introduced the study.

A central theme running through both these was the need to address a range of concerns and anxieties from leaders, managers, practitioners and, to a lesser extent, parents. I will explore this in more detail as I discuss each below, before extracting some key learning points.

Engaging professionals

Engaging gatekeepers at some level is inevitable in this field, and the outcome is often decisive. Our approach navigated a path through the various layers of gatekeeping that surround direct practice (see Figure 3.1).

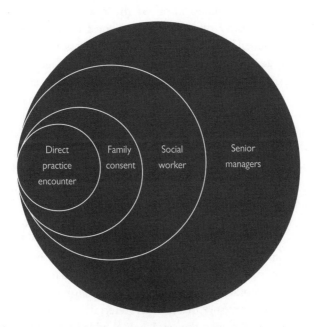

Figure 3.1: Layers of gatekeeping around direct practice

Two aspects of the RCT made this process particularly involved. First, the unusual proposal whereby the research team dictated significant parts of the allocation process in line with randomising families between groups. One can understand even the most research-minded managers having reservations about this (succinctly summarised by one service manager involved in our discussions who told us, 'If a child is at risk, you can stick your randomisation up your arse'). Second, our proposals would expose practice to an unprecedented level of scrutiny by embedding researchers within the CiN teams. At its heart the study was about how social workers engage parents, but the whole project rested on our ability to engage the social work staff.

Engaging senior managers involved a series of meetings, briefings and presentations where several issues were raised. Among these were ethical objections noted above, but other concerns were more practical – such as what would happen when workers take leave and where researchers would sit in the office building.

This process resulted in approval to conduct the study as planned, including a hugely important commitment to collaboration. This manifested in the accommodation of the research team within the primary local authority office, the use of local authority equipment, swipe cards, council email accounts and full access to the Integrated Children's System (ICS) recording system. These did more than make our lives easier – they were symbolic of the commitment of senior managers and undoubtedly influenced buy-in at team manager and social worker level. Part of this commitment was that all workers would participate and that this would be an expectation as part of their role as council employees. Of course, this alone did not automatically mean everyone participated enthusiastically. Nonetheless it helped a great deal as we began the process of engaging the workers we would be accompanying on home visits and their supervisors.

Upon senior management agreeing to the study we started to engage gatekeepers at every level of the organisation. This began with a series of briefings and presentations but it was an ongoing process through the seven-month data collection period. This was partly because the engagement of workers and teams varied throughout due to other forces, such as the pressure of increased referrals, and partly because a number of new staff joined the service. Embeddedness within the CiN teams increasingly bore fruit during this aspect of the project, and the good relationships we built with staff proved fundamental in how many families were subsequently involved in the study.

Engaging families

The process by which we approached each family in the RCT and invited them to take part is depicted in Figure 3.2. Crucially, we utilised our relationships with social work staff to introduce the study to them and invite them to be observed. We aimed to observe the second or third home visit, and cases that were closed prior to this point were excluded from the study. As I noted above, this opened the door to other elements of data collection. For example, 132 families (79.5%) involved in observations agreed to take part in a subsequent research interview – in contrast to other studies where these have been elusive (Forrester and Harwin, 2011).

Along with the embedded nature of the team, this may be the most innovative element of this approach. It came about as a response to dilemmas around how to recruit families to take part in interviews. An alternative way of approaching families is by contacting them directly by post but this can lead to lower response rates than we could afford (Ward *et al.*, 2012). The combination of observations and interviews matured towards the end of the Reclaiming Social Work study, and the final months of data collection there served as a useful pilot for the RCT.

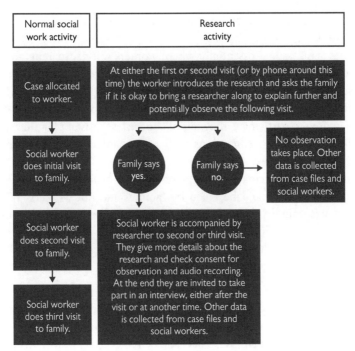

Figure 3.2: Process for inviting families to participate

Key learning points: real and imagined challenges of accessing home visits

1. Addressing practitioner anxieties

It is not difficult to see why large-scale observations of direct practice have proved elusive for researchers. These meetings are often fraught and emotional encounters both for practitioners and families. Most of those we observed took place during the initial assessment. During this time practitioners are under pressure to gather information and assess risk, as well as beginning to plan the work they will do in subsequent weeks and months. Meanwhile, parents are usually in the midst of some form of crisis that led to the referral. They may feel a range of emotions including anger, upset and grief, and that they are being victimised or blamed. Many also fear their children will be placed in care (Forrester *et al.*, in preparation).

The fact that direct observation opens up individual (and systemic) practice to an unusual level of scrutiny is unavoidable. This provokes anxieties that can manifest in problems elsewhere, the most obvious example being in the reluctance of workers to broach the topic with families. This issue – essentially where workers selected parents to ask or not ask, arose to some degree in the Reclaiming Social Work study. As such, it also came up during our 'premortem' (Klein, 2007) when planning the RCT. If workers were allowed to choose which families were invited to participate, they might choose less resistant families who would be 'easier' to engage. As well as jeopardising the balance of the sample, this raises ethical concerns because it denies parents the opportunity to participate. Both the research team and senior managers felt the decision should be taken by families and not workers. When framed accordingly, most workers understood that taking decisions away from families (in all but the most sensitive of circumstances) was unethical. As a result, parents in 90 per cent of cases were asked.

2. Gaining informed consent from parents

Fortunately we found engaging families in the research to be a far easier process. Although families can sometimes be resistant to social workers' involvement (Forrester, Westlake and Glynn, 2012), the majority of parents agreed for a researcher to observe and most of these also took the time to complete two research interviews afterwards. Some were so used to professional involvement that they were relaxed about another professional (the researcher) entering their lives. Many clearly appreciated speaking to independent researchers. They overwhelmingly reported finding the experience worthwhile, which indicates that low response rates may not be due to unwillingness to take part (Westlake and Forrester, forthcoming).

This inclination to participate even extended to families for whom the social worker felt circumstances were so severe that they were 'not up to' being asked. One example of this is the case of a mother who had recently been raped and had other difficulties including issues with drugs. The social worker initially felt she should not be asked, but the mother participated fully in both interviews and observation. Of course, this raises questions about the potentially throttling effect on service user participation that professionals may have. It suggests difficulties in recruiting to other studies may be a symptom of overly paternalistic gatekeeping. It is easy to imagine this kind of observation not going ahead. Two aspects of our approach were decisive in overcoming this challenge. First, through the ethical arguments and emphasis on the systematic approach needed and, second, through being embedded and therefore able to approach the worker informally and talk through concerns in the office.

3. Embeddedness

The embedded nature of the researchers was an enabling factor that facilitated all areas of data collection. It was a foundational element of both projects but it was more formalised in the RCT, where researchers sat within the six CiN teams. They got to know managers and other staff, occupied the same offices and attended team meetings. Embeddedness had a range of benefits, some more tangible than others. It became easier to identify and track new allocations and make arrangements with workers face to face, avoiding protracted email trails and wasted time. More broadly, effective relationships with people in research settings often smooth the way for success, just as poor relationships or key staff changing roles can interrupt or derail a study. The fact that some researchers were qualified social workers themselves helped in building trust between researchers and professionals. The importance of such trust has been highlighted elsewhere (Emmel *et al.*, 2007).

Strengths and challenges

Strengths and challenges apply to both the observational data itself and our protocol for collecting it. I outline these here before concluding with a broader discussion of the implications for social work research.

Observational data

Contrasting observational data with more commonly used alternatives is a useful way of illustrating its potential. An absence of observational approaches has led to a reliance on focus groups, surveys, interviews and diary recording to inform our understanding of practice. Although these are valuable in the right circumstances they have severe limitations in what they can teach us about key areas of practice, such as how social workers communicate with clients (Forrester and Harwin, 2011). They allow us to explore perspectives on practice but are not appropriate for analysing practice itself. This precludes exploration of important questions. For example, how do social workers talk to parents? How are concerns raised and discussed? How is resistance manifested and addressed? How do variables such as class, race and gender impact on the conversations that take place during home visits?

None of these questions can be satisfactorily answered by non-observational methods. Through audio recording we have a large dataset that is currently being analysed. The initial analysis aims to measure levels of skill in MI used by social workers using a quantitative method called the Motivational Interviewing Treatment Integrity (MITI) code (Moyers *et al.*, 2010). However, a programme of more qualitative analysis will follow and this will explore the questions raised above.

Although bias is an issue whichever method is used, it is particularly acute where practitioners are asked to recall information. In particular, shadowing workers to record how they spent their time (as we did in our initial study) is likely to produce more accurate data than asking workers to recall activity during a research interview or complete a diary (e.g. Holmes and McDermid, 2013).

Observational data suffers from a different kind of bias, emerging from the researchers' presence influencing the encounter. I have experienced this in various settings. When observing a team meeting it became clear that the structure of the session varied significantly from normal because of my presence as a researcher. Subsequent talks with individual staff supported my suspicions that team leaders had 'stage managed' the meeting to give me what they thought I wanted to see. Mundane discussions about printer problems, caseloads and administration gave way to an in-depth consideration of Freudian theory! Similarly, during home visits I have experienced social workers glancing over as if to ask, 'Am I doing it right?' Likewise, an angry father paused briefly during a torrent of abuse directed at his social worker and team manager, caught his breath and turned to me to ask, 'Did you get all that?' Sitting centimetres from him in a tiny room, my desire to be a 'fly on the wall' was stronger than ever but this remains an impossible ideal. Did he shout louder and swear more because I was watching? Perhaps, although I subsequently learned he was known for such outbursts. Either way, it is clear that some elements of performance can emerge and that these are a challenge for researchers. The altered dynamic of observation could make observation inappropriate or impossible for different reasons in other settings. One example is in professional supervision. While we observed a small number of supervisions in the Reclaiming Social Work study, there are obvious ethical challenges associated with observing a session where a supervisor may have to raise disciplinary matters or other challenging issues (the few that we observed were positive). The fact that more challenging sessions are likely to go unobserved may impact on how supervision is conceptualised in the findings.

While some bias is unavoidable and we must take account of these dynamics, we must also take steps to ameliorate it where possible – by reassuring workers that their practice would not be singled out, for instance. In our experience the level of anxiety decreased over time as practitioners became used to being observed; it seems logical that some other artefacts of observation would also diminish. This also reiterates the importance of a systematic sample inclusive of a wide range of encounters. Such a sample can be elusive even using our relatively successful approach. It is worth considering whether the 35 per cent of families who did not agree to take part were somehow different to those who did. It may be that those families were expecting a particularly tense meeting, for example, and therefore declined an observation. This could skew the sample, although a review of case file data suggested families who took part did not differ significantly from those who declined on any available measure. More broadly, non-participation, attrition and small sample sizes can be issues whichever method we use. This underlines the importance of triangulation where possible, which I discuss further later in the chapter.

Strategy for getting close to practice

Two self-evident strengths of our approach to gaining access stand out. First is the number of face-to-face encounters it allowed us to observe. The systematic sample of observations and recordings gathered gave sufficient statistical power to the experimental design. Over 65 per cent of families who were asked to take part in an observation agreed to do so (n=166) and 131 of these agreed for the observer to audio record the conversations for later analysis. This generated meaningful data that we are using to measure the quality of the intervention.

A second strength is the way in which it allowed us to involve service users, both in observations and beyond. In most cases when a parent agreed to an observation, they also took part in two research interviews. In this sense, the observations were a passage to other valuable sources of data, which allowed us to explore parents' views, family situations and child well-being. Data from family interviews illuminated the issues they faced and their views on the service. A key analysis we are working on correlates this with questionnaire data from social workers and the research observer to explore engagement from three perspectives (Waits *et al.*, in preparation).

A principle challenge is the extent to which delivering this complex strategy is transferable to other research settings. Of course, issues of generalisability more commonly arise when evaluating interventions than research methods. Nonetheless, the multiple contingent parts in this strategy make it unusually complex. Access to a given family depends upon their social worker approaching them, which in turn relies on their team manager approving, and so on. This has much in common with more traditional interventions and aspects of each would arguably be prone to local variations. Researchers looking to implement it elsewhere may be advised to consider such factors.

Chief among these is the nature of the local authority in which we undertook the RCT. Fortunately we chose a highly functioning and well-organised authority with a good inspection record. Senior managers are directive and preside over a culture of compliance. It is easy to see how this facilitated our approach; when workers were asked to engage with us a large majority did so. Senior staff also supported us when workers were reluctant to approach families, and a steering group met on a fortnightly basis to monitor progress. The relatively stable workforce also helped. Having worked in less organised, less hierarchical authorities with high rates of turnover among staff, it is difficult to envisage the study going so well in such a context. This underlines the importance of the research site in determining the success of innovative methods.

Another factor that worked in our favour was that the study featured a training course for staff that benefitted the local authority. Where appropriate and practical, other researchers would be advised to consider whether a similar 'quid pro quo' could be reached as this may help secure commitment. The nature of the relationship we built with the local authority facilitated other benefits for them, including numerous briefings on different areas of interest based on the research data. Such feedback has subsequently led to a further project, jointly proposed by the local authority and the research team. This is now funded and due to start in early 2015. It will build on the RCT and continue to collect data on direct practice through the observations of embedded researchers.

Conclusion

In this chapter I have set out a strategy for getting close enough to practice to observe face-to-face encounters. This evolved over time and across two studies of practice that had quite different designs. Key elements of observing practice and involving service users coalesced in the RCT and resulted in a successful programme of data collection. By way of a conclusion I will consider the implications for social work research more widely.

At an empirical level there is clear potential to adapt this strategy to explore other neglected aspects of these interactions. These could go beyond our focus on how social workers talk to parents and begin to address gaps in our knowledge of how they behave more generally during home visits (Ferguson, 2010). They could explore how they speak to and interact with other carers or with children, how they perform investigative work and how they navigate the home environment, among many others.

At a more conceptual level it reminds us that the best methods are strongly related to our research questions. There has been a preoccupation with qualitative and quantitative methods, which often boils down to their supposedly conflicting epistemological precursors (interpretivist versus positivist). From this perspective, there may be little in common between ethnographic research aiming to generate a 'thick' description (Geertz, 1973) (i.e. the Reclaiming Social Work study) and an RCT.

Broadly speaking, qualitative approaches have found favour among social work researchers, who have tended to be sceptical of experimental designs. This may be in part due to misunderstandings about how the two can complement each other. In a disparaging description of RCTs, Hollway argues, 'Actual people are nowhere to be found in this kind of research' (Hollway, 2009, p.463). The RCT described here contests this view, and more broadly there is an increasing recognition that mixed-method approaches are epistemologically rational (Bryman and Becker, 2012). Indeed, many contemporary studies use mixed methods to attempt theoretical triangulation, which is itself important in such a complex area (e.g. Forrester *et al.*, 2013; Pawson and Tilley, 1997; Pawson, 2013). I would therefore make the case for approaches such as ours, which combine observations with interviews and other sources of data.

Whether a method is quantitative or qualitative is really about analysis. This also shapes data collection, of course, but any chosen approach to gathering data should go beyond this. Closely relating the broader approach to the research questions is arguably more important. In the case of researching practice, this means whether research incorporates direct observation into the suite of methods or relies on second-hand accounts. The term 'practice-near' is widely used and would seem appropriate for making this distinction. Nevertheless, it has entered the current parlance without a consensus on the importance of observation.

'Practice-near' research has been the focus of an ESRC seminar series and a number of journal articles, including a special issue of the *Journal of Social Work Practice* (Froggett and Briggs, 2009). This helped to establish the centrality of an ethnographic element (e.g. Hingley-Jones, 2009), but defining 'practice-near' has not been straightforward (Froggett and Briggs, 2009). Elsewhere in the same issue somewhat broader definitions are proposed. The following, for example, could apply to almost any type of social work research: 'In social work we have been crucially concerned with social inclusion, values, anti-discriminatory practice and empowerment, and research that holds these in mind is practice near' (Aymer, 2009, p.444).

The areas cited here represent fertile ground for empirical work, but without observational methods the term 'practice-near' loses some of its meaning. Conceptually, there are areas for which accounts of practice are highly valuable, but for others discussed here direct observation is necessary. To answer these particular questions, accounts of practice are limited: it is akin to the difference between reading a theatre review and sitting on the front row during the performance. If we relied on such accounts in the RCT, the findings would be starkly different. Social workers were overwhelmingly positive about the MI training and several felt it had transformed their practice. Yet other data obtained through observations showed no such change. One important message to emerge from this is that 'practice-near' research needs to be both *about* practice and *near* to it.

If we recognise the value of this approach to learning about practice, accepting the necessity for mixed-method research designs, the strategy described in this chapter has considerable utility. It offers a blueprint for overcoming common practical and methodological challenges associated with doing research in social work. As well as being helpful in studies of face-to-face encounters, it may unlock doors to other types of data collection.

References

Allen, J., Mattson, M., Miller, W., Tonigan, J., Connors, G., Rychtarik, R., Randall, C., Anton, R., Kadden, R. and Litt, M. (1997) 'Matching alcoholism treatments to client heterogeneity: Project MATCH posttreatment drinking outcomes.' *Journal of Studies on Alcohol 58*, 7–29.

Aymer, C. (2009) 'Reflections at the waterhole: Black professionals researching together.' *Journal of Social Work Practice 23*, 443–450.

Bryman, A. and Becker, S. (2012) 'The Debate about Quantitative and Qualitative Research.' In: S. Becker, A. Bryman and H. Ferguson (eds) *Understanding Research for Social Policy and Social Work* (2nd edition). Bristol: The Policy Press.

Emmel, N., Hughes, K., Greenhalgh, J. and Sales, A. (2007) 'Accessing socially excluded people: Trust and the gatekeeper in the researcher–participant relationship.' *Sociological Research Online 12*, 2.

Ferguson, H. (2010) 'Walks, Home Visits and Atmospheres: Risk and the Everyday Practices and Mobilities of Social Work and Child Protection' *British Journal of Social Work, 40* (4), 1100-1117.

Forrester, D. and Harwin, J. (2011) *Parents Who Misuse Drugs and Alcohol: Effective Interventions in Social Work and Child Protection.* Chichester: Wiley-Blackwell.

Forrester, D., Mccambridge, J., Waissbein, C. and Rollnick, S. (2008) 'How do child and family social workers talk to parents about child welfare concerns?' *Child Abuse Review 17*, 23–35.

Forrester, D., Westlake, D. and Glynn, G. (2012) 'Parental resistance and social worker skills: Towards a theory of motivational social work.' *Child and Family Social Work 17*, 118-129.

Forrester, D., Westlake, D., Mccann, M., Thurnham, A., Shefer, G., Glynn, G. and Killian, M. (2013) *Reclaiming Social Work? An Evaluation of Systemic Units as an Approach to Delivering Children's Services: Final Report of a Comparative Study of Practice and the Factors Shaping it in Three Local Authorities.* Luton: University of Bedfordshire.

Forrester, D., Westlake, D., Waits, C., Thomas, R., Antonopoulou, P., Whittaker, C., Mccann, M., Killian, M. and Thurnham, A. (in preparation) *Engaging Parents and Protecting Children: A Randomised Controlled Trial in Motivational Interviewing in Child Protection.*

Froggett, L. and Briggs, S. (2009) 'Editorial.' *Journal of Social Work Practice 23*, 377–382.

Geertz, C. (1973) *The Interpretation of Cultures.* New York: Basic Books.

Goodman, S. and Trowler, I. (eds) (2012) *Social Work Reclaimed.* London: Jessica Kingsley Publishers.

Hingley-Jones, H. (2009) 'Developing practice-near social work research to explore the emotional worlds of severely learning disabled adolescents in 'transition' and their families.' *Journal of Social Work Practice 23*, 413-428.

Hollway, W. (2009) 'Applying the "experience-near" principle to research: Psychoanalytically informed methods.' *Journal of Social Work Practice 23*, 461–474.

Holmes, L. and Mcdermid, S. (2013) 'How social workers spend their time in frontline children's social care in England.' *Journal of Children's Services 8*, 123–133.

Irvine, H. and Gaffikin, M. (2006) 'Getting in, getting on and getting out: Reflections on a qualitative research project.' *Accounting, Auditing and Accountability Journal 19*, 115–145.

Klein, G. (2007) 'Performing a project premortem.' *Harvard Business Review 85*, 18–19.

Miller, W. R. and Rollnick, S. (2012) *Motivational Interviewing: Helping People Change* (3rd edition). New York: Guilford.

Moyers, T. B., Martin, T., Manuel, J. K., Miller, W. R. and Ernst, D. (2010) *Revised Global Scales: Motivational Interviewing Treatment Integrity 3.1.1* (MITI 3.1.1). (Unpublished manuscript). Albuquerque: Center on Alcoholism, Substance Abuse and Addictions, University of New Mexico. Available at http://c.ymcdn.com/sites/www.marrch.org/resource /resmgr/imported/02-09-MITI-3-1-1.pdf, accessed on 7 July 2015.

Munro, E. (2011) *The Munro Review of Child Protection: Final Report: A Child-centred System.* London: Department for Education.

Pawson, R. (2013) *The Science of Evaluation: A Realist Manifesto.* London: Sage.

Pawson, R. and Tilley, N. (1997) *Realistic Evaluation.* London: Sage.

Trevithick, P., Richards, S., Ruch, G., Moss, B., Lines, L. and Manor, O. (2004) *SCIE Knowledge Review 6: Teaching and Learning Communication Skills in Social Work Education.* London: Social Care Institute for Excellence.

Trowler, I. (2014) *Knowledge and Skills for Child and Family Social Work.* London: Department for Education.

UK Alcohol Treatment Trial (UKATT) Research Team (2005) 'Effectiveness of treatment for alcohol problems: Findings of the randomised United Kingdom Alcohol Treatment Trial (UKATT).' *British Medical Journal 331*, 541–544.

Waits, C. *et al.* (in preparation) *Engagement in Child and Family Social Work from the Perspectives of Parent, Worker and Observer.*

Ward, H., Brown, R. and Westlake, D. (2012) *Safeguarding Babies and Very Young Children from Abuse and Neglect.* London: Jessica Kingsley Publishers.

Westlake, D. and Forrester, D. (forthcoming) 'Adding Evidence to the Ethics Debate: Investigating Parents' Experiences of their Participation in Research'. *British Journal of Social Work.*

White, S., Broadhurst, K., Wastell, D., Peckover, S., Hall, C. and Pithouse, A. (2009) 'Whither practice-near research in the modernization programme? Policy blunders in children's services.' *Journal of Social Work Practice 23*, 401–411.

Chapter 4

ARCHIVAL RESOURCES FOR SOCIAL WORK HISTORY

PAT STARKEY
University of Liverpool

Is there any point in studying the history of social work? It is interesting and informative, certainly, but how relevant is it to contemporary concerns? Social work practitioners and policy makers involved with current issues and with devising practices and procedures to protect vulnerable people in the future may be justified in asking whether study of the past is any more than an indulgence. But so dismissive a view fails to consider what the past has to teach. Just as knowledge of their earlier experiences can help explain how and why individuals behave in certain ways, so the history of institutions and professions can illuminate the present and explain why we are where we are. An understanding of the past may even help to avoid repetition of its errors. This chapter will consider some of the resources relevant to the history of social work from the mid-19th century to the present day, their location, how they can be used and some restrictions that may be imposed on their use.

Understanding context is vital. History attempts to understand why and how events happened and there is no substitute for a basic understanding of the society in which developments took place; reference to general historical accounts of politics, society and the economy is essential. Equally important is an understanding of the history of professions with which social work intersects – among them law, local government, education and medicine – and of issues such as class, gender, ethnicity and disability. The past can also be brought to life by examining the experiences of workers and – often neglected, because they are challenging to recover – the experiences of service users. Utilising knowledge gained from wide exploration can help to identify and evaluate those forces brought to bear on previous generations and to appreciate why particular developments took place. Human nature and human problems may have changed little, if at all, but the ways in which they have been perceived have undergone significant alteration; understanding this process can enable us to map the ways in which the profession has evolved.

Biographies of notable pioneers may help to set the scene and stimulate historical imagination. Among the many notable figures whose lives are commemorated in the *Oxford Dictionary of National Biography* (ODNB)[1] are Josephine Butler, Octavia Hill, Eleanor Rathbone and Eileen Younghusband. Accessible through public and university libraries, the ODNB is a valuable tool but, although regularly updated, it is necessarily limited both in scope and detail. More detailed biographies, for example of Butler (Jordan, 2007) and Hill (Darley, 2010) in the 19th century or Rathbone (Pedersen, 2004) and Younghusband (Jones, 1984) in the 20th, alongside their writings, will greatly enhance the picture. Hill, for example, wrote about housing conditions in London (Hill, reprint, 1998) and Butler described her work with prostitutes (Butler, 1870). Both were concerned with 19th-century poverty and its impact on individuals. In the early 20th century, Rathbone described the experiences of Liverpool dockers and their families, and campaigned for the introduction of Family Endowment (the forerunner of Child Benefit) (Rathbone, 1904, 1924). Understanding of 20th-century social work is enhanced by Younghusband's accounts of 'the newest profession' (Younghusband, 1946, 1978, 1981). Although original material like this may be out of print, it is available at the British Library, which, through the legal deposit system, has received a copy of every UK print publication since 1662. Its website gives full instructions about applying for a reader's ticket and ordering material.[2]

Social work as we know it today is a young profession. Estimates of its age vary – it all depends what is meant by 'social work'. Legislation following the end of the Second World War accelerated a process whose evolution can be traced in developments of many earlier decades – or even centuries – and vital evidence lies in official records, which include central and local government records, material produced by professional associations and universities and voluntary organisations.

---

1   www.oxforddnb.com
2   www.bl.uk

Key innovative elements

New knowledge is often little more than the response to new questions. The skill lies in subjecting evidence to questions informed by wide knowledge and an appreciation of the complex processes inherent in the construction of any record. Preliminary questions to be asked of any document, whether in the public domain or an archive, whether handwritten or printed, must include: When was this written? Why? By and for whom? But the researcher who goes no further than formulating such fundamental questions will learn little. Material created in the past cannot change, but it may be interrogated in such as way as to yield new information.

Take, as one example, the verbatim account of a debate in the House of Commons, available online in public and university libraries.[3] The words on the page are those spoken during the debate – but that may tell us relatively little, even after the first-line questions have been answered. What is known about the social and economic context of the time? Who were the key speakers? To which party did they belong? Which constituencies were represented? Was the subject of that debate likely to win the approval of the voters – something that may be particularly important if a general election is on the horizon. Even in the heat of a debate MPs may still have an eye to the opinions of their party, the newspapers or their constituents and tailor what they say accordingly. A critical examination of even so choreographed an event as a parliamentary debate may uncover intentions and attitudes that are not immediately obvious. Of course, parliamentary activity extends beyond the confines of the debating chambers and the records of committees and working parties must be subject to similar scrutiny. Much of this material is in print and accessible through libraries, but original documents including committee minutes, memoranda, correspondence and other unpublished material is held in the National Archives, which house UK government records.[4]

Examination of the debates surrounding the Ingleby Report and the eventual passage of the Children and Young Persons Act 1963 reveals a range of opinions about child welfare and delinquency that can inform our understanding of demands made on social workers and the implications of changing legislation for local authority organisation (Hansard, 1956–63). Students of social policy, historians and others

3   http://hansard.millbanksystems.com
4   www.nationalarchives.gov.uk

have spent many keyboard hours considering the impulse for the legislation and its effects, not just on social work practice, but also on the organisation of local authority departments, voluntary agencies and public health bodies The trail can be followed through local authority record offices, which will hold the minutes of, for example, the Children's, Welfare, Education, Social Services and Public Health departments and the archives of relevant voluntary agencies (Hendricks, 1994; Starkey, 1998; Welshman,1996).

Many record offices provide online lists of their holdings and a search using the name of the relevant local authority will generally lead to the right place. 'Lancashire Record Office', for example, will lead to new.lancashire.gov.uk, while 'Bristol Record Office' will link to archives.bristol.gov.uk. Record offices frequently invite email or telephone enquiries about particular holdings. Such requests must be precise; most archives hold thousands of documents and archivists need clear descriptions of the researcher's needs in order to locate material. Because what we now call social work is an amalgam of a number of different occupations, official supervision of its work has varied from authority to authority and has changed over the years: an appreciation of how and when designations changed and local government organisation was altered is vital.

Further evidence can be found in the rich material held in the archives of voluntary organisations. A number of celebratory accounts exist but until recently the history of charities and voluntary bodies had been subjected to relatively little critical scrutiny. Studies of individual agencies (Lewis, 1995; Parker, 2010; Starkey, 2000; Todd, 2014; Welshman, 2008) have attempted to critique their activities and estimate their importance, but much more needs to be done. Because this sector is so large, and has been so significant, three examples may help to illustrate the sorts of records that a researcher may find, although no one organisation can be taken as truly representative. The first is a charity founded in mid-19th-century London to offer care to 'deserving' people in difficulty; the second an organisation working with families, which originated as a relief agency during the Second World War and influenced the development of post-war social work, and the third a counselling agency founded in 1977.

During the 19th century, official intervention in the lives of individuals was minimal, governed by the Poor Law and limited largely to the provision of workhouses (Brundage, 2001; Crowther, 1983;

Glasgow, 2012; Jones, 2006); extant records of some of which can be accessed at the National Archives. Designed to deter all but the desperate, they were avoided by those who could find other sources of aid. One such, the House of Charity in Soho, London (now the House of St Barnabas), still functions as a charity to help the homeless,[5] although the type of support offered has changed. Founded in 1846 by wealthy London residents, including the future Prime Minister, W. E. Gladstone, it offered temporary accommodation to respectable people who had fallen on hard times and to emigrant families waiting for their ships to sail to various parts of the Empire (Starkey, 2008, 2011). The archive contains case histories of almost every person admitted, notes made on them by staff and regular visitors, and minutes of the weekly meetings of the governing gouncil, which illustrate the ups and downs of a charity constantly needing to raise money. Kept on open shelves at the House of St Barnabas for many years, these documents, especially those in Gladstone's handwriting, attracted great interest and became soiled with the stains of many ungloved hands. Although a treasure trove for the historian allowed free access, the collection contravened legislation regarding the storage of personal data and has now been moved to the Westminster Archive Centre[6] where rules about access are observed and the risk of damage reduced.

Although kept inappropriately for many years, the records of the House of Charity were valued as an historical record. Family Service Units (FSU) can be taken to represent those agencies for whom preservation of their records was less important than their day-to-day work. From its origins in relief work in Liverpool, Manchester and Stepney in 1940 it developed into a social work agency working with families and has been credited with pioneering intensive family casework (Starkey, 1998, 2000). When files and other records were eventually collected for deposit,[7] some were found in bin bags in basements, while documents from the earliest days of the organisation were discovered on top of a water tank. Some had just disappeared.

Compass, the third organisation, is illustrative of many small voluntary agencies supporting people in difficulties. Operating on Merseyside, it is engaged in a range of activities alongside its primary function of providing a counselling service. It runs a charity shop, offers

---

5   https://hosb.org.uk
6   www.westminster.gov.uk/archives
7   www.liv.ac.uk/library/sca

benefits advice, organises anger-management courses and provides in-service training for counsellors. A café, where staff trained in listening skills can offer personal support, has recently been opened.[8] All records are stored in its main office, secure and catalogued. Relevant filing cabinets are locked, and a coded system of recording, to which only a few staff members have access, is in place. There are clear procedures for the retention or destruction of material, although measures for the conservation of its paper records have yet to be implemented.

The voluntary sector can also claim to have contributed to the development of modern social work through university settlements, where students and academic staff lived in poor urban neighbourhoods and aimed to provide facilities for local people. Some, like Toynbee Hall, still function.[9] The archives of Toynbee Hall, documenting more than 130 years of service in East London, are housed partly at its own premises and partly at the London Metropolitan Archive.[10] Manchester University Settlement, which operated in the 1890s, also has an accessible archive.[11] Internet searches will uncover similar projects, initiated by universities and public schools in the 19th century. Not all have extant archives.

If a study of individual organisations can throw some light on to the sort of work in which they were engaged, professional associations can be invaluable for illuminating the concerns and ambitions of those whose working lives were spent within them. The Modern Records Centre at the University of Warwick has extensive holdings relating to social work including the records created by the Association of Social Workers, 1936–1970; the British Association of Social Workers, 1970–1990s; the Central Council for the Education and Training of Social Workers, 1962–1980; the National Institute of Social Work, 1940s– 2002; the Association of Child Care Officers, 1951–1970; the Institute of Medical Social Workers, 1895–1971; the National Association of Social Workers in Education, 1897–1980; and the Health Visitors' Association. In addition, the Centre holds recorded interviews with significant social workers, and the personal papers of pioneers like Eileen Younghusband and Marjory Allen.[12]

---

8   www.compass-counselling.org.uk
9   www.toynbeehall.org.uk
10 www.cityoflondon.gov.uk
11 www.library.manchester.ac.uk
12 www.warwick.ac.uk

Further insight into the growth of the profession can be found in the experiences of its practitioners and use has sometimes been made of recorded interviews with both past and present social workers (Cohen, 1998; Burnham, 2012). Invaluable though it is, such material must be subjected to questions framed to uncover aspects of the past that may lie beneath the surface of simple, narrative memories and the risks of bias, of self-interest and of self-dramatisation must always be remembered. Moreover, memories fade or become distorted and any oral account must be studied alongside other forms of evidence.

Professional social work journals, invaluable for tracing discussions about practice, include publications such as *Social Work Today* and *Community Care* and may be found in university libraries. Valuable material may also be found in journals of other professional organisations, for example medical journals like the *British Medical Journal*, *The Lancet* or *Public Health*. Journals concerned with law and the history of education may also contain material relevant to social work history.

The ways in which practitioners were trained can also help in the understanding of a profession's view of itself and the shape it hoped to take. The archives of universities such as the London School of Economics and the University of Liverpool, which both claim to have initiated the university training of social workers in the early 20th century, hold records relating to the provision of courses and the students who enrolled on them. These help to illustrate the types of people attracted to social work, the gender balance of those admitted, the nature of the courses they studied and the varied types of work for which they were trained. Student placements from the University of Liverpool, for example, were wide ranging and included practical experience in personnel departments of local factories, child rescue agencies, various local authority departments and youth organisations (Starkey, 2006). These, and the records of other schools of social work, may be susceptible to a range of questions about social workers themselves, their training and their experience.

Newspapers, too, are an invaluable source of information, particularly about the social context of any development. The British Library holds a collection of national and international newspapers. Although they may reveal social attitudes, they must also be carefully interrogated. What is known about the ownership and political slant of any publication? What is its readership? What does the editorial policy tell us about attitudes among different sections of the public?

The voices of service users are seldom heard. Until recently, the narratives of their lives were constructed for them within social workers' files and, once constructed, were not accessible to their central characters who were, therefore, unable to correct misunderstandings, protest at misrepresentation or comment on the quality of care that they received; any grievances they had were necessarily 'privatised and unexpressed' (Mayer and Timms, 1970; Starkey 2007). Notable attempts were made during the 1970s and 1980s to discover service users' impressions of their encounters with social workers; John Mayer and Noel Timms, Eric Sainsbury and Peter Phillimore were all, independently, tasked to uncover the way that service users experienced their treatment by voluntary agencies (Mayer and Timms, 1970; Phillimore, 1981; Sainsbury, 1975). The timing is important. During the 1970s, voluntary agencies perceived themselves to be in competition with local authorities, which, in the aftermath of the 1963 Children and Young Persons Act, were thought to threaten the charities' near monopoly of preventive work. Some agencies set out to demonstrate that they provided superior service by interviewing their service users. The interviews are important, as much for what they unconsciously reveal about the process of the investigation as for the information they gathered. For the most part, the encounters were between educated men, representing aid-giving agencies, and poorly educated women, dependent on that aid. The interviewers appear to have taken the responses to their questions at face value; none seems to have considered the possibility that the women in front of them might have been anxious to stay on good terms with an organisation on which they were dependent and to have phrased their answers accordingly. Interpretation of the interviews becomes more nuanced and more complex once issues like gender, class and the respective positions of interviewer and respondent are taken into account. Recent attempts have been made to try to 'listen' to the voices of service users and to understand their experience, but much more imaginative work needs to be done (Koven, 2004; Starkey, 2000b, 2007; Welshman, 2008).

Experience of the present will inform questions about the past; changing social attitudes, changing legislation and changing professional concerns will prompt new queries. Inevitably, historians are affected by shifts in the cyclical concern about social problems and prompted to ask questions informed by the present. From the late

1940s, paediatricians and social workers often focused on the incidence of physical abuse and child neglect, partly as a consequence of increased use of X-ray examinations after the introduction of the National Health Service. Uncovering evidence of physical harm to children gave rise to alarm about what was sometimes known as the 'battered baby syndrome' and became an important feature of work with children, later reflected in historical studies (Hendricks, 1994). The period from the late 20th century has been characterised by concern about sexual offences, especially those involving children. The observation that punishment for abusive behaviour was more lenient 40 or 50 years ago has been interpreted as indicating changing attitudes to women and children. There may be truth in that. There is certainly nothing new about sexual exploitation, nor has it only recently been discovered; Josephine Butler shocked her contemporaries by describing sexual abuse, and the 1908 Children Act acknowledged and attempted to deal with the problem of incest, but it was not a major historiographical topic. However, the current interest in sexuality, the increased openness about aspects of personal life and greater awareness of what constitutes abuse haves led historians to ask about those areas of life that had been kept hidden by earlier generations. Seth Koven's examination of the records of night shelters and refuges, for example, has led him to argue that these were places of abuse and exploitation as well as relief (Koven, 2004).

If, from the late 20th century, social workers and doctors have had in mind questions different from or additional to those of their predecessors in the 1940s, researchers into medical and social work history may also follow current concerns as they revisit the past and interrogate afresh its records. They may also want to ask why moral panics occur as and when they do. Although, as Gareth Williams has recently noted, 'the lenses through which we view the past are invariably distorted by what we know now, and whatever we choose to focus on must be calibrated against what was usual and reasonable for the age' (Williams, 2013, p.297), Shirley Swain and Margot Hillel (2010) have argued that we must not be blind to the lessons it can teach. Their study of child rescue discourse in England, Canada and Australia from the mid-19th to the early 20th century, argues that the carefully constructed image of the lonely or abandoned child was built upon a denial or victimisation of the family and kin. In a challenge to aspects of past and current practice they argue that, properly supported, it is the family that is most likely to ensure a child's safety and that the future of those children 'for whom this recourse fails can only be guaranteed if romantic notions of substitute care are similarly deconstructed' (Swain and Hillel, 2010, p.175). In addition to more conventional records, Swain and Hillel have used fiction to demonstrate the way that particular images were fed into popular consciousness. The evidence that these authors choose to use demonstrates vividly a process of examining the past that may give pause. Swain, whose research into various forms of institutional care for children in the 19th and 20th century is combined with an attempt to draw out lessons for the present, has also argued that 'any institution that places adults in charge of vulnerable children has the potential to become abusive' (Swain, 2001, p.116).

Similar work has been done on the photography employed by Thomas Barnardo in his quest to solicit funds for his rescue work. Koven has demonstrated ways in which vulnerable young children were sexualised by being photographed in dirty clothes, torn and draped in ways that can be seen as provocative and, we must assume, in poses that were deliberately constructed. In Barnardo's publicity those images, made to represent the child's condition before reception into his care, are contrasted with photographs of the same child whose clean face, brushed hair and appropriate, clean clothing project an image of innocence once she or he has been 'rescued' (Koven, 2004). If, with Williams, the researcher must take into account what was reasonable for the age, she must also understand the messages that were being conveyed and use those insights to look carefully at current publicity.

Researchers will ask different questions, informed by their professional interests and their experience. The examples noted above point to a small selection of resources available to the researcher looking for evidence of the origins and development of the social work profession: some have received a great deal of attention; many have yet to be examined.

Strengths and challenges

Research is always hard work. As well as basic difficulties – like deciphering poor handwriting in a document written in fading ink on inferior quality paper – there are frequently trails that lead nowhere or evidence that challenges received ideas and necessitates careful rethinking. In addition, all archival resources need to be approached carefully. A collection may be incomplete and key documents may appear to be missing. Many explanations can be adduced. Personal papers are often carefully weeded, in order to ensure that the best possible impression of their author is left for posterity. On occasion, there may be unexplained gaps in an official record. Not all these gaps witness to malign intent; papers may simply have been lost or misfiled, but sometimes material will have been deliberately removed from an archive and the researcher may want to ask why and whether what is missing is as important as what is retained. In some cases, a catastrophe of some sort – fire or flood, for example – may have resulted in badly disordered or damaged files.

Paper records face a range of other hazards unless managed properly. Mice have been known to make nests in files that have been inappropriately stored; material may have been made unreadable because sticky-back plastic has been used to keep things tidy – once dry and discoloured this is almost impossible to remove without damaging the document. Paperclips can rust and damage paper, making sections illegible. Records may also be incomplete because the archive is divided between more than one archival centre. This is the case, for instance, with the records of FSU (1940–2005). Most of its records are housed at the University of Liverpool,[13] but some, including personal memories of staff members, are at the University of Warwick,[14] while others are housed at the London Metropolitan Archives, where they were deposited with those of Family Welfare Association (now Family Action) with which FSU amalgamated in 2006.[15] Following such a trail can be time consuming but is essential if a full picture is to be obtained.

Even if it is reasonably complete, all archival material must be read carefully. Just because something has become an official record and is housed at the National Archive this does not mean that it can tell us the whole truth – or even more than a small part of it. The official record is always composed with an eye to what future readers might think about those making decisions. Minutes of meetings are generally carefully phrased so as to give an account of the principal elements of discussion and the decisions taken; they often fail to record arguments and tensions. Sometimes the most illuminating official records are those that have handwritten comments in the margin, often notes taken

---

13 www.liverpool.ac.uk
14 www.warwick.ac.uk
15 www.lma.gov.uk

during the course of a meeting and throwing light on the views of the person whose copy has ended up in the official file.

Archives of the voluntary sector are an under-used resource. Large organisations like the Children's Society,[16] Barnardo's,[17] National Children's Homes (now Action for Children)[18] and Save the Children[19] are able to employ archivists or use the resources of universities to care for their records, which are catalogued, kept in environmentally controlled conditions and, sometimes, digitised. Many less fortunate agencies, including those working with older people or particular illness or disabilities, lack the funds to employ staff to manage their documents and preserve their history: some are in good working order, some have been kept in unsuitable conditions, while others may have been destroyed because the agency has nowhere to keep them or has not realised their importance. Records of small organisations, operating locally and providing valuable services, are often overlooked by social historians and other commentators; many such agencies have not been studied at all and offer a rich field for any researcher interested to discover the wide and varied range of support services outside the activities of local authority Social Services Departments.

Access to archival material is governed by legislation enshrined in the Data Protection Act,[20] essential to protect the identity of individuals, whether service users or staff. The 'closed period', during which access will normally be denied, is 100 years from the closure of records relating to clients, 75 years in respect of archives relating to staff and 30 years in respect of administrative archives. Researchers will sometimes be allowed access to records deemed to be closed, so long as guarantees are given that references to individuals are anonymised in published accounts and that their identity is protected. But some organisations will limit or refuse access to material, a situation exacerbated in recent years as scandals relating to abuse have increased agencies' reluctance to allow access to their records. The Children's Society, however, is in the process of digitising many of its records and making them widely available.[16]

---

16   www.childrensociety.org
17   www.barnados.org.uk
18   www.sca-arch.liv.ac.uk
19   www.savethechildren.org
20   www.gov.uk/data-protection/data-protection-act

Documents created for a wide readership are generally readily accessible and can be informative. As well as accounts of their work, magazines and annual reports will all be carefully worded, either because it is politically wise or, in the case of voluntary agencies, because they depended – and still depend – on donations from their supporters, so avoid making public anything that might discourage them from opening their wallets. They are, therefore, often upbeat and positive. A researcher, well armed with information about the social and economic context within which the charities were working and who has consulted newspapers and other contemporary journalism will try to read between the lines. Financial records, generally in the public domain because registered charities are required to publish their accounts, can also be very revealing. How was the organisation getting its money? How was it spending it? How healthy was its financial situation, especially if it was heavily dependent on time-limited grants?

In addition to the official sites already considered, there are other websites that may be useful in the search for particular archival holdings. For example the National Register of Archives[21] is an invaluable aid to discovering material and its whereabouts. The Archives Hub can also be a useful guide to a wide range of repositories.[22] DANGO (Database of Archives of Non-Governmental Organisations)[23] is a useful resource for those wanting to find out about charities and voluntary organisations, although its limitations must be recognised; it was funded only until 2011 and has not been updated since then.

Research can be a lonely business and opportunities to compare notes with others engaged in similar quests can be both supportive and stimulating. The founding of the Social Work History Network in 2000 demonstrates a growing interest in the history of the profession, and its members have begun to raise important questions about the way social work has evolved. Its website gives details about its journal and about its regular research seminars.[24] The Voluntary Action History Society can provide useful research and contacts;[25] it also hosts regular research seminars, which are published as webcasts, and organises conferences.

---

21 www.nationalarchives.gov.uk

22 www.archiveshub.ac.uk

23 www.dango.bham.ac.uk

24 www.kcl.ac.uk/sspp/policy-institute/scwru/swhn

25 www.vahs.org.uk

Other academic societies, like the Society for the Social History of Medicine,[26] Women's History Network,[27] the Society for Social Medicine[28] and the History of Education Society[29] may have within their membership those whose research interests intersect with aspects of social work, and their websites and journals can help to open up or elucidate new and perhaps collaborative lines of enquiry.

A short chapter like this can do no more than outline possibilities and provide a few signposts; it will have succeeded if readers are prompted to think of new and important areas to be researched and imaginative ways in which that research can be carried forward. If new knowledge lies in the results of imaginative interrogation, it cannot be limited to those records already known to exist, or those questions routinely asked, but must be extended into areas hitherto unexplored.

References

Brundage, A. (2001) *The English Poor Laws, 1700–1930*. London: Palgrave Macmillan.

Burnham, D. (2012) *The Social Worker Speaks*. Aldershot: Ashgate.

Butler, J. (1870) *The Duty of Women in Relation to Our Great Social Evil, and Recent Legislation*. Carlisle: Hudson, Scott and Sons.

Cohen, A. (1998) *The Revolution in Post-War Family Casework: The Story of Pacifist Service Units and Family Service Units, 1940–1959*. Lancaster: Lancaster University Press.

Crowther, M. A. (1983) *The Workhouse System: The History of an English Social Institution*. London: Batsford.

Darley, G. (2010) *Octavia Hill: Social Reformer and Founder of the National Trust*. London: Francis Boutle.

Glasgow, G. (2012) '*Pray Sir, How Many Paupers Have You Boiled.' Thomas Wakley, Workhouses and the Poor Law, c.1834-1847*. Cambridge: EAH Press.

Hansard (1956-63) *Parliamentary Debates* (Hansard) (1803-). London: HMSO.

Hendricks, H. (1994) *Child Welfare: England, 1872–1989*. London: Routledge.

Hill, O. (reprint, 1988) *Houses of the London Poor* (reprint). London: Institute of Economic Affairs.

Koven, S. (2004) *Slumming. Sexual and Social Politics in Victorian London*. Princeton: Princeton University Press.

Jones, K. (1984) *Eileen Younghusband: A Biography*. London: Bedford Square Press.

Jones, K. (2006) *The Making of Social Policy in Britain: From Poor Law to New Labour*. London: Continuum Press.

Jordan, J. (2007) *Josephine Butler*. London: John Murray.

Lewis, J. (1995) *The Voluntary Sector, the State and Social Work in Britain: Charity Organisation Society/ Family Welfare Association*. Aldershot: Edward Elgar.

---

26 www.sshm.org
27 http://womenshistorynetwork.org
28 www.socsocmed.org.uk
29 www.historyofeducation.org.uk

Mayer, J. and Timms, N. (1970) *The Client Speaks. Working Class Impressions of Casework.* London: Routledge and Kegan Paul.

Parker, R. (2010) *Uprooted: The Shipment of Poor Children to Canada: 1867–1917.* Bristol: Policy Press.

Pedersen, S. (2004) *Eleanor Rathbone and the Politics of Conscience.* Yale: Yale University Press.

Phillimore, P. (1981) *Families Speaking: A study of Fifty-One Families' Views of Social Work.* London: Family Service Units.

Rathbone, E. (1904) *Report of an Enquiry into the Conditions of Dock Labour at the Liverpool Docks.* Liverpool: Northern Publishing Co., Liverpool.

Rathbone, E. (1924) *The Disinherited Family. A Plea for the Endowment of the Family.* London: Arnold.

Sainsbury, E. (1975) *Social Work with Families. Perceptions of Social Casework among Clients of a Family Service Unit.* London: Routledge and Kegan Paul.

Starkey, P. (1998) 'The medical officer of health, the social worker and the problem family, 1943–1968: The case of family service units.' *Social History of Medicine 11.*

Starkey, P. (2000a) '"The feckless mother": Women, poverty and social workers in wartime and post-war England.' *Women's History Review 9.*

Starkey, P. (2000b) *Families and social workers: The work of Family Service Units: 1940–1985.* Liverpool: Liverpool University Press.

Starkey, P. (2006) 'Kindhearted and good with people – or skilled professionals? Social work training at the University of Liverpool.' *Transactions of the Historic Society of Lancashire and Cheshire 155.*

Starkey, P. (2007) 'Retelling the Stories of Clients of Voluntary Social Work Agencies in Britain after 1945.' In A. Borsay and P. Shapely (eds) M*edicine, Charity and Mutual Aid: The Consumption of Health and Welfare in Britain, c.1550-1950.* Aldershot: Ashgate.

Starkey, P. (2008) '"Temporary relief for specially recommended or selected persons": The mission of the House of Charity, Soho, 1846–1914.' *Urban History 35.*

Starkey, P. (2011) 'Change or Decay: the House of Charity for Distressed Persons in London, 1919-2000'. In C. Rochester, G. Campbell Gosling, A. Penn, and M. Zimmeck (eds) *Understanding the Roots of Voluntary Action: Historical Perspectives on Current Social Policy.* Brighton: Sussex University Press.

Swain, S. (2001) 'Child Rescue: The Emigration of an Idea.' In J. Lawrence and P. Starkey (eds) *Child Welfare and Social Action in The Nineteenth and Twentieth Centuries: International Perspectives.* Liverpool: Liverpool University Press.

Swain, S. and Hillel, M. (2010) *Child, Nation, Race and Empire: Child Rescue Discourse, England, Canada and Australia, 1850–1915.* Manchester: Manchester University Press.

Todd, S. (2014) 'Family Welfare and Social work in post-war England, c.1948-1970.' *English Historical Review CXXXIX.*

Welshman, J. (1996) 'In search of the problem family. Public health and social work in England and Wales, 1940–1970.' *Social History of Medicine 9.*

Welshman, J. (2008) 'Recuperation, rehabilitation and the residential option: The Brentwood Centre for mothers and children.' *Twentieth Century British History 19.*

Williams, G. (2013) *Paralysed with Fear: The Story of Polio.* Houndsmills: Palgrave Macmillan.

Younghusband, E. (1946) *Report on the Education and Training of Social Workers.* Edinburgh: Constable.

Younghusband, E. (1978) *Social Work in Britain: 1950–1975.* London: Allen and Unwin.

Younghusband, E. (1981) *Newest Profession: A Short History of Social Work.* London: Imprint unknown.

Chapter 5

A STUDY OF LONG-TERM OUTCOMES OF CHILDREN WITH HARMFUL SEXUAL BEHAVIOURS

Using Social Media to Reach and Engage a 'Hard-to-reach' Population

SIMON HACKETT WITH MYLES BALFE,
HELEN MASSON AND JOSIE PHILLIPS
Durham University and University of Huddersfield

The background to the research

Social workers' interventions are often relatively transitory when placed against the wider context of children's lives. The success of social work interventions with children should ultimately be measured not only by short-term goals, such as immediate improvement in family functioning, whether a child is re-referred or whether there is a repeat critical incident, but also by the child's longer-term developmental outcomes. However, the extent to which social work interventions meet the needs of children as they develop through adolescence and into adulthood is often poorly understood.

A particular example of this is the case of children and young people who come to the attention of professionals because of problematic or abusive sexual behaviours directed towards others. It has often been assumed that this group of children are at high risk of developing patterns of sexual deviance in later life and of becoming adult sex offenders. Although the past decade has seen significant advances in understandings of this group (Hackett, 2010), relatively little is known about what happens to such children and teenagers in later life.

Researchers investigating outcomes amongst this population have typically relied on analyses of criminal recidivism rates or other official data (Worling, Littlejohn and Bookalam, 2009). The approach most typically used in such studies involves the collection of information about a young person's behaviour at the point of initial referral or assessment and then obtaining recidivism data at a post-intervention follow-up through a search of official data, such as criminal statistics.

This approach has a number of limitations. First, official statistics relating to sexual offences are likely to represent only the 'tip of the iceberg' in terms of the true scale of abusive behaviour (ONS, 2014), therefore much reoffending committed by young people may not figure in official crime figures. Second, simply knowing whether someone has been convicted or not of another sexual offence does not, in itself, tell us very much about the processes that have led to recidivism or indeed the factors, such as social work interventions, that may have inhibited it. Third, approaches to establishing re-offence outcomes based on official statistics rarely give individuals opportunities to offer their own perspectives on their offence histories and life narratives.

In the research described in this chapter, we sought to address all three of these limitations by undertaking a long-term follow-up study of a sample of former service users, involving them directly in order that they could tell us their life stories, focusing not only on reoffending outcomes, but also examining the complex influences that shaped service users' lives following the end of social work involvement offered to them when they were children.

Aim and objectives of the study

The overall aim of the project was therefore to describe and analyse the experiences and current life circumstances of adults who, as children, were subject to professional interventions because of their sexually abusive behaviours. Key objectives were:

- to identify, trace and secure a total sample of 100 ex-service users who were known to welfare and/or criminal justice agencies at least ten years previously because of sexually abusive behaviours in their childhoods

- to undertake in-depth interviews with respondents about their experiences and life circumstances in the intervening years, complementing this data with an examination of their case records and interviews with professionals who knew the respondents

- to assess the current social circumstances and functioning of participants via the completion of a range of standardised measures and identify rates of recidivism

- to identify factors to explain why the life circumstances of participants who have continued to have significant psychosocial problems in adulthood may differ from those of participants who have not

- to give voice to a service user group that has been neglected in social research

- to synthesise findings in order to inform future policy, service provision and professional practice.

Methods

The study used both qualitative and quantitative methods, including documentary analysis, narrative interviewing and psychometric testing.

Stage One

We accessed and reviewed case files from nine participating sites that provided assessment and interventions services for children and young people with harmful sexual behaviours, based variously in the statutory, voluntary and private sectors. In total, 700 case files were analysed, comprising all referrals made to these services between the years of 1992 and 2000. This ensured that all participants in the follow-up study would be adults and that at least ten years would have elapsed since the intervention offered to them. For each of the 700 cases we collected data on age at referral, ethnicity and gender, the nature of the abusive behaviours, victim ages and gender, as well as the child's own family history including their experiences of victimisation.

Stage Two

We identified 117 cases for 'tracing' to represent the full range of young people with whom each of the services had worked. Cases were sampled purposefully to include young men and women, intra and extra-familial abuse, contact and non-contact offenders, male and female victims and violent and non-violent offenders. We reviewed the 117 case files in depth and produced case studies of each of the 117 young people. Key contact information for each case was extracted.

Stage Three

Using information from Stage Two, we searched for participants on publicly available data sources, such as the electoral register, commercially available databases, the internet and social network sites. Overall, we found reliable, up-to-date contact information on 69 per cent (n=81) per cent of people and/or their families.

Stage Four

The next stage was to contact individuals to invite them to participate in interviews. This was the most ethically challenging aspect of our work. It was vitally important not to compromise the current living situation of individuals who may not have disclosed their past histories to their current partners or employers, etc. We proceeded with extreme caution. Individuals were contacted by the agencies that had worked with them as children, rather than directly by us as researchers. Once initial contact had been established, permission was sought by the agencies for the researchers to contact the participant directly at a convenient and safe time in order to discuss the project in more detail. In this way, informed consent was negotiated with individuals in relation to their involvement and whether participants would prefer a face-to-face or telephone interview.

In total, we were able to gather information from 69 of the sample of 117 cases (59%). A mix of narrative and semi-structured interviewing was used to encourage participants to recall and reflect on key life experiences and the impact of the childhood sexual abuse.

Interviews typically lasted three hours or more. A range of questionnaires (including measures of satisfaction with life, mental health, depression, anxiety and self-esteem) was completed with participants. Permission was sought to check participants' criminal record history to compare official data on recidivism with self-report.

Findings

Key findings from our analysis of 700 case files indicate a higher than expected rate of sexual victimisation histories (50%) in the sample compared with previous studies. A wide range of sexually abusive behaviour was perpetrated by the sample. Eighty-four per cent of young people had inappropriately touched their victims. Non-contact abuse was prevalent in 50 per cent of cases, but in a further 52 per cent of cases young people engaged in penetrative abuse of their victims. Eighteen per cent used expressive violence in the commission of the sexually abusive acts. Whilst most young people had either one or two victims, 14 per cent had victimised three or more victims and a small proportion (3%) were prolific sexual offenders with ten or more victims.

A wide range of long-term developmental outcomes was reported by the follow-up sample. As far as could be ascertained by self-report and official records, most participants had not reoffended. Only a small proportion had reoffended sexually, with three reconvictions for sexual assault and one for child pornography, giving a six per cent sexual recidivism rate. However, general reoffending was more common, with a small number of participants having been reconvicted for serious offences of physical assault, violence and, in one case, murder.

Using Farrington and colleagues' (2009) resilient outcome factors, it was possible to classify overall life outcomes as successful (in 26% of cases), mixed (31%) or unsuccessful (43%). Successful outcomes were associated with individuals who were able to have ambitions and optimism for their future. Stable partner relationships or enduring carer and professional relationships were a feature of most adults with positive outcomes. Educational achievement and the ability to gain employment also constituted significant desistance factors. Poor outcomes, in contrast, were associated with individuals with poor body image and poor health. Relationship failure, chaotic or unstable living conditions and drug and alcohol misuse were common amongst those with the worst outcomes. Professional interventions offered to children with harmful sexual behaviours were largely well regarded, but the lasting significance of the work for these individuals in later life appeared to be related to the quality of the relationship that existed between the child and the professional concerned. This emphasises the vital importance of lasting 'social anchors' in the lives of children and adolescents at risk. Findings suggest that achieving carer and family constancy is an important part of professional interventions, as is general health promotion, though this area is as yet underdeveloped in the sexual abuse field.

For some participants, the research interview was the first time they were able to talk about their ongoing worries about their childhood experiences in their adult lives. The study therefore raised questions about the need for long-term supportive social work interventions with children at risk as they develop through adolescence into adulthood.

Key innovative elements

The project posed significant practical and ethical issues requiring us to be innovative in our approach. First, giving a voice to a largely invisible service user group was an important aim of our research, but this kind of research is very uncommon in the sexual offending field (Hackett and Masson, 2006). Second, it has been assumed that people with histories of sexually abusive behaviour are 'hard to reach'. Indeed, in discussing the research with experts in the field prior to embarking on it, we were advised that it would likely not be possible to retrospectively locate a sample of adults at such temporal distance from the commission of their childhood behaviours. Because of the nature of their offences and the social stigma attached to sexual crime, we were told, sexual offenders 'go to ground' following the end of professional interventions. Third, even if we located individuals, the extremely sensitive nature of the initial referral to services, i.e. the commission of an act of sexual abuse, meant that it would be very difficult to engage potential participants. How should we approach them in an ethically supportable way and would they talk to us?

In this section, we discuss the some of the ways we sought to overcome these methodological challenges.

Reaching the hard to reach

Retrospective tracing of respondents is not common in social work research. Kaltenborn (2001) traced children and young people who had previously been in residential establishments by sending a letter to their last known postal address. Fernandez (2008) followed up children in foster care. Tracing respondents after a considerable amount of time has passed between baseline and follow-up does, however, have a history in other fields, particularly in epidemiological and public health research (Lyons *et al.*, 2004). Weinberger *et al.* (2002) sought to trace 708 people who had participated in clinical studies 27 years previously and found 84 per cent, despite having no contact with study participants in the intervening years. Wilson *et al.* (2009) traced 70.1 per cent of 810 individuals who were treated for cancer during childhood. Wharton *et al.* (2006) traced 8583 children who were born in 1961 in Tasmania after 36 years and found 56 per cent of them. Such studies suggest that it is possible to trace and locate successfully a high proportion of individuals identified from historical case records.

It has been suggested that three populations are particularly hard to reach through retrospective tracing methods: people involved in illegal or deviant activities; those who were children at the baseline point; and women. Deviant populations may present particular tracing difficulties, as they tend to move addresses frequently, may be estranged from their families and may be wary about revealing information about their whereabouts (Kleschinsky *et al.*, 2009). Attempting to trace individuals who were children at baseline is also difficult, since the information that researchers have about them is likely to be out of date, for example they may have left home, changed their name, etc. (Cotter *et al.*, 2005). Women may also change their last or family names in adulthood. In terms of our study, adults who acted in sexually abusive ways in their childhoods were a particularly difficult group to trace. Although our sample was overwhelmingly male, they were often separated from their families and the communities in which they lived as children and their deviant sexual behaviours are amongst the most stigmatised in society.

Traditionally, a number of core sources of information have been used to trace research subjects retrospectively, including: dates of birth and last known addresses; court records; country-relevant databases; electoral databases and death records; and social services, medical and social security databases (Haggerty *et al.*, 2008). Techniques have included searching telephone directories (Wutzke *et al.*, 2000) and calling on last-known home addresses (Haggerty *et al.*, 2008).

Internet and social media based tracing methods

Recently, researchers have begun to argue that internet-based tools are likely to have significant benefits for locating participants (Barakat-Haddad *et al.*, 2009). Following other researchers who have trialled the use of internet-based approaches (Wutzke *et al.*, 2000), in our study we used internet and social media to locate our sample, as well as to invite them to participate and, in some cases, also as the medium for interviews. We believe that our use of such approaches is innovative and could be adopted as a social research tool in other contexts (Masson *et al.*, 2013), in particular in engaging populations that have traditionally been viewed as 'hard to reach'. Individuals often put significant amounts of information on their social network profiles. Such information is controlled by the individual and is changeable by them at any time. As a result, this information is often more up to date than more static, paper-based records or even other forms of online data, such as electoral rolls, which are updated relatively infrequently. There are therefore potential benefits of research methods that use social media sources, though there are many practical and ethical implications arising from their use.

Methods of tracing

In our study, 117 cases were identified for tracing. From our review of the case files, we extracted key contact information for each case including the subject's: name; date of birth; last known address; parents' and family members' names; and family members' addresses where available. Contact information for each case was at least ten, and in some cases approaching 20, years old.

Using this information, we searched for the person concerned on the most popular social network sites in the UK at the time of the research, including Bebo, Myspace, Friends Reunited and Facebook. We also searched the UK electoral register using two commercial databases: Tracesmart and 192.com. Our specific search strategy and approach is described in detail elsewhere (Masson *et al.*, 2013).

Results of tracing

We searched for 117 people (111 men, six women) and their families. Each individual and their family members were treated as one case; so, if we searched for, and found, a person and three members of a particular family, we treated this as one found case. Overall, we found up-to-date contact information (through a combination of social network sites and through the electoral register) on 69.2 per cent (n=81) of people and/or their families. Of the six female cases, we located five cases (83 per cent).

We found 29 per cent of the former service users (n=34) on Facebook, one per cent on Bebo (n=1) and two per cent on MySpace (n=2). We found 7.7 per cent (n=9) of the individuals on the electoral register using Tracesmart and 192.com. We found information on 5 per cent (n=6) of the ex-service users through Google. One per cent (n=1) were found through Friends Reunited.

We found 30 per cent (n=35) of service users' family members (e.g. a brother, sister or parent) through Facebook, 2.6 per cent (n=3) of their family members through Bebo and 1 per cent (n=1) of their family members through Myspace. We found 42 per cent (n=49) of family members on the electoral register using Tracesmart and 192.com. We found information on 1 per cent of family members through Google. No family members were found through Friends Reunited.

Making contact using social media

Once we had traced a former service user, we asked the service or, where still available, the original social worker or other professional who had worked with that individual to invite them to consider participating in the research. If we had located an individual through a social media source, we asked services to make contact with the individual through social media, setting up a separate Facebook account for the service to enable them to send their communications. Messages explained that 'a child health and family service' was following up the service users who had been in touch with it in the past. People who were interested in taking part in the study were asked to respond by social media message. Thirty-two such Facebook messages were sent in total. Of the 32 people who were messaged, nine agreed to be interviewed (28 per cent response rate). Facebook messages were also sent by services to 11 parents, and we had two positive replies (18 per cent response rate). Postal recruitment letters were also sent to 20 of the former service users and/or their parents identified through the electoral register, and again had two positive replies (one former service user, one parent – 10 per cent response rate).

Irrespective of how we sought to make contact with an individual, we assumed that all messages or letters could be opened and read by an individual other than the individual for whom the letter/message was intended (for example, a girlfriend or boyfriend) and that this other individual would not know anything about a person's past. Messages/letters therefore never revealed anything about the former service user's childhood behavioural problems and did not mention the name of the service that had worked with the young person.

We asked the people whom we later interviewed about how they felt about being contacted through social media and the response was overwhelmingly positive, though some were understandably initially surprised and anxious about being re-contacted by services 'out of the blue'. Nevertheless, those contacted generally felt that Facebook was a more secure and private way of being contacted than by telephone or letter. One 30-year-old male participant commented when asked how he felt about being contacted through Facebook:

I don't know, it was kind of a shock, I don't know, I never heard nothing from any sort of social services when I was an adult, so then I'm contacted... My wife she said well, you know, talk about it, you're not proud of your past, but, you know, you're not scared of it, you know, I can't change it, but you know, it's not something that you're worried about no more, so talk about it, get it out in the open.

Only one previous study as far as we are aware has explored the use of web-based search engines to locate a retrospective cohort of (former) children (Barakat-Haddad *et al.*, 2009) and none, as far as we are aware, has assessed the feasibility of using social network sites to trace in adulthood a cohort of former service users who, in childhood, had problematic or abusive sexual behaviours. The findings of our study indicate that it is possible to use social network sites to do this in combination with searches in other databases, such as the electoral register.

Using the combination of databases and social network sites described here, we found up-to-date contact information on 69.2 per cent of our sample. This figure compares well with other studies that have attempted to trace cases for research studies (Haggerty *et al.*, 2008; Weinberger *et al.*, 2002; Wilson *et al.*, 2009). It is especially promising given the length of time that had passed since these individuals had last been in contact with services and given that we were attempting to trace a sample that had engaged sometimes in highly deviant activities (Cotter *et al.*, 2005; Haggerty *et al.*, 2008).

Strengths and challenges

There are a number of practical lessons to draw from this study in relation to social research employing social network sites to trace people and for welfare services wanting to follow up cases they have worked with in the past.

First, it is important to consider whether searches should be conducted on both an individual and his or her family members. We found 30 per cent of the individuals whom we were looking for on Facebook, for example, but we found an equal number through immediate family members, usually parents, step-parents or foster carers. In terms of follow-up research, family members may well be able to direct researchers to the former service users, although it is important to consider information about family histories when contemplating such approaches. For example, in the current study, we felt it was appropriate to contact parents and former carers as we were also asking them take part in an interview with us (so that we could also understand something of the stories of carers of young people with harmful sexual behaviours). We also made sure from case records that parents were fully aware of the child's previous behaviours and the work undertaken with them by the service. However, we did not contact any parents where case history information indicated that the former service user may have been abused by them, nor did we make contact with any victims (such as siblings) of the young person. Researchers investigating less sensitive topics may be able to use family members more directly as a route to locating participants using social media. However, researchers will obviously need to be guided ethically and practically by the specific context of the research topic at hand.

Second, the response rate to Facebook messages in our study was higher than that to postal letters. This suggests that researchers undertaking follow-up work of this nature should consider social media to be an essential, rather than an optional, tool for contacting individuals. Whilst many of participants accessed Facebook through smartphones, very few had a landline phone and most had moved several times in the past two or three years. Contacting them by more traditional methods would have been very difficult indeed. At the same time, researchers should not underestimate the amount of time it takes to locate participants. It took six weeks of full-time work to search for our sample of 117 cases.

Third, many of the challenges we faced in safely and accurately locating potential participants were due to the necessarily retrospective, rather than prospective, nature of our approach. In future, it is important that welfare services who wish to learn more about the long-term outcomes of their work seek their service users' permission at the time of working with them to approach them in later life. This helps to ensure that both the services (and researchers undertaking follow-up studies) comply with the requirements of data protection legislation and should assist in making subsequent tracing and contacting ex-service users much easier.

Fourth, it is also important to consider the full ethical dimensions of this kind of approach to follow-up social research. Information on social networking sites is publicly available and individuals are free to conceal their profiles from public view. In essence, this is no different from people who choose to place their names on the electoral roll or in the telephone directory or not. As a result, we only found information about individuals that they wished to be broadcast publicly. However, there are legitimate concerns as to whether some individuals understand the full implications of making their personal details publicly visible through social networking sites. This concern has been voiced in relation to other areas of social work, such as in the adoption field, where adopted individuals or birth parents have been traced through Facebook and where access to such data through social networking sites is resulting in significant shifts in the nature of practice (Fursland, 2010).

Furthermore, Tregeagle and Darcy (2008) raise important points about respecting users' privacy on the internet. In our study, we proceeded with considerable care in partnership with the participating services, aware of the vulnerability of the group and the potential that individuals may be living in life situations where others are unaware of their childhood backgrounds. Our guiding principle was that the use of internet data sources to enable participants to give us a much needed first-hand account of how they had reshaped their lives following abuse should not be prioritised over, or compromise, their life circumstances. We were also aware that, however careful and sensitive our approach was, making contact and seeking to arrange an interview with someone could cause anxiety and distress. It is, therefore, important that researchers have an agreed support system set up prior to contacting a former service user in case such support is needed. In our study, having made the initial approach to the former service user, each of the services agreed to offer ongoing support or refer people to additional services, irrespective of whether the former service user had agreed to be interviewed or not.

The increasing impact of new technologies on social work practice and social work research

Over the past decade, social workers have begun to realise the importance of using the internet for social work practice, learning and social work research. Several themes have arisen in this literature: using the internet as an assistive technology (Blaschke, Freddolino and Mullen, 2009); using the internet to organise and monitor social work practice; using the internet to minimise risks to patients'/service users' health (Landau *et al.*, 2009); and using the internet as a public relations tool to advocate for service users' rights and shape how service users are portrayed (Brownlee *et al.*, 2010). Somewhat related to the current study, social work practitioners are increasingly having to embrace the new means available to make and maintain contacts with service users. For example, ChildLine now uses a variety of means to talk to its service users, including telephone, email, internet chat and social media sites such as Facebook. Such means have to be used with care and in line with professional ethics and data protection legislation but they offer much potential as ways of communicating with service users that complement more traditional means such as office-based meetings and home visits.

It is evident from the current study that the internet also has practical utility for social work research, enabling the retrospective location of service users many years after they last had contact with services. However, given the pace and scale with which these technologies have been adopted, particularly amongst young people and young adults, it is important that researchers who are thinking about tracing respondents keep up to date with the latest technological developments that could affect their cohort.

Conclusion

This study indicates that it is possible and feasible to use social network sites and web-based databases to trace a retrospective cohort of ex-service users who, in childhood, had sexually problematic or harmful behaviours, a group traditionally seen as 'hard to reach', ten years or more after their last known contact with children's services. Care and sensitivity is needed, but those working in the field of social work research should not be put off using these approaches as they may enable researchers and collaborating services to gain a fuller picture of the lives of those who have experienced social work interventions.

References

Barakat-Haddad, C., Elliott, S., Eyles, J. and Pengelly, D. (2009) 'Predictors of locating children participants in epidemiological studies 20 years after last contact: Internet resources and longitudinal research.' *European Journal of Epidemiology 24*, 8, 397–405.

Blaschke, C., Freddolino, P. and Mullen, E. (2009) 'Ageing and technology: A review of the research literature.' *British Journal of Social Work 39*, 4, 641–656.

Brownlee, K., Graham, J., Doucette, E., Hotson, N. and Halverson, G. (2010) 'Have communication technologies influenced rural social work practice?' *British Journal of Social Work 41*, 1, 1–16.

Cotter, R., Burke, J., Stouthamer-Loeber, M. and Loeber, R. (2005) 'Contacting participants for follow-up: How much effort is required to retain participants in longitudinal studies?' *Evaluation and Program Planning 28*, 1, 15–21.

Farrington, D., Ttofi, M. and Coid, J. (2009) 'Development of adolescence-limited, late-onset, and persistent offenders from age 8 to age 48.' *Aggressive Behavior 35*, 150–163.

Fernandez, E. (2008) 'Unravelling emotional, behavioural and educational outcomes in a longitudinal study of children in foster-care.' *British Journal of Social Work 38*, 7, 1283–301.

Fursland, E. (2010) *Facing up to Facebook: A Survival Guide for Adoptive Families.* London: BAAF.

Hackett, S. (2010) 'Children, young people and sexual violence.' In C. Barter and D. Berridge (eds) *Children Behaving Badly? Exploring Peer Violence Between Children and Young People.* London: Blackwell Wiley.

Hackett, S. and Masson, H. (2006) 'Young people who have sexually abused: What do they (and their parents) want from professionals?' *Children and Society 20*, 183–195.

Haggerty, K., Fleming, C., Catalano, R., Petrie, R., Rubin, R. and Grassley, M. (2008) 'Ten years later: Locating and interviewing children of drug abusers.' *Evaluation and Program Planning 31*, 1, 1–9.

Kaltenborn, K. (2001) 'Children's and young people's experiences in various residential arrangements: A longitudinal study to evaluate criteria for custody and residence decision making.' *British Journal of Social Work 31*, 1, 81–117.

Kleschinsky, J., Bosworth, L., Nelson, S., Walsh, E. and Shaffer, H. (2009) 'Persistence pays off: Follow-up methods for difficult to track longitudinal samples.' *Journal for the Study of Alcohol and Drugs 70*, 5, 751–761.

Landau, R., Werner, G., Auslander, G., Shoval, N. and Heinik, J. (2009) 'Attitudes of family and professional care-givers towards the use of GPS for tracking patients with dementia: An exploratory study.' *British Journal of Social Work 39*, 4, 670–692.

Lyons, K., Carter, J., Carter, E., Rush, K., Stewart, B. and Archbold, P. (2004) 'Locating and retaining research participants for follow-up studies.' *Research in Nursing and Health 27*, 1, 63–68.

Masson, H., Balfe, M., Hackett, S. and Phillips, J. (2013) 'Lost without a trace? Social networking and social research with a hard-to-reach population.' *British Journal of Social Work 43*, 24–40.

ONS (2014) *Crime in England and Wales, Year Ending June 2014: Statistical Bulletin.* London: Office for National Statistics. Available at www.ons.gov.uk/ons/dcp171778_380538.pdf, accessed 4 April 2015.

Tregeagle, S. and Darcy, M. (2008) 'Child welfare and information and communication technology: Today's challenge.' *British Journal of Social Work 38*, 8, 1481–1498.

Weinberger, M., Weinberger, M., Fineberg, N., Fineberg, E. and Wagner, U. (2002) 'Long-term follow-up of participants in clinical studies.' *Journal of Clinical Epidemiology 55*, 3, 230–234.

Wharton, C., Dharmage, S., Jenkins, M., Dite, G. and Hopper, J. (2006) 'Tracing 8,600 participants 36 years after recruitment at age seven for the Tasmanian Asthma Study.' *Australian and New Zealand Journal of Public Health 30*, 1, 105–110.

Wilson, C., Cohn, R., Johnson, J. and Ashton, L. (2009) 'Tracing survivors of childhood cancer in Australia.' *Pediatrics and Blood Cancer 52*, 4, 510–515.

Worling, J., Littlejohn, A. and Bookalam, D. (2009) '20-year prospective follow-up study of specialized treatment for adolescents who offended sexually.' *Behavioural Sciences and the Law 28*, 1, 46–57.

Wutzke, S., Conigrave, K., Kogler, B., Saunders, J. and Hall, W. (2000) 'Longitudinal research: Methods for maximizing subject follow-up.' *Drug and Alcohol Review 19*, 2, 159–163.

Chapter 6

INVOLVING PEOPLE WITH DEMENTIA IN A SYSTEMATIC REVIEW

NICOLETTE WADE AND MIKE FISHER
University of Bedfordshire

This chapter concerns a pilot research project undertaken with a group of seven people who had been diagnosed with dementia. The project had two overall aims – first to undertake the initial stages of a systematic literature review of the views of people living with dementia, and second to explore ways of ensuring that people living with dementia have a say in how reviews of this kind are undertaken. The systematic review relates to the researched and published views of people with dementia, while the group concerns participants' opinions on the criteria used in the systematic review and the key findings. This chapter focuses on how the group participants were recruited and enabled to 'have a say' in the systematic review and what their views were on what evidence should be used and if the findings made sense to them.

The research team received funding from the Averil Osborn Memorial Trust to undertake the pilot study, and fieldwork took place in August and September 2013. The Trust was established by the British Society of Gerontology in 1995 to support innovative research and dissemination projects that directly involve older people. Findings were disseminated by providing a report to the funders and by writing an article for *Generations Review*. Ethical approval for the project was obtained from the University of Bedfordshire Research Ethics Committee and by a NHS Research Ethics Committee (NHSREC).

Project overview

During the initial planning stage, a core team of seven was involved. This included three university-based members: a social work professor, a principal lecturer in social work and a social work Master's student. Two other members of the team were employed by the local mental health trust; a senior nurse who was the manager of the memory clinic based at the local general hospital and a psychologist also based there. In addition, during the planning and consultation stage, a second psychologist from the trust and a researcher from the Alzheimer's Society who had experience of involving people with dementia in organisational development and service user review panels (Tooke, 2012, 2013) were involved.

At the first meeting, we established our wish to be as facilitative as possible towards participants as a guiding principle. We drew on Tooke's work and on the literature on user involvement in research including older people in systematic reviews (Fisher *et al.*, 2005). We planned to undertake the work in a group setting, in order to provide a supportive environment for people to express their views. We were careful to make it clear that this was a time-limited group and not a support group (support was available from the memory clinic).

The participants were recruited from the memory clinic by the staff members based there. This involved a face-to-face discussion and a brief information leaflet was provided, which explained what the project was trying to do and how it would be conducted. In developing the information leaflet, and as was the case with any written materials used with the group, the emphasis was on plain, easy-to-understand language. We planned to recruit participants who had the capacity to consent to participate, and all the memory clinic staff possessed appropriate training in determining capacity. The basis for determining capacity is contained in the Mental Capacity Act 2005. The overarching principles contained in section 1 of the Act include that people must be assumed to have capacity unless it is established that they do not. Section 3 of the Act sets out the circumstances in which a person is unable to make a decision. In order to make a decision the person must understand information relevant to the decision, retain the information and use the information as part of the process of making a decision and finally they need to be able to communicate the decision.

Ten people with a diagnosis and who had capacity were approached while they attended the memory clinic or during other contact such as a home visit. Of the ten who were approached, seven agreed to participate. In two of the cases who declined, the reason was because informal carers thought it would not be appropriate; no further explanation was provided. The reasons for the third refusal were unclear.

Table 6.1: Characteristics of participants

	Age	Gender	Ethnicity	Living status	Diagnosis	Attended groups
01	77	M	White British	Married	Dementia with Lewy Bodies*	1
02	81	M	White British-Canadian	Married	Alzheimer's	1, 2
03	84	M	White British	Married	Alzheimer's	1, 2, 3
04	75	M	White British	Married	Alzheimer's	1, 3
05	74	F	White British	Married	Alzheimer's	1, 2, 3
06	67	F	Indian	Married	Alzheimer's	1, 2, 3
07	77	M	White British	Married	Alzheimer's	2, 3

* Dementia with Lewy Bodies is a type of dementia that shares symptoms with both Alzheimer's disease and Parkinson's disease.

The seven people recruited knew they had a diagnosis of dementia, as was the case with everyone who was approached. We initially considered including people with a diagnosis of mild cognitive impairment, but decided against this because we did not want to suggest, through our emphasis on dementia, that such a progression was inevitable.

Throughout all stages of this project we placed an emphasis on creating an environment in which those participating would, we hoped, feel valued and respected and therefore able to express their views. In part, this was achieved by a strong emphasis on practical arrangements. The groups were held at the local university campus. Initially this came about for pragmatic reasons, as rooms were available when we needed them. We wondered if this, in the event, had a positive influence on participants. Coming to university to participate in some research was rather different to attending the local hospital. We used two rooms, one for an informal gathering before the work phase began, where refreshments were offered. The group 'worked' for about an hour and always finished by noon so as to avoid any disruption to travel arrangements. An adjacent waiting area was made available for carers, with newspapers and refreshments, should they choose to stay. In the event only one carer remained during the first group. The refreshments room was available for breakout purposes in case any of the participants needed a break. This was not required over the course of the three meetings. Petty cash was available to reimburse any travel expenses that had been incurred. In addition participants were offered a £10 high street voucher to recognise their contribution. Follow-up support was made available at the memory clinic for any group member who felt in need of it; in the event nobody did.

The systematic review

We undertook the initial stages of a systematic review in order to generate questions for the review group. Initial work was based on 214 studies of the views of people with dementia, identified by means of a pragmatic search strategy (for the full report, see Fisher *et al.*, 2014). Systematic reviews are an integral part of evidence-based policy and practice, using systematic and transparent methods to assemble whole bodies of evidence, rather than relying on single studies (see Rutter *et al.*, 2010). While systematic reviews offer more reliable policy and practice messages, they are resource intensive and the participation of people who use services is often underdeveloped. In particular, the methodological processes of systematic reviews may appear to be so specialised as to be beyond the participation of people who use services, let alone people experiencing cognitive impairment. While there was no intention to train people living with dementia in research methods, involvement could be directed towards ensuring that their expertise is used to assist in some of the key questions. These included whether studies from other countries are relevant to the UK and what counts as high quality (for example, whether participants are approached directly or selected by gatekeepers). People with experience of living with dementia are also in a strong position to say whether they think the findings apply to them. User involvement in systematic reviews is thus about what evidence is used and whether the findings make sense to people who use services.

Using elements of dementia care mapping to measure participation and well-being

Involving people living with a diagnosis of dementia in this project meant accepting responsibility for their welfare as they would be asked to consider research findings that might well refer to the progress and outcome of their disease. Additionally, whilst we took care to ensure that the environment was as facilitative as we could make it, we did not know how the participants would react to the experience of being consulted using the approach that we adopted and therefore we wanted to take particular care to monitor, and if necessary safeguard, their well-being.

Dementia Care Mapping (DCM) (Bradford Dementia Group, 2005a, 2005b, 2005c) is a set of observational tools first developed by Kitwood and the Bradford Dementia Group in the early 1990s. It has been used extensively in formal dementia care settings such as hospitals, care homes and day care settings both in this country and internationally in order to develop person-centred practice. The most recent version of DCM was produced in 2005 and is referred to as 'DCM 8'. The basic principles of a person-centred approach, which provide the theoretical basis for DCM, are defined by Booker (2004) as follows: 'Person-centred care values all people regardless of age and health status, is individualized, emphasizes the perspective of the person with dementia, and stresses the importance of relationships' (quoted in Bradford Dementia Group, 2005a, p.11).

The way in which DCM was adapted and employed for this purpose is discussed in the section dealing with key innovative elements.

The groups

The project team members all had specific roles while the groups ran. Three members acted as facilitators to the group with one member taking a lead on introducing each topic and associated questions whilst the other two supported facilitating the discussion. Two other members took on the role of observers using elements of the DCM tool.

Seating was arranged around a small group of tables, with a view of a presentation screen. Participants had been provided with printouts of the presentation slides in a large font for ease of reading, showing the main issues for discussion. Being seated at the tables offered an opportunity to write notes. The small group of tables was designed to make it easier to hear one another and to bring people into conversation. Agreement had been sought and obtained from the group members to record each session. Due to a misunderstanding this did not happen for the first group but did for the next two. The two recordings were then transcribed.

The presentations gave participants background information on the research studies in plain language without technical terms and often using direct quotations. They consisted of eight to ten slides.

Changes made during the three sessions

The five research staff held a brief discussion after each group. As a result of these meetings, some refinements were made as the groups progressed.

Observational feedback at the end of the first meeting indicated that one participant was less involved. She pointed out that she used a hearing aid and had been unable to catch much of the discussion. While this showed the importance of gathering feedback as the group progressed, we should perhaps have checked this more thoroughly from the outset. This led to a decision to reduce the size of tables further so that the participants were more closely grouped and to place the person with a hearing aid next to one of the facilitators.

After group one, we also felt that we had allowed discussion to range too broadly and that we should try to achieve a closer focus on the tasks. We alerted the participants to this at the beginning of the second group and one facilitator took on the role of bringing discussion back to the task if it wandered. Lastly, we numbered the presentation slides to make them easier to follow.

Outcomes

This section focuses primarily on the outcomes from the third group with some references being made to the first two groups. By the third group people had got to know each other and felt more at ease in the environment. The questions are presented in the order given to the group. The intention is for the reader to get a sense of how the questions were structured and to give some insight into how, over the course of an hour, questions were introduced and responded to. The measurements taken by the two mappers showed that mood and engagement levels improved, from a high starting point, over the course of the three groups. By the third group people were familiar with how the sessions worked, each other and their role. These factors appeared to contribute to higher levels of focus and engagement than those shown in the first two groups.

In general when answering the questions most members of the group responded by relating personal experiences. For example, during group two, in response to the overall focus question 'What makes a good study?' supplemented by 'Are there any differences between men's and women's experiences?' individual members referred to their own experiences and views. A male member of the group suggested that women were more sociable than men and therefore had different and greater needs in this respect, whilst the two women in the group made quite a number of references to the dangers of cooking and ironing arising from forgetting what they were doing and burning things.

Most participants were unable to say in a direct sense whether studies should differentiate between men and women because they have different roles and needs, but located their responses in their own experiences, which showed that, amongst this group of people, men and women often did different types of things, for example women were more likely to cook. The upshot of this was that there was not always a direct connection between the question, or at least the intention behind the question, and the response. In order to try and make sure that we had understood correctly, responses were summarised by the facilitators and reflected back to the group members during the course of the group. This provided an opportunity for the group or individuals to make a correction if needed. Additionally, responses from groups one and two were summarised at the start of the following groups, in writing on the presentation slides as well as verbally, to check that we had understood correctly.

The focus of the third group was to see what the group members thought of some of the key themes arising from the literature review. Direct quotes from the studies that captured these themes were provided for the group. These included:

- 'I could shake myself for being so stupid.'

- 'I lose my temper with myself about it.'

- 'I feel stupid, a real nutcase.'

The question posed was 'Does it makes sense?' The group offered a range of views: some found that they resonated; others not at all.

Some members drew a distinction between having a positive outlook as opposed to a negative one. A distinction was also drawn between having a memory problem and being stupid or feeling stupid. The point is captured by this quote from one group member: 'Forgetful yes, stupid no, not really.'

The male members of the group seemed to demonstrate a more positive outlook than the women and this appeared to be associated with a greater sense of agency and personal control over their lives. The conclusion was that people vary in how they see things, with some members drawing a distinction between annoyance (either experienced by the carer or the person with dementia) arising from the circumstances rather than the individual. It is the disease that makes people angry, not the person.

The next set of quotes drawn from the literature review for the group to consider were as follows:

- 'I go from one day to the next because I never know what I'm going to have.'

- 'You just have to take what comes.'

- 'Well I take it from day to day. I think well what is to be will be.'

Again, there seemed to be a variation according to gender with male members of the group more likely to say that they could not relate to these points. They referred to plans extending over the coming days, weeks and months such as going on holiday, seeing children and grandchildren and attending appointments. Members also referred to using diaries to keep track of these arrangements.

An animated discussion developed from these initial responses on the question of driving. Some members of the group were still driving but the majority had had their license taken away. Again responses to this varied, with some people thinking that it was right and proper whilst others felt the loss of agency arising difficult to tolerate. The discussion also exposed the difficulty that people with dementia who live in rural and semi-rural areas can face when unable to drive.

The next set of questions related to coping strategies identified in the review:

- 'I'm ducking out of conversations more.'

- 'It feels like I'm insulting them by not remembering their name...I don't like that at all.'

Again we found that people varied in their response; one person admitted that he did 'duck out' sometimes, but this was linked to the topic under discussion not because he had forgotten someone's name. Three of the group said that this had not been their experience. As the discussion developed, a distinction was drawn between the people who had chosen to attend the group, and who were therefore more likely to be outgoing and sociable, and those who had declined to come. This reinforced the point that responses to the condition were personal and individual and probably linked to personality, previous life experience, identity and the current situation that people were in.

The next set of issues to be checked with participants concerned 'speak to me, not to others about me', again picking up on a key theme found in the literature. The group reported that they had not experienced this; their experience was of being spoken to. However, at the same time they made it clear that they were happy for spouses or other close family members to be present when meeting professionals and for them to be included in the discussion.

Key innovative elements

Despite the current drive for user involvement in health and welfare, we have few examples of involving people with dementia, a group whose views are rarely sought in policy making. As this group comprises primarily older women, their exclusion reflects gender and age-based prejudice as well as negative views of the contribution of people with cognitive impairment. The reasons for engaging with this group of people are therefore significant in overcoming ignorance, promoting inclusion and generating new insights and understandings.

As awareness of dementia increases and we screen people earlier, the population of people with dementia is changing, and people have a longer period when they are willing and able to make their voice heard. Nevertheless, involvement in national policy making remains rare (Toby, 2012). The main government report setting out the evidence base for dementia policy – *Dementia UK: The Full Report* (Knapp and Prince, 2007) – did not involve people with dementia and undertook no review of studies of their views. The subsequent report outlining government policy – *Living Well with Dementia: A National Strategy* (Department of Health, 2009) – involved two people with dementia but still failed to review studies of their views.

It would be wrong, however, to think that involvement is a recent issue in research with people with dementia. As long ago as 1993, Cotrell and Schulz argued that: 'Much can be gained from changing our view of the person with dementia from someone to be studied to someone whose perspectives can help us understand Alzheimer's Disease' (1993, p.210).

Since then, researchers have made significant efforts to involve people with dementia, including rethinking how to approach consent (Dewing, 2002) and outlining the conditions under which 'non-therapeutic' research might reasonably be undertaken (Berghmans and Meulen, 1995). Perhaps most significantly, the rise of person-centred thinking has reinforced the need for all professionals to work harder to understand the perspectives of people with dementia rather than to regard them as epistemologically worthless (Innes, 2009; Murphy, Gray and Cox, 2007).

Part of the reason for exploring how the views of people with dementia can be incorporated in research and policy is the sheer number of people involved. The most widely quoted figures – that there are 683,597 people with dementia in the UK – derive from the *Dementia UK: Full Report* (Knapp and Prince 2007, p.xiii). The report went on to project an increase to 940,110 by 2021 and to 1,735,087 by 2051. The current figure represents one person in every 88 UK citizens.

At the core of these estimates are the Medical Research Council studies of Cognitive Function in Ageing (CFAS) that reported in 1998 and 2013 (Matthews *et al.*, 2013; Medical Research Council Cognitive Function and Ageing Study (MRC CFAS), 1998;). The 2013 study contained a major surprise. Researchers found a prevalence figure of 6.5 per cent among over 65s, translating into some 214,000 fewer people with dementia than the 884,000 that would have been expected from the prevalence figure of 8.3 per cent in the 1998 study.

The 2013 study concluded that:

Although many factors could have increased dementia prevalence at specific ages (such as those associated with diabetes, survival after stroke, and vascular incidents), other factors, which could decrease prevalence, such as improved prevention of vascular morbidity and higher levels of education, seem to have had a greater effect. (Matthews *et al.*, 2013, p.7)

Despite the important public health message that we can reduce the prevalence of people with dementia, we need to remember that these remain huge numbers, with continuing implications for involvement in policy and practice. While there are no estimates of the proportion of people with dementia who retain the capacity to express their views, the drive towards person-centred approaches and the Mental Capacity Act 2005 provide a framework in which professionals should assume capacity unless there is contrary evidence and should use their communication skills to elicit the views of people with dementia. At a broad level an argument can therefore be made for including the views and opinions of people with dementia because of the numbers – currently this group of the population is not particularly engaged with influencing how knowledge is generated and lacks opportunities to become involved. The fact that people have a cognitive impairment should not be seen as a barrier to involvement but rather as a challenge to overcome in eliciting views. Issues of empowerment become pertinent as we consider how the optimum conditions can be created to allow contribution within this particular context.

Lessons from Dementia Care Mapping

DCM had relevance because the underpinning theoretical position of DCM was entirely consistent with the project goal of providing an environment that enhanced personhood and supported engagement. However, DCM had not been designed for our particular purpose; it was designed for use in formal group care settings and observations, using five-minute timeframes, are made for a period of some hours on a single day. Our project involved three one-hour groups spread over a three-week period. We reduced the number of behaviour categories substantially because most of them would not be relevant and settled on using behaviour categories that reflected the nature of the activity. These categories were intellectual activity, general engagement, passive onlooking, disengagement and reminiscence. We used the six-point mood and engagement scale to build up a general picture of how each individual was faring. A positive score ($+5$, $+3$, $+1$) means that an individual is showing signs of being very happy ($+5$) to neutral ($+1$) whilst being engaged with the activity. Conversely a minus score (-1, -3, -5) indicates at the upper end small signs of a negative mood through to significant signs of a negative mood at the lower end. DCM places a lot of emphasis on non-verbal communication (NVC) because of the impact of dementia as it progresses. All our participants were early stage and able to rely on their verbal ability, nevertheless being attuned to NVC was an important part of building up the picture of how participants were faring. Our results indicated that the review group enjoyed engaging in the activity – mood and engagement scores were predominantly in positive range and the handful of minus score were no more than –1. By group three mainly +3 and +5 scores were being recorded.

The value of this approach was that it provided a method for structuring our observations and recording them through using an established tool designed to put the person mapping in the shoes of the person being observed. This led to some small but important adjustments being made after the first group.

Strengths and challenges

The key strength of this project is that we managed to recruit and consult seven people who had a diagnosis of dementia about three key parameters of systematic review. In doing so we used a closely monitored process that the participants gave every appearance of actively enjoying. It is perhaps worth adding that the project was a very enjoyable one to be involved in as researchers.

In common with other efforts to seek the views of people living with a diagnosis of dementia (Smith *et al.*, 2009), we found that participants valued being asked and that as relationships developed so did people's ability to contribute and their sense of ease, in doing so, grew. This was significant – at the outset we did not know if it was possible to consult people who had a diagnosis for the purposes of a systematic review or how they would react once the 'work' started.

The views and experiences offered represented a spectrum of thought and these were sometimes at odds with the research findings presented to the group. For example, most members of the review group thought it was important to live life to the full: by that they meant going out, meeting people, going on holiday and socialising in general, whereas the findings that they were presented with suggested that sometimes people with dementia cope by avoiding social situations.

The fact that these participants did not find that the findings of the initial literature review resonated particularly well with their own experiences raises both challenges and opportunities. The participants were all at a relatively early stage probably reflecting the recent emphasis of early diagnosis. This suggests that there may, at this point in time, be some discrepancy between much of the existing research base and the new population of people with an early diagnosis. Looking ahead a number of possibilities become apparent. The recent (Matthews *et al.*, 2013) surprise findings on prevalence and the conclusion that there appear to be protective factors at play in reducing the incidence of dementia provide potentially fertile ground for future research. Involving people with a diagnosis so as to allow them to influence the topic selection, broad review questions, developing protocols, identifying exclusion and inclusion criteria and assessing the quality of studies will be important in the future. This is because we know from broader efforts in the field of disability (Albrecht and Devlieger, 1999), as well as specific work with people with a diagnosis (Alzheimer's Society, 2008), that new insights about how people cope, and what makes a difference in this respect, can only come from the voice of direct experience.

The demographic attributes of our group were fairly narrow. They were predominantly white British males and all married. This raises the question, as with any qualitative research, about generalisability. Nobody in our group was living alone and most spoke warmly about the support provided by their spouses. A person who lives alone with dementia is likely to have a very different experience and therefore what might be important to them is likely to differ from the views expressed in our group. The level of severity of the condition is another consideration. Our group were all at an early stage. Work developed by Murphy *et al.*, (2007) to gain the views of people with a more advanced state shows that it is possible to do this in a meaningful way. Again, if we look towards broadening out representation as fully as possible, we need to consider inclusion of this group.

Whilst there are good reasons for attempting to make the consultation group more representative of the population at large, there may be potential tensions on a number of levels in doing so. On the one hand, from a methodological perspective, gathering as diverse a group of people as possible is attractive because it becomes more probable that a broader range of views can be accessed. This needs to be balanced against the size of the group. Too large a group and individuals may lack the confidence to speak up and relationships may take longer to develop. We also need to recognise that receiving a diagnosis of dementia represents the start of a journey – one that can last many years. Inevitably people will have different needs, concerns and experiences along the way. It therefore becomes important to develop a more nuanced view about who is approached and for what purpose. For example, if the review is going to focus on a particular service intervention it makes sense that the people who are involved in developing the broad review questions have not only a diagnosis but also experience of that particular type of service.

A further challenge to involving people with dementia in systematic reviews is to raise awareness amongst research ethics committees about the population who have a diagnosis and capacity. The issues of capacity and getting approval are fairly well documented in the literature and reflect the fact that most research has involved people with more advanced dementia as subjects. What is less well understood is the inclusion of people an earlier stage as co-producers of research. It is important that the process of gaining ethical approval does not disempower people by imposing paternalistic conditions that limit their freedom to make choices for themselves.

What are the key lessons arising from this exercise for future researchers? Drawing on our experience, the following points appear significant:

1. A multidisciplinary approach is required. It is unlikely that those based in a university will have direct access to people with a diagnosis in the same way that nurses, psychologists, voluntary organisations and other care providers will have. Equally, the expertise in systematic review methodology tends to reside in universities. Aligned to this point, and perhaps true of any innovation, is that establishing as broad a base of support as possible to take the initiative forward promotes confidence in what one is doing. Additionally, by involving a range of perspectives, checks and balances come into play, which is important when working with any vulnerable population.

2. Establish clarity of purpose and role within the project and maintain it. We were clear from the outset that we were not offering a support group but also recognised that some of our participants appeared to be seeking this type of function during the first group meeting. We responded by reiterating the purpose of the group and by having one of the team take on the role

of bringing the discussion back to the point under discussion for the subsequent groups. Follow-up support was also offered if required. Aligned to this is building in time after the 'work' phase to review how it went and to agree adjustments for the next group. Each member of the project team had a clear role, understood by them and understood by others, which meant that we could offer consistency and a sense of security as the groups ran. Using two rooms, one for refreshments and socialising and the other for 'working' in, reinforced the sense of purpose whilst allowing time and space for building relationships in a more general social sense.

3. Pay attention to practical details. The purpose is to create an environment in which people, including carers, feel at ease and therefore more able to contribute and support the activity. This involved an emphasis on trying to provide facilities in such a way as to reduce the impact of cognitive impairment, i.e. active facilitation, plain English, written prompts such as name badges and providing paper copies of the material being presented, sticking to a predictable format, making sure that people can see and hear, seating round a table and providing notepaper and pens so that people could make notes as we went along. It is also advisable to check if there are any particular requirements prior to the first meeting. This could relate to other disabilities (not uncommon as most people with dementia are older people) or special dietary requirements if refreshments are being offered.

4. Observation and monitoring. There is an inherent responsibility not to cause harm when conducting research. We adapted an established tool, DCM, to monitor the well-being of the review group during the course of the 'work' phase. The benefit of using DCM is that it has an established theoretical base, a clear structure with associated definitions and explanations of scales – it provides a particular type of lens through which to view what is happening, predicated on respect for the person. We would argue that it is important in future work of this type that some method of observation and monitoring of well-being is adopted.

5. Use a group format for the discussion, length and timings of the groups. As explained earlier, we were building on expertise developed by Alzheimer's Society in settling on a group format

for the work. Our findings support this approach and it is less resource intensive than conducting individual interviews. It appeared that the members enjoyed being in each other's company, took an interest in each other's point of view and were stimulated by this. The timing of the group work phase – one hour – appeared to suit the members, as did the time of day – mid to late morning. An important point for future researchers to note is to check with those who know the person with dementia as to when they are most likely to be alert.

6. Check accuracy and interpretation of what is said. We did this verbally, in writing and over time. The first check would take place within the group, by summarising during and at the end of the group what had been said. This was followed up in the next group by capturing the point in the presentation slides. Sometimes the links between the question and the responses were ones that had to be inferred, so this gave an important opportunity to check that the inferences were correct.

References

Albrecht, G. and Devlieger, P. (1999) 'The disability paradox: High quality of life against all odds.' *Social Science and Medicine 48*, 977–998.

Alzheimer's Society (2008) *Dementia: Out of the Shadows*. London: Alzheimer's Society.

Berghmans, R. L. P. and Ter Meulen, R. H. J. (1995) 'Ethical issues in research with dementia patients.' *International Journal of Geriatric Psychiatry 10*, 8, 647–651.

Bradford Dementia Group (2005a) *Dementia Care Mapping Principles and Practice*. Bradford: University of Bradford.

Bradford Dementia Group (2005b) *Dementia Care Mapping 8 User's Manual*. Bradford: University of Bradford.

Bradford Dementia Group (2005c) *Dementia Care Mapping 8 Self Update Pack*. Bradford: University of Bradford.

Cotrell, V. and Schulz, R. (1993) 'The perspective of the patient with Alzheimer's disease: A neglected dimension of dementia research.' *The Gerontologist 33*, 2, 205–211.

Department of Health (2009) *Living Well with Dementia: A National Dementia Strategy*. London: Department of Health.

Dewing, J. (2002) 'From ritual to relationship: A person-centred approach to consent in qualitative research with older people who have a dementia.' *Dementia 1*, 2, 157–171.

Fisher, M., Kelly, R., Lawrie-Skea, A., Randall, J. and Wade, N. (2014) *Involving People Living With Dementia in Systematic Reviews*. Luton: University of Bedfordshire. Available at www.beds.ac.uk/__data/assets/pdf_file/0019/308602/Report-to-Fund-v5.pdf, accessed on 4 April 2015.

Fisher, M., Qureshi, H., Hardyman, W. and Homewood, J. (2005) *Using Qualitative Research in Systematic Reviews: Older People's Views of Hospital Discharge.* London: Social Care Institute for Excellence.

Innes, A. (2009) *Dementia Studies: A Social Science Perspective.* London: Sage.

Knapp, M. and Prince, M. (2007) *Dementia UK: The Full Report.* London: LSE, Kings College and the Alzheimer's Society.

Matthews, F., Arthur, A., Barnes, L., Bond, J., Jagger, C., Robinson, L. and Brayne, C. (on behalf of the Medical Research Council Cognitive Function and Ageing Collaboration) (2013) 'A two-decade comparison of prevalence of dementia in individuals aged 65 years and older from three geographical areas of England: Results of the Cognitive Function and Ageing Study I and II.' *Lancet 382,* 9902, 1405–1412.

Medical Research Council Cognitive Function and Ageing Study (MRC CFAS) (1998) 'Cognitive function and dementia in six areas of England and Wales: The distribution of MMSE and prevalence of GMS organicity level in the MRC CFA Study.' *Psychological Medicine 28,* 319–335.

Murphy J., Gray, C.M. and Cox, S. (2007) *Communication and Dementia: How Talking Mats can Help People with Dementia to Express Themselves.* York: Joseph Rowntree Foundation.

Rutter, D., Francis, J., Coren, E. and Fisher, M. (2010) *The Conduct of Systematic Research Reviews for SCIE Knowledge Reviews* (2nd edition). London: SCIE.

Smith, E., Donovan, S., Beresford, P., Manthorpe, J., Brearley, S., Sitzia, J., and Ross, F. (2009) 'Getting ready for user involvement in a systematic review.' *Health Expectations 12,* 197–208.

Toby, W. (2012) *A Stronger Collective Voice for People with Dementia.* York: Joseph Rowntree Foundation.

Tooke, J. (2012) *Connecting Staff and Service Users: A Relational Approach to involving People with Dementia in the Work of an Organization.* London: Alzheimer's Society.

Tooke, J. (2013) 'Involving people with dementia: Service user review panels.' *Quality in Ageing and Older Adults 14,* 1, 56–65.

Chapter 7

ACTING AS A CRITICAL FRIEND

Developmental Evaluations, Service Users
and the Role of the Researcher

ROGER SMITH
Durham University

Overview – the search for authenticity

In this chapter, I want to explore the complex dynamics that infuse the relationship between the professional researcher and service users when working on a common project, in this case what I will term a 'developmental evaluation' of a 'training for trainers' project. For me, this was a new experience, and like the service user/trainers themselves, I was involved in a process of exploring and adaptation as we undertook the programme of work in our respective roles. What I think I learnt, and I hope they would agree, is a strategy for building a collaborative relationship that enabled me as an 'outsider' to offer an informed and constructive, but still critical, contribution to the implementation of the project and the evaluative process associated with it. In doing so, I became increasingly convinced of the virtues of adopting the role of 'critical friend', as articulated by Swaffield (2002, 2003).

As has been acknowledged quite widely, there are a number of pressing challenges to be faced in initiating and carrying out collaborative research activities, involving those with credentials as researchers on one side, and those who have direct experience of the subject of inquiry on the other. This kind of tension is particularly acute, of course, where there are clear differentials of power, experience and 'expertise' (although this is a contested term) between the different partners, such as where the research involves children and young people (Smith, Monagan and Broad, 2002), people who use mental health services (Tew, 2008) or those involved with social care services in general (Fleming *et al.*, 2014). Of central significance in negotiating effective partnerships is the nature of the relationship between participants: 'Collaborative research highlights the necessity to reconsider relationships between academics and service users...and can lead to reducing power differentials between partners' (Fleming *et al.*, 2014, p.708).

In the example presented here, I want to explore some of the elements involved in establishing and maintaining a successful collaborative relationship. The subject of the evaluation was a project that had been funded by the Department of Health and involved an established self-advocacy organisation that was seeking to develop and deliver a 'training for trainers' project with people with learning difficulties. This involved a process of programme development, piloting, evaluation, delivery, re-evaluation, revision and so on. I was invited to act as an independent (but sympathetic) evaluator/consultant to the project, partly because I was already fairly well known to the organisation. Thus, whilst the relationships between those involved were themselves constituted formally, in terms of a conventional contractual requirement, there were also in place certain mutual and informal understandings, in that all those involved had worked together previously and had some prior knowledge of each other.

Despite this, the way in which the project was structured created a clear demarcation between areas of activity and expertise, affording a distinctive advisory role to the academic researcher involved, with the inherent potential for this to lead to unhelpful divisions and a formalised separation of roles and competencies. Simply expressed in these terms, it is clear that the process of negotiating and sustaining an equitable working relationship in relation to the project in question raised a considerable number of questions and potential challenges. In what follows, I will offer an outline account of the training for trainers project itself, what it achieved and how it was evaluated; and, subsequently, I will reflect on what this might tell us about the process of establishing a workable and (I hope) 'authentic' research relationship between the external (professional) researcher and people who use services.

The research project – a collaborative, developmental evaluation

The substantive training project itself was commissioned by the Department of Health in 2003, as part of the National User Training

Development Project, to promote the role of service users as active trainers of those involved in providing services. Central England People First (CEPF)[1] applied for and was successful in gaining funding under this project umbrella; it then set about designing and delivering a two-day 'training for trainers' programme to be delivered to people with learning difficulties who might themselves want to take on a training role with service providers and others. In setting up the project, CEPF approached me to take on the role of evaluator for the project, as required by the funder. I had worked with them previously and also knew them from my former role as an elected member and Chair of Social Services in the area. We agreed from the outset that the evaluation would be developmental, in the sense that I would provide feedback and advice on a continuous basis throughout the life of the project, with the aim of supporting the incorporation of learning from each phase of its implementation.

The first phase of the project involved the development and testing of a range of training materials and activities and an initial survey of organisations and practitioners to gain some insight into what sort of training they would like service users to provide. Two survey tools were developed for this element of the project – an open-ended questionnaire for service user-led organisations and a more specific questionnaire for provider agencies and staff. While I assisted with 'technical' advice at this stage, the data gathering aspect of this exercise was carried out entirely by the four members of CEPF who comprised the project delivery team. At this stage, we had effectively already begun to demarcate those areas in which my advice and distinctive expertise would be drawn upon, and those where the team would retain control (essentially around substantive content and process).

I was called upon again to carry out analysis of the survey responses, but assisted by team members who were able to draw on their own interpretations of respondents' comments. This represented an early attempt to avoid an unhelpful separation of responsibilities for different aspects of the process, which Walmsley and Johnson (2003) have warned against. They warn us, particularly, of the risks of what might seem easy assumptions, for example that academics who are used to undertaking analytical and theoretical work might take this over

1   Central England People First is a self-advocacy organisation of people with learning difficulties, established in 1991, which by the time of this project included a number of members with substantial experience as trainers.

exclusively, leading to the risk of building in hierarchies of knowledge and expertise.

In practice, it was the project team who drew on the survey findings to decide how they should go about devising and delivering the training programme. Not only was this the preparatory stage for the project as a whole, but it was also the phase during which the working relationship between myself and the team was established, with an understanding that I would act as observer/advisor and wouldn't be involved in any more of a substantial way in the direct delivery of the training workshops.

The next step was for the team to devise a two-day programme, based on their own previous experience and use of training techniques such as role plays and structured exercises (such as 'The Road'), which was then piloted within the local area. This was another instance in which the nature of the role between evaluator and project team became the subject of further negotiation, in effect. Although I was acting as an observer in these sessions, in reality it became impossible to achieve invisibility, or to avoid being called upon to provide an 'extra pair of hands' in carrying out the practical requirements of the training activities. The recurrent question of course was to do with the fine distinction between 'supporting' the team in this delivery phase and straying across the line and 'taking control' or otherwise significantly influencing what was happening – and of learning not to jump in every time the thought occurred that: 'I wouldn't do it like that.'

In fact, the pilot phase itself was relatively reassuring, and our joint review of this phase of the project led to very few substantive changes to the planned programme – in this context, I certainly felt more comfortable about offering feedback because here it was possible to act more easily in accordance with our initial agreement about my role.

In the delivery phase of the project, the four-member CEPF team (with a support person) went on to deliver the two-day programme to over 80 participants in eight locations around England. Participants were usually recruited via local authority services for learning difficulties, and delivery sites included a number of day service settings, a 'care village' and another user-led organisation with whom CEPF had an existing relationship. In my role as observer, I attended some of these training events. The training programme itself followed a fairly conventional format, with presentations from the delivery team, exercises, small group activities and some practical workshops (use of video recording, speaking in public, using quizzes, for example). One of the challenges here was to find a way of presenting the programme that took account of the needs of those attending (with or without their own support people), and the programme did include frequent breaks, for example, and incorporated short presentations where these were required.

Undertaking the evaluation – in search of collaboration

In my role as evaluator, I was asked to undertake both a formative role in terms of providing feedback and supporting enhancements of the programme as it was delivered on repeated occasions, and, at the same time, generating summative feedback to inform the final project report to the funder (Department of Health). Thus, observation was combined with more standard feedback methods, such as the use of suitably designed response forms for participants (as previously developed and used by CEPF) to complete at the end of the programme and comments gleaned in more informal settings during the course of delivery. The team was comfortable with this approach as it was consistent with their previous experience and use of this kind of feedback method. On the other hand, the collation, recording and analysis of responses was a task for which I took responsibility, presumably because this was an area of activity seen to be consistent with my (assumed) professional expertise. I also acquired responsibility for the initial drafting of project reports and the accompanying accessible accounts of the work undertaken by the team, and I took on the task of editing the accompanying training pack, which had always been an intended 'product' of the project. As Tew (2008) has acknowledged, though, this highlights one of the challenges in securing a genuinely participatory and democratic approach in 'service user-led' research, if certain aspects of the task (analysis, 'writing up', for example) are reserved for those with the assumed expertise (or time and facilities) to carry them out – thereby reflecting and reproducing embedded power differentials that may not be acknowledged.

In practical terms, I took on my consultative role from the very early stages of project development, commenting on the initial project proposal, joining planning meetings to design the format of the two-day training workshop, discussing possible delivery sites and agreeing my role in the process as observer and provider of continuous feedback. This meant that my involvement would need to be continuous, and active, in the sense that I would be presenting thoughts and suggestions orally in meetings, rather than in the form of paper-based reports (which were largely for the funder's benefit). We agreed that the most important written material to be produced jointly in the delivery stage would be the programme content and participant evaluation tools. In the event, I attended a number of meetings at the planning stage, a pilot delivery event and several of the 'live' project workshops in order to be able to provide ongoing feedback, as well as obtaining observational material for the final project report. I was also able to draw extensively on the feedback obtained from workshop participants.

As the programme was delivered and refined over the lifetime of the project, it was clear both that the team became more comfortable and confident in what they were doing and that the approach they were taking was extremely well received (by service users and staff who sometimes chose to attend). Participants were very welcoming of the opportunity to see themselves in a more authoritative and influential role as trainers of those providing their services. They clearly understood this as a means of enabling them to 'speak out' about the things that mattered most to them, the direct services provided and other aspects of their lives (dealing with and challenging 'bullying on the bus' proved to be a much appreciated role-play exercise, for example).

In fact, the chance to learn how to design and conduct a role-play exercise proved to be a very popular element of the programme, and post-event evaluations showed that participants valued both practical skills development and the chance to develop their own ideas. One respondent from the user organisation that hosted the programme highlighted learning about how 'to do role plays' and stated: 'Now I will be able to train other people', whilst another participant from this organisation said: 'I liked all [of the activities], especially the warm up and "speaking up"' (quoted in Weeks *et al.*, 2006, p.52). Another participant at a training event held in the West Midlands said that it would help her/him to train others in 'problem-solving'. It was clear, too, from my observations that participants welcomed practical aspects of the workshops, such as using video recorders (not phones, it was a few years ago!) and learning about how to make presentations.

Although most responses were positive, some of the feedback received was less so; sessions were 'long', and one respondent complained of 'not being able to get a word in edgeways'. However, such complaints were in the minority, and at the conclusion of the project, it was possible to identify a number of consistently positive outcomes, at least in terms of immediate feedback. It did seem that respondents appreciated the distinctive quality of a training programme presented by people with learning difficulties, and this may well have had an effect in the sense that others felt empowered by this. In a broader sense, the level of engagement and the detailed nature of the feedback suggested that this model of 'training for trainers' did offer indications of its continuing potential value, especially in terms of providing a practical resource for promoting service user empowerment.

We were careful however to ensure that the positive achievements overall did not lead to an unrealistic idealisation of the project. Although in this case, the team of trainers generally worked well together and demonstrated considerable skills in delivering the programme, this cannot be taken for granted, clearly. The team had to work on their delivery skills and learn from the feedback received. Similarly, there are likely to be specialist areas of knowledge ('welfare rights', for example) where specialist input is needed and that the limits of the team's capacities have to be recognised. The approach taken necessitated the commitment of time and resources to provide support to the core team, as indeed is often the norm in service provision, although the support role needs to be clearly demarcated and its limits recognised. Finally, the benefits of the CEPF programme depended on the skills of the training team and the quality of the programme they delivered – service user-led training could not be assumed simply to be a 'good thing' by definition; indeed, this would be a rather patronising assumption.

Overall, though, the evaluation concluded that the model offered some powerful advantages that should be recognised: it provided a site for dialogue and mutual learning distinct from and not circumscribed by the service setting – there was clearly a greater degree of freedom for participants than they may have felt elsewhere; some aspects of learning, such as improved communication, seem particularly well suited to a user-led approach; the role reversal implicit in taking on and leading a training activity is inherently empowering for service users, who find that their knowledge and expertise is valued and that they can take on 'leadership' roles. And, finally, in simple pedagogic terms, the series of training events delivered by the CEPF team appeared to meet their learning objectives consistently.

Methodological reflections – a learning relationship

In carrying out this piece of work, I feel that I, too, had several objectives. First, I did want to support and facilitate the achievement of a successful project outcome, and this was the primary objective. But, in addition, this was a vehicle for testing my own assumptions (and values) in relation to the researcher role in user-led projects. At the time of the project (the early 2000s), and since, there has been a growing interest in participatory approaches, in practice and in research; these are quite often seen as inherently virtuous and perhaps subject to less substantive criticism than research carried out from other methodological positions. On the other hand, it is undeniably the case that a great deal of thought has been given by those involved to addressing the challenges of establishing fair, respectful and equitable relationships, in a context where service users in particular may be in a vulnerable position (Tew *et al.*, 2006, for example). Power is recognised as a recurrent issue in this context, and it is argued that it is important initially to 'recognise' differentials in this respect, as a first step towards overcoming them:

> Empowerment inevitably means that those situated in potentially oppressive positions of 'power over' may need to hold back from deploying it in order to allow the emergence of more effective forms of 'power together' between people with different backgrounds and experiences.' (Tew *et al.*, 2006, p.18)

Practical dimensions of this include 'acknowledging the expertise of service users (Walmsley and Johnson, 2003); being prepared to 'give up' control over certain aspects of the design and implementation of the research (evaluation) strategy (Smith *et al.*, 2002); and reversing the relationship between service users and the researcher (who becomes a reactor rather than an initiator; Healey and Walsh, 1997).

It was undoubtedly helpful in the case of my working relationship with CEPF that we already knew each other and believed that we could establish an appropriate working relationship. However, none of us knew at the start how this would develop, so the work we did in the early stages to agree a formal contract was of considerable benefit in terms of clarifying expectations and setting out a framework for the evaluation itself. The contract itself was probably never consulted again, but the work undertaken in drawing it up enabled us to address and resolve some of the inbuilt imbalances in the researcher–service user relationship, including subsequent dissemination and use of the outputs generated. The transfer of power may necessitate an active process of engagement on the part of the researcher:

> [A]s I write this I am conscious of where the power still lies. *I* will think about how to include people. *They* are not demanding inclusion. As long as this is the case, then it remains the responsibility of the non-disabled researcher to think of ways in which inclusion can happen. (Walmsley and Johnson, 2003, p.122)

This is not just a one-off exercise, but necessarily a continuing feature of the research relationship – renegotiation and reflection on the question of power differentials remain central to the process throughout. Concrete examples of this would have included the decision to adapt existing feedback gathering tools from CEPF's previous work, rather than to introduce an alternative tool, perhaps with a more academic pedigree. Equally, it was important to ensure that the findings generated at this point and subsequently were the subject of regular dialogue between myself as evaluator and the training team – both in the sense of refining the analysis and also ensuring that they were able to draw on and respond to the messages emerging. Thus, in making sense of the initial survey (of potential participants and users of the training), the 'collated responses...provided some important guidance to the team, enabling them to decide how they should go about delivering the training programme itself' (Smith, 2004, p.340). We detected, for example, a level of anxiety amongst service providers about the capacity of the training team to deliver the two-day programme; which meant that the team were aware of the possibility that any staff members in attendance might be 'too helpful' in trying to ensure that sessions went well.

Whilst power imbalances are clearly bound up with structural (positional) inequalities, they are also linked to implicit assumptions about 'expertise' and who holds it. In this respect, it was clearly helpful to incorporate the use of the organisation's own tools for obtaining feedback, since this did represent recognition of their expertise in this respect. On the other hand, my experience (in common with that of others – see Walmsley and Johnson, 2003, for example) is that certain aspects of the collaborative task seem to 'stick' to us, notably the analysis and writing of reports or articles for dissemination. In the present example, this was partly at my collaborators' request – they asked me to edit the training guide to accompany the programme, for instance – but in such cases it remains important that a consultative process is built in and consideration is given to underlying requirements, such that material should be produced in accessible formats as far as possible. Equally, though, there is a case for allowing those with the relevant 'technical' skills to take on specific aspects of the overall task, and there is no particular merit in simply carving up responsibilities purely to comply with an idealised notion of parity. The important point here is that these decisions are the subject of discussion and are revisited when necessary.

These reflections have, in turn, led me back to the relationship as the fundamental determinant of the degree to which service user participation and/or control of the research process can be ensured. The checks and balances that are built in act as a sort of template or verification tool, but what they are really measuring is the continuing quality of that relationship rather than whether or not a particular function was carried out appropriately.

It is the quality of the relationship, too, that enables collaborators to express themselves honestly and openly. In the course of the evaluation, it was inevitable that I would make observations or receive feedback that might lead to critical observations about aspects of the programme or its delivery – for instance, about the tendency sometimes for the training team to be focused on delivery at the expense of dialogue, or the need to pace sessions and allow for regular breaks. It seemed important to be able to share these points constructively and in this case, it did seem appropriate for me to draw on my 'expert' status to do so. Clearly, the manner of this kind of exchange and its outcome are also dependent on the working relationship between those concerned. In reflecting on this subsequently (Smith, 2004), it seemed to me that it might be possible to define this relationship in a number of ways in order to clarify its essential characteristics. The researcher can take one of the following roles: contractor, expert, supporter or critical friend.

1. A contractual arrangement

It may seem relatively straightforward to treat the working relationship between external researcher and service user organisation as a formal contractual arrangement, whereby mutual responsibilities are clearly specified from the outset and fixed. This might be felt to build in the kind of safeguards and guarantees that would protect service users from exploitation whilst ensuring that the researcher delivers a service as specified. In practice, though, this limits the potential for establishing an effective developmental relationship, which depends on a continuing process of negotiation and adaptation to changing circumstances. Would constraining the researcher's input in this way prove to be counter-productive?

2. A 'client' relationship

From this perspective, it might seem reasonable to rely on the external researcher to bring the 'expertise' to the arrangement (as with a plumber fixing a tap), underpinned by the assumption that the partner organisation could not reasonably be expected to understand or apply the techniques to carry out legitimate and valid research. Indeed, it might be argued that this is just the sort of expertise that should be expected, shaping the project in order to ensure that the evaluation process is effective and methodologically robust. In a pure sense, this may be a route to more readily demonstrable compliance with conventional rules of valid research practice, but it does build in problematic assumptions about a hierarchy of expertise and privileges researcher judgement in a way that is not compatible with the principle of service users taking the lead.

3. Acting as a support worker

In some ways, the most attractive role for the intending researcher/ evaluator is to adopt the kind of 'support' role that is well accepted in the field of learning difficulties, where the task is defined as one of giving substance to service user expectations and providing nothing more than assistance in achieving these. It is not part of the support role to question aspirations or to substitute one's own judgement for that of the service user. This is a role that is likely to be familiar to the user-led organisation and it appears to offer the opportunity to act in a suitably empowering manner without unduly compromising the aims of the project being undertaken. But it would seem, here, that the specialist skills of the external researcher would be almost redundant, with no capacity to offer constructive suggestions for fear of compromising the purity of the service user-led initiative. It is also difficult to sustain this position should the need arise to question or challenge the attitudes or approach of the project team on ethical grounds. It seems that to eschew critical comment of any kind is itself potentially problematic if and when it may diminish the quality of the project overall.

4. Being a 'critical friend'

By contrast, it is perhaps more fruitful to see the role of the external researcher as being a 'critical friend'; that is to say, the relationship is to be seen as organic and negotiable, albeit within an agreed framework. In this way, the researcher puts her/himself at the disposal of the user-led organisation without denying her/his own expertise and capacity to influence the process in light of this. The term 'critical friend' is most closely associated with research in the field of education (Swaffield, 2002), but it provides a helpful way of conceptualising the balancing act that is a key component of the task of providing external input to a project in which service users are in the lead, but remain characterised by power imbalances. A 'critical friend':

> Asks provocative questions, provides data to be examined through another lens, and offers critiques of a person's work as a friend. A critical friend takes the time to fully understand the context of the work presented and the outcomes that the person or group is working towards. The friend is [also] an advocate for the success of that work. (Costa and Kallick, 1993, p.50)

In the project in which I was involved with CEPF, this understanding allowed me to make comments about aspects of the training for trainers programme that were 'critical', but that could also be accepted as standing within a framework of shared commitment to improving the programme and of offering constructive suggestions rather than substituting my judgement for theirs; as in the case of suggesting that the programme allow rather more space for participants to share their own ideas.

But, as Swaffield (2002) has pointed out, this requires an adaptive strategy on the part of the researcher:

> Even when the critical friend's comments are judgemental and are welcomed as such, there is a sequence of support and judgement, and the latter is not delivered in isolation. 'Although I want him to be supportive, I also want him to criticise, to be judgemental. But, there is a third step. Once he has been judgemental and critical, I want him to go back to be supportive'. (Swaffield, 2002, p.14)

Concluding thoughts – the value(s) of a collaborative relationship

It is clearly a fundamental aspiration of research carried out under the banner of social work that it should be strongly grounded in the core values of the discipline and that it should therefore seek to be anti-discriminatory, empowering and led by the interests of service users. On the other hand, as already acknowledged, giving substance to this in a collaborative research project is itself challenging. The central argument here is that it is the quality of the relationship between partners that is the critical element in determining how effectively the project will be delivered, but that it is also likely to be crucial in determining the quality and validity of the findings in conventional research terms. A relationship of trust constructed on an equal footing equalises different sources of knowledge, for example, rather than privileging any one (Fleming *et al.*, 2014). Interestingly, as already mentioned, this affords legitimacy to the researcher, acting as critical friend, when s/he does offer critical comments or challenges the 'knowledge' of service users – the important point here is that this is a two-way street and challenges can travel in both directions. As a result, it certainly appeared that the project generated a number of significant benefits: first and foremost, I think everyone thought of it as a rewarding (and sometimes enjoyable) experience; the team appeared to gain demonstrably in skills and confidence over time; the workshops were very well received wherever they were presented – service users were visibly encouraged by the message that they, too, could be 'trainers'; and a detailed and workable two-day programme with accompanying materials was developed.

We didn't achieve everything we wanted. In terms of the evaluation, I did feel that some of the conventional assumptions about who does what (I got to do most of the analysis and writing, for example) were not overturned (but see Fleming *et al.*, 2014, which is more encouraging in this respect), and, disappointingly, the funder showed little or no interest in the outcome, irrespective of its demonstrable successes. Nonetheless, as a test-bed for ideas about how to promote effective collaboration between the researcher and service users, this experience did demonstrate for me that underlying everything, it is the relationship that is fundamental, and of course this is tested and proved through the experience of 'making it happen'.

References

Costa, A. and Kallick, B. (1993) 'Through the lens of a critical friend.' *Educational Leadership 51*, 6, 49-51.

Fleming, J., Beresford, P., Bewley, C., Croft, S., Branfield, F., Postle, K. and Turner, M. (2014) 'Working together – innovative collaboration in social care research.' *Qualitative Social Work 13*, 5, 706–722.

Healey, K. and Walsh, K. (1997) 'Making participatory processes visible: Practice issues in the development of a peer support network.' *Australian Social Work 50*, 3, 45–52.

Smith, R. (2004) 'A matter of trust: Service users and researchers.' *Qualitative Social Work 3*, 3, 335–346.

Smith, R., Monaghan, M. and Broad, B. (2002) 'Involving young people as co-researchers: Some methodological issues.' *Qualitative Social Work 1*, 2, 191–207

Swaffield, S. (2002) 'Contextualising the Work of the Critical Friend.' Paper presented at *15th International Congress for School Effectiveness and Improvement*, Copenhagen, 3–6 January.

Swaffield, S. (2003) 'The role of a critical friend.' *Managing Schools Today 12*, 5, 28–30.

Tew, J. (2008) 'Researching in partnership: Reflecting on a collaborative study with mental health service users into the longer term impact of compulsory admission to psychiatric hospital.' *Qualitative Social Work 7*, 3, 271–287.

Tew, J., Gould, N., Abankwa, D., Barnes, H., Beresford, P., Carr, S., Copperman, J., Ramon, S., Rose, D., Sweeney, A. and Woodward, L. (2006) *Values and Methodologies for Social Research in Mental Health*. London: SCIE.

Walmsley, J. and Johnson, K. (2003) *Inclusive Research with People with Learning Disabilities*. London: Jessica Kingsley Publishers.

Weeks, L., Shane, C., MacDonald, F., Hart, C. and Smith, R. (2006) 'Learning from the experts: People with learning difficulties training and learning from each other.' *British Journal of Learning Disabilities 34*, 49–55.

Section 2

INNOVATIONS IN
RESEARCH METHODS

Chapter 8

OBSERVING SOCIAL WORK PRACTICE

Using Ethnographic and Mobile Research Methods with Social Workers and Service Users

HARRY FERGUSON
University of Nottingham

Social work is a human enterprise. While the internet and information technology have expanded the opportunities for people to communicate and get closer without being in the same place, effective social work still largely depends on practitioners and service users being physically together (Broadhurst and Mason, 2012). Thus, in order to understand what social work is, how it is done and aspects of its effectiveness it is essential for research to get as close as it possibly can to those practice encounters. A vital method for achieving such closeness is for the researcher to participate in and observe what social workers do. Participant observation is the defining feature of ethnography. An ethnographic study of social work may include examining documents such as case records and interviewing social workers and service users for instance, but it is the focus on observation of people, events and processes that defines ethnography. What distinguishes ethnography within the broad range of qualitative methods is some degree of direct observation and participation (Hammersley and Atkinson, 2007). In recent years increasing attention has been given to recognising the movement that characterises everyday life (Urry, 2007), including social work (Ferguson, 2008), and mobile methods are emerging for studying such movement (Buscher, Urry and Whichger, 2011; Fincham, McGuinness and Murray, 2010). This chapter focuses on ethnography as a research method in social work and the importance of incorporating attention to movement into such research. The chapter's claim to innovation is the approach of combining ethnographic and mobile methods to get as close as possible to social work practice, to deepen understandings of how it is practised and experienced by those who receive it. Drawing on my ethnographic research into social work and child protection, the chapter considers the approach of shadowing social workers wherever they go, observing and audio recording their face-to-face interactions with service users. I have set out elsewhere the core theoretical and practical components of using ethnographic and mobile methods in researching social work (Ferguson, 2014a). Here I want to provide further insights into the method, how to use it and the nature and depth of data that it produces. After providing an overview of the approach and what is original about it, the chapter then focuses in detail on a single case and goes on to provide some general research findings and critical reflections on the method.

Observing social work and being mobile

Simply put, ethnography is the study of people as they go about their everyday lives. It focuses on observing phenomena that occur naturally in that the researcher seeks to be present when people are doing what they normally do. Floersch, Longhofer and Suskewicz (2014) note the growth that has occurred in recent years in ethnographic research in social work that focuses on a wide range of types of social work delivery and service user groups, including mental health, homelessness, addiction, neighbourhood work and child welfare (for instance, Floresch, 2002; Longhofer, Kubek and Floersch, 2010; Stanhope, 2012). Studies of social work differ, however, in the focus of their observations. Many social work researchers have observed and interviewed practitioners and managers in their offices, inquiring into what social workers do there and the impact of contemporary developments such as computerisation and hot-desking. They listen in to how staff talk about their cases and generally try to make sense of the culture of the organisation, office designs and their effects on social work (Broadhurst *et al.*, 2010; Buckley, 2003; Gillingham and Humphreys, 2009; Helm, 2013; Jeyasingham, 2014; Pithouse, 1998; Scourfield, 2003). What hasn't received as much attention is practice in the sense of what goes on between social workers and service users. Longhofer and Floersch (2012) refer to an approach that seeks to observe actual social worker–service user encounters as 'practice ethnography' and have used it to draw out the ways that social workers have engaged and worked creatively with people experiencing mental health problems (Longhofer *et al.*, 2010). Some practice goes on with service users within the office, but most practice encounters occur outside of it: on hospital wards, in residential care homes, prisons, daycentres and, most common of all, on home visits. This requires social workers to be *mobile*. To be able to see, understand and help service users involves leaving the office, making a journey and entering their communities and homes. If research is to fully capture what social work is – and does – it, too, must be mobile and follow social workers wherever they go (Ferguson, 2011a). Movement is central to participant observation, yet it is under-recognised and some social scientists argue that correcting this makes it crucial to foreground movement by referring to a distinct approach of 'mobilised ethnography' (Gottschalk and Salvaggio, 2015). This involves participation in the 'natural' work that goes on, including patterns of movement as well as stillness. The basic idea is that 'the researcher can be co-present within modes of movement and then employ a range of observation, interviewing, and recording techniques' (Sheller and Urry, 2006, p.218). Using ethnographic and mobile methods in social work research is innovative therefore in its insistence on the necessity to focus on researching *practice* in the sense of the encounters that go on between professionals and service users and its commitment to following and gathering data from practitioners wherever they go, within and beyond the office. There is a social work research approach that refers to itself as seeking to get 'near practice' and this has produced valuable insights, especially into the emotional dynamics of social work (Froggett, 2012; Ruch, 2013). However within this approach getting 'near practice' can be taken to mean near to workers' emotional experiences through interviews and case discussions and there is no absolute requirement to conduct close up observation of social work practice encounters in real time. On the other hand, the method of what Longhofer and Floersch (2012) call practice ethnography in combination with mobile methods is about getting as close as it is humanly possible to get to social workers and moving with them as they conduct their work with service users, while ensuring the research is ethical.

I began conducting participant observations of social worker–service user interactions on home visits in 2008 and used some of this data in my book *Child Protection Practice* to illustrate what social workers do and to theorise their actions (Ferguson, 2011b). A researcher being present to observe practice encounters in people's homes had never been done in this way before in child protection and I was very fortunate to gain the help of enlightened and generous senior managers and social workers in a local authority who granted me access and worked with me on developing an ethically sound research procedure (Ferguson, 2014a). In 2012–13 I undertook a larger funded study where I observed social workers from two local authorities on a total of 87 practice encounters, 71 of them on home visits. It is from this data that this chapter draws. The research questions were concerned with: what do social workers do, how do they perform child protection, especially on home visits? Do they see children alone? If yes, where? If not, why not? How do social workers, children and parents relate to one another? What are social workers' lived experiences of the work and what enables and constrains practice that keeps children safe? I conducted all the fieldwork myself. The research was granted ethical approval by my university and the social work agencies involved. Only social workers and service users who consented were included. All the access to observations of practice was negotiated through the social workers, who asked for parents' consent for the researcher to accompany them to the visit. Where consent was given, on arrival at the home I provided an explanation of the research and if the family were happy for me to stay, permission was then sought to audio record the interview. All of the families who agreed to me visiting signed consent forms, a copy of which was left with them, with contact details should they wish to withdraw at any time or make other inquiries.

The fieldwork lasted for six months (three months in each local authority) during which time I spent an average of 2.5 days per week in the teams. I 'hung out' in the office and did some observation of routines and noting conversations, but my main aim was to observe the social worker's practice and they knew it. Once my participation in a visit had been set up I followed the social workers from the moment they left their desks, and I began recording discussion with them as we moved together. I drew from the repertoire of mobile research methods being developed to capture everyday movements and practices, by using 'walk-alongs', where interviews are conducted while walking (Clark and Emmel, 2010) and 'ride-alongs' in cars or other vehicles (Kusenbach, 2003). Ross *et al.* (2009) used both these 'go-along' methods to good effect in their research into the experiences of young people in care. I went along with the social workers on their journeys from the office to see service users. The majority were by car, a small number were close enough to the office to walk, one was a bus journey and one was a bicycle ride. During the journey the social worker was interviewed about their plan for the encounter, expectations and feelings. One of the best decisions I made was to continue to interview the worker about what they were experiencing on the 'walk-along' from the car to the doorstep. I accompanied the social worker into the family home and observed and audio recorded their encounters with children, parents and others present (such as ubiquitous family friends). The worker was then interviewed about the encounter and their feelings about it immediately after on the way from the house to the car (the first thing they said on leaving the home was often very significant) and in the car on the journey back to the office or next visit. Back at the office I also observed the interactions between workers and team managers and interviewed some managers about the casework.

The findings produced by ethnographic and mobile methods

I will now show how the methods were used in practice by focusing on a single case that has been chosen randomly from the sample of 71 home visits in the study. While all cases were different and a wide variety of findings emerged, the research methods were applied in the same way in all cases and my aim in using a single case is to convey the kind of journey into the heart of social work practice that the research typically took and show the kinds of data and insights these produced. All information that could possibly identify those involved has been changed.

The case involved a father, here called 'Michael' and mother, 'Mel', who was arrested a week prior to the home visit in the research for allegedly assaulting her six-year-old stepson, here called 'Barry', who had some severe bruising. There are three other children, a three-year-old boy, here called 'Andrew', a two-year old girl, 'Bethany' and a five-month old boy, 'Niall'. Mel is on bail but is allowed to live at home because Barry is staying with relatives for his own protection. The assessment so far led social work to conclude that the other three children were not at a level of risk from their mother that required them to be removed to safety, but the children were only allowed to stay at home with an agreement that their father must be their carer and that Mel was not to be left on her own with them. Although it was closed when this new referral came in, the family had social work involvement in the past, mainly regarding neglect, and standards of childcare were once again a cause for concern. Before the social worker, here called 'Louise', left the office jokes were made about the state of the home conditions: a colleague quipped 'You've got your jeans on [Louise] so you're ready for the visit' – meaning that she was going into a dirty house. When I posed the question of what kind of a father is Michael, 'like does he share the housework?', the answer came back that nobody does any housework.

The social worker had home visited once before, the previous week. On the journey there she told me that her plan for this, her second home visit, was to have a good look around upstairs and to talk to the father about how he's coping and how things are going.

> I want to see the rest of the house because I've not seen the rest of the house yet and see how Dad is and what Dad's wanting to say about, if he's got any questions about [the case] conference or how he's feeling about the police investigation, if [Mel] said anything else to him about choosing between her or Barry and the kids and just getting a bit more of a general feel of how he's coping.

Her intention was to observe two-year-old Bethany and three-year-old Andrew who has language difficulties and 'observe really how they are with Dad'.

The family have a large dog and as the car got closer to the housing estate the social worker explained her intention to park at the back of the house so she could listen out and look into the garden to see where the dog was.

> Normally if you can hear the dog barking as you're walking past the house you know he's already in the garden, but they normally tend to put him away before they let us in.

When we got out of the car and walked towards the home the dog could be heard barking ferociously and Louise expressed worry that it was in the house. On arrival it was in the garden. This shows how interviews while driving and walking to see service users give valuable insights into the lived experience of doing the work and the workers' state of mind and emotional state as they are about to knock on the door and engage with service users.

Michael let us in and led the social worker into the sitting room where she sat beside him on the settee. Louise knew that Mel wouldn't be there because she had to go out. Niall the baby was sleeping in the cot in the living room and two minutes into the visit the social worker got up and walked over to look at him. Bethany and Andrew followed her and the social worker touched Bethany on the head as the child looked into the cot. The baby was unwell and slept for the entirety of the 30-minute visit. The social worker returned to the settee and for the next eight minutes interacted with Michael, exploring issues around the baby's health, how he was coping with the three children, him wanting contact with Barry and his request for financial help. Eleven minutes into the visit, the social worker asked for father's permission to see upstairs.

Social worker (SW): Do you mind [Michael], because I've not seen upstairs in the bedrooms, do you mind if I have a look?

Father: No, that's fine.

SW: Do you want the children to take me? Are you going to show me where your bedrooms are? Are you going to show me your bed? Are you going to show me?

SW: Are you going to show me upstairs? Are you coming? Are you going to show me and Harry? Are you all right with that [Michael], yeah?

The manner in which the social worker engaged the children about showing her their bedrooms was a common tactic employed by social workers in the study. Another was to allow parents to lead the way around the house. Louise explained afterwards (as did many other social workers) how the aim of these strategies is to be respectful and give families at least a semblance of control in a situation where the worker is painfully aware that such practices can be experienced as unduly invasive. The quotation also shows how the social worker asked the father if it was alright for me to accompany her upstairs. This was something I always asked permission from parents to do but social workers knew my aim was to observe them everywhere they went and this shows how they often assisted the research by asking too.

Michael first led the social worker into the toddlers' bedroom where it emerged that three-year-old Andrew had wet the bed. Michael explained that although it was midday it was the first time today he'd been in their bedrooms. The social worker's rather upbeat response was: 'He did, bless him. They'll need to be cleaned up and changed – more washing for you there, Michael!' She could have challenged him about why he and Mel were not systematically checking first thing a child who wets the bed three times a week. The worker addressed it in the spirit of trying to understand the circumstances from father's perspective, accepted that he'd been caring for a sick baby and quickly shifted to engaging with the children about their toys. Then Louise asked to see where the baby sleeps and was taken to the parent's bedroom, which had a cot in it, positioned beside the double bed. The father entered the bedroom first and positioned himself in a way that blocked the social worker from moving beyond the threshold and she could only gain sight of the child's cot from a distance. She never actually crossed the threshold of the bedroom. Afterwards in the car the social worker said that going into any parents' bedrooms feels much more intrusive and here she was trying to respect their privacy. Michael seemed to feel the same and enacted his resistance by effectively using his body as a barrier and blocking her access. He never said anything that expressed overt hostility or resistance; he embodied it. The worker reasoned afterwards that she saw enough of the cot from a distance to feel satisfied with the standard of care. This is a good example of how focused attention to mobilities and the dynamics of movement/non-movement deepens understandings of social work. Inspecting the bedrooms was only possible through the worker purposefully enacting movement, while blocked movement also had a profound influence on the shape of the practice and what it was able to achieve.

Exiting that situation left Michael and the social worker standing on the landing and beside another bedroom door that was closed and had a duvet sticking out of the top of it. I could sense the social worker momentarily pausing and thinking to herself shall I ask to get into this room? I put this to her in the car afterwards and she agreed that she was hesitant and put it down to dilemmas about her role as Barry had another social worker of his own and this left her uncertain about whether to enter his room:

> I did feel I was [hesitant], I did, because I did question myself in my head, I did question myself whether to ask or not, so you were right, you did pick up on that because I was. And that was all about whether I was [engine turned off] whether I could, because I'm not Barry's worker and mother knows I'm not there for Barry, and I didn't want that then to clash and us then get more on conversations about Barry, but I wanted to, to see the difference between the bedrooms.

I have left the reference to '[engine turned off]' in to show how the transcript captured the point when the talk was going on at the end of the car journey as we arrived back at the office. These drive-along interviews provide vital data about the worker's perspective on what they did and felt on the visit and how they are feeling right now when the experience is still very much alive for them. The car provides a productive space for research because the worker doesn't have to find time to give an interview but is engaging in the research while going about what they would be doing anyway. The dynamics of car journeys create intimate spaces for research discussions and disclosures in ways that are similar to how children will speak of things in cars that they won't discuss in other spaces (Ferguson, 2010a).

The issue for the social worker on the landing was not just one of roles but also of privacy and as far as possible minimising intruding into the family. The right to occupy space is central to negotiations around privacy and it is important to dig below the surface to consider the psychodynamics of these encounters and the emotional experience of workers as they conduct these navigations (Froggett, 2012). The worker had just had an experience of blocked movement and this is likely to have (unconsciously) compounded her ambivalence and uncertainty about asking to see the bedroom and perhaps also her fear about what was behind the door, given that it was Barry, the injured child's bedroom. The social worker did ask and established that the duvet was hanging up to dry. She entered the room, had a look around unobstructed by Michael and in the car afterwards said that she felt it was quite well presented.

A total of six minutes were spent upstairs. On going downstairs, the social worker asked to see the kitchen and spent two minutes in there checking in the fridge, freezer and cupboards to see what provisions there were for the children. After the visit she said there was not as much food as the father had suggested but this wasn't challenged or fed back to him. The social worker then moved back into the sitting room and assumed the same position as before on the settee. The baby was still asleep and Bethany and Andrew were very active and playful. While talking to Michael the social worker had two moments of direct interaction with the children – one in a playful way that involved some tickling and the other where they were climbing on her and she settled them on the settee as they played so that she could speak to Michael. She also observed them interacting with their father. Before ending the

30-minute visit the social worker reminded Michael that she would see if she can get him some help with money (she did manage to get him a small amount) and arranged to come back in a few days at a time when Mel would be there.

The strengths and challenges of mobilised ethnography

As this analysis of a practice encounter and the journeys before and after it illustrate, ethnographic and mobile research methods provide knowledge about core aspects of social work. The researcher can observe how interactions occur and the social context (such as signs of poverty, lifestyles, standards of care and so on) and they can sense the emotional climate (such as anxiety about dogs, parental anger, resistance) and its affects on participants. The audio recording of practice encounters enables analysis of forms of talk, questioning styles (on the above visit the social worker asked 137 questions, 75 of which were leading and 62 were open-ended) and learning about key issues such as how authority is used and challenging requests are made (Hall, *et al.*, 2014). There is also scope to rate practice in terms of how effective it is at engaging families and motivating change (Forrester, *et al.*, 2008; 2013). Longhofer *et al.*'s (2010) important practice ethnography of mental health social work shows how the method can produce knowledge about how to enable service user engagement and change over periods of years. Analysing transcripts also provides a means to timing when particular actions occurred, such as social workers' requests to see upstairs, the amount of time spent in different rooms and the time spent working directly with children and with all family members together. The method enables a comparison to be made of the worker's intentions prior to meeting service users with what they actually did and achieved in practice and analysis of the reasons for any discrepancies, a process that begins in earnest straight afterwards while walking to the car and travelling in it.

The human presence of the ethnographer gives privileged access to participants' lived experiences and the existential dilemmas they face. The research drew on Sarah Pink's (2009) approach of 'sensory ethnography', which encourages an openness to exploring how participants and interactions are affected by all the senses and for researchers not to rely merely on sight and sound but to record smells, touch and how such lived experiences *feel* and use this as a form of data. This enabled my research to observe and sense parents wrestling in their minds and bodies with how far to allow access to their private space and children. Social workers could be observed communicating in skilful non-verbal as well as verbal ways and struggling with whether and how to ask the difficult questions, how to overcome parental resistance that is physical in blocking their access to spaces and children, whether and how to ask to see into a room and get their body to move enough to be able to turn a bedroom door handle and take just a few short steps into and across the room and how to move to get close enough to children to really know what they are experiencing. These existential dilemmas constitute what I have elsewhere called 'fateful moments' where workers can go either way in whether they ask difficult questions or move, or not (Ferguson, 2004; 2011b). As that moment where the social worker Louise hesitated on the landing before asking and going into Barry's bedroom illustrated, how fateful moments are negotiated is bound up with rational thinking, such as wanting to protect people from undue intrusion, but of equal if not greater importance is the non-rational – in terms of emotional and unconscious experiences and the kind of atmospheres within which the encounters and relationships go on (Ferguson, 2010b). In ways that mirror the findings from inquiries into child deaths, the research found that sometimes social workers get stuck and don't move, ask the challenging questions or pay attention to what they need to. In a small number of home visits in the study, social workers were observed not relating to children at all or achieving what they regarded as effective work. This finding shows what can happen when workers are unable to overcome their fears, hostile atmospheres and the high levels of anxiety and emotional demands of the work and when their organisations fail to provide them with the necessary support to do effective child protection.

Despite the existence of a huge literature, in the UK 40 years of inquiry reports into the deaths of children in child protection cases that have made countless recommendations for changing practice and the development of huge amounts of procedures and practice texts directing and theorising practice, at the outset of this research little was known about what social workers actually do when they are face to face with children and families in the place where most practice goes on, their homes. A striking example of this is how during the 2000s policy guidelines became much more explicit in directing that children suspected of being at risk must be seen on their own (Department for Education, 2013), yet no knowledge existed about where children were usually seen and no advice or direction was given or even discussion undertaken about where the best place to see children on their own was. Participant observation that is committed to movement and shadowing workers wherever they go provides knowledge about patterns of practice, even those that go on in individuals' and families' most private places, such as bedrooms.

The research found that children's bedrooms were the most common place where social workers saw them on their own, followed by the living room, kitchen and garden. On assessment visits generally small amounts of time were spent with children on their own, which resulted from a combination of factors. Workers were expected to adhere to a timescale of ten days for completing assessments and this caused them to feel they had to rush through gathering information from children and other family members. Some sessions would have been longer but were cut short by parents interrupting by walking into the room or making loud noise outside it to communicate the message that the social worker's time was up. On a minority of visits the social workers did not even introduce themselves and explain their role, but went straight into asking children about specific concerns. This points to how the quality of practice was not just determined by time and other organisational factors but also by how practitioners had varying levels of communication skills with children and comfort at playing with and getting close to them. Some were highly skilled at it and had a capacity to explain their role to children, develop rapport with them and use toys, play and charisma to get them to talk about their experiences and problems, even in short periods of time and all while managing parents' anxious feelings about and sometimes resistance towards what was happening. A high proportion of children were not seen by social workers on their own because they were viewed as being too young and, as in the Michael and Mel case study, practitioners spent the majority of their time working with parents and children together (Ferguson, 2014b). The data shows that a crucial skill in contemporary social work is to be able to perform creatively a complex array of tasks and achieve a huge amount, usually in short amounts of time.

The presence of a researcher at encounters that go on in deeply private places like people's bedrooms and where there are concerns about children's safety and parents' integrity is obviously highly sensitive research. It was made clear at the outset of observations of practice that if anyone felt that the researcher's presence was adversely affecting any family member or the social worker's safeguarding practice or if the researcher felt there was any sign of this then they would leave. Some complex and emotionally charged interactions and atmospheres were encountered and on a couple of occasions I did step out of rooms to protect people's privacy. However, it was never felt necessary that I should leave a visit and encounter completely. Staying right up close to social workers wherever they go means travelling into the unknown with them as they very often do not know what is behind the doors they walk through. This can easily be used by research ethics committees as a justification for not granting such research ethical approval. Such risk aversion is not in the interests of promoting learning for social work or finding out more about service users' experiences of services. My experience shows that mobilised practice ethnography that gets right up close to encounters can be done ethically as long as the core ethical condition of ensuring that research does no harm is very closely monitored at all times.

Conclusion

It was only possible to find out what social workers do and gain the kind of knowledge presented in this chapter by observing them, staying right up close to them and going wherever they went. The innovation in the mobilised ethnography approach is that it goes beyond those ethnographies and other kinds of research methods that have been 'immobile' and not gone with the flow of practice by studying face-to-face social work wherever it goes on. There will always be a place for classic qualitative research methods like interviews in social work research; they were an important part of my own research discussed here. But we seem to be entering a period in the development of research approaches where the limitations of the researcher and researched meeting for a sedentary interview in a fixed space like an office are more evident, certainly as a stand alone method for understanding the nature of social work. There is so much knowledge and understanding to be added by the social work researcher going along with research subjects and observing them on journeys into the heart of practice.

References

Broadhurst, K. and Mason, C. (2012) 'Social work beyond the VDU: Foregrounding co-presence in situated practice – why face-to-face practice matters.' *British Journal of Social Work*, DOI: 10.1093/bjsw/bcs124.

Broadhurst, K., Wastell, D., White, S., Hall, C., Peckover, S., Thompson, K., Pithouse, A. and Davey, D. (2010) 'Performing "initial assessment": Identifying the latent conditions for error at the front-door of local authority children's services.' *British Journal of Social Work 40*, 2, 352–370.

Buckley, H. (2003) *Child Protection Work: Beyond the Rhetoric.* London: Jessica Kingsley Publishers.

Buscher, M., Urry, J. and Whichger, K. (eds) (2011) *Mobile Methods.* London: Routledge.

Clark, A. and Emmel, N. (2010) *Using Walking Interviews.* Manchester: National Centre for Research Methods, University of Manchester.

Department for Education (2013) *Working Together to Safeguard Children.* London: HMSO.

Ferguson, H. (2004) *Protecting Children in Time.* Basingstoke: Palgrave.

Ferguson, H. (2008) 'Liquid social work: Welfare interventions as mobile practices.' *British Journal of Social Work 38*, 3, 561– 579.

Ferguson, H. (2010a) 'Therapeutic journeys: The car as a vehicle for working with children and families and theorizing practice.' *Journal of Social Work Practice 24*, 2, 121–138.

Ferguson, H. (2010b) 'Walks, home visits and atmospheres: Risk and the everyday practices and mobilities of social work and child protection.' *British Journal of Social Work 40*, 4, 1100-1117.

Ferguson, H. (2011a) 'The Mobilities of Welfare: The Case of Social Work.' In M. Buscher, J. Urry and J. Witchger (eds) *Mobile Methods.* London: Routledge.

Ferguson, H. (2011b) *Child Protection Practice.* Basingstoke: Palgrave.

Ferguson, H. (2014a) 'Researching social work practice close up: Using ethnographic and mobile methods to understand encounters between social workers, children and families.' *British Journal of Social Work* 1–16, DOI: 10.1093/bjsw/bcu120.

Ferguson, H. (2014b) 'What social workers do in performing child protection work: Evidence from research into face-to-face practice.' *Child and Family Social Work*, DOI 10.1111/cfs.12142.

Fincham, B., McGuinness, M. and Murray, L. (2010) *Mobile Methodologies.* Basingstoke: Palgrave.

Floresch, J. (2002) *Meds, Money and Manners: The Case Management of Severe Mental Illness.* New York: Columbia University Press.

Floersch, J., Longhofer, J. and Suskewicz, J. (2014) 'The use of ethnography in social work research.' *Qualitative Social Work 13*, 3–7.

Forrester, D., Kershaw, S., Moss, H. and Hughes, L. (2008) 'Communication skills in child protection: How do social workers talk to parents?' *Child and Family Social Work 13*, 1, 41–51.

Forrester, D., Westlake, D., McCann, M., Thurnham, A., Shefer, G., Glynn, G., and Killian, K. (2013) *Reclaiming Social Work?: An Evaluation of Systemic Units as an Approach to Delivering Children's Services.* Luton: Tilda Goldberg Centre, University of Bedford.

Froggett, L. (2012) 'Psychosocial Methods in Action.' In S. Becker, A. Bryman and H. Ferguson (eds) *Understanding Research for Social Policy and Social Work.* Bristol: Policy Press.

Gillingham, P. and Humphreys, M. (2009) 'Child protection practitioners and decision-making tools: Observations and reflections from the front line.' *British Journal of Social Work 40*, 2598–2616.

Gottschalk, S. and Salvaggio, M. (2015) 'Stuck inside of mobile: Ethnography in non-places.' *Journal of Contemporary Ethnography 44*, 3–33.

Hall, C., Juhila, K., Matarese, M. and van Nijnatten, C. (2014) *Analysing Social Work Communication: Discourse in Practice.* London: Routledge.

Hammersley, M. and Atkinson, P. (2007) *Ethnography: Principles in Practice* (3rd edition). London: Routledge.

Helm, D. (2013) 'Sense-making in a social work office: An ethnographic study of safeguarding judgements.' *Child and Family Social Work,* DOI: 10.1111/cfs.12101.

Jeyasingham, D. (2014) 'Open spaces, supple bodies? Considering the impact of agile working on social work office practices.' *Child and Family Social Work,* DOI: 10.1111/cfs.12130.

Kusenbach, S. (2003) 'Street phenomenology: The go-along as ethnographic research tool.' *Ethnography 4,* 3, 455–485.

Longhofer, J. and Floersch, J. (2012) 'An Example of Social Work Practice Ethnography.' In S. Becker, A. Bryman and H. Ferguson (eds) *Understanding Research for Social Policy and Social Work.* Bristol: Policy Press.

Longhofer, J., Kubek, P. M. and Floersch, J. (2010) *On Being and Having a Case Manager: A Relational Approach to Recovery in Mental Health.* New York: Columbia University Press.

Pink, S. (2009) *Doing Sensory Ethnography.* London: Sage.

Pithouse, A. (1998) *Social Work: The Social Organisation of an Invisible Trade.* Aldershot: Ashgate.

Ross, N., Renold, E., Holland, S. and Hillman, A. (2009) 'Moving stories: Using mobile methods to explore the everyday lives of young people in public care.' *Qualitative Research 9,* 605–623.

Ruch, G. (2013) '"Helping children is a human process": Researching the challenges social workers face in communicating with children.' British Journal of Social Work, DOI: 10.1093/bjsw/bct045.

Scourfield, J. (2003), *Gender and Child Protection.* Basingstoke: Palgrave.

Sheller, M. and Urry, J. (2006) 'The new mobilities paradigm.' *Environment and Planning A 38,* 207–226.

Stanhope, V. (2012) 'The ties that bind: Using ethnographic methods to understand service engagement.' *Qualitative Social Work 11,* 4, 412–430.

Urry, J. (2007) *Mobilities.* Cambridge: Polity.

Chapter 9

USING MOBILE METHODS TO EXPLORE THE LIVES OF MARGINALISED YOUNG MEN IN MANCHESTER

ALASTAIR ROY, JENNY HUGHES, LYNN FROGGETT AND JENNIFER CHRISTENSEN
University of Central Lancashire and University of Manchester

Overview

Social work and welfare practices are founded on mobilities, as practitioners must move between and within the different areas of practice not only to be co-present with service users, but also to understand the safety and well-being of those they are professionally responsible for (Broadhurst and Mason, 2014; Ferguson 2008; 2010a, 2010b). In this respect, walking is not simply a physical and behavioural activity ('a means to transport the brain from one place to another'[1]), it is a kinetic way of thinking and knowing, an activity done through the feet (Ingold, 2010; Phillips, 2014; Sheets-Johnstone, 1998). We argue these ideas have important implications for the embodied *practices* of research and social work. In this chapter, research and social work are seen as sharing common problems and we conceive them as forms of *praxis* – thinking *in* movement (or, perhaps more appropriately, thinking *through* movement). The value of mobile methods for informing social work practice are examined through data from a research project conducted in Manchester, England, which used walking tour interviews to explore the lives of young men in the city (Hughes, Roy and Manley, 2014). The interviews offered insight into the routines, habits and practices of

---

1   This paraphrases Ken Robinson's Ted Talk on how schools kill creativity www.ted.com/talks/ken_robinson_says_schools_kill_creativity?language=en

young men surviving in the city, which were indexed to a series of city centre sites including car parks, public gardens, casinos, statues, canal sides and service locations. The methods allowed for a meaningful exploration of the ways in which the young men's social, psychic and embodied worlds are intertwined, thus generating the kind of client-centred knowledge needed not only to understand individual stories of survival, but also to inform appropriate and timely practice interventions. The chapter argues that mobile methods are of relevance to social work researchers because harnessing movement and the relationship between humans and place can alter the conditions of knowledge making and uncover new meanings and understandings of people's lives that are psychosocial: structural, cultural *and simultaneously* 'deeply embedded in subjectivity' (Back, 2014; Frosh, Phoenix and Pattman, 2004, p.42; Ingold, 2010).

The agency context

The Men's Room is an arts and social care agency in Manchester, England, which uses creativity as a means of engaging and supporting highly marginalised young men. It offers involvement in high-quality artistic projects whilst also providing wider support. The agency engages different groups of young men including those with experience of sexual exploitation and/or sex work and those with experience of homelessness and/or the criminal justice system. Across the year it collaborates with various artists to create diverse projects, delivered via two creative sessions each week.

From its inception in 2004, the Men's Room's peripatetic and creative approach has helped it to engage many young men not accessing other support services in the city. The men commonly share experiences of being looked after by the state, alcohol and other drug use, mental health problems, educational failure and involvement in crime. Generally speaking, the young men live outside normative social and familial contexts and are often not in secure accommodation (Hughes, 2013). The Men's Room also provides a safe space to meet other young men with similar experiences. At the time of writing, 45 young men attend the project regularly.

Research design

The research was commissioned by the Lankelly Chase Foundation and aimed to explore the young men's routes into the Men's Room and their lives beyond the service as well as how they defined successful service provision.

The methodology employed in this project is written up in detail elsewhere (Hughes, Roy and Manley, 2014). Here we present an overview of the methods used and the rationale for them. The research involved nearly 12 months of fieldwork conducted by Jenny Hughes and Alastair Roy as well as a specific contribution to the visual matrix component by Julian Manley. It began with a residential with staff, volunteers and young men from the Men's Room in January 2013. The residential was crucially important in initiating the relationships that sustained the work and responding to the framework already established by the Men's Room staff. During one discussion about the research one of the men asked the following question: 'How the fuck could something like this be useful to someone like me?' Whilst the directness of the question was intended as a challenge to the researchers, its content fuelled a highly productive discussion. Working with it together, we came up with the idea of a research project based around producing a 'Survival Guide to Manchester'. The methodology sought to generate a detailed and contextualised understanding of the lives of the young men in the city of Manchester and also of the life of the organisation. The main methods used were as follows.

Participant observation at regular sessions run by the Men's Room
We began the research by trying to develop an understanding of the life of the organisation in as naturalistic a manner as possible and we needed to develop an appropriate observational technique. We conducted more than 12 months of ethnographic participant observation (Spradley, 1980), which allowed us to be involved in the Men's Room sessions whilst observing the quotidian life of the organisation – its internal processes, personal interactions and relationships, modes of communication, 'emotional climate' and day-to-day conventions and rituals. Minimal notes were taken during the session, but detailed self-reflexive ethnographic diaries (Sanjek, 1990) were written up afterwards and maintained throughout the work. Through this we developed a detailed understanding of the day to day processes and relations of the organisation as a cultural milieu.

Walking tours

We conducted seven 'walking tours' as part of the research. In each case, young men were invited to lead a researcher and a Men's Room staff member on a walking tour of city centre sites they associated with their own survival. We walked and talked together and on arrival at each stop, we asked them to take a photograph and, if they were happy to, tell a story about the site. All tours were audio recorded and transcribed.

Visual matrix with staff and volunteers

We also conducted a visual matrix with staff and volunteers, which allowed them to reconsider the work of the organisation creatively and associatively, avoiding cognitively oriented familiar forms of discussion and debate. This methodology is written up in detail elsewhere (Froggett *et al.*, 2014) as well as in this volume (Chapter 11).

Ethical issues

'Ethically important moments' inevitably arise in sensitive research such as this (Guillemin and Gillam, 2004). Elements of the young men's narratives were uncomfortable and upsetting for the men, the researchers and the staff members. However, it is our view that upset should not be conflated with harm. It was our experience that the young men felt that the tours provided a space in which their stories had been heard and many of them commented to this effect. The researchers collaborated with the Men's Room in a cycle of planning, realising and reflecting on each tour. This was critical to the realisation of an ethical research practice; one that could be considered in advance but had to be delivered in the moment and reflected on afterwards. In this respect we agree with Ferguson (2014) who observes that:

> The critical issue is for researchers to be clear about what constitutes ethical research behaviour, to reflect very hard on it on the spot and to have a repertoire of responses at the ready to respond appropriately to ethically important moments when they arise.

The research plans and methods for this project were reviewed and approved by the Psychology and Social Work Ethics Committee at the University of Central Lancashire. All potential participants were provided with written information about the focus of the study, confidentiality and data protection a few days before. Verbal consent was taken in all cases. Details that would potentially identify the young men to those outside the organisation have been changed.

Key innovative elements

Walking tour interviews

Walking as a research method has been adopted in anthropology and ethnography (Ingold and Vergunst, 2008; Pinks, 2008), cultural geography (Anderson, 2004; Butler, 2006) and qualitative social science (Ferguson, 2008, 2010a, 2010b; Hall, 2009) as an innovative way to produce knowledge. This body of work is based on two central ideas: first, the oft-cited notion of the 'co-ingredience of people and place' (Casey, cited in Anderson, 2004, p.257) – the idea that identities, experiences and behaviours are embedded in the places a person inhabits. And second, that getting mobile with research participants can change research relationships, altering the staging of power and opening out new possibilities of making knowledge (Anderson, 2004; Back, 2014).

A significant body of knowledge argues that the human condition is profoundly influenced by place and space (Anderson, 2004; Casey, 2000, 2001; Ingold, 2011). This work originates, in part, from Heideggerian (1988) philosophies of 'Being-in-the-World' and Merleau-Ponty's (1962) exploration of the phenomenology of perception. These ideas have been developed most extensively in the field of human geography, where a series of studies have explored the interrelationship between people and place (Anderson, 2004; Davidson, 2003; Hillier, 2001; Sack, 1997). For example, Casey argues that:

> The relationship between people and place is not just one of reciprocal influence...but also, more radically, of constitutive coingredience: each is essential to the being of the other. In effect, there is no place without self and no self without place. (2001, p.684)

As Anderson (2004) argues, these ideas recognise that place is integral to human identity and hence that when researchers engage with place through movement the interrelationships between place and human identity can help uncover important new meanings and understandings of the lifeworlds of those they seek to understand.

There were two sources of impetus for walking tours in this project. First, previous research had suggested the Men's Room's peripatetic approach was key to its successful engagement with young men and we wanted to reflect this approach in our own research (Hughes, 2013), to better capture the nature of the experience. Second, the walking tours were inspired by a comment made by a young man to the researchers during the participant observation that, if we wanted to find out how people survive in the city, we would need to go out and talk to young men in the city centre. This appeared to be a provocation to get mobile with young men in the city.

Prior to this we had been fearful that trying to conduct face-to-face interviews with the young men – whether semi structured or narrative pointed – would initiate highly defensive performances. We felt that they associated interview situations with the police and other forms of authority and hence we were concerned about how they would feel in, and respond to, these interview situations.

We also wanted to destabilise the traditional hierarchy between researcher and researched by giving young men control of the encounter in the role of tour guides (Anderson, 2000; Back, 2014). We found that 'walking and talking' set up a companionable relationship, which encouraged attentiveness to sensual and embodied meaning, facilitating collaborative knowledge making (Myers 2010).

Walking tour findings

The seven walking tours provide a kaleidoscopic view of the challenges of survival in the pasts, presents and futures of the young men taking part. We have given each tour a title taken from the conversation that accompanied it. A full account of the seven narratives can be seen elsewhere (Hughes *et al.*, 2014). Here we choose one tour that gives a good sense of the type of data produced as well as introducing some of the issues raised across the seven tours.

Jeff: Immovable object, irresistible force
Jeff took us to two spaces in the city, both made of concrete and metal – the statue of Alan Turing in Sackville Gardens (a small public park

in the Gay Village)[2] and a corner of the third floor of a multi-storey car park, which once provided a sheltered spot to sleep as well as a good vantage point to survey the street below.[3] Jeff explained that both sites were spaces where he had been able to express intense and overwhelming feelings in ways that did not solicit unwelcome responses or interventions. These sites, and the isolation they represented, provided respite from the pressure of life on the streets. As part of this tour, Jeff told us that being homeless can feel like getting a break to sort your head out and that isolation was sometimes a welcome relief as it meant staying out of trouble.

Figure 9.1: Alan Turing statue, Sackville Gardens: 'This is where I sometimes come, when I just want someone to chat and listen.'

---

2   Alan Turing was a mathematician and computer scientist. He worked at Bletchley Park in Buckinghamshire during the Second World War, developing code-breaking methods, and from 1949 for the University of Manchester, where he helped develop the first computer. In 1952, Turing admitted to a sexual relationship with another man (illegal in the UK at the time) and was convicted of gross indecency. His conviction ruined his reputation and on 8 June 1954 he killed himself by eating an apple poisoned with cyanide. Alan Turing received a posthumous Royal Pardon in 2013.

3   This was the same car park that Albert Kennedy fell to his death from in 1989. He had been in care and suffered from depression, and may have been engaging in sex work. The Albert Kennedy Trust was set up in 1989 to support lesbian, gay, bisexual and transgender (LGBT) young people who are homeless or living in a hostile environment.

The first site – the Alan Turing statue in Sackville gardens – was described as peaceful, but also connected to crime, violence and sex work, especially at night. In the day time, this was a place that Jeff could express feelings in the company of another who, helpfully, did not answer back:

> It's where I come. Some people think I'm mad because I sit talking to him. But he gets my head straight … He don't pass judgement, that's the one thing.
>
> I used to sleep in the car park over there and then in the day time I'd come and sit here and then just talk to Alan. Sometimes it was like, he was the only one that listened, at one point. Because I went through a bad patch in my life, but I didn't see any point, any way round it. And then like when I started getting into a bit more trouble with different people, it was like sometimes I'd just come sit here for a day or so. And then even just sitting here, watching things go past you're not on your own because you got someone sat next to you. And yeah, looks a bit creepy but it's, sometimes it's all you need, someone that's just there. You know what I mean?

The solidity, immovability and isolation of the statue's presence feels more secure and comforting than an unpredictable, moving and movable person here. This feeling of solidity and immovability is explicitly contrasted to the discomfort Jeff experienced when referred to a counsellor:

> …they put me through for counselling and then they went, it was [the counsellor] went off sick and then by the time she'd actually come back I'd found myself more at ease [at the Men's Room] than I did talking to her. Because [with the counsellor] it was like meet up in a café to discuss like personal problems. So it was like you're talking in cafés about your feelings and it didn't feel right at the time…

The phrase 'didn't feel right' may reflect something of the importance of companionship rather than a therapeutic intervention at this point in Jeff's life. In addition, the statue is in the Gay Village and very close to where Jeff accessed support from the Men's Room. All three sites provide accepting spaces for this young man, in which his experiences of sex work are recognised as familiar rather than exceptional. There is also a sense in which Alan Turing's own biography, and the suffering caused to him by homophobia, which Jeff was aware of, provides an important avenue of support for a young man who identified as gay. The referral into the Men's Room had provided a regular point of contact and support – a specialist service operating in the area of the Village that did not expose him to other interventions. There is also a good sense here of voluntary sector agencies working in partnership – Jeff had been referred to the Men's Room by the counselling agency.

A feature of the tour, prominent in the second site but also present in the first, was that these sites provided a place of retreat from the social world as well as a vantage point from which to watch movements in the street. Jeff connected these vantage points with a capacity to protect others as well as feel protected. On the third floor of the multi-storey car park, he commented: 'so this bit, yeah, you can watch down the street, and up the street, and keep your eye on like things that is going on about'; 'it's like, you're kind of like the eyes and the ears'. He reported that he had phoned the police when he saw people at risk in Sackville Gardens, and intervened from his vantage point in the car park to stop inebriated men being taken down the canal path and attacked late at night. It was our interpretation that this overarching protection may have been imagined, or desired, as much as a reality, but it also, perhaps, is indicative of the ground-level, informal kinds of support that the Men's Room nurtures.

Figure 9.2: Chorlton Street car park, facing Bloom Street: 'You feel like you're on top of the world here.'

The third floor of the multi-storey car park, like the Alan Turing statue, provided a safe place to express intense emotions. Here, Jeff described how he placed himself above and away from the street, and it is almost as if this is necessary in order to express himself safely (both for himself and others). The intensity of his feelings had led him into confrontations with others, including with the police; a concrete place up above the streets provides an environment infused with the resistant material, distance and anonymity necessary for containing destructive feelings:

> The best thing is, you can stand here and just scream, like, all your emotions out and nobody hears it. It's like a release…

> When I started getting like really wound up and stuff, because it used to like, I'd get tugged every night. As soon as you get accused of one thing, that's it, you're tarnished with the brush by the police. The police are all over you like there's no tomorrow. But then I found like I could come here like if I felt like things were getting on top. I could just sit down, scream, let it all out and then go back down when I feel better.

These two sites represent a search for secure immovable objects in the face of overwhelming feelings. The concrete and metal facades of the city provide moments of relief and respite – they do not answer back, move or intervene. This solidity creates a feeling of release, but also perhaps reproduces a sense of, 'I am not worth listening to' or, 'it is not safe for me to talk to another person'. Perhaps the permanent presence of the Men's Room in these sites, with its consistent offer of a protective, compassionate, non-interventionist, 'not answering back' style of contact, might provide a valuable stepping stone from Alan Turing's comforting presence to more responsive forms of support and interdependence.

Summary

In this chapter we only present a single case study. We have decided to do this rather than providing a summary of a number of tours because the emphasis in working in this way has been on depth rather than breadth. Looking at Jeff's tour allows us to understand the highly specific and idiosyncratic survival strategies that he has developed. However, even this single case gives important glimpses towards the mechanisms of support that might be needed in supporting and working with marginalised young men. As Rustin (1991) argues, it is through the analysis of single cases that self-reflection, decision making and action in human lives can best be explored and represented; the ontological assumption being that individual biographies make society and are not merely made by it.

Taken together, the seven walking tours provide different pathways – of sorts – mapped out by the men, which contain contrasting, competing and overlapping narratives of moving on, getting stuck, going backwards and going round in circles as well as articulating a need to keep on moving. As we discovered whilst undertaking the tours, the demand to 'move on' shapes the daily experience and life histories of many young men engaging with the Men's Room, who move in and out of care, in and out of custody, in and out of domestic environments, away from the police and in and out of scenes of opportunity, crime and threat. Here, 'moving on' can be a tactic of survival in a risky environment, a means of eluding control, an affirmation of lack of self-worth and an assertion of personal agency, as much as a step towards a positive future. The walking tours helped us to understand that the process of supporting these young men is fraught with difficulty therefore, and there is a need to ask who is being moved, why, from where, where to and in the service of whose ends? The tours highlighted a need to better understand the 'self made maps' and 'trajectories of movement' experienced by young men facing severe and multiple disadvantage in order to develop appropriate models of support.

New knowledge developed

We now examine the data from the Men's Room research in relation to three questions.

1. How does walking and talking alter research relationships?

Walking and talking together with young men in this research profoundly altered the dynamics of the research relationships. There were several interesting elements to this: first, it was our experience that, in each case, the young men were the tour guides and as researchers, we literally did not know where we were going at the beginning of the tour, whereas our tour guides generally did. Second, whilst we walked and talked together, we also paused at certain points either to elaborate on an issue or to hear a site-specific recollection. Some of these stops were planned and some happened simply because a memory emerged at a certain location often prompted by a lamppost, road sign, building or other visual provocation. In this way some of the stories the men told us had been thought about in advance, but many simply emerged in ways that could not have been anticipated either by our tour guides or ourselves. Third, the side-by-side dynamics of the encounter allowed for moments of intense and intimate exchange and also moments of reflection in which we quietly walked together. This seemed important in providing a containing emotional environment for stories that were sometimes upsetting and difficult. Finally, we were interested that at the end of the tours many of the respondents said thank you to us. This seemed to show that the experience of walking and talking together had a quasi-therapeutic quality to it and that tour guides had felt having their stories attended to had been personally beneficial in some way (Hollway and Jefferson, 2000).

2. What might be the value of a movement-based social science?

Our findings are in line with those of a series of other researchers, artists and journalists who have used mobile methods in exploring different possibilities of making knowledge (Anderson, 2004; Ferguson, 2008, 2010a). For example, in a recent Radio 4 programme – Cover from View – the writer and journalist Horatio Clare and producer Jeremy Grange used walking tour interviews as a means of understanding the ways in which ex-servicemen use the environment of the Brecon Beacons as a part of their recovery from service life. Clare walked with infantry soldiers, trained, challenged and shaped by the Brecon Beacons, in order to see the Welsh mountains through their eyes. In this respect there is much about Clare's journalistic practice that is relevant to the practices of research and social work. Two important ideas emerge in the programme relevant to this research: first, one of the ex-servicemen describes beautifully how walking and talking together allows for forms of intimate exchange that he feels would not emerge when sitting face to face:

> So many deep conversations can happen between service folk on hills, shoulder to shoulder, you know, there's the concept of 'shedding', two blokes in a shed together...a bit like standing at the bar together. There's a quality of conversation, particularly between

blokes…which happens when you are not face to face and when you have got a dynamic of movement with that. And maybe as difficult feelings come up there is an opportunity for silence and also possibly to tread some of those feelings back into the earth and offer it back. [And] then I would argue it's a really valuable place to do that stuff. (Quote from Ex-Serviceman, BBC Radio 4, 2014)

Second, by walking and talking together in the environment of the Brecon Beacons, Clare is introduced to a particular 'way of seeing' and understanding the lives of these men in which identity and environment are intricately enmeshed. After Casey (2001), we might say that this relationship is one of 'reciprocal co-influence'. One of the ex-servicemen describes the environment as 'a place of safety', 'where you can shout and scream…completely away from society and its expectations' (Hughes *et al.* 2014, p.15). Through this, we see how the identities of the two servicemen have been shaped by and also shaped this environment.

In the Men's Room research, something very similar happens as the walking tours allow us to experience the 'ways of seeing' of young men trying to survive in the city of Manchester. Each walking tour provides a different pathway of sorts, in which contrasting, competing and overlapping narratives of moving on, getting stuck, going backwards and going round in circles emerge through stories that were heavily indexed to a series of sites in the city (Cresswell, 2004). In common with the ex-servicemen in Cover from View, these young men's sense of themselves is intensely rooted in the spaces and places infused with personal significance (Casey, 2001). We see how they use the different elements of an intensely urban environment as a means to find places to sleep, eat, meet, graft, work, rest, escape and take time out. For example, Jeff describes how the concrete and metal facades of the city provide moments of relief and respite from the pressures of day-to-day survival. In a different tour we are told by Jimmy that he has developed his own 'way of seeing' and his own practice of looking, acting and attending – 'I've got my own eyes, I can do what I want' – which is intrinsic to his sense of self, his sense of agency, his own strategies around survival and the style of service provision that he might engage with.

3. What might be the implications of these arguments for research and social work when viewed as forms of praxis?

Taken together the tours provide a rather desolate articulation of how disconnected most of these young men are from interpersonal, familial and societal networks of support. We feel that what is intensely relevant to both research and social work – when viewed as forms of praxis – is something first identified by bell hooks (1989), namely that the problem of *speaking* cannot be separated from the problem of *listening*. If young men such as these are to speak in their own voices then audiences – in this case researchers and practitioners – must learn to hear in new ways. Walking and talking together with young men in this research helped us to see that for many of them there is a tension between going forward and being held back – both by circumstance and their own actions. This tension between resilience, productive and destructive agency, and external threat presents real challenges for professionals in agencies working with these young men. In the Men's Room the subtle difficulty of knowing how to accompany someone's journey without inciting fear, rejection or anger is one element of an incredibly complex practice domain. This is made even more complex in working with young men who are so disconnected from structures of support, some of whom are phobic about reaching out to other people.

Strengths and challenges

In this chapter we argue that a movement-based social science is of distinct value in informing social work and welfare practice. In doing so, we have addressed important epistemological questions about the possibilities of knowledge making as well as methodological questions about how such knowledge might be made. In addressing the possibilities of *making knowledge*, Ingold (2010, p.S122) makes the following observation:

> If knowledge is indeed made, then making has to be understood in the sense implied when we say of people that they 'make their way' in the world. It is not a construction, governed by cognitive mechanisms of one sort or another, but an improvisatory movement – of 'going along'…that is open-ended and knows no final destination.

Ingold (2010, p.S134) identifies profound problems with 'psychologistic' approaches to making knowledge, based on construction and grounded cognition, suggesting that knowledge is not 'built *up*' and established, but 'grows *along* the paths' we take in the world. Ingold's ideas about making knowledge are relevant to the arguments made in this chapter for two reasons: first, because researchers and practitioners face quite similar challenges in trying to understand and make sense of the world that confronts them in their day-to-day practice; and second, because, for both groups epistemological concerns – assumptions about the possibilities of making knowledge – and methodological concerns – strategies for making knowledge – are of great significance. In this project we have adopted a psychosocial perspective (Froggett 2012) where the subjectivity of our research participants is understood as being formed, in significant part, by the way they move through the socio-spatial environment of the city where they live.

Recently, and informed by the mobilities paradigm, some social work academics have begun to theorise and conceptualise practice through the lens of movement (Broadhust and Mason, 2014; Ferguson, 2008, 2010a, 2010b, 2014; Phillips, 2014). For example, Harry Ferguson (2008) employs a mobile orientation – both conceptually and methodologically – in an attempt to offer a new lens on child protection practice, by understanding the daily lives of movement of practitioners, including the sights, smells, feelings and affects of practice. In doing so, he employs 'go-along interviews', which encourage practitioners to reflect on their feelings and professional actions/inactions and approaches in the moments immediately before and after client interactions, as well using ethnographic observation of practice itself. The upshot is a set of arguments of the need to view social work as rhythmic, liquid, fluid and hence 'unthinkable and unrealizable' without mobility (Ferguson, 2008, p.577). Ferguson (2008, p.561) argues:

> ...social work interventions in late-modernity are best understood in terms of a flow of mobile practices between public and private worlds, organisations and the home, at the heart of which is the sensual body of the practitioner on the move.

We argue that, for researchers, employing mobile methods can involve an altered conception of what interviews are and how and where they should be realised, as well as how they might be recorded and analysed – and to what effect? David Silverman (2007) has heavily criticised what he describes as the 'interview society', suggesting interviews often involve a socially stylised and quite particular mode of relating life.

Furthermore, Back (2014) draws our attention to the ways in which modes of authority are staged and socially performed in interviews, often for the benefit of the researcher and his or her equipment. In this chapter, we are interested in the arguments put forward by Silverman (2007) and Back (2014) amongst others for two main reasons. First, because they help make the case that all researchers should (re)consider the social conditions of knowledge production and the ways in which power is staged and socially produced in their research practices. And second, because they indicate that a number of the issues faced by researchers in making knowledge mirror important issues also faced by social workers in the practice of understanding the lives of their clients and responding appropriately. In particular, it is argued, that both research and social work are forms of praxis in which 'social forms are staged' and performed (Back, 2014) and in which process and movement – or lack of it – heavily influences the possibilities of knowing (Ingold, 2010). In fact, Polsky's (1967/1998, p.119) observations about the characteristics of successful field research might easily be cut and pasted into a text describing the characteristics of successful social work practice:

> Successful field research depends on the investigator's trained abilities to look at people, listen to them, think and feel with them, [and] talk with them rather than at them.

It is for these reasons, that we argue that the context, mode and form of research practice is critical to knowledge making. We argue that walking and talking together with research participants can allow us to be co-present with their ideas and environments, helping us to be more observant and attentive to spaces and places (the social and physical world) in which ideas, arguments and understandings emerge and to which identities and stories are often indexed.

Conclusion

We conclude by identifying three clear benefits to walking and talking with research participants. First, walking and talking involves a rhythmic relaxation of mind and body, which can free the imagination, making for more open forms of dialogue (Anderson, 2004). Second, that the associations between people and place that emerge whilst walking can 'excavate' ideas and meanings not anticipated by the researcher or the participant (Anderson, 2004). And third, that walking and talking together can help overcome the traditional power relationship between researcher and researched, allowing a different staging of power and facilitating more collaborative knowledge making. In fact, walking and talking with research participants embodies Kvale and Brinkman's (2009) proposal that the researcher is a *traveller,* which as Back (2014, p.251) notes, brings to mind the Latin definition of conversation as 'wandering together with'.

References

Anderson, J. (2004) 'Talking whilst walking: A geographical archaeology of knowledge.' *Area 36,* 3, 254–261.

Back, L. (2014) 'Tape Recorder.' In C. Lury and N. Wakeford (eds) *Inventive Methods: The Happening of the Social.* London: Routledge.

BBC Radio 4 (2014) 'Gone to Earth - Cover From View, Episode 2 of 2.' 16 July. Available at www.bbc.co.uk/radio/player/b0499dl1, accessed on 22 June 2015.

Broadhurst, K. and Mason, C. (2014) 'Social work beyond the VDU: Foregrounding co-presence in situated practice – why face-to-face practice matters.' *British Journal of Social Work 44,* 578–595.

Butler, T. (2006) 'A walk of art: The potential of the sound walk as practice in cultural geography.' *Social and Cultural Geography 7,* 6, 889–908.

Casey, E. (2000) *Remembering: A Phenomenological Study* (2nd edition). Bloomington: Indiana University Press.

Casey, E. (2001) 'Between geography and philosophy: What does it mean to be in the place-world?' *Annals of the Association of American Geographers 91,* 683–693.

Cresswell, T. (2004) *Place: A Short Introduction.* Oxford: Blackwell.

Davidson, J. (2003) *Phobic Geographies: The Phenomenology of Spatiality and Identity.* Aldershot: Ashgate.

Ferguson, H. (2008) 'Liquid social work: Welfare interventions as mobile practices.' *British Journal of Social Work 38,* 561–579.

Ferguson (2010a) 'Walks, home visits and atmospheres: Risk and everyday practice and mobilities of social work and child protection.' *British Journal of Social Work 40,* 1100–1117.

Ferguson H (2010b) 'Therapeutic journeys: The car as a vehicle for working with children and families and theorising practice.' *Journal of Social Work Practice: Psychotherapeutic Approaches in Health, Welfare and the Community 24,* 2, 121–138.

Ferguson, H. (2014) 'Researching social work practice close up: Using ethnographic and mobile methods to understand encounters between social workers, children and families.' *British Journal of Social Work,* DOI: 10.1093/bjsw/bcu120.

Froggett, L. (2012) 'Psychosocial Research.' In S. Becker, A. Bryman and H. Ferguson (eds) *Understanding Research for Social Policy and Social Work: Themes, Methods and Approaches.* Bristol: Policy Press.

Froggett, L., Roy, A., Manley, J., Prior, M. and Doherty, C. (2014) *Public Art and Local Civic Engagement, Final Report.* Project Report. Swindon: Arts and Humanities Research Council.

Frosh, S., Phoenix, A, and Pattman, R. (2004) *Young Masculinities: Understanding Boys in Contemporary Society.* London: Palgrave.

Guillemin, M. and Gillam, L. (2004) 'Ethics, reflexivity and "ethically important moments" in research.' *Qualitative Inquiry 10*, 2, 261–280.

Hall, T. (2009) 'Footwork: Moving and knowing in local space(s).' *Qualitative Research 9*, 5, 571–585.

Heidegger, M. (1998) *Being and Time*. Oxford: Blackwell.

Hiller, J. (2001) 'Imagined Value: The Poetics and Politics of Place.' In A. Madanipour, A. Hull and P. Healey, (eds) *The Governance of Place: Space and Planning Processes*. Aldershot: Ashgate.

Hollway, W. and Jefferson, T. (2000) *Doing Qualitative Research Differently*. London: Sage.

hooks, b. (1989) *Talking Back: Thinking Feminist, Thinking Black*, London: Routledge.

Hughes, J. (2013) 'Queer choreographies of care: A guided tour of an arts and social welfare initiative in Manchester.' *Research in Drama Education: The Journal of Applied Theatre and Performance 18*, 2, 144-154.

Hughes, J., Roy, A. and Manley, J. (2013) *Surviving in Manchester: Narratives on Movement from the Men's Room, Manchester*. Manchester: University of Central Lancashire/University of Manchester/The Men's Room.

Ingold, T. (2010) 'Footprints through the weather world: Walking, talking, breathing, knowing.' *Journal of the Royal Anthropological Institute 16*, S1, S121–S139.

Ingold, T. (2011) *Being Alive: Essays on Movement, Knowledge and Description*. London: Routledge.

Ingold, T. and Vergunst J. L. (eds) (2008) *Ways of Walking: Ethnography and Practice on Foot*. Burlington and Hampshire: Ashgate.

Kvale, S. and Brinkman, S. (2009) *InterViews: Learning the Craft of Qualitative Research Interviewing* (2nd edition). London: Sage.

Merleau-Ponty, M. (1962) *The Phenomonology of Perception*. Routledge: London.

Myers, M. (2010) '"Walk with me, talk with me": The art of conversive wayfinding.' *Visual Studies 25*, 1, 59-68.

Phillips, C. R. (2014) '"Seeing the child" beyond the literal: Considering dance choreography and the body in child welfare and protection.' *British Journal of Social Work,* DOI: 10.1093/bjsw/bct070.

Pinks, S. (2007) 'Walking with video.' *Visual Studies 22*, 3, 240–252.

Polsky, N. (1967/1998) *Hustlers, Beats and Others*. New York: Lyon Press.

Rustin, M. (1991) *The Good Society and the Inner World: Psychoanalysis, Politics and Culture*. London: Verso.

Sack, R. D. (1997) *Homo Geographicus: A Framework for Action, Awareness and Moral Concern*. Baltimore: John Hopkins University Press.

Sanjek, R.(1990) *Fieldnotes: The Making of Anthropology*. Ithaca: Cornell University Press.

Sheets-Johnstone, M. (1998) *The Primacy of Movement*, Amsterdam: John Benjamins Publishing Co.

Silverman, D. (2007) *A Very Short, Fairly Interesting and Reasonably Cheap Book About Qualitative Research*. London: Sage.

Spradley, J. (1980) *Participant observation*. London: Holt, Rinehart and Winston.

Urry, J. (2007) *Mobilities*. Polity: Cambridge.

Chapter 10

BEING BRAVE, DOING CREATIVE

*Using Visual Ethnography in Social Work
Research to Explore the Impact of Space and
Environment on Organisational Culture*

JADWIGA LEIGH
University of Sheffield

Introduction

Last year I completed a comparative ethnography that explored how culture affected the ways in which social workers situated in England and in Flanders, North Belgium, constructed their professional identity (see Leigh, 2013a). I chose this subject as my focus because as a practising social worker who was working for the agency where the research would take place, I was intrigued as to the extent culture affected the way my colleagues and I perceived ourselves as professionals and practitioners.

Initially, my aim was to use the 'traditional' methods of data collection such as participant observation, interviews and document analysis. However, my PhD supervisor suggested that I also consider including photography as he wanted to gain a sense of what 'culture' looked like for those working in child protection in Belgium; it is because of what we see that we can then establish 'our place in the surrounding world' (Berger, 1972, p.7). Although we may use words to describe what a particular kind of culture means to us, we can never undo the fact that we are surrounded by what we see.

At first this suggestion puzzled me. I could not understand why pictures of a child protection agency would be of any interest to anyone. The social work agency I worked for in England was housed in a building that had formerly been a primary school. The interior had been decorated with neutral colours such as cream and grey; it was, therefore, not the most vibrant of settings. In fact when I thought about all the agencies I had ever worked for, or been on placement with, not one of them stood out as being particularly appealing. In fact I had once worked in a building that had formerly been a morgue!

But it wasn't just the bland and uninspiring setting that was perplexing me; I realised that there was also the issue of ethics to consider. Interview data and field notes for observations felt as if they were 'safe' ways of conveying information. They would produce extracts that were relatively straightforward to anonymise and could be, at the same time, powerful ways of delivering the unpolished, yet-to-be analysed views of the participant. Whereas taking photographs of the locations in which participants were situated meant I would need to deliberate the uncomfortable aspects of data collection because, after all, pictures are more easily recognisable. They are the kind of representations that could also lead to breaches in terms of confidentiality and anonymity.

However from what I read, it seemed that if I implemented plans before commencing the visual research, issues surrounding confidentiality could be overcome (see Pink, 2007). And I learned that there were ways in which visual data could be disguised so that privacy and anonymity of participants could be maintained. For example, when using videotaping to record midwives carrying out consultation visits with their clients, Lomax and Casey (1998) concealed the identities of their participants by blurring their faces. The concerns I had relating to ensuring confidentiality therefore seemed relatively straightforward providing I sought consent, ensured I followed my plan and grew familiar with my environment. In the case of the agency in England, I felt assured this was not going to be a problem as I already worked there.

However, what I became more concerned about, the more I read into using visual methods in research, was the realisation that photographs can't just be classified as being one dimensional. Rose (2007) and Banks (2001) have argued that the meanings of photographs are 'arbitrary and subjective' – they depend entirely on who it is that is doing the looking (Pink, 2007, p.67). One photograph may be viewed differently by other audiences simply because the viewers will be situated in different historical, spatial and cultural contexts. This forced me to consider something I had not previously thought of: if I were going to use pictures to enable others to understand what I had seen, how would I know for sure that they would see it the same way as I had?

Indeed, it is also a dilemma that the majority of visual methodologists face (Banks, 2001; Pink, 2007; Rose, 2007). Yet reflexivity, a process that enables the researcher to be open and self-aware so that the reader can make judgements about their views, is not only an integral part of doing ethnography but also a method of learning for the ethnographer (Agar, 1996). Thinking about these kind of questions led me to the world of visual research, and the more I read, the more informed I became. Rather than feel anxious about this aspect of the project I started to feel convinced that using photographs would add that extra element to my work: they would enable me to capture a certain level of 'texture' that words alone would not be able to convey (see Latham, 2003). And although pictures can encapsulate so much visual information, they can also provide us with the kind of details that would just take pages of writing to describe (Rose, 2007).

This chapter, therefore, will continue by reviewing how visual methods have been used by others in social work. I will then discuss how I used photographs in my research and will go on to explore some of the challenges I faced and subsequently overcame. In doing so, I will draw from theories that underpin the way in which ethnography is conducted in order to demonstrate how important 'reflexivity' or 'reflexive vigilance' is for a researcher who wishes to incorporate visual materials (Rose, 2007, p.253). Although visual ethnography has been used as a powerful instrument in social research both in the present and past century (Szto, Furman and Langer, 2005), it has only recently become a popular method to undertake or integrate into a social work research project. In this context, I intend to use some of my data to demonstrate how particular dilemmas can be overcome in certain situations. My aim, in doing so, is to encourage others in the social work field to embrace photography, or other visual methodology, when undertaking their future research.

The use of visual methods research in social work

Although using visual methods in social work is a relatively new concept, social science research, in particular, has been 'enhanced' by the integration of creativity into methodology as it has been found to add 'expression' to research findings (Russell and Diaz, 2013, p.434). In Russell and Diaz's (2013) grounded theory study with lesbian women that aimed to explore participants' experiences of identity, culture and oppression, the authors found that using images not only increased access and offered opportunities in social work research, in terms of visual representation, but it also added an element of empowerment, which in turn supported social work practice. In this study the authors discuss the multiple benefits associated with using photographs and frame these within a discourse that seeks to overcome oppression as they ensured that participants felt 'valued and heard'. In addition, the authors felt that readers of the research would also benefit from their use of visual images, since the majority of people in society are considered to be 'visual learners' (Russell and Diaz, 2013, p.449).

Chapman *et al.* (2013) support some of these concepts in their study, which aimed to identify the ways in which images could support and facilitate difficult discussions. They used photographs with social workers to decide whether visual representations could alter expectations and attitudes. Their findings were also positive as they demonstrated just how images could successfully engage participants in debate, inspire openness and reflection and augment a certain level of understanding that did not formerly exist. Chapman *et al.* (2013) noticed that when social workers were presented with photographs in combination with a narrative, it evoked compassion, interest and understanding for both the children and their families. So essentially, what this meant was that it was only when participants saw an explanation in conjunction with the photograph that the image developed more meaning for them.

Collectively, Chapman *et al.* (2013) and Russell and Diaz (2013) found that using photographs was not just beneficial for research purposes but as Phillips and Bellinger (2011) found, they were also a useful way to be creative in social work teaching. In their study, which examined photographic works on the subject of asylum seeking, Phillips and Bellinger used the work of Diane Matar to develop conversations that could provide texture and in-depth understanding of others' experiences. Phillips and Bellinger (2011, p.96) discovered that Matar's visual representations forced them to consider the social relation of 'them to us, and us to each other'. It was through the use of visual images that the authors then began to reflect on the spaces they occupied and this encouraged them to make connections between their own lives and the lives of those they were observing.

Together the findings from these studies suggest that an understanding of social-environmental cues does prompt individuals to respond to a new stimulus in ways that are consistent with the experiences and expectations of others. Yet when I read this literature I became aware that the images that had been used in these contexts had been employed quite differently to the ones that I would be using in my research. The ones in this review tended to focus on the emotional impact that images could have on research participants, whereas the photographs that I wanted to employ were to be integrated into the study so as to provide information about relationships between practice materials, the research site and people. Although other disciplines, such as anthropology, found it orthodox to study the way in which 'relationships flow constantly between persons and things' (Miller, 2008, p.12), I started to realise that this particular approach was a more contentious issue in social work research due to the setting in which these relationships and things were situated: a context that needed to ensure confidentiality and data protection due to the deeply sensitive nature of work that was being carried out.

Despite recognising that there would be a difference between my work and the work of others, I felt undeterred and became instead even more enthusiastic about exploring the private and hidden environment in which social work takes place – that area of practice that is not normally seen by those who have never been involved with a social worker. Pink (2007) has noticed that only recently has there been an increasing amount of ethnographic fieldwork carried out on the domestic interior, which has, in turn, developed great opportunities for researchers 'to create data archives and reveal the detail of everyday experience and practice' (Pink, 2007, p.28). Therefore, by focusing on the material and sensory prompts, I was hopeful that my participants would be more likely to talk about their self-identities and experiences as social workers.

My aim therefore was to use photographs in such a way that I could relate some of these theoretical concepts to this study. By offering a visual dimension of both the English and Flemish setting I hoped to provide the reader with an understanding of what space and environment embodied for me, the ethnographer. The literature I had read up until this point discussed how beneficial using visual methods could be. There appeared a lot to gain from using this method and, providing I was prepared, it seemed to involve little risk. This knowledge provided me with the confidence to proceed and deliver, what I thought might be key contributions to the area of social work. In fact, because I was so keen to produce original work, what I was not ready for was the unexpected ethical dilemma that was waiting for me.

Key innovation elements

However, before deliberating what this unexpected dilemma consisted of, I want to spend some time discussing the key innovating elements of photography in this project. As I mentioned earlier, when the idea was suggested to me that I use photographs in my research I had no real understanding as to what would be of interest to the reader about the seemingly featureless setting in which I worked. I think, upon reflection, that this must have been the case for those who consented to me using photographs as part of my data collection. Whenever I asked if I could take a photograph, no one objected but I did receive a strange look in response.

As a novice researcher I took this to mean that they too felt it was a pointless venture, but what I did not properly consider was a question Braun (1998) posed and that is, when people do consent to being filmed or photographed are they really informed about how they will be represented and how others will interpret this? This was not a question I think troubled the participants or myself as I felt reassured that I had planned sufficiently to protect their identities by instead focusing on the building in which they worked, and the way in which it was used. In fact one of the key drivers that inspired me to use photography turned out to be using this unremarkable setting as a comparative. The reasons as to why will be revealed shortly.

When I arrived in Flanders it became abundantly clear that photographs would have to play a fundamental part in my project. Although I found that the Flemish child protection agency was also based in a primary school, there were a number of distinct differences between the two settings. First, in Flanders the school was still open and functioning. The team who worked at this agency had chosen this site specially so that those who were visiting them would not be distinguished by others in the community as families involved with child protection services. When their families visited the centre for their appointment, they did not stand out from those parents whose children were pupils at the school.

In England, however, everyone in the neighbourhood knew that our office was a place that housed children and family social workers because of the huge sign we had erected in the car park indicating who we were and what our role was. Although the Flemish tried desperately hard not to stigmatise their service users, in England we unabashedly defamed those who were coming to visit us by making no overt attempt to disguise our identity and, in turn, then protect theirs. Although this had not been a consummate act of malevolence, it was evident that we had not properly considered how our building could have had an adverse impact on the way we went about trying to build relationships with our service users.

It was this distinct difference in how both contrasting agencies used their buildings to develop, or hinder, the relationships with service users that was key to me taking my first photograph. However, it is also important to acknowledge at this point that what I saw at that moment was significant to me, and to me only, because of the relationship I held with the agency I worked for in England. Berger (1972, p.9) recognised that we never look at 'just one thing; we are always looking at the relation between things and ourselves'. What I saw when I stood outside the agency in Flanders was a number of distinct differences between this setting and the one I was familiar with at home; these emerged because I had found something that could unmask and, subsequently, reveal to me distinguishing features of the England site.

Miller (2008, p.283) has suggested that, in a way, our 'state operates too efficiently' because services can be delivered 'without any of us having to know anything much about how this came to be'. Although we, as a society, become aware of these forces when they fail or disappoint us, we do not seem to pay attention to these abstract images that lie close to the way we go about our daily lives. It was by being somewhere else and seeing something different that I was able, for the first time, to recognise what kind of impression we created, as a child protection agency, on our community and society at home. I had seen the building I worked at in England as simply a place from which we did child protection work from; I had never properly paused to consider the impact that structure may have had on those people we were trying to work with.

Others standing outside that Flemish building may have seen something quite different; they may have focused on the architecture of the building or the place in which it was located or the fact that there appeared to be limited parking spaces for staff. Not one of these views would have been wrong or inaccurate, they would have just been their own unique perception of what they saw before them. Therefore, not only do we look at the relationship between things and ourselves, but also the positioning and experiences of the researcher will also have a strong influence over the pictures that are taken. As well as, of course, how they will be subsequently analysed and presented to the external world as 'research'.

Although there is no established methodological framework to discuss the uses of photography in social science research (Becker, 2004; Rose, 2007), Gillian Rose has developed two groups of methods that might help the novice researcher, which she calls the *supporting* and the *supplemental* (Rose, 2007, p.239). In the first of these groups, *supporting,* photos are subordinated and worked over to see what they offer in support of the research question. Most photo-elicitation studies fall into this group because they seek to use photographs to encourage, for example, interview talk.

The second of these groups, *supplemental,* is when the visual qualities of the pictures taken are allowed to display themselves rather more on their own terms thus supplementing and complementing the written text of the researcher. It was this second group, supplemental, that I would use when presenting the photographs that I had taken. This was not a purposeful move on my behalf. Although I had followed the advice of Pink (2007) prior to taking photographs of the settings, by planning in advance, seeking the appropriate consent and familiarising myself with the research contexts, I did not read up to the data analysis stage until after I had taken the photographs. I realised in hindsight that the supplemental approach would be most beneficial to the study as I had taken pictures to provide an extra level of texture to the stories I was told by the participants in my study.

To demonstrate this point further, take a look at Figure 10.1. This is the first photograph that I took in Flanders and, as I have mentioned earlier, what struck me initially was the way in which the agency concealed itself behind the facade of the school. But in order to explain and clarify to the reader what the Flemish building meant to me, as a researcher, I used an interview extract in my presentation of the data so that I could elucidate this meaning further.

Figure 10.1: The outside of the Flemish agency

Jadwiga (J): Why did you decide to base yourselves here?

Social worker (SW): When we were looking for somewhere to base ourselves, we knew it had to be of benefit for the families and not for us. They are the ones, after all, who are the most important and so we wanted them to feel comfortable when they come here and so that people passing by don't know why they are coming here.

The picture of the building as it stands would represent different meanings to different people. But when it is accompanied with the interview extract it brings that certain level of texture, an element that was missing before; by supplementing one with the other, two separate bits of data are consolidated and used as a way of clarifying each other's purpose. The interview extract alone is interesting but when it appears alongside the photograph its meaning is crystallised (see Leigh, 2014b).

Also, by comparing two photographs of similar settings, it was easier to describe how one location differed so contrarily to another. When people move into new cultures it is inevitable that they will compare the new with that which is familiar. It may be a subconscious process but it will inevitably occur as we seek to measure that which we know with that which we do not (Leigh, 2013b). When I moved inside the Flemish building, I felt comfortable with certain areas of familiarity such as the receptionist situated at the front door, the staff room, corridors leading to different offices and the number of meeting rooms that were available for use. But I also became instantly aware of those places or things that were different to the agency I worked for at home.

These differences had a significant impact on me. They made me stop and stare. Some made me laugh and smile. But some left me with a distinct feeling of despair. These reactions can be considered as data for the visual ethnographer; rather than be ignored, they should be listened to and recorded. In qualitative methods the experiences of the researcher should never be ignored (Coffey, 1999). In this case I recorded the reactions I felt in a diary and later used them to show the reader how two distinct settings could affect professional identity, organisational culture and the way in which child protection practice was carried out, as the following pictures demonstrate.

Figure 10.2: A door in the English agency

This is a picture of a door in the agency I worked for in England. There is nothing spectacular about this door and I expect many readers have seen many similar doors in and around social care agencies in England today. But as we can see, this isn't a blank door; it has a sign on it, which is there to indicate to any newcomer visiting the agency who or what will be behind that door. In this case this office is designated to a 'social work team'. As I worked in this agency I know, from experience, that behind this door there are 12 desks and two offices. The offices are for the two managers and the 12 desks are to be shared amongst 15 members of staff who are made up of social workers and support workers.

This may seem like insignificant information to the reader who may be asking themselves right now, 'Why on earth has she shown me a picture of a door? What relevance does it have to learning about professional identity and organisational culture?' These are pertinent questions to ask and are similar to the questions I asked myself when my PhD supervisor initially asked me to take photos of the environment in which I worked. But Figure 10.2 is very telling and the messages it conveys only become distinguished when we take a look at the next picture (Figure 10.3).

Figure 10.3: A door in the Flemish agency

The beauty of ethnography is that it is a method that can be successfully used as a comparative way of collecting data as it allows researchers to connect human beings in their experiences of similar situations from across cultural settings. It is a process that enables those involved to respond by either 'converging on their cultural similarities' or 'conserving, even emphasizing, their cultural differences' (Gingrich and Fox, 2002, p.7). Comparative ethnographic visual data does not seek to elicit 'the truth' from the data but by juxtaposing two diverse settings simultaneously, it can make the differences between the two more obvious or visible. In Figure 10.3 we see a picture of a door from the Flemish agency. It is very different to the door in the English organisation. To begin with, it has a caricature on the front of it that represents the person to whom the office belongs. Each professional in the Flemish agency has their own office. Each door has a caricature of that practitioner on the front of it. The idea of the caricature was to create a little humour for the family who are coming to visit. The practitioner who worked behind this door had relatives in Scotland and was an avid fan of the English sitcom 'Allo Allo' hence the inscription 'Listen carefully, I'll say this only once.' These gestures are there to show us that these practitioners are human and they do have a fun side. It also acts as a guide as it shows newcomers and regular visitors which door they need to knock on when they do visit.

But there is also something else that is quite significant; it is the fact that behind the door each practitioner has their own space to practise in. This provides them with room to talk and be creative with those with whom they are working. When they need to access information or add comments to the case notes from their families they can do so in the presence of the client. This contributes to an emancipatory form of practice, something that we recognise is beneficial and that we do strive for in social work practice in England but, in many cases, have yet to achieve.

This a complete contrast to Figure 10.2, in the English setting, where there are 12 desks for 15 people to share. Not one of those social workers has their own space; instead they have to use the space that is available when they arrive at work. Yet although it has been recognised that having your own 'private space' is important in social work practice as it enables social workers 'to exercise discretion and sustain their own ways of working' with families, it is not an aspect of cultural practice that is generally considered essential in this context (Jeyasingham, 2014).

Although to begin with Figure 10.2 showed nothing of significance, we can now see that when it is accompanied by Figure 10.3, it has developed meaning. By comparing and contrasting these two doors in these different agencies, we not only learn a little bit more of how child protection practice is carried out in both countries but we also gain a picture of what 'being a professional' might mean to those who work there.

Being prepared for challenges and overcoming barriers

In the previous section I discussed a few ways of how photography might be used in social work research. In this part, I want to deliberate some of the challenges I faced whilst using photography as a data collection tool and how I then went about overcoming these. The first of these barriers that I want to discuss is issues relating to ethical considerations.

Gaining ethical consent to take photographs in my study was not a problem. When photographs are taken of people in a research project, it is only natural to expect that certain ethical issues will arise in relation to those pictures (Rose, 2007). But when it was explained to the relevant persons that I wanted to take pictures of the interior and exterior of the organisation and not of people, consent was a relatively straightforward process. However, despite avoiding complexities initially, I have since learned that ethical issues can still occur even when pictures do not contain images of human beings.

Although the photos I have used in this chapter have not identified the exact location in which they were taken, it never properly occurred to me that this piece of information could still be revealed to someone who read my work – someone who is familiar with the organisation. This is a dilemma I experienced when I gave a presentation to a group of academics at the university where I was studying for my PhD. As I happily flicked through the slides that day providing spectators with a story of what each photograph revealed to me, I came to a picture of the agency building in England. Without any warning I heard someone from the audience shout out 'I know that place!' and before I could gain composure, s/he then proceeded to tell the others in the room the name of the organisation. At the time I was so shocked that I didn't know what to do and so rather abruptly I just asked that person to, 'Be quiet.'

Although, it materialised, there was no one else in the room who was familiar with the agency or had any connection with it, this revelation left them with a piece of information they had not been previously aware of: the identity of the agency. It also meant that I had, inadvertently, breached one of the six key ethical principles devised by the major funder of social science research in the UK, the Economic and Social Research Council (ESRC), which reads as follows (ESRC, 2006, p.1): 'All information supplied by informants should be confidential, and all informants guaranteed anonymity.'

By announcing the name of the organisation, the promise I had made to protect the identity of those social workers who took part in my study had become compromised. At the time there was little I could do about it. But once I overcame the initial shock, I realised that I could have prevented this from happening and I could have done what Lomax and Casey (1998) did and replaced the photograph with a drawing of the building to conceal its identity (see Figure 10.4).

Figure 10.4: An amended image of the building in England

This lack of consideration led me to realise there was another ethical implication that I had not seriously considered before this event: the importance of reflexivity. Reflexivity, or 'reflexive vigilance', has been described by Rose as 'the careful and consistent awareness of what the researcher is doing, why, and with what possible consequences in terms of power relations between researcher and researched' (2007, p.253). Being aware of our positioning within a study is a matter that the researcher needs to consider seriously when using visual methods as it has a number of implications on their findings.

In my case, having reflexive vigilance prior to experiencing this dilemma meant making it clear to the reader the kind of relationship I had with these agencies. It will now be evident that a particular kind of analysis has been developed from the way in which I used these photographs; one that has highlighted the positives in one setting and a number of negatives in the other. I am very aware that these findings convey messages about the professionals working in those settings and will most certainly influence the opinions of those who read my work.

Interpretive research such as ethnography acknowledges the active role of the researcher in the processes of research (Taylor, 2006). Yet this has led researchers to question what kind of impact their position has had in relation to that research (Hammersley and Atkinson, 2007). The notion of reflexivity recognises that texts do not simply and transparently report the social order of reality; they are produced and interpreted by the social actors (the researchers) who were also part of the field under observation (Atkinson, 1990). Undoubtedly my relationship with both agencies has played a part in the way I have analysed these photos and being reflexive means making it clear what that relationship entailed. This is an area I have written extensively about elsewhere (see Leigh, 2013a, 2013b, 2014a, 2014b) and it is also in this work that I have documented some of the challenges and difficulties I have faced whilst in the position of a practitioner/researcher. Yet even though I had been reflexively vigilant elsewhere, it is because of this work that I became even more troubled about having revealed the identity of the agency I worked for in the presentation that day.

Conclusion

Using photography in social work research can undoubtedly present the researcher with a number of complications. I now recognise that reading about visual methods prior to commencing research, is not like following 'a recipe book for successful visual research' as it cannot prevent dilemmas from occurring (Pink, 2007, p.5). It is learning from doing that creates experience, and I have now learned to expect the unexpected. This chapter has attempted to demonstrate that, like most methods, challenges will arise when using visual methods but they can be overcome. When they are they can leave the researcher with exceptional material: visual information that can be used to enhance the written word. The visual material I have collected in this study has created new opportunities for social workers, service users and for me as a researcher keen to take on another project.

And this experience has also taught me that whilst it is important to be reflexive and be clear about the possible consequences my findings may have, it is equally important to remind myself when doing so just how these outcomes may have been reached. It was not until I started to compare like with like that I started to realise that the English agency I worked for had flaws. The saying 'ignorance is bliss' is appropriate in this instance; before I visited Flanders, I had never been aware that there could exist something quite different beyond those organisation(s) I had worked for in England. It was only when I saw how professionals and families were treated in Belgium that I then started to realise how social workers and families were treated in England. Therefore, had I not visited Flanders and only focused on England, these photographs would have been analysed in an entirely different way.

Also, a researcher in a different position with a more objective view may have seen something completely different. My view is not the only true way of seeing but it is still an innovative way of using my position to generate new knowledge through an enhanced understanding. In doing so, I have tried to demonstrate that when using visual material in research, the researcher does not need to feel that the images used have to be the most inspiring or aesthetically pleasing. In my experience, it is the meaning derived from the picture that is the nugget of information that holds the most significance. Rose (2007) has argued that if visual methodology is to be truly effective then the researcher needs to have the ability to take fine photographs. This is certainly beneficial, but I would add that what is also needed, in certain situations, is an aptitude to recognise disparity between that which is familiar and that which is not. This will not just produce engaging material but also original and meaningful data.

References

Agar, M. H. (1996) *The Professional Stranger: An Informal Introduction to Ethnography.* Berkeley: Academic Press.

Atkinson, P. (1990) *The Ethnographic Imagination: Textual Constructions of Reality.* London: Routledge.

Banks, M. (2001) *Visual Methods in Social Research.* London: Sage.

Becker, H. (2004) 'Afterword: Photography as Evidence, Photographs as Exposition.' In C. Knowles and J. Sweetman (eds) *Picturing the Social Landscape: Visual Methods and the Sociological Imagination.* London: Routledge.

Berger, J. (1972) *Ways of Seeing.* London: Penguin.

Braun, K. (1998) *Passing Girl: Riverside - An essay on camera work (24 mins).* (Video essay.) Waterside, MA: Documentary Educational Resources.

Chapman, M. V., Hall, W. J., Colby, R. and Sisler, L. (2013) 'How images work: An analysis of a visual intervention used to facilitate difficult conversation and promote understanding.' *Qualitative Social Work,* DOI: 10.1177/1473325013496597.

Coffey, A. (1999) *The Ethnographic Self: Fieldwork and Representation of Identity.* London: Sage.

ESRC (2006) *Research Ethics Framework.* Swindon: ESRC. Available at www.esrc.ac.uk/_images/framework-for-research-ethics_tcm8-33470.pdf, accessed on 17 June 2015.

Gingrich, A. and Fox, R. G. (2002) *Anthropology by Comparison.* London, Routledge.

Hammersley, M. and Atkinson, P. (2007) *Ethnography: Principles in Practice* (3rd edition). Exeter: Routledge.

Jeyasingham, D. (2014) 'Open spaces, supple bodies? Considering the impact of agile working on social work office spaces.' *Child and Family Social Work,* DOI: 10.1111/cfs.12130.

Latham, A. (2003) 'Research, performance, and doing human geography: Some reflections on the diary-photograph, diary-interview method.' *Environment and Planning A 35,* 1993–2017.

Leigh, J. (2013a) *Constructing Professional Identity in Child Protection Work: A Comparative Ethnography* (unpublished thesis). Salford: University of Salford.

Leigh, J. (2013b) 'A tale of the unexpected: Managing an insider dilemma by adopting the role of outsider in another setting.' *Qualitative Research Journal,* DOI: 10.1177/1468794113481794.

Leigh, J. (2014a) 'The story of the PPO Queen: The development an acceptance of a spoiled identity in child protection social work.' *Child and Family Social Work,* DOI: 10.1111/cfs.12157.

Leigh, J. (2014b) 'Crossing the divide between them and us: Using photography in child protection social work.' *Qualitative Social Work,* in press.

Lomax, H. and Casey, N. (1998) 'Recording social life: Reflexivity and video methodology.' *Sociological Research Online 3,* 2. Available at www.socresonline.org.uk/3/2/1.html, accessed on 8 April 2015.

Miller, D. (2008) *The Comfort of Things.* Cambridge: Polity Press.

Phillips, C. and Bellinger, A. (2011) 'Feeling the cut: Exploring the use of photography in social work education.' *Qualitative Social Work 10,* 1, 86–105.

Pink, S. (2007) *Doing Visual Ethnography* (2nd edition). London: Sage.

Rose, G. (2007) *Visual Methodologies: An Introduction to the Interpretation of Visual Materials* (2nd edition). London: Sage.

Russell, A. C. and Diaz, N. (2013) 'Photography in social work research: Using visual image to humanize findings.' *Qualitative Social Work*, 12, 433.

Szto, P., Furman, R. and Langer, C. (2005) 'Poetry and photography: An exploration into expressive/creative qualitative research.' *Qualitative Social Work 4*, 2, 135–156.

Taylor, C. (2006) 'Practising Reflexivity: Narrative Reflection and the Moral Order.' In S. White, J. Fook and F. Gardner (eds) *Critical Reflection in Health and Social Care*. Maidenhead: Open University Press.

Chapter 11

RESEARCHING RECOVERY FROM SUBSTANCE MISUSE USING VISUAL METHODS

JULIAN MANLEY, ALASTAIR ROY
AND LYNN FROGGETT
University of Central Lancashire

Social work and welfare practice is beset by challenges to effective communication (Ferguson, 2010) and social work researchers have been addressing the place of communication in good practice, examining the skills and abilities of professionals and how these might be enhanced in training as well as enacted in practice (Forrester *et al.*, 2008a, 2008b; Lefevre, Tanner and Luckock, 2008). However, for practitioners and service users, there are difficulties in finding languages that capture experience that is often misunderstood, unknown and unsayable. This is problematic for both social work practitioners and social researchers (Froggett, 2001, 2002; Hoggett, 2000; Roy *et al.*, this volume).

Scheff (1997) characterises this problem in his description of the 'cultural convention of common sense', arguing that much social science operates on the assumption that research respondents: 'think clearly, are conscious of their own motives and those of others, and [that in talking to researchers they]…mean what they say and say what they mean' (p. 220).

Much social-science-led research on substance misuse is rooted in objectivist epistemologies which, while simplifying the task of conducting research (Roy, 2009), obfuscate the complex and affective components of drug related issues (Roy, 2012a, 2012b). Lloyd (2010, 2013) and Coomber (2006) emphasise that the topic of illegal drug use is infused with affect, with problem drug users often castigated and pathologised. Sadie Plant (1999) highlights some of these complexities and ambiguities:

> To write on drugs is to plunge into a world where nothing is as
> simple or stable as it seems. Everything about it mutates as you try
> to hold its gaze. Facts and figures dance around each other; lines
> of enquiry scatter like expensive dust. The reasons for the laws, the
> motives for the wars, the nature of the pleasures and the trouble
> drugs can cause, the tangled web of chemicals, the plants, the brains,
> machines: *ambiguity* surrounds them all (p.248, our emphasis).

The visual methodology discussed in this chapter attempts to address
some of these issues. Crucial to our discussion is the distinction
between emotion and affect. We are using affect to mean the complex,
cumulative and embodied sense of 'emotion' as defined by Deleuze and
inspired by Spinoza, as opposed to basic 'feelings' that are easier to put
into words, (Deleuze, 1978; Manley, 2010). The research is located
in a wider field of psychosocial research, which attempts to capture
aspects of experience that are elusive, unrecognised and not easily
expressed in words (Manley, 2009; Froggett and Hollway, 2010). Until
recently, social researchers interested in tacit dimensions of experience
have often relied on interpretations of qualitative interviews. There
are exceptions such as the Biographical Narrative Interpretive Method
(Wengraf, 2001) and the Free Association Narrative Interview (Hollway
and Jefferson, 2012/2000) and these methods have been used in the
field of substance misuse (Roy, 2012a, 2012b). However, semi-structured
interviews – arguably the most commonly used method in qualitative
social science – tend to assume the research participant has a 'unitary'
sense of self, is transparent to herself and is able to give a rational verbal
account of her motivations and behaviours, (see Henriques *et al.* (1984)
for an epistemological critique of the Rational Unitary Subject). This is
an ontological position that has been questioned by psychosocial and
postmodern thinking on human subjectivity and by psychoanalytically
informed inquiry. This 'unitary' sense of self does not describe well the
social worker, the researcher or the people who use welfare services, for
whom words are not always the most obvious form of self-expression.

Being unable to give a complete and rational account of ourselves
is not necessarily a question of education or ability: we do not always
think and act in our own interests; we are often not aware why this
is so and if we are, we cannot necessarily explain it (Hoggett, 2000).
The epistemological implication is that we have to find other means of
getting close to the experience of our research participants. One way of
doing this is to acknowledge that besides thoughts and words people

live in a rich sensory world and this creates opportunities for researchers to use a wide range of sensory data, including visual, alongside methods that rely on language.

There are various sources for the idea of 'visual thinking', but the immediate antecedent for the method described in this chapter is the practice of social dreaming, which has been developed since the 1980s as a means of allowing dream images to be shared in a group setting called a 'matrix'. In social dreaming (Lawrence, 2005; Manley, 2014), the participants engage with dreams and 'associative thinking'. This allows thoughts and feelings to flow with as few obstacles or second thoughts as possible and has its origins in Freud's idea of 'free association' as a method for allowing thoughts and feeling to be expressed without hindrance (Freud, 1991/1900, pp.174–175). The word 'matrix', used to describe the participatory process, was chosen as an alternative to 'group' in social dreaming in order to encourage this flow of free association into a shared space ('matrix') as opposed to an engagement in group dynamics. Since free association is a crucial element of the visual matrix, the same structure and name have been used. The visual matrix and the social dreaming matrix share many procedural features, the principal differences being that rather than dreams the visual matrix is stimulated by images and associations that bear on a research problem and can be interpreted to yield research findings.

We argue that 'experience-near' methods (Geertz, 1974) are needed to research recovery processes – methods that do not burden people with explaining what they themselves only partly understand. The visual matrix has the potential to be experience-near and 'practice-near' (Froggett and Briggs, 2012) by getting close to the experience of the participants it can enhance practice strategies. Not only does it provide a research setting for hitherto unspoken aspects of recovery journeys, it also gets beyond the fact that recovery processes *feel* idiosyncratic, enabling expression of experiences common to all.

Design

The research project – 'Researching recovery from drug and alcohol addiction with visual methods' – was designed to understand the potential benefits of using the visual matrix in the context of recovery from substance misuse. Visual matrices were conducted in Greater Manchester, Merseyside and London, with people at different stages of recovery and in different recovery environments (Manley, Roy and

Froggett, 2014). Acorn Recovery Projects (the focus of this chapter) provides shelter and treatment for their clients. The overall aims were:

1. to research a drug and alcohol recovery programme by engaging participants in visualisation and reflection on their addictions

2. to develop the visual matrix as a research method.

We conducted a visual matrix on site for each of the organisations. Each visual matrix, including the post-matrix discussion, lasted about two and a half hours. Numbers varied between 7 and 15 clients, who were recruited by the organisations themselves. Written information prior to the events was passed on to the prospective participants through the respective staff members of each organisation. In line with ethical practice, the researchers sought verbal and written consent and guaranteed anonymity.

In the two case studies described in this chapter, one group of clients taking part was 'early' and the other group 'longer' in recovery. By working with two groups with the same provider but at different stages of recovery, we hoped to understand how the visual matrix was sensitive to the experience of groups at different points in their recovery journeys.

Method

Below we describe the organisation and process of the matrix through the example of the recovery project. We present some of the 'data' produced and explain the interpretative process that follows.

1. Visual matrix

The stimulus material – pictures of local streets, Acorn, country scenes, nightclubs and others – for the matrix in this project were selected from photos taken by a service user. They were then made into slides by the researchers and projected onto a screen. Participants were encouraged to sit quietly and to allow the slides to stimulate their own images and associative thinking in preparation for the visual matrix. (5 minutes)

For the visual matrix participants sit in a 'snowflake' formation that constitutes the 'matrix' described above (Figure 11.1). The snowflake arrangement is designed to discourage people from speaking directly to each other.

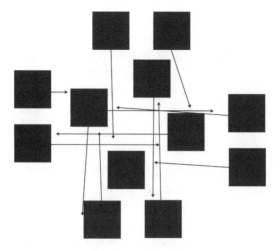

Figure 11.1: Snowflake seating arrangement; the arrows indicate how the formation interrupts a group dynamic

Participants are encouraged to contribute mental images, feelings and associations as they emerge. These might be images that seem to arise spontaneously within an individual or emerge as a result of others' contributions. Images or associations are offered whenever anyone feels the need to contribute. The whole matrix is transcribed in real time by one of the researchers. People are asked not to make overt interpretations of the possible meanings of the images in the course of the visual matrix itself. Instead, the experience is one of images and feelings beginning to (e)merge in a collage-like way. These are then worked into meaning in subsequent interpretation sessions, as described below. (40–60 minutes)

2. The post-matrix session: drawings and discussion
The post-matrix session is an opportunity for participants (including the researchers) to begin to make sense of the visual matrix. In this project the process began with a session in which participants were asked to work independently to create drawings of images they felt were important to them from the visual matrix. Subsequently, the group sat in a circle – which differentiated the process from the matrix 'feel' of the snowflake pattern – and these drawings were placed on the floor in the middle of the room. The group worked together with the drawings, moving them to make connections between the different images. These created

'collages' that expressed affects and ideas through the combinations (these could be similar objects, colours or shapes) in the configurations on the floor. The final collage of images was photographed to retain a record for future analysis. This was followed up by group discussions with the participants, to consider possible interpretations of the visual matrix. (20 minutes)

Analysis

Immediately after the workshop, the researchers met to consider their initial impressions, highlighting important images, thoughts and feelings. At a later date, the researchers worked in a series of research panels. The objective of these was to allow meanings to emerge and hypotheses to be formulated, and to have interpretations corroborated. Each panel had four phases:

1. A 're-living' of the visual matrix experiences, achieved by rereading out loud the visual matrix transcript.

2. Each researcher panel member was allowed about five minutes to make their own response to the material, allowing their thoughts to flow freely and without interruption, followed by comments, feelings and associations from the other researcher members of the panel.

3. The drawings were placed on the floor and the panel worked with the original arrangement of the material as well as considering new connections between the images. This resulted in different configurations from the original collage, which brought to light other ways of understanding the material.

4. Finally, the panel took a step back from the 'experience-near' associative work of the previous phases and worked in a discursive and analytical fashion to consider the emergent ideas.

The interpretation process is designed to allow the visual thinking of the matrix to 'speak in its own language'. That is to say, it respects the emotional and image-based expression of the visual matrix. It does so by allowing the images to retain their multiple meanings and complexity by incorporating further association and returning to the original material as part of the analysis. In this way, the process attempts to avoid foreclosure through premature interpretation. In line with other psychosocial approaches to research, the process of interpretation in panels allows the ideas of all panel members to be challenged. This helps to avoid wild analysis and the blind spots of individual panel members (Hollway and Jefferson, 2012/2000; Wengraf, 2001). Further discussion of the visual matrix and its interpretation can be found in Froggett *et al.* (2014b) and Hughes, Roy and Manley (2013).

Findings

VM1: Acorn, 23 January 2014; Attendance:
7 secondary clients (longer in recovery), 2 researchers
OVERVIEW
The visual matrix brought out dilemmas and paradoxes related to recovery: the sense of old and new was represented in photographs of a lost past and family comforts. At the same time there was the problem of trying to make a fresh start in middle age and a yearning for a time when things were somehow simpler and had survived the passing of time, as symbolised by an image of an antique jug and bowl. There was a wariness of the kind of containment represented in monumental buildings – such as courts, libraries or hospitals – contrasted to small buildings such as squats, with little in between. The shelter provided by the recovery organisation (Acorn) was compared, in this context, to the 'impossible-made-possible' containment of the Amish community, discussed below. The desire to love and be loved was difficult to grasp, as symbolised in an image of a heart-shaped trinket, dancing in the wind of a market stall. Potential transformation was expressed in images of oil into petrol and fire into smoke. True and false identities were explored through images of different kinds of masks. Interestingly, the participants themselves considered the differences between words and images, feelings and thought, making the process of the visual matrix part of the potential for recovery too.

EXTRACTS
The clients were able to express an intense desire for an ideal community represented by the Amish, which could be seen as both ideal and real in comparison to Acorn.

- 'The Amish suggest a pure sense of life, simple, cleaner, ordered, safe, secure, no worries.'

- 'I remembered coming from prison to Acorn and thinking this is just another rehab, now I feel gratitude, a safe house.'

Feelings of the care and protection of community were associated to memories and photos of family.

- ' ...an old picture of my Gran and Great Gran and my uncle in the middle.'
- 'My Great Grandfather and Gran in Trinidad...and images of beaches and sunshine.'
- 'Pictures of my Mum and Dad when they were younger.'

The participants' understanding that photos are old but depict 'younger' selves (and, through association, compared to the Amish who are an 'old-style' community but contemporary too) commented on idealised comforts of family past.

Finding a new community and home and making a fresh start in life require a transformation, where such transformation has to be weighed against the fear of losing one's identity (behind the surgeon's mask or the beautician's face pack).

- 'Images of oil and the process to petrol, a chemical...'
- 'Surgeons wearing masks.'
- 'Treatment is better than rehab.'
- 'Face brush...images of beauticians, face packs, hairdressers.'

Associated to this idea of transformation without loss is the question of the image of the brain that 'thinks' and the words that can come from it (related to the mask that hides something real and the doubt cast upon the word 'treatment' that needs transforming into something new):

- 'Separating the word 'Treat-ment', meant to treat you...'
- 'People being pampered.'
- 'Seeing a brain.'
- 'I can see little sign next to the brain, "think, think, think..."'

In the post-matrix session the drawings reflected this sense of journey, with a past left behind and a future unknown. In the example that follows, the journey is envisaged as a calm reflection of an observer who contemplates a dreamscape. The back of his head looks through the paper to the other side and views a sea of red and purple.

Figure 11.2: Front and reverse image of back of man's head and sea of colour

VM2: Acorn, 2 April 2014; Attendance: 10 primary clients (in early recovery), 3 researchers

OVERVIEW

This visual matrix was relentless in its flow of stark, undeveloped images compared with VM1. Attempts at building alternative images soon gave way to anger. A feeling of breathlessness was conveyed in the incessant rapid fire of the images with barely a pause for any kind of reflection. The rush of excitement, which was mimicked by momentum of the contributions, was also expressed through images related to films and music: images of careering dangerously in a fantasy car like the Batmobile, images of Glastonbury and a sense of freedom combined with living dangerously. Through the linking of film images, however, opportunities were created to consider other images and complex emotions related to time and the feeling of 'hanging on', as symbolised in images of a man hanging from a clock face.

EXTRACTS

The following example provides a short excerpt from the transcript in which there is a continued rebalancing, in this case of aggression with calm, where alternative images of the potential for recovery (in bold) are worked and reworked.

- 'Bins.'

- **'Calendar: organisation.'**

- 'Bins.'
- 'Shooting gallery.'
- 'The posh bedroom, all lies.'
- 'Bedroom: sex.'
- 'Metal, abuse.'
- **'Traffic lights, stop and think which way you are going to go.'**

Although there was little of the multi-layered interconnectivity of images that was displayed in VM1, there was still an opportunity for a development of themes through the use of film imagery from A Clockwork Orange.

- 'The Clockwork Orange outfits, all mixed up, penis, smashed your head in and that was just foreplay.'
- 'The film Clockwork Orange, and the car like the Batmobile, the car racing along lanes.'

Film images are used to represent the 'mixed-up' experience of addiction and recovery, describing elements of overwhelming experience including moments of disturbing excitement, as in the car scene alluded to from the film and the experience of brutality and violence. These ideas were developed through other film references.

- 'Reminds me of the film with the fellow hanging off the clock, trying to stop time moving.'

This image, possibly a reference to the Harold Lloyd scene of a man hanging on to a clock face, connects with the 'clock' in A Clockwork Orange and combines the morbid scenes of the latter with the time struggle symbolised in the former.

The post-matrix drawing session depicted images of substance misuse, and some reference to alternative possibilities, such as the traffic lights and the organisation of the timetable/calendar reminiscent of the opening of the VM cited above.

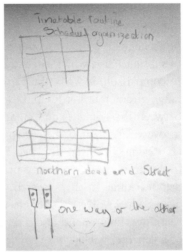

Figure 11.3: Substance misuse and recovery alternatives

Discussion

There are two emergent points in relation to the visual matrix method applicable to substance misuse policy and practice.

1. The value of a method that allows the expression of complex elements of experience

Both matrices allowed people the opportunity to express complex affect and ambiguous ideas related to recovery. In this way people are freed from the need to provide a coherent and rational account of their own experience. The matrix creates a setting in which experiences – many of which might be mis- or partially understood – can be expressed collectively via imagery and associations. The method assumes that there are many feelings, affects and experiences that 'await a vehicle' through which they can be expressed and thought about (Hoggett, 2000, p.121). In researching addiction and recovery, this helps to avoid what Keane (2002) refers to as 'textual production', where certain tropes, which have already found expression, are continually reworked and reproduced in research and treatment discourse. In comparison, the visual matrix provides rich data for research team interpretation and new possibilities of knowing.

For example, in VM2 the short, fast-paced contributions are rich in affect. They create a staccato feeling that conveys a combined sense of excitement, anger, discomfort and anxiety interspersed with images of substance use, which circle the contributions throughout the matrix. In comparison, in VM1 the participants were able to weave together a range of different images and they were also able to make comparisons between these images and emotions and their actual situations in the recovery agency and their own lives. Neale, Nettleton and Pickering (2012) suggest that for people in recovery the future can seem frightening and hence many prefer to adopt a strategy of taking one day at a time. In this research we see that shifting participants' self-perception involved a struggle with conflicting impulses, confusions, yearnings, failures and also a sense of mourning related to the passing of a version of self whose comforts and coping strategies had become familiar and which had its own complex and contradictory pleasures.

2. The value of an associative and affect-rich shared process

Consumers of illegal drugs are often castigated and pathologised (Coomber, 2006). For Buchanan (2000) this hostile climate is responsible for casting some drugs users as an 'enemy within', describing a 'wall of exclusion' that perpetuates their marginalisation from mainstream society. Stereotypes about people who use illicit drugs are embraced by the wider community and some health professionals. Stigma diminishes citizenship opportunities and is internalised by people with drug problems, significantly impeding recovery (Buchanan and Young, 2000; Lloyd, 2013; Roy, 2012b). The expression of complex affect and situations that provide containers for understanding recovery could help people in recovery understand their anxieties and emotions. The matrix offers a participatory process that attenuates the judgementalism that attends substance misuse. Neale *et al.* (2012) suggest that many people early in recovery feel overwhelmed and that 'one unhelpful response is to revert to drug use' whilst 'another is to try to suppress emotions and hope that they will go away' (p.101). In this research participants were able to express shame and a sense of degradation, as well as the illicit excitements they experienced through addiction, extending self-reflection beyond 'coping'. The potential to explore a range of contradictory affects may make the overwhelming nature of early recovery more manageable.

Both matrices in this project allowed for the open sharing of complex affect and a movement towards sense making. The main difference between the two was in the quality of reflection. Those service users who were 'longer' in recovery demonstrated greater capacity to attend to personal and shared feelings. Those in 'early' recovery were still able to use visual thinking to express complex feelings. The short, staccato-like contributions enabled these participants to think together. By interlocking disparate images, the visual matrix enabled a fusion of collages into meaning. This was achieved through extensive use of images from films and other cultural reference points in place of the participants' own images.

Innovation

Researching with innovatory visual methods

THE IDEA OF VISUAL THINKING

The visual matrix is an innovative research method that puts into practice the idea of 'thinking visually' in relation to an empirical research field. However, the importance of visual thinking has long been recognised. For example, Ludwig Wittgenstein suggested that there were some aspects of experience that could not be expressed in words (Wittgenstein, 1953). Later, Susanne Langer, a philosopher of art, described these experiences as 'presentational', and used the example of artistic creations, especially music, to make her point that there are things that can only be experienced, not described (Langer, 1942). The French postmodern philosopher, Gilles Deleuze, claimed that some experiences are impossible to describe in words due to the complex emotions they entail. He called these complexities in emotion 'affect' to distinguish them from simpler feelings that *could* be described. He also claimed that 'affect' in its purest form is directly expressed as an image without narrative, as opposed to images that are used to illustrate or support a story (Deleuze, 1981). For the German philosopher, Alfred Lorenzer (Bereswill, Morgenroth and Redman, 2010; Froggett and Hollway, 2010; Hollway and Froggett, 2012), the world is first understood visually as a 'scene' in the unconscious, rather than through sequences of words. Words only come into being for the purposes of symbolisation.

A VISUALLY INFORMED RESEARCH METHOD

Both the visual matrices described above demonstrated the potential for new ways of understanding affect through the use of images. For example, the idea of home and shelter was not a simple matter for the participants in VM1. It would take us many pages of description to express the subtle combinations of yearning and gratitude; the sense of loss and hope beyond hope; of a future through a seeking for some past, a past that is both unreal and real; the sense of limbo and a fear of the unknown. All of this, and possibly more, was expressed in the images, without which it would be difficult to capture the depth, nuance and complexity of thought and feelings of the service users in our research project. This affect is expressed in individual images and also in the way the images interconnected and merged with each other – for example the combination of images of masks and of the Amish community that together subtly questioned the authenticity of an 'impossible' community.

A RESEARCH PROCESS ABLE TO GIVE MEANING TO
DIFFERENT STAGES OF RECOVERY THROUGH 'REVERIE'

In VM1 the participants were able mentally to weave together images and make comparisons between the images and their actual situations in the recovery agency. The service users who were 'longer' in recovery demonstrated imaginative and reflective abilities, through what Wilfred Bion called 'reverie' (1962, 1970) or free-floating attention, with thoughts and affects arising from pre-conscious experience as images or associations. The impression is one of interlinked philosophical and emotional complexity, similar to the 'condensation' (the combining of various themes into one) Freud identified as a feature of dream images (Freud, 1991/1900).

Innovation for research

The particular innovatory qualities of the visual matrix for research are:

1. the combination of creative, open-ended, non-directional, interconnected and imaginative thought and affect in a research method

2. the facilitation of the expression of complex emotions through images

3. the way the method works through sharing, participation, collaboration and relative anonymity. Meaning is co-created by the bringing together of disparate images. In this way, possibilities are opened out for the piecing together of meaning through participation where the vulnerability of the individual is attenuated through the collaboration of others.

Strengths and Challenges

One of the main strengths of the visual matrix is the facilitation of expression through image and affect. It also allows the expression of shared vulnerability of participants, including researchers and staff. In the context of recovery, Anderson (1981) suggests that: 'if one can accept oneself as limited, if one can give up trying to be omnipotent, it is from this very admission of limitation that one can give to and contribute to other limited human beings' (p.30). Participants can work with researchers and their 'limitations' towards sense making without the 'omnipotent' certainties of many other methods.

The visual matrix is a method that combines the individual and the social, and in doing so provides an insight into how participants relate to an intertwined personal and social world, consisting of peers (with each other), different communities (the Amish), friendship groups (in Glastonbury), family (old photographs) and eventually the person's role within society (expressed through the 'whole' of the matrix collage). Drawings created by participants gained expression through their combination with other drawings and shared images offered by others in the matrix (see Figures 11.2 and 11.3).

The method reveals the complexity of affective experiences – in this case the person's path to recovery from substance misuse and the shared nature of the 'journey'. Other methods that are based around words – whether in group settings such as focus groups or in one-to-one situations such as interviews – may be insufficient in gathering some of the most meaningful expressions of affect. Focus groups allow for the sharing of opinions and attitudes but in the form of intellectual – rather than affective – debate. Interviews, if they are styled to be biographical, narrative or associative, may indeed open out avenues of affect, but in an individualised rather than shared fashion.

The visual matrix can be used on its own if the research is directed towards the understanding of complex affect in a group-based setting, but also as a complement to and in conjunction with other research methods. We have argued elsewhere (Froggett *et al.*, 2014b) that researchers may wish to consider using the visual matrix in a multi-method approach that affords opportunities for triangulation.

The method is applicable, therefore, not only to social work research, but also to a range of areas where complexity makes it difficult for the subject matter to be expressed verbally. It has been successfully employed, for example, in the area of community engagement with public art (Froggett *et al.*, 2014b). Although this might at first seem to be a completely different field, the key to its application is not so much in the subject matter, but in the tackling of thoughts that are difficult to articulate.

Working in this way stimulates a creativity that arises when the visual matrix approaches Winnicott's (1971/2005) 'potential space', the space where transformations of reality enable participants to turn their affect into images in a playful, enjoyable fashion. If the researcher is dealing with sensitive issues with service users who are vulnerable and might easily feel open to negative feelings, choosing a research method that 'feels good' is more likely to elicit the kind of previously hidden data that is especially useful to researchers.

The interpretive process understands meaning through shared thinking and the creation of working hypotheses within a rigorous interpretive process. This is usually undertaken in a panel, whose task is to ensure that researchers challenge one another thus avoiding over-interpretation and 'wild analysis' (Clarke and Hoggett, 2009). One of the challenges, however, is to ensure that there is enough time and commitment from the research team for analysis, to ensure that the interpretations are thoroughly tested and supported in iterative return to the data. The process is demanding of the researcher who will also need to confront the difficulty of interpreting multi-layered data with an emphasis on images, which makes it difficult to reach clearly defined conclusions.

Furthermore, the task of verbally synthesising the quality of imagery and affect of a whole matrix is a particular skill. In another context, the Psychosocial Research Unit has developed creative writing techniques for this particular research task (see Froggett *et al.*, 2014a). Such techniques need to be reconciled with a research-based rigour afforded by an open self-reflexive stance and a willingness to have personal interpretations challenged by other research analysts and through a constant return to the data. A further issue is that in order to extrapolate findings for an applied field, a degree of critical researcher distance must be combined with a sensitivity to the totality of the data in its original state. That is to say, the necessary interpretive distance must be tempered by a necessary nearness to the data, uninhibited by the foreclosure of meaning that may be inherent in analysis. Effectively the research analyst is in a position of oscillating between an experience-near immersion in the data and experience distance from it as the analysis proceeds.

A further challenge lies in the researcher adopting a facilitating, non-intrusive role, designed to elicit material, and requiring 'containment', that is to say the ability to accept uncertainty and withstand anxiety; to hold on to unconscious thoughts; and a willingness to avoid a premature move to conclusions. These may all be skills that are unfamiliar to researchers more accustomed to adopting leading and guiding positions in relation to their research subjects.

Finally, although this is untested, the visual matrix might be employed as a practice method by recovery agencies and in other areas of social work. Feedback from staff and service users bears witness to the potential of the visual matrix as a sensitive, group-based communicative tool beyond research. Feedback also pointed to how the visual matrix encouraged new thoughts – 'I enjoyed it, made me start thinking out of the norm' – and a different sense of calm - 'Everybody was more relaxed and in the drawing exercise, a feeling of sharing and being connected, bonded...'

Conclusion

The visual matrix can contribute significantly to the expression of complex affect, imaginative thinking and communication in situations where this expression is important but difficult to express in words. With this new understanding, researchers may be in a position to produce recommendations for better communication and for therapeutic practice. This may be accompanied by an awareness of the settings in which experiences can be shared. Within these settings, staff are then potentially able to apply the visual matrix to their efforts to support their clients in their recovery journeys. For example, knowledge about the intensity of the service user's fear of the loss of identity through treatment and transformation discussed in VM1 above, could be used by staff to encourage recovery journeys that explicitly deal with issues of identity. In terms of research in human services, where subjective sensitivities of the participants to the research are fundamental to the understanding of the research question or problem, the visual matrix provides a valuable addition to the methodological repertoire. In terms of social work practice, the visual matrix may also have significant benefits in therapeutic settings as a form of practice that offers new ways for people to express experience. This itself is a question for further research.

Acknowledgements

We thank our funders, the Richard Benjamin Trust. We also thank Mark Prest, Artistic Director of Portraits of Recovery – a social enterprise company that focuses on visual arts and addiction recovery – for his advice, support and contribution; thanks also to the staff and clients of Acorn Recovery Projects.

References

Anderson, D. J. (1981) *Perspectives on Treatment: The Minnesota Experience.* Center City, MN: Hazeldean Information Education.

Bereswill, M., Morgenroth, C. and Redman, P. (2010) 'Alfred Lorenzer and the depth-hermeneutic method.' *Psychoanalysis, Culture and Society 15*, 3, 222–252.

Bion, W. R. (1962) 'A theory of thinking.' *International Journal of Psychoanalysis 43*, 306–10.

Bion, W. R. (1970) *Attention and Interpretation.* London: Maresfield.

Buchanan, J. (2000) 'The war on drugs a war on drug users?' *Drugs: Education, Prevention and Policy 7*, 4, 409–422.

Buchanan, J. and Young, L. (2000) 'Examining the Relationship Between Material Conditions, Long Term Problematic Drug Use and Social Exclusion: A New Strategy for Social Inclusion.' In J. Bradshaw and R. Sainsbury (eds) *Experiencing Poverty.* London: Ashgate Press.

Clarke, S. and Hoggett, P. (eds) (2009) *Researching Beneath the Surface.* London: Karnac.

Coomber, R. (ed.) (2006) *The Control of Drugs and Drug Users: Reason or Reaction.* Amsterdam: Harwood Academic Publishers.

Deleuze, G. (1978) *Lecture transcripts on Spinoza's concept of Affect.* Available at www.gold.ac.uk/media/deleuze_spinoza_affect.pdf, accessed on 8 July 2015.

Deleuze, G. (1981) *Francis Bacon.* London: Bloomsbury.

Ferguson, H. (2010) 'Walks, home visits and atmospheres: Risk and everyday practice and mobilities of social work and child protection.' *British Journal of Social Work 40*, 1100–1117.

Forrester, D., Kerhaw, S., Moss, H. and Hughes, L. (2008a) 'Communication skills in child protection: How do social workers talk to parents?' *Child and Family Social Work 13*, 41–51.

Forrester, D., McCambridge, J., Waissein, C. and Rollnick, S. (2008b) 'How do child and family social workers talk to parents about child welfare concerns?' *Child Abuse Review 17*, 1, 23–35.

Freud, S. (1991/1900) *The Interpretation of Dreams*. London: Penguin.

Froggett, L. (2001) 'From rights to recognition: Mental health and spiritual healing among older Pakistanis.' *Psychoanalytic Studies 3*, 2, 177-186.

Froggett, L. (2002) *Love, Hate and Welfare: Psychosocial Approaches to Policy and Practice*. Bristol: The Policy Press.

Froggett, L. and Briggs, S. (2012) 'Practice-near and practice-distant methods in human services research.' *Journal of Research Practice 8*, 2.

Froggett, L. and Hollway, W. (2010) 'Psychosocial research analysis and scenic understanding.' *Psychoanalysis, Culture and Society 15*, 3, 281–301.

Froggett, L., Conroy, M., Manley, J. and Roy, A. (2014a) 'Between art and social science: Scenic Composition as a methodological device.' *Forum: Qualitative Social Research 15*, 3.

Froggett, L., Manley, J., Roy, A., Prior, M. and Doherty, C. (2014b) *Public Art and Local Civic Engagement: Report for the Arts and Humanities Research Council: AH/ L006189/1*. Swindon: Arts and Humanities Research Council.

Geertz, C. (1974) 'From the native's point of view: On the nature of anthropological understanding.' *Bulletin of the American Academy of Arts and Sciences 28*, 1, 26–45.

Henriques, J., Hollway, W., Urwin, C., Venn, C. and Walkerdine, V. (1984) *Changing the Subject: Psychology, Social Regulation and Subjectivity*. London: Routledge.

Hoggett, P. (2000) *Emotional Life and the Politics of Welfare*. London: Macmillan.

Hollway, W. and Froggett, L. (2012) 'Researching in-between subjective experience and reality [45 paragraphs].' *Forum Qualitative Sozialforschung/Forum: Qualitative Social Research 13*, 3.

Hollway, W. and Jefferson, T. (2012/2000) *Doing Qualitative Research Differently: Free Association, Narrative and the Interview Method* (2nd edition). London: Sage.

Hughes, J., Roy, A., and Manley, J. (2014) *Surviving in Manchester: Narratives on movement from the Men's rooms, Manchester*. London: Lankelly Chase Foundation.

Keane, H. (2002) *What's Wrong with Addiction*. Melbourne: Melbourne University Press.

Langer, S. K. (1942) *Philosophy In A New Key: A Study in the Symbolism of Reason, Rite, and Art*. Cambridge, MA: Harvard University Press.

Lawrence, W. G. (2005) *Introduction to Social Dreaming: Transforming Thinking*. London: Karnac.

Lefevre, M., Tanner, K. and Luckock, B. (2008) 'Developing social work students' communication skills with children and young people: A model for the qualifying level curriculum.' *Child and Family Social Work 13*, 166–176.

Lloyd, C. (2010) *Sinning and Sinned Against: The Stigmatisation of Problem Drug Users*. London: UK Drug Policy Commission.

Lloyd, C. (2013) 'The stigmatization of problem drug users: A narrative literature review.' *Drugs: Education, Prevention and Policy 20*, 2, 85–95.

Manley, J. (2009) 'When Words are Not Enough.' In S. Clarke and P. Hoggett (eds) *Researching Beneath the Surface*. London: Karnac.

Manley, J. (2010) 'From cause and effect to effectual causes: Can we talk of a philosophical background to psycho-social studies?' *Journal of Psycho-Social Studies 4*, 1.

Manley, J. (2014) 'Gordon Lawrence's social dreaming matrix: Background, origins, history and developments.' *Organisational and Social Dynamics 14*, 2.

Manley, J., Roy, A. and Froggett, L. (2014) *Researching Recovery from Drug and Alcohol Addiction with Visual Methods*. Preston: UCLan. Available at http://clok.uclan.ac.uk/11397/, accessed on 8 February 2015.

Neale, J., Nettleton, S. and Pickering, L. (2012) *The Everyday Lives of Recovering Heroin Users*. London: Royal Society for the Arts.

Plant, S. (1999) *Writing on Drugs*. London: Faber and Faber.

Roy, A. (2009) 'New Methods – Old Problems: A Practical and Philosophical Analysis of Participatory Approaches to Qualitative Drugs Research.' In T. Decorte, J. Fountain, D. Korf and Z. Demotrovics (eds) *Old and New: Qualitative Social Research on Substance Use*. Amsterdam: The European Society for Social Drugs Research.

Roy, A. (2012a) 'Avoiding the involvement overdose: Drugs, race, ethnicity and participatory research practice.' *Critical Social Policy, 32,* 4, 636–654.

Roy, A. (2012b) 'The life narrative of a mixed race man in recovery from addiction: A case-based psycho-social approach to researching drugs, "race" and ethnicity.' *The Journal of Social Work Practice, 27,* 4 375–392.

Scheff, T. J. (1997) *Emotions, the Social Bond, and Human Reality: Part/Whole Analysis*. Cambridge: Cambridge University Press.

Wengraf, T. (2001) *Qualitative Research Interviewing*. London: Sage.

Winnicott, D. W. (1971/2005) *Playing and Reality*. London: Routledge.

Wittgenstein, L. (1953) *Philosophical Investigations*. Oxford: Blackwell.

Section 3

INNOVATIONS IN
DATA ANALYSIS

Chapter 12

VALIDATING MEANING MAKING

The Potential of Phenomenological Inquiry

SUE THOMPSON
Avenue Media Solutions

Introduction and overview

Before embarking on an overview of my phenomenologically grounded study, I want to make it explicit that, though I am a social worker, the study itself was not framed *specifically* within a social work research context. Rather, it was conceptualised in terms of a development in the social theory of ageing. However, given that my intention has been to challenge decline and deficit models of ageing that focus on old age as negative, and highlight the potential for old age to be a time of continuing growth and 'usefulness', the implications for social work theorising and practice are many and relevant, as I will go on to refer to later in the chapter.

For those new to phenomenology, it is: 'the study of phenomena, of things or events, in the everyday world. Phenomenologists study situations in the everyday world from the viewpoint of the experiencing person' (Becker, 1992, p.7).

Furthermore, because the focus is on the experiential aspect of social life, phenomenology is also concerned with perception. A paradigm is a set of theories that have an assumption or assumptions in common and a shared assumption within the phenomenological paradigm is that there is no fixed 'truth' – no undisputed reality – but rather a multitude of 'truths' because knowledge is not fixed and 'known' but interpreted through layers of meaning. As I have suggested elsewhere: 'Key to this paradigm are the concepts of interpretation and meaning making which provide a challenge to the positivist assumption that

social phenomena can be studied in an objective and value-free way'
(Thompson, 2013, p.29)

Given that I intended to situate my study within an empowerment
paradigm which recognises that unheard or marginalised voices need to
be listened to, validated and acted on, I had looked for a methodological
approach that would support those aims and found it in phenomenology.

The study itself

This research was an exploration of:

1. the significance that dependent older people who are reliant on
    formal care support attach to reciprocity in their lives

2. whether they perceive its contribution to their spiritual well-
    being to be recognised by others who have the capacity to
    facilitate opportunities for them to continue to 'give back' in
    some way.

It comprised an analysis of literature in the fields of reciprocity and
eldercare policy in the UK and Tamil Nadu, India, and an empirical
study using samples drawn from the over-70 population in those
countries. Though not designed or claimed as a comparative study,
taking advantage of the opportunity to interview elders in differing
cultural contexts offered the potential to add an extra layer of richness
to the data and informed the adding of a second strand to my thesis. As
a result, it became concerned with not only the potential for spiritual
enhancement or diminishment, but also the promoting of a sociological
dimension to broaden the largely psychological focus that predominates
in this particular research field.

The study was very broad ranging, and space here is limited, so
my focus in this chapter is on the potential for practice to be informed
in a positive way by research that is grounded in a phenomenological
paradigm and that draws on phenomenological concepts. Because these
are part of what I consider to be the innovative elements of the research,
I will elaborate on these aspects in the next section. Meanwhile, I
highlight some key points relating to design, method, analysis and
dissemination.

Design

Given that my focus was on getting a better understanding of the participants' experience and perception of reciprocity – generally understood as a relationship of give and take and manifesting itself in this case as a 'sense of usefulness' – then hearing their subjective accounts of what it means to them was crucial. One-to-one interviews were chosen as an appropriate method of data production and guided by a schedule constructed with the intention of persuading the participants to relate their aspirations and experience both before and after becoming significantly dependent on others. While this method generated fascinating and relevant 'rich' data (in the sense of data rich in detail and emotional depth) the process was not without its difficulties. For example, I had to take account of the fact that the participants' meaning making was being 'filtered' through that of others involved, including myself. However, from a phenomenological perspective, complete neutrality is not possible, the researcher's meaning making being part of the research dynamic and acceptable as long as it is made transparent (Gadamer, 2004).

Choosing a method of data analysis proved to be more difficult, given that my focus was on exploring the meanings that people attach to their experiences and therefore a very subjective phenomenon. Favouring a constructivist approach (in that my aim was to construct new knowledge, rather than set out to prove or disprove existing knowledge) latent thematic analysis (LTA) appealed: thematic because it involves identifying themes within texts – in this case, interview transcripts – and latent because the focus is on 'surfacing' underlying meanings. As the following comment suggests, it was a flexible enough approach to incorporate both the participants' individual meaning making and the broader social contexts in which those psycho-spiritual processes took place:

> [it] can be an essentialist or realist method, which reports experiences, meanings, and the reality of participants, or it can be a constructionist method, which examines the ways in which events, realities, meanings, experiences and so on are the effects of a range of discourses operating within society. (Braun and Clarke, 2006, p.81)

To some extent the underlying or 'latent' themes were predefined, or at least informed, by the four phenomenologically significant concepts that I had incorporated into a model that I was proposing as a useful analytical framework for understanding social phenomena, including reciprocity. These four concepts:

1. social space

2. social time

3. meaning making at the level of the individual

4. meaning making at the level of discourse and institutionalised patterns of power

informed both the construction of the interview schedule and the data analysis.

Method

Both sets of research samples were purposive in that non-random samples were drawn from populations chosen to reflect experience of the phenomenon I was studying. Seven significantly dependent older people in Chennai and seven similarly dependent people in the UK were interviewed. The sample size was deliberately small in both countries, consistent with a qualitative form of inquiry that has individual narratives at its core. Given that some of the Indian participants did not speak English as a first language, or at all, an interpreter was used on some occasions. To guard against yet another layer of meaning making (that of the interpreter choosing how to convey what they are hearing) from compromising the data I was trying to produce (the older people's perspective) I used the interpreter services of a research-minded social worker, whom I believed to have both an understanding of my methodology and values, and the necessary skills to ensure that the transcripts were as accurate a representation as possible of the participants' reported lived experience.

Adapting LTA to my particular purpose, I undertook a four-stage process whereby I:

1. read all 14 transcripts twice over to sensitise myself to emerging themes

2. annotated the transcripts in relation to emerging concepts, which were 19 in total. An experienced colleague undertook the same process on two transcripts chosen at random, and these were

compared as a way of checking that my annotations were not idiosyncratic, but reflected a shared cultural understanding

3. allocated each identified concept to relevant section(s) of the analytical model

4. identified each concept as 'significant', 'very significant' or 'particularly significant', depending on the number of times it was raised by the participants during the interviews.

Findings and discussion

Available space allows for only a selective overview of the findings but most significant to my mind were that:

1. opportunities to operate in environments where connecting with other people might provide opportunities for 'giving back' were often limited by practical or ideological constraints

2. being able to reciprocate was important to the vast majority of participants but aspirations to continue operating as valued citizens, and to feel good about that, often went unrecognised

3. the consequence for older people on the receiving end of care appears to have been one of spiritual diminishment – of feeling undervalued despite being capable of reciprocity in some form

4. assessments of need had been experienced as often having lacked consideration of aspirations for the future

5. a mismatch between the older people's aspirations, and other people's expectations of them, is likely to have been influenced by differing social constructions of old age and associated differences in expectations of reciprocity in the two different cultures of India and the UK.

Dissemination

The findings have been disseminated through the publication of the thesis in its entirety in book form (Thompson, 2013).

Key innovative elements

A phenomenological approach in itself is not innovative within social work research, though I would suggest that it is very much underrepresented.

My claim to innovation and the basis on which I would wish to promote phenomenologically grounded research are founded on my development of a phenomenologically informed model that provides:

1. a 'sensitising framework' (Sibeon, 2004) to aid knowledge development and understanding

2. a tool for analysis not only of reciprocity in eldercare, but also of other social phenomena in the broad field of 'people work'.

So what is a sensitising theory and why is it significant for social work research? Sibeon (2004) differentiates between substantive theories that provide new empirical information and sensitising theories that provide ways of thinking about the world and the knowledge we produce. I consider my social work practice to have been enhanced by having studied sociology. My aim in undertaking this research therefore has been to develop an analytical model that has the potential to enhance the sociological dimension of social work theorising, research and practice – a recognition that individual lives and the cognitive, emotional and spiritual processes that are enacted at a psychological level within those lives – are lived within broader and changing social contexts and influenced by meaning making at levels beyond that of the individual. While much of phenomenologically based research *does* focus on individual meaning making, I could see that, as an approach, it allowed for the broader macro analytical perspective I was seeking but without losing the significance of the micro-level processes of individual experience, perception and meaning making. In terms of social theory there has long been a tension between the two poles of:

1. human agency (the recognition that we can make decisions and take actions) and;

2. social structure (the recognition that our decisions and actions are constrained by wider political and social forces).

For example, psychological theories in general have often attracted criticism from a sociological point of view for their tendency to inadequately consider wider social concerns (Stones, 2005; Thompson, 2010) while, on the other hand, some sociological theories have been criticised for neglecting to adequately consider human agency. In his account of structuration theory Giddens (2009) emphasises that it is the interplay between structure and agency that is key to understanding social life – describing that interplay as a dialectical interaction whereby conflicting forces come together to produce change. In his work relating to PCS analysis, Thompson (2011) offers a development of Giddens' structuration theory, in that he proposes the existence of a *double* dialectic, whereby there exists one dialectical relationship between the levels of human agency (consistent with the personal level of PCS analysis) and culture (the level of shared understandings and expectations within a culture) and a second dialectical relationship between the cultural level and structural considerations such as the bases on which societies are divided up – for example, gender, ethnicity and, of course, age.

As I travelled along my research journey I began to see how both PCS analysis and a methodology based on a phenomenological 'lens' could inform my study of the relationship between reciprocity and dependency in a way that could bridge the two points of focus – the macro and micro, social structure and human agency – without neglecting the significance of either, so that I might arrive at the end of my research journey with a coherent and useful analytic framework rather than just a collection of individual narratives, useful though those would be in their own right. In essence, given that it had the potential to enhance the ways in which practitioners understand knowledge and the situations with which they engage, I began to see that my phenomenologically grounded model could be considered a sensitising theory that could inform the following in an innovative way:

1. practitioners' understanding of the spiritual significance of meaning making – in this particular case, the significance of feeling 'useful' while also dependent – but also a more general appreciation of the significance of clients' 'takes' on situations and how these may differ from those of practitioners with their different frameworks of meaning

2. eldercare practice in general, by highlighting dialectical relationships between different levels of analysis

3. the theorising of ageing itself, by challenging the dominant focus on advanced old age as being characterised by decline rather than personal growth. This point also draws attention to how it is not only social work research that has relevance for social work practice. In this case, the phenomenologically grounded research paradigm used highlighted the relevance of social theory in general, and the social theory of ageing in

particular, as legitimate fields in which to locate social work research (Garrett, 2013).

From my own perspective, and I fully accept that this is a value-based position not necessarily shared by all social work researchers, I find it difficult, and not necessarily useful, to conceptualise social work research and social work practice as two completely discrete entities. Consistent with the concept of theory-practice integration (Thompson, 2010), it would seem to me that a primary function of social work research is to inform, and be informed by, social work practice in positive ways. On that basis, I consider social work research and social work practice to be inextricably linked also. If we accept best practice as a primary motivating force for both the theory-practice and the research-practice dynamics then the usefulness of a theoretically underpinned research paradigm shows promise for enhancing theory-practice integration. Therein, to my mind, lies the usefulness to social work research of an innovative 'sensitising framework' such as the one I offer – one which both a) addresses a relative neglect in social work research of theoretical frameworks by highlighting theoretical complexity, and b) offers a framework for helping to make sense of that complexity.

It is not my contention that social work research should adopt a theoretical orientation at the expense of social work practice, but rather that it considers the usefulness of a research paradigm which facilitates an understanding of the dynamics between individual lives, the contexts, constraints and opportunities in which those lives play out, and the part that social work plays in that dynamic. Drawing on the insights that the phenomenological paradigm offers has been innovative in relation to the particular field of research in which my study was located – reciprocity in eldercare – and I would suggest that it is innovative in the social work research field in general because of the its combination of theoretical depth and breadth and accessibility as a tool for both research and practice.

Having made my claim to innovation in social work research, I now return to the specifics of my study and to how four key phenomenological concepts both aided my understanding of the relationship between dependency and reciprocity and, to my mind, highlight a phenomenologically grounded methodology as being consistent with the social work endeavour and values.

Social space

This refers to the space in which we live out our lives. As such it can incorporate a range of considerations, including relationships (as in the 'space between people'); physical space (as in living environments and so on); virtual spaces (consider the internet and changing definitions of 'community', for example) and also space in a more spiritual sense, as in where we feel we fit in our social world.

Incorporating this concept helped to surface a number of issues that seemed to be playing a significant role in the participants' meaning making about reciprocity or its absence.

These included that:

- their dependency made them more likely to have little or no access to the communities in which opportunities to 'give back' exist and therefore few opportunities to feel valued through positive feedback

- where living with similarly dependent people, there was the potential for a sense of 'home' to become synonymous with a sense of 'dependency' rather than of interdependency

- their experience of having no or only limited access to a range of new technologies that are redefining the concepts of social space and relationships may have contributed to their being denied opportunities for giving back via virtual communities.

Social time

As we have seen, one of the assumptions that underpins the phenomenological paradigm is that we do not live our lives in a social vacuum. But nor do we live in a temporal one. By incorporating the significance of social time into my analytical framework I became sensitised to more issues that appeared to be informing the meaning making of the participants and therefore, to my mind, need to be heard by policy makers and practitioners. They included that:

- at a time of change in their lives it can be difficult for dependent older people to maintain a positive sense of self: that is, to 'stay me' as it were (Tanner, 2010). It was clear from my findings that this was a concern for the vast majority of the participants

- research around life history work and so on has produced valuable insights but research that brings the future into the dynamic seems less in evidence. Yet several writers have theorised this dynamic from perspectives influenced by phenomenology. For example, Heidegger (a philosopher who drew heavily on phenomenology) proposes the thesis that we 'project' ourselves into a future we aspire to, while being constrained by having been 'thrown' into the world in an era beyond our choosing and within which a particular set of assumptions about social norms, mores and so on are dominant (Heidegger, 1962). And Thompson (1992), drawing on the work of Sartre, suggests that taking account of our past experiences and our intentions for the future *both* have significance for the sense we make of the present.

It was clear from my analysis of the reciprocity and eldercare literature bases I explored, and in the findings from the empirical research, that the part that ambition and aspiration plays in the lives of dependent older people is under-researched. Gaining insight from those writing about time from a phenomenological perspective once again sensitised me to the existence of layers of meaning making that might otherwise have remained invisible to me and therefore not have informed my methodological perspective.

Meaning making at the level of personal spirituality

Though one of the stated aims of my research was to broaden the predominantly psychologically focused emphasis in reciprocity studies by incorporating a sociological dimension, this is not to say that meaning making at a personal level is insignificant. Indeed, from empowerment and personalisation perspectives, I suggest it is crucial that we seek to understand how older people make sense of what is happening to them. Findings from my study highlight the following issues, chosen from many, as significant.

- It can feel spiritually diminishing to have one's aspirations unrecognised or ignored – in effect for it to be assumed that you don't have a future. Almost all of the participants reported a desire to continue being 'useful' in whatever ways they could manage. They wanted to continue to contribute to family, community and society but their responses indicated that discussion of such aspirations to reciprocity were rarely, if ever, initiated by those undertaking assessments of need or providing support.

- That eldercare providers who attended to the physical and mental well-being of older people by helping them to stay active often overlooked the significance to their *spiritual* well-being of not just being active for its own sake, but of finding ways to continue being the person they had always considered themselves to be, or still wanted to become.

Interestingly, in relation to what follows, there emerged from the findings some evidence that a different set of assumptions were influencing how each of the two different cultural groups were making sense of their dependency in old age and their sense of self-worth. For example, those in the UK appeared to have been heavily influenced by an assumption that that old age is different from adulthood (as conceptualised by Midwinter (1990) through the use of the term 'post-adulthood'), while the Indian elders tended only to see old age as different from adulthood where there was an associated problem such as declining health.

Meaning making at the levels of discourse and institutionalised patterns of power

This is the level of meaning making that throws into particular prominence the concept of power because it brings to the surface questions about whose takes on what constitutes 'reality' are the ones that become dominant and influence popular thinking, policy and practice. The phenomenological perspective that underpinned my research alerted me to two considerations that had the potential to throw further light on the relationship between dependency and reciprocity.

THE POWER OF DISCOURSES

Discourses are language-based ways of representing phenomena or events that 'persuade' us to view something in a specific light. When certain discourses become dominant in a society, they serve to portray a particular way of making sense of something as the *only* way. For example, it was clear that ageist discourses (underpinned by the assumption that older people are a burden rather than a resource) were influencing even the older people themselves. Having become sensitised to the power of dominant discourses to influence meaning making I began to see how bio-medical discourses (promoting the assumption that old age is an illness) and citizenship discourses (relating to rights and obligations) were very significant considerations when researching a social phenomenon such as reciprocity.

THE RELEVANCE OF INSTITUTIONALISED PATTERNS OF POWER

This relates to the need to consider the dialectical relationship, described earlier, between taken-for-granted assumptions about old age and reciprocity at a cultural level, and the ways in which societies are structured in such a way that some groups are more powerful than others. Influenced by the idea of a double dialectic, I could surmise that negative stereotypes of older people as useless, and a structure where age is used as a basis for social division, had the potential to be mutually reinforcing. That is, while it remains 'acceptable' at a cultural level to describe dependent older people as a burden, there is unlikely to be a push for change that would result in their becoming less marginalised at a structural level and therefore less likely to become dependent in the first place.

Earlier I claimed my methodology to be innovative in the sense that it provides and draws on a sensitising framework that facilitates an overarching theoretical coherence to counterbalance the postmodernist trend for deconstruction and microanalysis. I hope this very brief overview of the phenomenologically significant concepts that informed its construction will have convinced you that, in a profession where it is recognised that life is complex and needs to be meaningful if people are to thrive, a methodology that is premised on the significance of meaning making and the management of complexity has much to offer.

Strengths and challenges

It is probably clear to you by now that I consider a phenomenologically informed methodology to have a number of strengths and I will make some of these explicit below. However, I have also made the point that I consider it to be underused in social work research and this might be partly because it is not without its challenges. Again, I will make some of these explicit below, though space only allows for a selective overview.

Strengths

- Precisely because it is premised on meaning making, a phenomenologically informed methodology has a degree of symmetry with many key policy and practice agendas that are current in social work, in the UK at least. For example, person-centred practice can arguably only be enacted if the meaning making of the person on the receiving end of social work intervention is understood and validated. Similarly, the dignity in care agenda that is, or should be, informing the care and support of vulnerable adults relies on an appreciation of what is understood to constitute dignity. A focus on meaning making allows for both what policy makers and practitioners understand dignity to mean and how vulnerable adults make sense of its presence or absence in their lives to inform what happens at policy and practice levels. One of social work's key premises is that we should 'start where the client is at' (Alinsky, 1989) and a research focus on meaning making would seem to be consistent with that value statement.

- It provides a challenge to positivist assumptions that social life can be understood in terms of the existence of objective 'truths' and in which there is no place for subjective interpretation. By helping to bring to attention that there are differences of perspective on, and interpretation of, any given social phenomenon – in this case the significance of reciprocity for spiritual well-being – a phenomenological approach to research has the potential to promote critically reflective practice by posing the question, 'Whose perspective is informing practice, and indeed policy making, the most?' In recognising the value of multiple perspectives on what constitutes 'reality' a phenomenological methodology is consistent with the conceptualising of older people as research partners – co-constructers of new knowledge rather than objects of research.

- Because the phenomenological paradigm in general incorporates and validates the fluidity and complexity of social life, and supports innovation in the challenging of orthodox ways of looking at the world, a phenomenologically informed methodology allows for a degree of flexibility in terms of research processes too. This fits well with the concept of *phronesis*, or practice wisdom, as Barsky (2010) points out:

> For SWRs [social work researchers] phronesis has implications for research design and implementation. SWRs do not simply rely on textbook information and research protocols for how to design and implement research. They make use of their experience working with clients and research participants to determine how to act in particular situations. (p.5)

- Given that social work is concerned with spiritual well-being – our sense of who we are or want to be – and that spirituality is increasingly becoming a social scientific, as well as theological, research interest, the phenomenological paradigm's emphasis on meaning making is a useful vehicle for raising the profile of the spiritual dimension of people's lives. In doing so, it can very usefully inform research into the holistic nature or otherwise of needs assessment processes and social work responses.

- And finally, a phenomenological focus to social work research has the potential to be transformative to a degree. That is, where there is a focus on validating differing perspectives, there is the potential for each perspective to inform the other in a dialogical relationship of two-way learning.

Challenges

- While the validation of multiple sets of meaning making is one of phenomenologically informed research's strengths, it does leave the methodology open to accusations of vagueness. That is, the fact that a phenomenological perspective recognises that people construct their own versions of reality by interpreting what they experience poses a problem for those influenced by positivistic science to assume that there is only one version of reality and that the research endeavour is to find that 'truth' through processes of proving, disproving, and so on.

- One of the challenges faced by phenomenological researchers then is to make the case that no one form of knowledge, or way of discovering or creating it, should claim primacy over others. Having been alerted by my study of phenomenological methodologies to the relevance of epistemology (broadly speaking, the study of knowledge) I began to consider early on in my research journey whether I was trying to prove evidence of academic rigour by reference to an established set of criteria, which are, after all, only one perspective on what constitutes academic rigour and, indeed, one heavily influenced by the very paradigm I was seeking to challenge. Another challenge for phenomenological researchers, then, is to make obvious their claim to academic rigour in whatever ways they feel appropriate: the concept of 'the virtuous social work researcher'

(Barsky, 2010) influenced my own claim to academic rigour but, of course, there are many more ways. The challenge is to remain confident about the epistemological value of knowledge produced or co-produced by phenomenologically grounded research.

- Linked to this is the challenge of convincing others that research findings are valid knowledge *in their own right,* such that triangulation of evidence is not necessary for the research results to be accepted as valid. This is not to say that findings such as mine could not have been supplemented and possibly enhanced by being part of a mixed-methods approach but it *is* to say that the findings can stand alone.

- Social work is, of course, people work – we are people working with people. The same can be said of social work researchers who, like their subjects or research partners, do not live in a bubble and so will be open to influences such as prevailing dominant discourses about research, professional practice, the empowerment of vulnerable adults, and so on. The early phenomenologist, Husserl, argued that it is possible to 'bracket' one's own experience when exploring phenomena (Moran, 2000) – that is, to take one's own meaning making out of the equation so that this element of potential bias can be removed (Becker, 1992). Another perspective in the phenomenological tradition, however, is that this is neither possible nor desirable (Gadamer, 2004). Some approaches seek to minimise or eliminate researcher bias but for my own part, I explored my own meaning making as part of the research dynamic, rather than dismissing it from it. One of the biggest challenges, then, is to resist attempts to frame researchers' meaning making as a problem and instead to promote it as a positive contribution to reflexive research.

Conclusion

With the limited space available I have been able to provide only a very brief overview of my research study and the phenomenological paradigm that informed the methodology. I hope it has been enough to inspire you to find out more about the latter. Phenomenology poses very interesting existential questions about what it means to be an individual living in a social world. For example, do we construct our world by being part of it, rather than the world, and our experience of it, being two different things? The philosophical ideas that underpin the phenomenological paradigm can sometimes be a challenge to get one's head around but I would argue that it is well worth the effort if the empowerment of vulnerable people, surely a key social work aim, is also the aim of social work research.

References

Alinsky, S. D. (1989) *Rules for Radicals*. New York: Vintage Books,

Barsky, A. E. (2010) 'The virtuous social work researcher.' *Journal of Social Work Values and Ethics 7*, 1, 1–10.

Becker, C. S. (1992) *Living and Relating: An Introduction to Phenomenology*. London: Sage.

Braun, V. and Clarke, V. (2006) 'Using thematic analysis in psychology.' *Qualitative Research in Psychology 3*, 77–101.

Gadamer, H.-G. (2004) *Truth and Method* (3rd edition). London: Continuum.

Garrett, P. M. (2013) *Social Work and Social Theory: Making Connections*. Bristol: The Policy Press.

Giddens, A. (2009) *Sociology* (6th edition). Cambridge: Polity Press.

Heidegger, M. (1962) *Being and Time: A Translation of Sein und Zeit*. New York: University of New York Press.

Midwinter, E. (1990) 'An ageing world: The equivocal response.' *Ageing and Society 10*, 2, 221–228.

Moran, D. (2000) *Introduction to Phenomenology*. London: Routledge.

Sibeon, R. (2004) *Rethinking Social Theory*. London: Sage.

Stones, R. (2005) *Structuration Theory*. Basingstoke: Palgrave Macmillan.

Tanner, D. (2010) *Managing the Ageing Experience: Learning from Older People*. Bristol: The Policy Press.

Thompson, N. (1992) *Existentialism and Social Work*. Aldershot: Avebury.

Thompson, N. (2010) *Theorizing Social Work Practice*. Basingstoke: Palgrave Macmillan.

Thompson, N. (2011) *Promoting Equality: Working with Diversity and Difference* (3rd edition). Basingstoke: Palgrave Macmillan.

Thompson, S. (2013) *Reciprocity and Dependency in Old Age: Indian and UK Perspectives*. New York: Springer.

Chapter 13

THE ELEPHANT IN THE ROOM

Taking Language Difference Seriously in Research

BOGUSIA TEMPLE
University of Central Lancashire

The research discussed in this chapter grew out of an awareness of the lack of engagement with issues of language, representation and identity by many social researchers. This is surprising given the huge growth in interest in culturally appropriate service provision and research that includes people who speak a variety of languages. Writers across disciplines who are concerned with issues of cross-language representation have developed a body of literature in this area. I refer to some of this briefly below. Suffice it to say here that researchers are increasingly careful not to ignore gender, sexuality or religion, for example, as possibly important in people's lives, including in research, but the same respect for the importance of the actual language used by people is rarely shown. It is assumed that users of different languages view their worlds in a similar way. This view neglects the active role of language in constructing social reality. Although the language we use does not determine how we view social reality, it does provide the resources we use to shape how we think and live through language. It follows that no one can stand outside of the social world to objectively analyse it (Temple and Young, 2004). This position is now accepted by many social researchers outside of social work research and necessitates an exploration of how different languages may produce differences in understanding concepts within research. Finding a word match in a language dictionary may be straightforward. This does not mean people understand the concepts in the same way. Researchers have found many examples of this, including when researching understanding of terms such as child maintenance, social care, drugs or family.

The research I discuss in this chapter had two overall aims: to develop conceptual thinking on the place of language in constructions of identity; and to contribute to developments in methodological and epistemological debates on cross-language research (Temple, 2008).[1] The research was with people who identified themselves as Polish in Greater Manchester and included topics such as views on the desirability and definition of integration, relationships with speakers of other languages and the significance of preferring to use one language over another. It was designed from the outset to foreground the actual language people used in their everyday lives and in the research. A theoretical sampling strategy was used (Mason, 1996). The aim was to include people who identified themselves as Polish in any way, including being second or third generation born in England but identifying in some way as Polish. The sample was drawn up to include men and women who came to England before the fall of the iron curtain either as refugees or to marry or work as well as those who had come more recently. It also included people who did not describe themselves as Catholics as well as those who were practising Catholics. Some people were active in Polish organisations such as the Polish Parish Clubs whilst others were not. Second and third generation men and women born in England also formed part of the sample, as being born in Poland has been shown in previous research as not necessarily a defining characteristic of Polish identity (e.g., Temple 2001). For example, migrants born in Poland may define themselves as European or British if they settle in England and children of Polish migrants may occasionally consider themselves as Polish depending on context. Ethnicity is not determined by place of birth and is not necessarily an either/or choice (Temple, 2008).

Interviews were undertaken with 30 people aged over 18 about how Polish and English languages (and others if relevant) impacted on identity and influenced the desire as well as the ability to integrate. For people whose first language was not English, the interviewer asked about the process of learning English and the changes people saw in themselves and their lives as the languages they used changed. For bilingual Polish speakers the interviews covered the place of different languages in their lives and the effects on their identity. The researcher asked about people's expectations and experiences of being Polish and/or English, the networks people had and their use of English

---

1   My thanks to the ESRC for funding this research (*Language and Identity in the Narratives of Polish People*, RES-000-22-2187). We would also like to thank the participants for their time and hospitality and the Research Assistant for her hard work on the research.

and Polish. In order to ground the interviews, participants were asked about specific examples of their contacts with English speakers and what they thought settling and contributing to English society involved. This included discussion of media and government debates about migration, integration and citizenship.

Each interview was in the respondent's preferred language and transcribed if in English and translated if in Polish. The bilingual Research Assistant (RA) and bilingual Principal Investigator (PI) discussed each transcription/translation and after the research was complete the PI interviewed the RA about her views on the research topics and interviews. This was in line with a theory of how knowledge (epistemology) is produced that challenges the possibility of objectivity, that is of any researcher standing outside of their research. We are all part of the social world and there is no 'god's eye' view outside of it. My research therefore aimed to extend reflexivity to the translation process by exploring everyone's influence on how the research was produced. This reflexivity was premised on Liz Stanley's (1990, p.62) concept of 'intellectual auto/biography', defined as 'an analytic (not just descriptive) concern with the specifics of how we come to understand what we do, by locating acts of understanding in an explication of the grounded contexts these are located in and arise from'. That is, the influences working on the research were explored by looking at the views of everyone involved, not just the research participants, as the RA and PI were also seen as affecting the research process in their role as interviewers, transcribers and translators. Recognising that objectivity is not possible in research or in life generally meant that issues of understanding were placed at the heart of the translation process.

The data was analysed by recording themes on a grid for each participant. These provided cross-sample comparisons of participants' views on themes within language and identity. Conceptual and methodological issues of interpretation, translation, representation and the narrative structure of interviews were noted on the transcripts/translations as well as on the grids for each participant. This helped to maintain as far as possible the integrity of individual cases in line with the narrative approach being used. Participants were offered copies of the transcripts of the interviews and of the report to the ESRC. No one took up this offer. The research did not involve returning to participants to discuss our interpretation of what they had said. This was due to a number of factors. First, for qualitative researchers the issue of feeding back to participants is not one of validation in the sense of confirmation but of opening up debate about perspective and interpretation (Silverman, 1993). Participants may not necessarily agree with a researcher's interpretation. Any new interview to discuss transcripts would involve a new context and another version of the issues and not a 'truer' account of the original interview. Discussing agreement and difference may provide a valuable reassessment of perspective on all sides but not a confirmation or otherwise of the stable reality of the context of the original interview. Second, the issue of language would again come to the fore as some participants would not understand the translations into written English. Third, returning to participants would have proved difficult, as many were highly mobile. Fourth, as I discuss below, this kind of research is very expensive and unfortunately funders often consider the number of participants overall when they make a decision to fund or not.

The sample was made up of 16 men and 14 women. Their ages ranged from 20 to 89. Four participants had come to England as refugees after the Second World War, one had come to marry in the 1960s, two were students, 14 had come to find work either before or since Poland joined the EU and nine had been born in England, one of whom was third generation. Many of the recent migrants were highly mobile and had lived in a number of areas around Greater Manchester. Only one migrant, a student, definitely wanted to stay in England and three hadn't decided whether to stay or not. Three intended to stay for a long time and considered living in England permanently and one was unsure. All the other migrants intended to return to Poland. The older participants had always wanted to return to Poland. All but two participants from the second and third generation were professionals. It was more problematic to classify people who came over from Poland. Many considered that they were working in temporary jobs that did not match their skills and defined themselves according to previous rather than current occupations.

Although there were differing views on the definition of, and desire to, integrate, everyone acknowledged the importance of which language/languages they choose to use in terms of their sense of who they were, enabling them to differentiate themselves from people who used other languages and influencing how and to what extent they integrated (Temple, 2010). The research findings (Temple, 2008) showed that participants defined integration in different ways and that many factors influenced their desire to integrate. These included English language ability, everyday experiences of meeting people from other backgrounds, views about the values they attributed to the communities they encountered, reasons for coming to England and the kinds of social networks used. Fluency in English alone did not necessarily lead to an increased desire to mix with English speakers. There were many examples in the research of participants' recognition that the language/languages they chose to use were important for their sense of who they were. For example, Bozena Stanczyk,[2] a 29-year-old student who came from Poland in 2003, felt that she needed to be able to speak the language of the country she was living in to be part of that society: 'Jeżeli ja nie mam języka ja nie istnieję. Istnieję tylko dla siebie. (If I don't have the language I don't exist. I do exist but only for myself) – translated by Katarzyna Koterba, the RA in the project.' Alongside this need to learn a new language was the desire to retain the language that had made them who they were. Moreover, language was used to differentiate between 'us' and 'them' with judgements being made about people's values according to the way they spoke Polish or whether English or other languages were used. For example, some migrants preferred to mix only with Polish speakers as they did not like what they saw to be the 'English values' of excessive drinking and promiscuity. Others had come to England because they preferred the values they saw as 'English' such as the lack of interference of religion in the way people lived their lives as well as the care given by the state to vulnerable people. In the example I give above, I chose to signal the actual language used in the interview and to limit the extent to which I tidied up the grammar in participants' quotes for reasons I discuss below. Writing in the language participants used acknowledges its significance as well as giving other Polish language users the chance to challenge the translation presented.

How findings were constructed was a key aspect of this research (see above). How the research was to be presented was also considered an important consideration from the outset. It would be ironic to wipe out all signs of the actual languages used during the research whilst at the same time arguing, and showing in the findings, that these were central to people's lives. This is in effect what many cross-language researchers do when they argue about the importance of culture and then wipe out any sign of a significant aspect of it – language. An attempt was made therefore to retain some of the Polish language when quotes were used and to provide discussion of concepts or words where

---

2   All participants have been given pseudonyms.

there were possible alternative meanings or contexts that needed to be explained.

Key innovative elements

In this section I focus on three aspects of the research that I argue are innovative: first, the cross-disciplinary approach that questions some of the prevalent practices in cross-language social research; second, the focus on the usually non-problematised nature of working with interpreters, translators or bilingual researchers; and third, an engagement with the politics and ethics of writing about others in languages they did not use.

In a rare focus in social work on language difference, Gai Harrison argues that:

> despite the pivotal position of language to many social work activities, its significance has rarely been explored in terms of difference. Moreover, the linguistic diversity that characterizes the local and global contexts in which many practitioners operate has been given minimal attention in the social work literature' (2006, p.401; see also Dominelli, 2004; Harrison, 2009).

These points apply to cross-language social research generally where researchers marginalise the actual language used by participants, often only stating that interpreters or translators were used or that bilingual researchers were employed (Temple, 2006). However, researchers from a range of disciplines, including sociology, philosophy, sociolinguistics, interpretation and translation studies (see Young and Temple (2014) for a review of some of this literature) have argued that the actual languages used are significant. Calls for 'cultural sensitivity' or 'anti-oppressive' practices are meaningless if only one language perspective is ultimately used to understand social reality.

Across the disciplines researchers have shown that language is not neutral, is central to our views of ourselves and others, and is political. Within the social work literature Harrison (2006) points out that monolingual English speakers often mistakenly assume that all languages describe a common reality. However, Lena Dominelli (2004) puts it well when she states that 'language structures not only thinking but the ways in which individuals perceive and make sense of their world and subsequently use these understandings in their interactions with others' (p.515). Different languages provide different resources for expressing and understanding and may result in different views on social reality. Some concepts may appear to be straightforward to translate in the sense that there are accepted translations available. For example, the word 'family' and 'social policy' may appear unproblematic. However, the social reality that these concepts refer to may vary. Families are not the same the world over; neither are understandings of the meaning of social care. There is therefore no single objective place from which to understand the social world; it depends where you are looking from. In my research the actual language used by participants was visible *by design* in that the translation process formed part of the overall research inquiry. Sometimes this involved producing whole sentences in Polish with the translation used and who carried out the translation noted alongside. At other points, words or concepts that had proved challenging to translate or appeared easy to translate but meant something specific in the Polish language were explained in notes or in the text itself. At the very least this was meant as a means of signalling that languages other than English were used and that the meaning ascribed could vary between languages. Using literature from disciplines where researchers understand the need to address language use, such as sociolinguistics or translation studies, helped in arguing the case for including Polish and suggested ways of presenting findings. Using literature from outside my own discipline, sociology, opened up new ways of looking at how my research was produced and reflecting on part of the process that is often neglected, even when the focus is on different cultures. My research also specifically foregrounded the act of writing in cross-language research using research from disciplines such as philosophy and translation studies (see below). Decisions such as how far sentences conformed to English language structures rather than Polish language structures, for example, became an aspect to be considered. How do researchers write about others?

Second, the reflexivity that researchers argue for in research generally but rarely apply to cross-language research was extended to include the role of the bilingual RA and myself as PI as producers of the research rather than objective spectators. In other words, *who* works on the research as an interpreter, translator or bilingual researcher is significant in the construction of research findings. There is a fascinating literature on the different ways in which bi-multi lingual people experience and use language (Pavlenko, 2006), which shows that it is possible to be bi-multi lingual in a variety of ways, for example, being proficient in a spoken language whilst lacking confidence in the written medium, being a second generation Polish speaker with a variety of Polish learnt in England or a new migrant with Polish that has evolved and changed in Poland. The way the RA and I differed in our use of Polish and English and these differences formed part of the research with translations discussed and viewpoints challenged. As I was born in England my use of Polish and English differed from that of the RA who had been born in Poland. Moreover, our biographies influenced our relationships with Polish speakers and therefore the composition of the research sample and our translations. For example, the tensions within Polish communities meant that the RA found it difficult to contact second/third generation participants, some of whom resented the new arrivals from Poland. I found it difficult to translate the slang used by younger Polish people. As a feminist I note the gendered use of language within my research, for example, when people use 'man' to represent all Polish speakers. The RA was less concerned with this. It matters, therefore, *who* is employed as an interpreter, translator or bilingual researcher as we use our languages in different ways that affect how people interact with us and how we represent what has taken place. We are not interchangeable. This approach involves more than asking how proficient multi/bilingual researchers are in using a particular language. Although this itself is not straightforward (what language register, dialect, only oral or written proficiency?) a serious attempt to engage with language involves exploring, for example, how the language was learnt and where, what language affiliations are at play and what ties if any exist with others using the language. Being a cultural broker is not as simple as is sometimes implied when one person is chosen from a culture that is not homogeneous to interview within communities. How does their background affect who speaks to them and what they are told? There is a substantial literature on being an 'insider' or 'outsider', which muddies the boundaries between the two suggesting that ethnicity/language may not be the only marker of significance in cross-language research (what of gender, class or sexuality?) and that there may be advantages to being an 'outsider' (Young and Temple, 2014). This research sought to bring some of these issues to the fore.

Third, writers have shown that the *actual language* used is important for political and ethical reasons. Gayatri Spivak (1993), for example, argues that how languages are treated is important for political reasons

– the stronger language often being used to dismiss the voices of those using less valued languages. This is what happens when researchers wipe out of existence the language used in research and provide readers with only neat translations with no indication of the process used to produce them. She argues that the translator must be able to distinguish between 'resistant and conforming writing' (Spivak, 1992, p.186). As Gail Wilson (2001) has shown in relation to power and translation in social policy research, an important issue is: whose history or culture is relevant? She argues that pan-European statistical data are likely to incorporate top-down values and common patriarchal and racist attitudes, for example failing to count unpaid work in gross domestic product (GDP) figures, which then discriminate against women and older people. In a similar way, what is considered 'fair' child maintenance is not the same in Denmark and the UK. Even though the term 'fair' may not be difficult to translate, its contextual meaning may nevertheless differ (Corden, 2001).

In a similar way to Spivak, Lawrence Venuti (1998) argues that this is a form of domestication in translation in which the act of translation itself is erased and the 'linguistic and cultural differences of the foreign text' (p.31) are assimilated into the values of the target culture making the text seem as if it has not been translated. The results of this domestication can be significant. For example, Jan Blommaert (2001) has shown how languages may have different structures and that there are consequences in judging people's stories according to a language structure that may not be appropriate. He gives examples of the results of asylum seekers' accounts in court being judged according to criteria such as logic and facts when in their own language other criteria such as emotional engagement are used to try to convince the listener/reader of the authenticity of accounts. In my research some of the Polish used is presented and the translations are not represented as grammatically 'correct' English. They were often not grammatically 'correct' Polish and I wanted to present their speech and not a tidied up written account.

Strengths and challenges

The approach and concepts I use are not the only way to address cross-language moves within research (for other approaches and concepts see Edwards, 1998; Threadgold, 2000; Wolf and Fukari, 2007). These researchers all share a conviction that although there is no deterministic link between a language and the meaning of words and concepts, it is intellectually naïve to assume that there are no possible differences in how we construct our social realities using language. However, there are challenges in any attempt to understand and present the words of others in ways that recognise their language use. Not least of all, other readers or speakers may not be prepared to engage with other languages and researchers may be unwilling to take on board the time consuming and expensive process of allowing other languages into the dialogue about the translation process and possibly different understandings. Moreover, some publishers are reluctant to accept 'untidy' quotes and word limits often mean that only the language that readers use is included. However, technology now means that source languages quotes, can, for example, be attached via hyperlinks, although arguably anti-oppressive practice would mean that the source language remained in the primary text and translations into the target language should be linked rather than reintroducing English as a baseline by the back door. Research funders are also difficult to persuade. The focus tends to be on the number of interviews promised rather than whether the research opens the door to other language users' views on what the researchers 'found'. Employing someone to carry out interviews and go away and translate them is much easier and cheaper. Some researchers may try to circumvent translation issues by only including people who can speak English in research. This exclusionary practice discriminates against other language users and assumes that speaking a language enough to get by is inclusive. However, Craig Murray and Joanne Wynne (2001) sum up research that shows that communicating in a second language may require extra effort and can result in 'impoverished accounts... as well as making the grounded accuracy and value of the data uncertain' (pp.158–159). This means that it is still necessary to explore possible differences in understanding. Both the practice of employing someone to translate without an interest in the process and the attempt to bypass other language users involve an oppressive and hierarchal approach to other language users.

As well as practical publishing and funding challenges, there are always challenges in presenting 'the other' in any language. I have argued above that neglecting to use participants' own language may dismiss any possibility of signalling difference in understanding as well as ignoring an important part of self and other identification. However, there are also dangers in trying to present source languages or translations that try to retain the structure of the source language rather than use that of the target language or of providing quotes in a 'foreign' language that are ignored. Such presentations of others may reinforce stereotypes of incoherent and strange people (for a review of these issues see Young and Temple, 2014). The issue is not one of domestication or not. Umberto Eco (2003) suggests that all translators make decisions about the extent to which they wish to domesticate other languages and have to grapple with these issues, whether they specify their strategies or not. Farming out translations to people not included in trying to understand and present the research moves the burden of deciding how to present people in languages they did not use on to the lone translator. Which words to choose, where to make the break in sentences, how to portray lack of understanding of the question or hesitation or emotion, how to signal awareness that some concepts are understood differently or that the interview was uncomfortable and the person reluctant to discuss aspects of the research question – all this may be hidden in an attempt to present a 'perfect' translation.

In this chapter I have put forward an approach that involves debating possible meanings rather than assuming one translator holds the key to understanding what it means to speak a particular language. Accepting that there is more than one way to view the social world can be uncomfortable. In order to persuade the reader that a version of the research or translation is at least plausible involves spelling out how the account of the research was produced, that is, reflecting on the research process rather than merely stating that participants' words were translated. This opens up the translation to the possibility of challenge and disagreement. How do readers know that the concepts chosen to discuss are the most relevant ones to be picking up on? Has the researcher missed possible differences in meaning or stressed difference when similarity may have been equally important? The answer is that we do not know. This is the case in all research. All researchers select what they present and how they present it. This has been the basis of the argument for reflexivity in research generally. The approach I put forward in this chapter and other approaches that attempt to let the reader 'in' on the research process have the strength of attempting to engage with possible differences in situated understanding and starting debate about meanings across languages. This is the opposite of claiming an impossible objectivity that positions the researcher as arbitrator of meaning across cultures and languages. The uncomfortable lack of finality in translation may be seen as a weakness of approaches that try to point to the translator's active role in research. I view the lack of finality as a strength bound up with an ethics and politics that challenge hierarchies of understanding, including in the choice of language used to present research. It shows the researcher as human, fallible and part of society rather than standing aloof outside of it.

The approach centres ethics and politics in research. It is unethical to present the researcher/translator as judge of what other language speakers mean using only one language baseline, usually English/ American English. The research I discuss shows the significance of *who* is doing the translating. What is their relationship to the languages used? What are their language affiliations? Which language users do they mix with and how are they engaged, if at all, with language communities? Researchers should at least be open to the idea that there are different communities rather than any one community of language speakers. Differences include those of dialect, generation, gender, sexuality and religion. What is the translator's position on, for example, the use of gender-specific language in translation? Whom you employ to translate does matter. However, following on from the view that there is no objective point outside of society from which to do research, no one translator or bilingual researcher will present the view of all speakers of a language. It is the researcher's responsibility to investigate as far as possible the influence of all involved in research and not to hide behind the shield of objectivity.

My approach of looking at how all participants in the research influenced the process may not be a solution and indeed I am arguing that there is no solution, just methods that can be used to signal the demise of the omnipotent researcher/translator. Researchers are used to exploring the influence of the gender and class of participants, for example, as well as increasingly accepting that these and other factors may influence the perspective of the researcher. They are less used to taking into account that anti-oppressive practice and participatory research must involve a serious attempt to include language as possibly important in the lives of participants.

References

Blommaert, J. (2001) 'Investigating narrative inequality: African asylum seekers' stories in Belgium.' *Discourse and Society 12*, 413–449.

Corden, A. (2001) 'Comparing child maintenance systems: conceptual and methodological issues.' *International Journal of Social Research Methodology 4*, 4, 287–300.

Dominelli, L. (2004) 'Crossing international divides: Language and communication within international settings.' *Social Work Education 23*, 5, 515–525.

Eco, U. (2003) *Mouse or Rat? Translation as Negotiation*. London: Weidenfeld and Nicolson.

Edwards, R. (1998) 'A critical examination of the use of interpreters in the qualitative research process.' *Journal of Ethnic and Migration Studies 24*, 197–208.

Harrison, G. (2006) 'Broadening the conceptual lens on language in social work: Difference, diversity and English as a global language.' *British Journal of Social Work 36*, 401–418.

Harrison, G. (2009) 'Language politics, linguistic capital and bilingual practitioners in social work.' *British Journal of Social Work 39*, 1082–1100.

Mason, J. (1996) *Qualitative Researching*. London: Sage Publications.

Murray, C. and Wynne, J. (2001) 'Researching community, work and family with an interpreter.' *Community, Work and Family 4*, 2, 157–171.

Pavlenko, A. (2006) *Bilingual Minds: Emotional Experience, Expression and Representation*. Clevedon: MultiLingual Matters Ltd.

Siverman, D. (1993) *Interpreting Qualitative Data: Methods for Analysing Talk, Text and Interaction*. London: Sage Publications.

Spivak, G. (1992) 'The Politics of Translation.' In M. Barratt and A. Phillips (eds) *Destabilizing Theory: Contemporary Feminist Debates*. Cambridge: Polity Press.

Spivak, G. (1993) *Outside In the Teaching Machine*. London: Routledge.

Stanley, L. (1990) 'Moments of writing: Is there a feminist auto/biography?' *Gender and History 2*, 58–67.

Temple, B. (2001) 'Polish families: A narrative approach.' *Journal of Family Issues 22*, 386–399.

Temple, B. (2006) 'Being bilingual: Issues for cross language research.' *Journal of Research Practice 2*, 1, 1–18.

Temple, B. (2008) *Language and Identity in the Narratives of Polish People: ESRC End of Award Report RES-000-22-2187*. Swindon: ESRC. Available at www.esrc.ac.uk/my-esrc/grants/RES-000-22-2187/read, accessed on 8 April 2015.

Temple, B. (2010) 'Feeling special: Language in the lives of Polish people.' *The Sociological Review 58*, 286–304.

Temple, B. and Young, A. (2004) 'Qualitative research and translation dilemmas.' *Qualitative Research 4*, 161–178.

Threadgold, T. (2000) 'When home is always a foreign place: Diaspora, dialogue, translations.' *Communal/Plural 8*, 193–217.

Venuti, L. (1998) *The Scandals of Translation: Towards an Ethics of Difference*. London: Routledge.

Wilson, G. (2001) 'Power and translation in social policy research.' *International Journal of Social Research Methodology 4*, 4, 319–326.

Wolf, M. and Fukari, A. (2007) (eds) *Constructing a Sociology of Translation*. Amsterdam: John Benjamins Publishing Company.

Young, A. and Temple, B. (2014) *Approaches to Social Research: The Case of Deaf Studies*. New York: Oxford University Press.

Chapter 14

DATA ANALYSIS IN PARTICIPATORY RESEARCH WITH ADULTS WITH ASPERGER'S SYNDROME

JACKIE ROBINSON
De Montfort University

This chapter explores a participatory research study where a researcher and three co-researchers with Asperger's syndrome worked together to design research tools, conduct the research, analyse the data and disseminate the findings. The study will be introduced and then the data analysis stage will be discussed in more depth to understand how a shared analytic framework was agreed. Finally, the strengths of this approach will be discussed with suggestions for other research studies.

Thinking behind the research

The motivation for this study was to demonstrate that the principles of participatory research can be applied to working with adults with Asperger's syndrome. I was unaware of any studies that had demonstrated this at the time of starting the research project in 2009. My understanding of participatory research is based on an understanding of power. As part of the preparation for this research study, I had read about the operation of power and how it is multidimensional and operates through different levels of influence and takes different forms, operating for example through families and communities (Dominelli, 2002). I had read Lukes' (2005) book on power and his description of what he called the 'third dimension of power' (Lukes, 2005, p.26). This dimension is concerned with power operating through cultural practices as well as through social structures. I had also read about what Smith refers to as 'relational power' (Smith, 2008, p.53). This aspect of power is concerned with the practitioner's professional standing and authority and how this comes into play in interactions with service users (Smith, 2008). The more I read about power, the more daunting the task of working in a participatory way with service users with Asperger's syndrome seemed to be. I was also aware of the accounts from people with Asperger's syndrome of their experiences of living in a neuro-typical world[1]. The titles of some of the books written by people with Asperger's syndrome indicate how they view their relationship with the world of neuro-typical people: *Through the Eyes of Aliens* (O'Neill, 1999), *Inside Asperger's Looking Out* (Hoopmann, 2013), *Martian in the Playground* (Sainsbury, 2009) and *Women from Another Planet: Our Lives in the Universe of Autism* (Miller, 2003). The insight that authors with Asperger's syndrome gave me of their sense of isolation in society added to my desire to work in a participatory way but also added to my understandings of the complexities of how power could operate in any interactions between myself as a neuro-typical researcher and a registered social work practitioner and a group of adults whose experiences in society were likely to be ones of isolation, misunderstanding and powerlessness.

I had read many criticisms of participatory research. Zarb (1992) wrote of the retention of power by professionals, including utilising their knowledge rather than the knowledge of any co-researchers. Walmsley and Johnson (1998) described how the 'voice' of service users can be packaged in such a way that it actually just reflects what the professional researcher wanted to say. Oliver (2009) wrote of how, despite the good intentions of some researchers, disabled people are still left in positions in research that are oppressive.

One of the main criticisms of participatory research seemed to be the control that is retained by the researcher over the co-researchers. Kindon, Pain and Kesby (2007, p.21) detail what they believe can be 'some negative power effects of participatory approaches':

- Retention of researcher's control whilst presenting them as benign arbitrators of neutral or benevolent processes.

- Re-authorisation of researchers as experts *in* participatory processes.

---

1   Neuro-typical refers to people who do not have Asperger's syndrome or autism.

- Reinforcement of pre-existing power hierarchies among participating communities. (Kindon *et al.*, 2007, p.21)

The challenge of this research project was to work in a way that did not replicate the power relationships that the co-researchers had experienced outside of the research. The power differentials between myself and the co-researchers was significant. We had to find a way to work together where they did not experience the alienation they experienced in wider society and that also addressed the power imbalance between us of professional researcher/academic and service users. From my reading of the literature about power and participatory research, the key seemed to be in getting the process of the research right. Chappell (2000) cites Oliver's discussion of the 'social relations of research production', that there is a:

> ...firm distinction between the researcher and the researched...the belief that it is the researchers who have specialist knowledge and skills; and that it is they who should decide what topics should be researched and be in control of the whole process of research production. (Chappell, 2000, p.39)

Given that this research was part of my PhD thesis, I was unable to meet the second part of Oliver's statement. I had to have a research question prior to forming a research group and I was also aware that I had to conform to principles of ethical approval as well as meet the requirements for the award. However, I was concerned that myself and the group of adults with Asperger's syndrome who were the co-researchers would use the specialist knowledge and skills of all involved in the research design, data collection, analysis and dissemination.

The considerations above informed the design of the study. I recruited a group of three adults with Asperger's syndrome. This was achieved through an open invitation to join to members of existing support groups for adults with Asperger's syndrome and also through recommendations from social workers. The co-researchers did not know each other or me prior to joining the group. I did not know at the beginning of the project how we were going to work together as I did not know the co-researchers and also had not worked with adults with Asperger's syndrome in a group situation before.

Setting the scene

The first meeting was a very important one as this set the tone for how the group would work together. We discussed the nature of an 'expert' and I explained that they had expertise that I did not have. Although I had worked with adults with Asperger's syndrome, I am neuro-typical so cannot know what it is to have Asperger's syndrome. My methodology was informed by the insights offered by phenomenology. According to phenomenologists, researchers are not able to detach themselves from their own presuppositions (Groenewald, 2004). I was aware of both my knowledge and experience of working with people with Asperger's syndrome. I wanted to 'bracket' myself off (Giorgi, 1970, quoted in Dyson and Brown, 2006, p.16) from these presuppositions and put them to one side. How far this can be achieved is an interesting point, but it was my intention to try and utilise the expertise of the co-researchers without making assumptions about them and how they experienced the world. I did want to use my expertise in working with groups and my knowledge of how power operates and how people with Asperger's syndrome can be oppressed within society. As a neuro-typical researcher, I had knowledge of how people with Asperger's syndrome can be viewed and an awareness of being in a society that is not generally concerned about including people with Asperger's syndrome.

The co-researchers were very enthusiastic about being regarded as the 'experts'. One co-researcher had been a participant in a research project with a very different methodology where he had been observed to see how he made eye contact with people. He explained that this felt like being a 'guinea pig', whereas in this research he was the 'expert'. The importance of this initial discussion cannot be overestimated.

Developing a way of working together

All three co-researchers had been members of groups previously and had all experienced them as oppressive. One co-researcher later expressed the view that she just expected this to be another example of a group where she felt ignored. Building on the discussion of the status of the co-researches as experts, we discussed how we were going to work together. People with Asperger's syndrome often have a desire for routine and we established a pattern that we adhered to in order to make the sessions predictable. We met at the same venue and worked to the same times, with breaks being at the same time every session.

Each co-researcher chose to do the same activity every lunchtime. We also agreed the roles for each group member. This was a real learning point for me as my social work practice has been predominantly with adults with a learning disability. In my social work practice and in my practice as a social work academic, I had been concerned to support service users in taking up positions of responsibility, for example in chairing meetings. Although I was concerned to 'bracket off' my own assumptions, I had not extended this to areas of my previous practice, which I regarded as sound. The co-researchers and I discussed what roles they might have in our group and I did have in mind that they could chair the meetings. I was also concerned to make the research process as much in line with the principles of participatory research as I could. My presuppositions were challenged as none of the co-researchers wanted to chair the meetings. In fact, one of them expressed the view that if I were to insist on this, that would end their involvement in the research. The reason for this was that this would have provoked anxiety in the co-researchers. I had learnt a valuable lesson.

Research method

My original aim had been to find out what support adults with Asperger's syndrome wanted from services. I presented this to the co-researchers and we worked on what areas of support we were going to focus on. We did this by writing down all the areas of support that they felt were important. We had a list of areas, but they were too many and wide ranging for the purpose of the study. I asked them which areas they thought it was possible to achieve change in and this narrowed the areas down. One example is that they were concerned about the benefits system, but thought it beyond any influence that we could exert. From the list of areas, we devised a questionnaire, which was piloted with other adults with Asperger's syndrome and then made available to over 200 adults with Asperger's syndrome who lived in the area in which we were based. We received back 19 completed questionnaires and we analysed the data together. Having analysed the data together, we designed questions for focus groups for more adults with Asperger's syndrome based on the main themes from the data analysis from the questionnaires. We held two focus groups, which the co-researchers also took part in and then we analysed the data from this together. The purpose of this second stage of data collection and analysis was to gain a greater depth of insight into the themes from the questionnaire stage.

Dissemination

Having completed all the stages of the research together, I was particularly concerned that the co-researchers were involved as much as possible in the dissemination of our findings. We discussed as a group how the findings should be disseminated. The co-researchers chose to have their own webpage,[2] which they have since changed to a blog and a Facebook page. They also chose to present our findings at a conference, and in July 2012 we held a conference where the co-researchers and I spoke about how we had conducted the research and what we had found. Nearly 100 people attended the conference, including many professional workers as well as carers of adults and children with Asperger's syndrome and adults with Asperger's syndrome. The findings were very well received and the co-researchers enjoyed the experience of presenting what we had achieved together.

Key innovative elements

In this chapter, I will focus on one stage of the research: the questionnaire analysis. My role in this was to facilitate the analysis sessions. As part of this, I asked questions to help with the task of coding the data. I asked two questions.

- How would you summarise what the respondent is saying?

- How do you understand what they are saying?

As I reflect in my thesis:

> These questions asked two different things and this was indicative of what we were trying to achieve. They asked for an understanding of the data and a response to it. The first question was asked in order to encourage an understanding of how the respondent was answering the question and the second to encourage the 'filter' to be applied by the co-researchers. I tried to encourage a response from the group where they also used their own experience to make sense of the data. (Robinson, 2015, p.190)

The 'filter' I refer to is the understanding of the data from the perspective of a person with Asperger's syndrome, rather than a neurotypical perspective. The difference between the way that we used the 'filter' or 'lens' of the co-researchers is that this was achieved wholly

---

2   www.aspergersconsultationgroup.org

as a group. A shared meaning was arrived at through discussion. Space does not permit a consideration of the focus group data analysis as well. However, the principles applied at this stage of the research were the same as those applied throughout. These principles were developed through an application of the principles of participatory research and a consideration of the epistemological positioning of the research. The challenge that had been posited by the literature on participatory research was in relation to my own power as the researcher and that of the co-researchers. This in turn led to a consideration of the use of experience, of the co-researchers as adults with Asperger's syndrome and of my own as a neuro-typical researcher. Mason (2002, p.16) poses a pertinent question: 'What might represent knowledge or evidence of the entities or social "reality" that I wish to investigate?' The design of all parts of the research was driven by a concern to use the experience of all the researchers, but in different ways. We wanted to ascertain what the experience of people with Asperger's syndrome is and understand from them what support they think they need. I did not want to use my neuro-typical knowledge or way of thinking to interpret the data and so impose on it my own meaning. I wanted the co-researchers to interpret the data from other adults with Asperger's syndrome. Nind (2014, pp.73–74) cautions against training whom she refers to as 'lay researchers' to 'look at the world through our lens'. It was not the lens of a neuro-typical person that I wanted to interpret the data, but that of other people with Asperger's syndrome. The question was: how could this be achieved?

The concept of an 'interrupted space' is useful in a consideration of this. This term was coined by Bolzan and Gale (2011) in relation to their research with young people. The term refers to a metaphorical space that 'provides the opportunity for social actors to experience something different, something outside of their usual daily routine, and make meaning of it' (Bolzan and Gale, 2011, p.505). In Bolzan and Gale's research, the young people were given opportunities where they could explore 'new ways of being' and have their insights valued by adults (Bolzan and Gale, 2011, p.505). An essential element of creating this space was giving the young people as much power as possible. As a result of this redistribution of power, the young people assigned meanings to activities that could not have been predicted by the adults involved (Bolzan and Gale, 2011). We wanted to achieve insights that neuro-typical people could not predict. We tried to achieve this through a redistribution of power, hence giving credence to the views and experience of people with Asperger's syndrome.

It is in the extent of the redistribution of power that this research is innovative. I was not aware of any other participatory research projects involving people with Asperger's syndrome when we commenced our project, but there have been other studies published. In one of the studies (Bagatell, 2007), observations were made of an individual with Asperger's syndrome as well as an interview with the same person. The script of the interview was given to the participant for checking in relation to accuracy. In a second study (MacLeod, Lewis and Robertson, 2013) participants with autism and Asperger's syndrome were interviewed and the participants were then given the opportunity to comment on the data analysis. These studies are valuable as they included people with Asperger's syndrome in the process more than have previously been documented. As detailed above, this research project aimed to make the adults with Asperger's syndrome central in all the parts of the research, including the data analysis.

Data analysis of the questionnaires

The co-researchers and I discussed how we wanted to analyse the data. I did not have any preconceptions about how we would do this, as I had not read of any previous examples of research with people with Asperger's syndrome as co-researchers. Through the previous stages of the research we had developed a way of working together that the co-researchers found to be enabling. We had produced together an 'interrupted space' in which their experience was valued and was used to shape the research. I was not sure how we could extend this to the data analysis and suggested that each of us take the questionnaire responses away, 'make sense' of them and then come together to discuss them. I had read Cotterell's (2008) account of a research study where he and his group of co-researchers with life-limiting conditions had worked in this way and it had worked well. However, the co-researchers did not like this idea and had the view instead that they wanted to continue to work as a group and complete every aspect of the data analysis together. My concern had been that I did not unduly influence the way they interpreted the data and I thought that if they gained their own perspectives and then shared them this was less likely to happen. I had underestimated the importance of the way we worked together.

Our agreed way of working (our 'interrupted space') provided safeguards against me imposing a neuro-typical way of understanding the data. What we had created between us was a 'space' in which we used the experience of the co-researchers to understand and interpret the data we received from the questionnaire respondents with Asperger's syndrome. We had also created a way of working together that gave a structure that the co-researchers were happy and familiar with.

We were concerned to achieve a shared meaning in the data analysis. Shared meaning has been achieved in data analysis involving co-researchers in different ways. Cotterell (2008, p.9) describes two phases of the data analysis: the first, where the researcher conducted an initial analysis of the data, and the second, where the data together with suggested themes were given to the co-researchers for more detailed analysis. Cotterell's study differs from mine in a number of ways: first, in relation to the initial analysis that the researcher conducted and second in relation to the work conducted by co-researchers outside of the group in Cotterell's study. Co-researchers in Cottrell's study shared their understandings of the data in 'interpretation sessions'.

Stevenson (2013) writes of a similar way of conducting data analysis with co-researchers. She outlines a research study with people with Down's syndrome. Two co-researchers were given written scripts of the data with a margin for them to write their own comments or highlight words they thought to be important. Having analysed the data individually, a shared meaning was developed through discussions as a group. This approach and Cotterell's approach are different to the one that we adopted in that we arrived at a shared consensus of meaning through the discussion solely in our group and the data was coded according to the consensus of the co-researchers.

This consensus was arrived at through my promptings of discussion and the co-researchers considering the data together. The co-researchers had discussed their experience with each other throughout the earlier stages of the research and continued to do so throughout the data analysis stage. The co-researchers had formed a strong sense of identity in our group and they felt that this identity was valued by other group members.

I asked the co-researchers how they wanted to analyse the data together. They chose that I would read aloud each question and as I have described above, the group answered two questions that I posed.

- How would you summarise what the respondent is saying?

- How do you understand what they are saying?

For each questionnaire response, we agreed on a summary statement, which we recorded. In this way we developed a set of codes. The wording of each code was discussed. For some codes we used the words of the respondent and for others we used the experience and understanding of the co-researchers. One example of the name for a code that came from the experience of the co-researchers was 'Understanding neuro-typical behaviour'. This was a statement that the group wrote to summarise what they believed the respondents were saying. In this way we built up a list of codes, which we added to every time we met when we considered more questionnaire responses.

I was presented with some dilemmas during the coding of the questionnaires. The co-researchers disregarded answers that they felt did not answer the questions. I knew that this could have consequences for the data analysis, as some data would inevitably be missed. However, I thought it important not to interfere in the way that the co-researchers understood the data. I was aware of the systemising abilities that adults with Asperger's syndrome can have (Baron-Cohen, 2004) and I did not want to interfere in the way that the co-researchers made sense of the data. I regarded this lack of intervention as being a part of creating an 'interrupted space'.

Although we conducted all of the data analysis as a group, the co-researchers expressed different preferences for how this analysis was recorded. One co-researcher preferred to use numerical values for the codes rather than the phrases or words that were agreed. For this co-researcher to make sense of the data, he assigned numbers to our codes and devised his own spreadsheet. He regularly shared this with the group, although the other co-researchers and myself found it easier to think in terms of phrases.

From codes to themes

After we had coded all the data from the questionnaires, we continued our work as a group to try and categorise the codes. I found that the co-researchers had a great ability for this process. We devised 16 categories or themes into which we could place all of the codes. We achieved this by discussing each code and deciding what it was concerned with. The categories were:

- Me understanding me
- Practical skills
- Communication skills
- Individualised support
- You understanding me
- One-to-one support
- Support from being in a group
- Volunteering opportunities
- Encouragement to be social
- Me understanding others
- More contact with people with Asperger's syndrome
- Practical support
- Emotional support
- Opportunity to be social
- Better promotion of services
- More responsive services.

We wanted to have a smaller number of themes, as there were too many. We reduced the number of themes by looking at each of the categories above and discussing how the group understood each one. It became apparent that the co-researchers believed that what lay behind each category was a lack of understanding, either on the part of the adult with Asperger's syndrome understanding themselves or others or a neuro-typical person understanding them. We decided that three themes stood out as they summaries all the others. These three themes were:

- Me understanding me
- Me understanding you
- You understanding me.

We re-worded these slightly as the co-researchers were not happy with our original choice of the word 'you'. They wanted the themes to refer more specifically to a person with Asperger's syndrome, so we renamed them:

- Me understanding myself
- Me understanding others
- Others understanding me.

We discussed the other 13 themes in the light of these three themes and it became even more apparent that they summarised all our data. However, I struggled to understand some of the links until one of the co-researchers explained them to me. One example of this was where a respondent had answered 'Far less bureaucracy' to a question about what would help in relation to services. We had given this the code 'practical support'. It was explained to me that this was concerned with 'Others understanding me'. Society was organised by neuro-typical people and so bureaucracy had resulted that favoured the way neuro-typical people think and it caused anxiety to people with Asperger's syndrome, i.e. they were misunderstood by 'others' and did not themselves understand others.

The moment where we agreed the three main themes was a significant one for the group and an excellent example of using the perspectives of the co-researchers together with mine as a neuro-typical researcher. The co-researchers agreed that these three themes summarised how they understood the data in relation to what support adults with Asperger's syndrome needed in order to cope with living in a society dominated by neuro-typical people. They also stated that the three themes summarised what they themselves thought they needed in terms of support. I was familiar with the triad of impairment (Wing, 1991), which is often used to understand adults with Asperger's syndrome, but from the perspective of what they are unable to do. I saw the potential for a reframing of how people with Asperger's syndrome are thought about. I drew a triangle on flipchart paper and put a theme in each corner (see Figure 14.1).

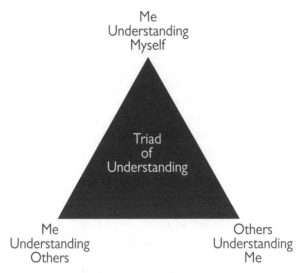

Figure 14.1: The triad of understanding

The co-researchers were very enthusiastic about the representation of the themes. I suggested that we call the model the 'Triad of Understanding', as I saw the potential for this to provide a model for understanding as well as support for people with Asperger's syndrome. What it shows is that there is a mutual responsibility for neuro-typical people and people with Asperger's syndrome to understand each other. It also highlights the areas that are needed for support in order for someone with Asperger's syndrome to cope in their lives. This is a significant contribution to knowledge in relation to Asperger's syndrome.

Strengths and challenges

The strengths in this research lay in its application of the principles of participatory research and its use of the experience and understanding of living in a neuro-typical society from the perspective of people with Asperger's syndrome and the perspective of a neuro-typical person. The way the data was analysed and then constructed into the model of the Triad of Understanding was due to the influence of both perspectives. Without the systemising talents of the co-researchers and their use of their own experience of misunderstanding and being misunderstood, the data would not have been themed in the way that it was. Without the facilitation of the data analysis sessions by myself and the encouraging of the co-researchers to use their own experience to interpret the data, the coding or theming of the data would not have been as rich. Without the understanding of myself as the neuro-typical person with a practice and academic background in working with people with autism and Asperger's syndrome, we would not have put the three themes together in the way that we did into a model of understanding. The crucial point here is that the research was successful in terms of its data analysis and hence findings, because it utilised the strengths and experience of all. Researchers considering how to conduct participatory research with co-researchers should consider with the co-researchers what each person can contribute.

There are a number of traps into which it is possible to fall, even when the researcher is fully intentioned to work in a participative way. I would have fallen into one of them, had not my co-researchers been clear with me about how they wanted to work within the research group. I would have continued to work in a way that I had done before because I regarded it as good practice. I would have encouraged the taking on of roles that were unwanted by the co-researchers. I was trying to empower them, whereas in fact what I learnt was that they were able to empower themselves. My role in that was to work with them to provide an environment in which this could happen. The principle of self-empowerment was advocated by Oliver (1992) and it is an appropriate one to apply to all stages of the research. The question: 'How can research be conducted in way that enables co-researchers to empower themselves?' is a useful one to consider for every stage. In our case this was attained in the data analysis through using the abilities of the co-researchers and working in a way that they found helpful. For other groups of people, the way this is achieved may well be different, but a consideration of this with the co-researchers should always be beneficial. A second trap a researcher can fall into is to underestimate their own contribution to the research. I was so concerned to provide conditions for the co-researchers that were helpful and to recognise fully their contribution that I had a tendency to leave unacknowledged the contribution that I made to the success of the research. It took challenges from my supervisors for me to consider what my role had been. It was only when I considered this that I began to see how essential the partnership that we had developed was to every stage of the research.

Participatory research has been criticised for 'merely tinkering at the edges rather than transforming the social relations of research production' when compared with emancipatory research (Nind, 2014, p.73). This research has demonstrated that the social relations of research production can be transformed. Other research that has gone before has also shown how these relations can be transformed (Browne, Bakshi and Lim, 2012; Fleming, 2012). This research has shown what can be achieved by working with co-researchers with Asperger's syndrome when they are given the opportunity to be involved throughout the whole process. The co-researchers and I have written an article in which we outline exactly how we worked together (Martin *et al.*, 2014[3]). One statement made in this article is particularly striking: 'Group members believe that it is their Asperger's syndrome that has made their group successful. It is successful *because* they have Asperger's syndrome, not *in spite* of it' (Martin *et al.*, 2014, p.78). This is so striking because people with Asperger's syndrome are usually regarded as not being able to work in groups due to their difficulties in understanding other people and in communicating with them. What this research has shown is that it is possible for people with Asperger's syndrome to work in groups if the groups are organised in a way that is enabling to them.

The Triad of Understanding

After we had developed the Triad of Understanding, the co-researchers saw it as an explanation as to why our group had been so successful in working together. It is a model that could be adopted in participatory research, with co-researchers with Asperger's syndrome or with any group of co-researchers. A consideration of all three themes as represented in the triad would be valuable as they can raise questions that are useful in working together. Below are some suggestions for questions based on the triad, from the perspective of co-researchers, but they could easily also be applied to the researcher.

Me understanding myself

- How do I work best with others?

- What role do I like to play when working with others?

- What do I need to happen for me to use my full potential when working with others?

---

3 I previously wrote under the surname Martin, but have since changed my name to Robinson.

- What experience and skills do I possess that can be useful for this research?

- How can I use my experience and skills in this research?

Me understanding others

- How well do I understand what the purpose of the research is?

- How well do I understand the others involved in this research and what their roles are?

Others understanding me

- Do other people involved in the research understand what contribution I can make to the research?

- Do other people understand the role I like to play in working with others?

- Do other people understand what I need in order to take a full part in this research?

These questions are by no means exhaustive and will need to be adapted for each group of co-researchers. The process of doing this adaptation with the co-researchers at the beginning of the research could add valuable insights on which to build.

Conclusion

The success of this research was due to the way in which it was conducted. It was a true partnership between a neuro-typical researcher and co-researchers with Asperger's syndrome. Future participatory research may be conducted in very different ways, but the principles on which this research was based are sound principles. The Triad of Understanding offers one way of considering these principles at every stage of the research.

References

Bagatell, N. (2007) 'Orchestrating voices: Autism, identity and the power of discourse.' *Disability and Society 22*, 4, 413–426.
Baron-Cohen, S. (2004) *The Essential Difference*. St Ives: Penguin.

Bolzan, N. and Gale, F. (2011) 'Using an interrupted space to explore social resilience with marginalised young people.' *Qualitative Social Work 11*, 5, 502–516.

Browne, K., Bakshi, L. and Lim, J. (2012) '"There's No Point in Doing Research if No One Wants to Listen": Identifying LGBT Needs and Effecting "Positive Social Change" for LGBT People in Brighton and Hove.' In P. Beresford and S. Carr (eds) *Social Care, Service Users and User Involvement.* London: Jessica Kingsley Publishers.

Chappell, A. (2000) 'Emergence of participatory methodology in learning difficulty research: Understanding the context.' *British Journal of Learning Disabilities 28*, 38–43.

Cotterell, P. (2008) 'Exploring the value of service user involvement in data analysis: "Our interpretation is about what lies below the surface."' *Educational Action Research 16*, 1, 5–17.

Dominelli, L. (2002) *Anti-oppressive Social Work Theory and Practice.* Basingstoke: Palgrave Macmillan.

Dyson, S. and Brown, B. (2006) *Social Theory and Applied Health Research.* Berkshire: Open University.

Fleming, J. (2012) 'Service User Involvement: What It Is and What It Could Be: Lessons from the Standards We Expect Project.' In P. Beresford and S. Carr (eds) *Social Care, Service Users and User Involvement.* London: Jessica Kingsley Publishers.

Groenewald, T. (2004) 'A phenomenological research design illustrated.' *International Journal of Qualitative Methods 3*, 1, 1–26.

Hoopmann, K. (2013) *Inside Asperger's Looking Out.* London: Jessica Kingsley Publishers.

Kindon, S., Pain, R. and Kesby, M. (eds) (2007) *Participatory Action Research Approaches and Methods: Connecting People, Participation and Place.* Abingdon: Routledge.

Lukes, S. (2005) *Power: A Radical View* (2nd edition). Basingstoke: Palgrave.

MacLeod, A., Lewis, A. and Robertson, C. (2013) '"CHARLIE: PLEASE RESPOND!" Using a participatory methodology with individuals on the autistic spectrum.' *International Journal of Research and Method,* DOI: 10.1080/1743727X.2013.776528.

Martin, J., Fox, K., MacGregor, D. and Hickman, L. (2014) 'People with Asperger's syndrome lead the way in how to work in a group.' *Groupwork 24*, 2, 63–79.

Mason, J. (2002) *Qualitative Researching* (2nd edition). London: Sage Publications Ltd.

Miller, J. (2003) *Women from Another Planet: Our Lives in the Universe of Autism.* Bloomington, IN: 1st Books Library.

Nind, M. (2014) *What is Inclusive Research?* London: Bloomsbury.

Oliver, M. (1992) 'Changing the social relations of research production?' *Disability, Handicap and Society 7*, 2, 101–114.

Oliver, M, (2009) *Understanding Disability: From Theory to Practice.* London: Palgrave Macmillan.

O'Neill, J. (1999) *Through the Eyes of Aliens: A Book about Autistic People.* London: Jessica Kingsley Publishers.

Robinson, J. (2015) *Participatory Research with Adults with Asperger's Syndrome: Using Spatial Analysis to Explore How They Make Sense of Their Experience* (unpublished doctoral dissertation). Leicester: De Montfort University.

Sainsbury, C. (2009) *Martian in the Playground: Understanding the Schoolchild with Asperger's Syndrome.* London: Sage.

Smith, R. (2008) *Social Work and Power.* Basingstoke: Palgrave Macmillan.

Stevenson, M. (2013) 'Participatory data analysis alongside co-researchers who have Down's syndrome.' *Journal of Applied Research in Intellectual Disabilities 27*, 1, 23–33.

Walmsley, J. and Johnson, K. (1998) *Inclusive Research with People with Learning Disabilities.* London: Jessica Kingsley Publishers.

Wing, L. (1991) 'The Relationship between Asperger's Syndrome and Kanner's Autism.' In Frith, U. (ed.) *Autism and Asperger Syndrome.* Cambridge: Cambridge University Press.

Zarb, G. (1992) 'On the road to Damascus: First steps towards changing the relations of disability research production.' *Disability, Handicap and Society 7*, 2, 125–138.

Chapter 15

QUANTITATIVE RESEARCH AND THE SECONDARY ANALYSIS OF LONGITUDINAL DATA IN SOCIAL WORK RESEARCH

MARTIN ELLIOTT
Cardiff University

This study investigated whether there is a statistically significant relationship between the presence of certain socio-economic factors within a household and child welfare concerns (Elliott, 2013). The hypothesis being tested, that such a link exists, is one drawn from an evidence base derived primarily from US literature. The intention within the study was to test that hypothesis within a UK population. Using the third wave of the British Cohort Study 1970, a quantitative analysis of this secondary dataset was undertaken using binary logistic regression. The British Cohort Study 1970 is a large-scale longitudinal study following a cohort of babies born in one week in April 1970 (n=16,500). Wave three of the study was undertaken in 1986 and is referred to as the '16-year follow-up'. In undertaking this wave of the study the primary researchers were able to trace 11,615 young people of the 16,500 children and their families recruited to the study at birth, who agreed to take part in this phase of the study. All the variables used within this analysis were derived from data collected from the Parental Interview (British Cohort Study (BCS), 1970). Information included data on the child's environment, health, family finances, accommodation and neighbourhood.

In this study the outcome variable, contact with a statutory social worker, has been used as a proxy measure for child welfare concerns. Within their study of the impact of adverse childhood experiences on adult service use, McGavock and Spratt (2012) suggest that 'social services contact, alone, acts as a proxy indicator for the presence of multiple adverse childhood experiences' (p.1) and it was this that was settled upon as a suitable outcome measure for use within this study. The legal framework within which statutory social work services are provided means that those included within this measure would encompass those with additional support needs, such as disabled children and their families, those who have been subject to child protection procedures and children who have spent periods of time on public care thus providing a defined framework. In addition, the choice of outcome variable was also in part to overcome the definitional issues around what constitutes child abuse or maltreatment identified within previous studies (Gambrill and Shlonsky, 2000; Wald and Woolverton, 1990).

The study tested whether there was a statistically significant relationship between various risk factors – household income level when the children participating in the study were five years of age; the absence or presence of birth parents, also at five years of age; poor housing; and the sex of the child – and those same children having contact with statutory social work services between the ages of 10 and 16 years. These 'predictor' variables were identified based on the literature review undertaken to inform the study, those chosen being the ones that were most frequently identified in the findings of the studies identified. The studies, whilst all seeking to explore the nature of risk factors in relation to child welfare, are heterogeneous in the ways in which they have sought to explore this concept. Many have sought to identify those factors correlated to specific forms of child maltreatment, such as physical abuse (Finkelhor *et al.*, 1997; Wolfner and Gelles, 1993) or sexual abuse (Bergner, Delgado and Graybill 1994; Boney-McCoy and Finkelhor, 1995; Finkelhor, 1980) whilst others have looked more widely at child welfare and abuse (Chaffin, Kelleher and Hollenberg, 1996; Greenland, cited in Corby, 2006; Sedlak, 1997; Sidebotham and Golding, 2001). A further group of studies are those that have sought to consider risk factors in relation to use or involvement with services or systems such as child protection (Bywaters, 2013; Gordon and Gibbons, 1998; Winter and Connolly, 2005) or placement in public care (Bebbington and Miles, 1989; Bywater, 2013). It is perhaps this latter group of studies, along with those that have looked more broadly at child maltreatment risk factors (Chaffin and Valle, 2003; Greenland, cited in Corby, 2006; Sedlak, 1997; Sidebotham and Golding, 2001) with which this study is most closely aligned given its focus on possible correlations between socio-economic factors and contact with social work services rather than particular forms of child maltreatment or additional support needs that may of themselves necessitate contact with a social worker.

The most striking results provided by the data relate to the statistically significant relationship between family income and contact with a social worker. With regards to those households within the lowest family income band, the study has identified that the children within these households are almost 14 times more likely to be in contact with a social worker than children living in households with the highest level of joint income after controlling for other variables included in the model. The data also appears to demonstrate a negative correlation between income and contact with a social worker. As levels of income increase there is an incremental decrease in the likelihood of contact with a social worker. The correlation between low income and contact with statutory social work services identified reflects the key finding of Sedlak (1997) who stated that children in households with an income of less than $15,000 were at far greater risk of all the categories of child maltreatment used within the study. Similarly, these findings support those of Finkelhor (1980) whose findings identified low income levels (in the Finkelhor study less than $10,000) as a significant 'risk' factor albeit in specific relation to the likelihood of the sexual abuse of girls.

The results from the regression model also show statistically significant results between the absence of either both natural parents or one natural parent at age five and contact with a social worker between the ages of 10 and 16 years after controlling for other variables included in the model. With regard to the absence of both natural parents the model predicts that children are over 3.5 times more likely to have contact with a social worker between the ages of 10 and 16 years than those children living in households with both natural parents at age five. However, children living with neither natural parent at five years of age are likely to be explained it could be argued, in some of these cases, by those children being in some form of public care, such as foster placements or residential care, or having been adopted. Based on this explanation the correlation identified between the absence of birth parents and contact with a social worker would appear to be unsurprising. Potentially of more interest is the identified relationship between children living in households with one natural parent at age five and contact with statutory social work services. The study has identified that the odds of a child in a single birth parent household having contact with a social worker are twice that of a child living with both birth parents at the same age. This finding is similar to that of Boney-McCoy and Finkelhor (1995) who suggested that children living with only one parent were just over twice (2.2) as likely to be at risk of sexual victimisation. However, it is not reflective of the significantly increased odds highlighted in the study by Bebbington and Miles (1989). In considering the family backgrounds of children entering public care Bebbington and Miles (1989) found that children from single parent families were eight times more likely to enter care than those living in two-parent families. What has not been explored within this study and warrants further investigation is the effect of reconstituted families and step-parents within these cases.

With regard to the sex of the child the results indicate a statistically significant relationship between this variable and contact with a social worker. The regression model suggests that boys are 36 per cent more likely to have contact with a social worker than girls at the same age after controlling for other variables included in the model. This finding is contrary to those of Gordon and Gibbons (1998) who in their study of children being placed on the child protection register suggested that a child was more likely to be the subject of an initial child protection case conference if they were a girl. The finding does however concur with those of Wolfner and Gelles (1993) whose study suggested that being a boy placed a child in the high-risk checklist of variables in terms of being a victim of physical abuse.

One predictor variable that was found to not be statistically significant within the analysis of this study was that of overcrowding. Unlike a number of previous studies (Bebbington and Miles, 1989; Chaffin and Valle, 2003; Franzen, Vinnerljung and Hjern, 2008; Taitz *et al.*, 1987), this study found no statistically significant link between 'overcrowding', as it was defined and operationalised within this study and contact with a social worker between the ages of 10 and 16 years.

It would clearly be simplistic and ill advised to draw inferences of direct causal relationships between factors identified by this study such as low household income and the likelihood of contact with statutory services such as social work. What needs to be explored is the potential presence and effect of other, unmeasured, mediating factors. For example, Gordon and Gibbons (1998) suggest that the poorest families might be more visible to community agents, increasing their chances of referral and it is this level of additional surveillance that could potentially act as a mediating factor between low income and involvement with statutory social services. Similarly, Bebbington and Miles (1989) who suggest that the findings of their work should be seen as associative and not indicative of direct causal relationships, when looking at the relationship between single parent families and entry into public care and suggest a number of explanations for this correlation. One such explanation is that single parents lack not just a partner but also a social support network that enables them 'to cope during times of adversity, and in general with the tensions of raising a family' (Bebbington and Miles, 1989, p.365).

Key innovative elements

The study outlined within this chapter was undertaken using logistic regression as the method of data analysis. As such, arguably this study is unremarkable. The use of logistic regression and other forms of multivariate analysis within research undertaken across a wide range of disciplines is fairly common. That said, within the social sciences it has been identified that there is a paucity of quantitative research being undertaken, arguably linked in no small part to a lack of quantitative skills amongst social scientists. This lack of quantitative skills was most clearly articulated in recent years in the position statement *Society Counts* (British Academy, 2012), which raised deep concerns that 'the UK is weak in quantitative skills, in particular but not exclusively in the social sciences and humanities' (p.1). Acknowledgement of this lack of quantitative skills has led to a range of initiatives being implemented to attempt to redress this balance.

When the field of social work research in the UK is focused upon, this wider situation is reflected just as strongly. In the 2001 Research Assessment Exercise (RAE) it was highlighted that 'quantitative work, while sometimes of very high quality is rare and not always good when found' (Higher Education Funding Council for England (HEFCE), 2001, p.4). By the 2008 report, whilst there were some improvements noted in regard to quality, the low volume of quantitative research in social work was still highlighted (RAE, 2008). Further evidence of the relative dearth of quantitative research in social work is provided by McCambridge *et al.* (2007). In a study exploring the use of quantitative methods in papers published in the *British Journal of Social Work* during a five-year period, the researchers found that of the 262 papers or research notes analysed, less than a quarter used an element of quantitative analysis. Of the 67 papers categorised as having used quantitative or combined quantitative/qualitative analyse, less than a third used multivariate analysis, such as the logistic regression undertaken in the example outlined within this chapter. In the five-year period studied therefore, less than eight per cent of the total number of studies published in this journal utilised multivariate analysis. Furthermore, UK-only studies were found to be more likely to use only descriptive statistics and 'less likely to use bivariate or multivariate analyses than studies conducted entirely or in part in other countries' (McCambridge *et al.*, 2007, p.267). This relatively limited use of quantitative analysis in the UK within the context of social work research is in stark contrast to research undertaken in the US, where arguably it provides a significant proportion of research evidence for the field of social work. This fact provided one of the focuses for the research undertaken and its aim of testing research findings from US-based research within a UK population.

The issues highlighted regarding quantitative analysis skills amongst social work researchers have, I would argue, a knock-on effect for the use of certain types of often readily available data. As Maxwell *et al.* (2012) highlighted there are a range of large-scale, non-social-work-specific, longitudinal studies that are readily available within the UK that include information regarding children, young people and their families and their use of social work and social care services. Arguably the lack of exploration of the research opportunities provided by these data could be attributed to both a lack of awareness of such datasets and the social work information they contain, and a lack of sufficient social work researchers with the quantitative skills necessary to make best use of the opportunities that they provide. That is not to say that there are no researchers making use of this type of data. In fields such as adoption research, studies such as that undertaken by Wijedasa and Selwyn (2011) have used secondary analysis of longitudinal data. In this example, analysis of the Longitudinal Study of Young People in England (LSYPE) was used to explore outcomes for children and young adults who have been adopted relative to their non-adopted peers. Similarly, longitudinal data from studies such as the ALSPAC study undertaken in Bristol, whilst derived from a study with a predominantly health focus, has been analysed using quantitative methods to explore the socio-economic backgrounds of families who come into contact with statutory services (Sidebotham and Golding, 2001).

The intention in highlighting and discussing these issues is not to privilege one ontological or epistemological standpoint over another. The range of ontological and epistemological standpoints and their attendant quantitative and qualitative approaches all have a role to play in providing insights into the social world. What I would argue however is that perhaps some of those insights provided by the analysis of quantitative data are currently under-utilised within the context of UK social work research.

Strengths and challenges

The methodological strengths and challenges that are presented by studies undertaking this type of quantitative analysis can be broadly broken down into three areas: those relating to using longitudinal data; issues around using secondary data; and factors that influence the analysis of data and interpretation of findings from such studies.

Longitudinal studies are very resource intensive and expensive to run. Few social work researchers will have access to the resources necessary to undertake primary research collecting data from a representative sample of children, young people and their families, particularly at a country level. However, this is exactly what secondary analysis of available longitudinal datasets, such as the example provided, potentially gives the social work researcher. These studies give researchers at all levels of their academic careers access to large-scale, robust and academically well-recognised representative samples. Maxwell *et al.* (2012) highlighted a number of existing UK panel studies that included information of interest to social work researchers. The British Cohort Study 1970 was one of the examples highlighted, but others included the Longitudinal Study of Young People in England (LSYPE), the Millennium Cohort Study, the Growing Up in Scotland Study and the British Household Panel Study. Each of these datasets provides researchers with detailed information on between 10,000 and 20,000 individuals. In the case of the British Cohort Study 1970 it provides access to data collected across eight 'sweeps' of all cohort members between 5 and 42 years of age. The data is often accompanied by extensive documentation, explaining data collection procedures and other technical information relating to the study, has been cleaned and is available in a readily usable electronic format.

However, as with all aspects of research design there are trade-offs. In seeking to use longitudinal data within research the issue of attrition, 'the drop out of participants through successive waves of a prospective study' (Alasuutari, Bickman and Brannen, 2008, p.235) is a perennial one and that needs consideration, particularly with respect to drawing conclusions from the findings of a study. In the example used of the British Cohort Study 1970, the primary researchers recruited 16,500 participants and their families at birth. By the time these participants had reached 16 years of age the number of participants had dropped to 11,632, a drop-out rate of 27.3 per cent. One of the issues this raises is that it is clearly not possible to establish the reasons for this level of drop out or whether there was contact with social work services by individuals within those households that ceased involvement in the study. What this introduces is the issue of non-response bias to any consideration of a study's findings. In the case of this study, consideration was given to exploring the socio-economic backgrounds of those participants that dropped out from the study in order to attempt to assess the impact of attrition on the study's findings. The birth wave data held no comparable income data to that used in this study and the only possible comparator that could be used was the social class of fathers, which was felt not to be a usable measure. The impact of attrition on the study's findings remains therefore, largely unknown.

The issue touched upon above, of what information is available within the data being used, provides a starting point for discussion of factors associated with undertaking secondary analysis of data, which need to be considered and managed within this type of research. One of the ever-present tensions of undertaking analysis of secondary data is one that is inherent in the nature of such data, which is that it was collected by someone else. The data was not collected with the questions that the researcher undertaking the secondary analysis has in mind. Information that may be seen as central by a secondary researcher to exploring the research questions they are seeking to answer may not have been collected. Related to this issue, within the original research, concepts may have been framed and operationalised differently to how the researcher undertaking the secondary analysis would seek to use them and as a consequence variables within the data may be defined or categorised differently. Recoding and other approaches may enable the researcher to address some of these issues, but in some instances it may result in the secondary researcher not being able to analyse the data in the ways in which they would have liked or indeed answer certain research questions at all. As a result, compromises have to be made. An example of such a compromise and the issues inherent in secondary analysis is provided by the predictor variable used within the example study to represent household overcrowding. Within the data available the variable 'How many other people share the same bedroom as the study teenager' was identified as a potential proxy for overcrowding and/or poor housing conditions. The identification of this variable was based on a decision to use the Bedroom Standard as an appropriate measure of overcrowding. As stated by Shelter, 'this measure has been used in Government and social research since the 1960s and is widely accepted as the "bare minimum" a family requires' (Shelter, 2005, p.38). It was therefore felt that this was an appropriately robust measure, which is well defined, academically recognised and easily replicated.

The Bedroom Standard states that the following should have one bedroom:

> Married or cohabiting couples; Single people more than 21 years old; Pairs of children under 10 years old, regardless of gender; Pairs of children aged 10 to 21 years old of the same gender. Any unpaired person aged 10 to 20 is then paired if possible, with a child under 10 of the same sex (if that is not possible, he or she is counted as requiring a separate bedroom, as is any unpaired child). (Shelter, 2005, p.38)

Bedroom sharing outside of these definitions would therefore constitute 'overcrowding'.

Whilst the use of this measurement of overcrowding makes sense for a number of reasons its use within the context of the secondary analysis undertaken was not without its issues. The research team undertaking the primary research has clearly collected data on whether the young person is sharing their bedroom with someone else. The age of the young person taking part in the study is known, as all survey participants were 16 years old at the time the data used was collected. However, as collected, the data does not allow the age of the person(s) sharing with the teenager to be established. Under the Bedroom Standard, decisions on whether bedroom sharing would constitute overcrowding, is dependent to an extent on knowing additional information such as the age and gender, which is not available within the data. In applying the Bedroom Standard to the data, if the teenager was sharing with only one person, but that person was over 21 years of age that would be considered overcrowding. The lack of age data, which if the study was undertaken as primary research would have been seen as important information and collected, means that some cases will be inaccurately coded, which introduces issues of construct validity.

The study has used data from a wave of a well-established and academically well-recognised longitudinal study providing robust data. However, the use of the dataset chosen also brings with it limitations and these are acknowledged. The data is clearly now quite old, with the wave of the study used for this research having been collected in 1986. It could be argued that data from a more contemporary longitudinal study, for example the Millennium Cohort Study, would have been more appropriate. The rationale for using the British Cohort Study was based on a number of factors. The most recent publicly available data from the Millennium Cohort Study at the time this analysis was undertaken was that from the fourth survey, collected in 2008. Whilst more recent, this dataset would not have allowed the type of consideration of risk factors over time that have been afforded by the British Cohort Study data, given that the children were only eight years of age at the time of collection. That said, it is acknowledged that because of the age of the data used, in terms of looking at a phenomena such as use of statutory social services, the legislative and societal landscape has clearly changed in the intervening years. The clearest example of this is provided by the Children Act 1989, which has had a fundamental impact on the way child welfare is legally defined and responded to by statutory services. There is clearly therefore an element of caution required in translating the study's findings to the present.

One of the strengths of the approach outlined within this chapter is that the research has a good level of internal reliability. The research design and tests used within the study, as described in full in Elliott (2013), have been described in detail, including for example, how a concept such as 'overcrowding' has been defined and operationalised within the study. The level of explanatory detail associated with this type of analysis enables repeated administrations by others of the tests performed on the data to replicate the same results.

The final methodological area to be explored in terms of the challenges and considerations associated with this type of research is factors that influence the analysis of data and the interpretation of findings derived from such studies. When drawing conclusions from the findings of this study and others of its type, it is necessary to be careful to avoid falling into the trap of 'ecological fallacy' with regard to the generalisability of the relationships identified by the analysis. As Sayer (1992) suggests, the researcher needs to avoid the tendency to draw spurious inferences about the characteristics of individuals from group level characteristics. For example, the significant result with regard to low income families within this study clearly does not indicate that all low income households are affected by child welfare issues that require contact with statutory services or that those households with higher joint income levels are not. There are clearly considerable practical, moral and ethical issues with any attempt to apply simplistically the results of such predictive models, which need to be guarded against, given this potential for high levels of false positive and false negative cases when applying such predictors to populations (Corby, 2005).

A further interpretational consideration when reflecting on findings such as those of the study outlined here is the nature of odds ratios, as produced by this type of analysis, versus absolute risk. The study's findings clearly indicated that children living with one birth parent at age five are at a greater 'risk' of coming into contact with a social worker between the ages of 10 and 16 than those living with both birth parents. Single birth parent families also proportionally represent the biggest group having contact with a social worker. Of the 812 families where the child was living with one birth parent at the age of five included in the model, 83 had contact with a social worker, representing 11 per cent of families in this category. In contrast, 287 families where the child was living with both parents at age five had contact with a social worker out of the 8092 such families included in the model, representing only 3 per cent. However, what these figures also demonstrate is that whilst children living in households with one natural birth parent are in the 'higher' risk category and are proportionally the biggest group, in absolute terms those children living with both natural parents are still the largest group experiencing the outcome overall. This clearly raises interesting questions regarding not only how study results are interpreted but also how those findings are used to inform practice. For example, the efficacy of policy and practice approaches that target risk factors alone and that may therefore prove ineffective for the majority of cases at 'risk' of being affected by a particular outcome.

References

Alasuutari, P., Bickman, L. and Brannen, J. (eds) (2008) *The Sage Handbook of Social Research Methods*. London: Sage.

Bebbington, A. and Miles, J. (1989) 'The background of children who enter local authority care.' *British Journal of Social Work 19*, 349–368.

Bergner, R., Delgado, L. and Graybill, D. (1994) 'Finkelhor's risk factor checklist: A cross validation study.' *Child Abuse and Neglect 18*, 4, 331–340.

Boney-McCoy, S. and Finkelhor, D. (1995) 'Prior victimisation: A risk factor for child sexual abuse and for PTSD-related symptomatology among sexually abused youth.' *Child Abuse and Neglect 19*, 1401–1421.

British Academy (2012) *Society Counts: A Position Statement*. London: British Academy. Available at www.britac.ac.uk/policy/Society_Counts.cfm, accessed on 9 April 2015.

British Cohort Study (BCS) (1970) 1970 British Cohort Study: Sixteen-Year Follow-Up – Parental Interview (Document O), 1986. Colchester, Essex: UK Data Archive. Available at http://discover.ukdataservice.ac.uk/catalogue/?sn=3535&type=Data%20catalogue, accessed on 9 April 2015.

Bywaters, P. (2013) 'Inequalities in child welfare: Towards a new policy, research and action agenda.' *British Journal of Social Work,* DOI: 10.1093/bjsw/bct079.

Chaffin, M. and Valle, L. A. (2003) 'Dynamic prediction characteristics of the child abuse potential inventory.' *Child Abuse and Neglect 27*, 463–481.

Chaffin, M., Kelleher, K., and Hollenberg, J. (1996) 'Onset of physical abuse and neglect: Psychiatric, substance misuse and social risk factors from prospective community data.' *Child Abuse and Neglect 20*, 3, 191–203.

Corby, B. (2005) 'Risk Assessment in Child Protection Work.' In K. Kemshall (ed.) (2005) *Good Practice in Risk Assessment and Risk Management 1*. London: Jessica Kingsley Publishers.

Corby, B. (2006) *Child Abuse: Towards a Knowledge Base* (3rd edition). Maidenhead. Open University Press.

Elliott, M. (2013) *The Social Determinants of Child Welfare: An Analysis of the BRITISH Cohort Study 1970* (MSc dissertation). Cardiff: Cardiff University.

Finkelhor, D. (1980) 'Risk factors in the sexual victimisation of children.' *Child Abuse and Neglect 4*, 4, 265–273.

Finkelhor, D., Moore, D., Hamby, S. L., and Straus, M. A. (1997) 'Sexually abused children in a national survey of parents: Methodological issues.' *Child Abuse and Neglect. 21*, 1–9.

Franzen, E., Vinnerljung, B. and Hjern, A. (2008) 'The epidemiology of out-of-home care for children and youth: A national cohort study.' *British Journal of Social Work 38*, 1043–1059.

Gambrill, E. and Shlonsky, A. (2000) 'Risk assessment in context.' *Children and Youth Services Review 22*, 11/12, 813–837.

Gordon, D. and Gibbons, J. (1998) 'Placing children on child protection registers: Risk indicators and local authority differences.' *British Journal of Social Work 28*, 423–436.

Higher Education Funding Council for England (HEFCE) (2001) Overview Report on Social Work: Research Assessment Exercise 2001. Bristol: HEFCE. Available at www.rae.ac.uk/2001/overview/docs/UoA41.pdf, accessed on 8 July 2015.

Maxwell, N., Scourfield, J., Gould, N. and Huxley, P. (2012) 'UK panel data on social work service users.' *British Journal of Social Work 42*, 165–184.

McCambridge, J., Waissbein, C., Forrester, D. and Strang, J. (2007) 'What is the extent and nature of quantitative research in British social work?' *International Social Work 50*, 2, 265–271.

McGavock, L. and Spratt, T. (2012) 'Prevalence of adverse childhood experiences in a university population: Associations with use of social services.' *British Journal of Social Work, 1–18.*

RAE (2008) *UOA 40 Subject Overview Report.* Bristol: RAE Team. Available at www.rae.ac.uk/pubs/2009/ov, accessed on 9 April 2015.

Sayer, A. (1992) *Methods in Social Science: A Realistic Approach* (2nd edition). London: Routledge.

Sedlak, A. J. (1997) 'Risk factors for the occurrence of child abuse and neglect.' *Journal of Aggression, Maltreatment, Trauma 1*, 149–187.

Shelter (2005) *Full House: How Overcrowding Affects Families.* London: Shelter. Available at http://england.shelter.org.uk/__data/assets/pdf_file/0004/39532/Full_house_overcrowding_effects.pdf, accessed on 9 April 2015.

Sidebotham, P. and Golding, J. (2001) 'Child maltreatment in the "children of the nineties" a longitudinal study of parental risk factors.' *Child Abuse and Neglect 2*, 9, 1177–2000.

Taitz, L. S., King, J. M., Nicholson, J. and Kessel, M. (1987) 'Unemployment and child abuse.' *British Medical Journal 294*, 1074–1076.

Wald, M. and Woolverton, M. (1990) 'Risk assessment: The emperor's new clothes?' *Child Welfare 69*, 483–511.

Wijedasa, D. and Selwyn, J. (2011) *Transition to Adulthood For Young People in Adoptive Care.* Bristol: Hadley Centre for Adoption and Foster Care Studies. Available at www.bristol.ac.uk/sps/research/centres/hadley/research/transitiontoadulthood.pdf, accessed on 9 April 2015.

Winter, K. and Connolly, P. (2005) 'A small scale study of the relationship between measures of deprivation and child-care referrals.' *British Journal of Social Work 35*, 937–952.

Wolfner, G. D. and Gelles, R. J. (1993) 'A profile of violence toward children: A national study.' *Child Abuse and Neglect 17*, 197–212.

Section 4

INNOVATIONS IN DISSEMINATION AND IMPACT

Chapter 16

PARTICIPATORY ACTION RESEARCH

Empowering Women to Evaluate Services

LENA DOMINELLI
Durham University

Introduction

Women's services have become important vehicles for empowering women. Assessing the benefits of such interventions is important for funders and policy makers wishing to ensure money is spent wisely and women benefit from these expenditures. Evaluating services raises questions about who will undertake the evaluation; who will be involved in it; how it will be conducted; and how the results will be used. The values of the evaluator or researcher will impact on the answers to these questions and determine whether an expert, top-down approach or a grassroots one utilising local and/or indigenous knowledges is practised. Those aiming to empower residents or service users have focused on engaging them collectively in the research process to collect data that will help solve problems they have identified and in ways that are acceptable to them. This occurs through an empowerment process that has been termed the co-production of knowledge.

Participatory action research (PAR) is a qualitative methodology for involving people in doing research and is used in collaborative ventures that co-create evidence-based knowledges and solutions. For women working with women, Feminist Participatory Action Research (FPAR) draws upon the tenets of PAR and illuminates the way forward in doing research involving women as service users and/or residents. FPAR emphasises qualitative and interpretive methods that highlight subjectivity and meaning. Its stance challenges mainstream positivist approaches that are heavily quantitative and treat participants in research processes as objects rather than subjects (Belenky *et al.*, 1998;

McIntyre, 2008). Positivists assume that participants hold little knowledge or information of value to strict scientific approaches that glorify objectivity, quantitative methods and measurement. They also deny the role of human agency in creating, interpreting and using knowledge.

In this chapter, I consider PAR and its use in participatory evaluation by focusing on a project entitled Affirming Women Project (AWP), which evaluated services for women in a voluntary agency in England, using FPAR, to involve and empower marginalised women in research processes to evaluate the services they used, and disseminate the recommendations they have for improvements.

The key tenets of Participatory Action Research

Kurt Lewin (1946, 1948) is credited with devising Participatory Action Research and engaging people in resolving social problems. There is no universally shared definition of PAR, nor of the processes integral to it (Cullen and Coryn, 2011). However, I have distilled a diverse literature on the subject to highlight areas of commonality centring on collaborative participation for the purpose of taking action that enhances the lives and livelihoods of marginalised groups. One of PAR's key tenets is the integration of reflection and action in the co-production of knowledge and solutions to problems. It adopts an action-based method whereby research is conducted as collaboratively as possible and respects those participating in the research as subjects. The emphasis on collaboration and participation has popularised PAR among critical theorists, practitioners committed to empowering reflective practice and social movement activists. Chevalier and Buckles (2013) expand this idea by postulating that PAR involves participation, action and research to generate new knowledge. Or, as Reason and Bradbury (2008, p.1) put it, PAR involves 'communities of inquiry and action [to] evolve and address questions and issues that are significant for those who participate as co-researchers'. Cousins and Whitmore (1998) argue that PAR used to evaluate services should be termed participatory evaluation and encompass questions about: who controls the evaluation process; which stakeholders are invited to participate; and the depth of stakeholder participation.

PAR involves 'members from 'the affected communities in all stages of the research including research design, implementation, analysis and dissemination of findings' (Sullivan *et al.*, 2005, p.978). In practice, participation varies at different points in the research process because participants determine their willingness to participate in each stage of the process, and researchers are obliged to respect their preferences as occurred in this study (William and Lykes, 2003).

PAR encourages participants to reflect upon their experiences and situations and acquire a critical understanding of these as articulated by Paulo Freire (1972) in critical pedagogy. This can result in new self-created learning among participants. Kemmis (2001, p.92) describes how PAR can create a critical consciousness that helps participants to 'develop a critical and self-reflective understanding of their situation'.

PAR was deemed relevant to the women in the AWP because it ensured that the evaluation was not 'something done "on" or "to" them' (Kemmis, 2001, p.90). PAR seeks a more empowering approach that shares control of research processes with individuals, groups and communities participating in these (Joyappa and Martin, 1996). The evaluators emphasise reciprocity, dialogue, collaboration and the co-creation of knowledge between researchers and research participants (Gannon, 2013; Gatenby and Humphreys, 2000; Genat, 2009).

PAR researchers encourage participants to ask questions important to them and propose solutions for improving their services. This combination of reflection and action provides a process of 'reflection and action upon the world so as to transform it' (Freire, 1972, p.51). Critical thinking also becomes an 'action' in itself (Crotty, 1998). An open discussion around 'shared topical concerns, problems and issues' leads to 'mutual understanding and consensus' (Kemmis, 2001, p.100), enabling collaborative action to be undertaken while knowledge production yields 'knowledge that will be used to solve problems identified by both researchers of programs and the people who participate in them' (Penuel and Freeman, 1997, p.176). However, implementing major recommendations is funding and resource dependent. This highlights a flaw of PAR because not securing the necessary resources can raise expectations that cannot be met. Yet, participatory evaluation can give voice to women's experiences and reveal women's resilience and positive life changes, which may be personally transformative and life enhancing. Transforming adverse socio-economic and environmental or structural challenges remains difficult for PAR to achieve (Dominelli, 2005).

Feminist Participatory Action Research (FPAR)

Feminist Participatory Action Research (FPAR) was specifically developed to empower women. FPAR combines critical feminism and PAR to facilitate a critical understanding of women's multiple experiences and perspectives, and work towards women's inclusion, participation and action (Langan and Morton, 2009). PAR had traditionally treated the social world as 'gender neutral' (Gatenby and Humphries, 2000, p.90) until feminists queried this state of affairs. There remain similarities between PAR and feminist approaches. Gouin *et al.* (2011, p.265) argue that the commonalities between feminist research and participatory approaches cover values and theory, and emphasise emancipation, participation and knowledge for political action (Gatenby and Humphries, 2000). Both PAR and FPAR include 'an explicit focus on learning, transformation and action' (Gouin *et al.*, 2011, p.265). Other characteristics that they share are:

- viewing individuals and groups as active subjects
- offering alternative forms of research
- sharing control of research processes with participants
- giving voice to marginalised groups and their experiences. Women-centred feminist evaluation focuses on women's varied experiences, multiple voices and the meanings given to patriarchal oppression (Genat, 2009)
- acknowledging that marginalised groups are socially situated and better able to express their lived experiences and ask questions than non-marginalised groups
- emphasising experience and consciousness-raising. This approach becomes 'political' in that it exposes power relations and challenges existing social structures and orders (Gavey and McPhillips, 1999)
- being 'empowerment-orientated' to enable individuals and communities to initiate action that results in social change.

Crucially, PAR-informed evaluations are concerned with action – producing knowledge that can be used to improve practices or organisations (Whyte, 1989) and transform situations. The insights of PAR and feminist theory underpinned the evaluation processes in the AWP.

Woman participants take control

Valuing women

A participative methodology places participants in charge of the research process wherever possible. Achieving this requires relationships of trust and collaboration between groups with diverse concerns, varying social positions and power, and different responsibilities involving a range of stakeholders with an interest in the research. Valuing women's strengths and potential contributions facilitate building rapport and trust. In the AWP, women assumed control of research processes, participated in each research stage, and chose what to do. Additionally, the evaluation encompassed multiple stakeholders to cover several objectives set by service providers around the 'value and impact of their work' and identifying 'learning opportunities'. Key questions that the evaluation addressed included the following:

1. What is being delivered and how? Who attends the services?

2. Has the project achieved the aims and anticipated outcomes for women service users? These outcomes covered:

    a) improved *emotional* well-being, for example building self-esteem, confidence, raising aspirations and motivation

    b) increased *life opportunities*, including encouraging progression into education, training or employment and accessing housing

    c) developing *skills* including social skills and creative skills

    d) improved *awareness and knowledge* about domestic violence, other issues pertinent to women's lives and existing support services

    e) *self-expression* of needs and experiences, providing opportunities for mutual support and sharing experiences in a group context

    f) creation of *strategic networking* for organisations and groups providing services for women in the city, including the provision of training events, raising awareness of gender violence and participation in activism campaigns

    g) the establishment of *informal support networks* for and by women.

3. What value do the people receiving services place on them? What value do the professional workers place on the services offered? How satisfied are service users and professional workers with these services?

4. What is the impact of these services on the lives of women and girls in relation to anticipated project outcomes?

5. What are the implications of the findings for improving services?

These questions were developed and clarified through the participation of women service users, involvement of professional workers, visits to individual groups and discussions with individual women and staff members. These deliberations suggested adding further people to the sample.

Research processes

In the first stage, a 'research group' was formed among women who attended groups/sought services and wished to engage in the evaluation. A professional worker and neighbourhood manager facilitated the initial meetings by approaching women prior to researcher involvement. The two researchers both had social work experience and were sensitive to the women's needs, which could include multiple problems and low research confidence (O'Connell, 2003). 'Vulnerability' was not assumed, because these women participated in groups that emphasised strengths. However, the issue of possible vulnerability existed.

In the introductory meeting, women, staff and researchers heard narratives about the women's groups and services offered. The researchers explained their commitment to: engage women fully in the research; hear their experiences and opinions of the services received; gain women's views on changes they would like; and make recommendations for achieving these. The researchers also emphasised that they had 'not come to tell the women what to do and how to do it' (King *et al.*, 1999). The women would define the research topic, the research processes and which individuals to engage and how.

The researchers conveyed the message that involvement in the evaluation was an opportunity for women to participate at all levels of the research, including design, research methods, conducting the research, analysis and dissemination. They stressed that levels of participation were a choice for the women to make individually and/or collectively (Sullivan, 2005). A conversation about women enjoying being creative in producing leaflets and posters developed into a mutual decision for the women to produce posters about their services for the next research group meeting. These were to explore the concept of 'evaluation' by presenting women's opinions (positive and negative) of the services offered.

In their interactions, researchers and participants followed the dialogical method in which both groups are 'simultaneously teachers and students' or 'equally knowing subjects' (Freire, 1972, p.72). This developed an atmosphere that facilitated dialogue between the women and researchers as part of data collection, and is central to participatory evaluation.

Women felt more comfortable in their own groups, so these, rather than a central 'research group' provided the settings for the evaluation that engaged them as co-participants in designing and conducting it. Professional workers in each women's group conducted a session where they introduced the concept of 'evaluation' and enabled women to understand what the research was about, and begin to think about research questions, including overarching questions and sub-questions, that they wanted to ask. Involving participants in setting research questions is integral to participatory methodological approaches that recognise that those affected – individuals and/or communities – are 'experts' of their own experiences and cognisant of 'local contexts, needs and understandings' (Gannon, 2013, p.343). This approach enriched the experiential data collected.

The women were also asked whom they wanted to involve as research participants and 'how they wanted to ask the questions', thereby contributing to the research methods. The women decided that research participants should include women who attended the groups; staff members; those not currently attending groups, but using services; and agencies that referred women to these groups. The professional workers helpfully produced a written summary of the session for the researchers who then collated the women's feedback. Draft interview schedules that incorporated the women's questions were written down and shared with them for further discussion, making the AWP a qualitative participative study involving women service users. The agency was separately collecting quantitative data about the numbers of women using services.

The interview schedules incorporated questions that encouraged critical reflection by enabling women to share experiences and opinions.

For example, following collective discussions about domestic violence, disadvantage, difficulties in accessing appropriate services and life experiences including their social and economic realities, women reached different levels of understanding of their predicaments. This process of critical reflection and confrontation with issues and problems allows women to identify and challenge the lack of control over their lives and resources (Crotty, 1998). Critical reflection enables women to see their 'situation as one which they can transform' (Dalrymple and Burke, 1998, p.15). This allows a more hopeful and empowering attitude to emerge.

Forming a research group, building trust and rapport and addressing challenges

Resolving tensions

PAR does not always run smoothly. Competing interests can complicate research processes and leave researchers exposed. They then have to negotiate and smooth over relations in contexts they cannot control. Finding allies becomes crucial in such situations. One particular professional worker played a special role in facilitating the evaluation of the women's services at every stage of the research by encouraging women service users and other professional workers to contribute. Without this support and input, the evaluation would have been impossible. This assistance included:

- identifying potential participants

- organising meetings and rooms

- providing helpful suggestions for introducing the evaluation project to women, liaising between women and researchers, giving voice to the wants and wishes of women and enabling one researcher to visit the groups as a volunteer.

This invaluable helper enabled the researchers to gain access and establish relationships with the women, unpack understandings of research as a concept, and increase women's acceptance of the evaluation before data collection began.

Prior to data collection, ethical approval was gained from Durham University. The anticipated participatory processes were compromised when ethical approval was delayed and impacted upon the planned timeframe because data could not be collected until formal ethical approval had been granted. Mismatches can happen in time-limited participatory research projects and reveal that researchers may not control important processes. For the AWP, data collection through poster activities could not proceed as women participants and researchers had agreed and plans had to be altered at the last minute. This upset the women who had been looking forward to doing posters together and had prepared to do this task during the second meeting. They could not understand this shift within a participatory framework, enthusiasm dropped and some re-evaluated their willingness to engage with the research. Others felt uncomfortable about being 'out of their group environments'. Recovering from this situation required retracing the path for the proposed research and rebuilding trust. The professional worker described above became the ally who brokered the trust rebuilding process and reengaged the women.

Collaboration between the group facilitators and the researchers led to negotiations in which the women agreed that the researchers would step back, and one would attend the women's groups to rebuild trust and relationships as a group volunteer, maintain a reflective diary, visit different centres, participate in group activities and explain the research face to face. This ethnographic period re-enthused the women, and the researcher gained additional valuable knowledge by talking to women and observing different groups, activities and sessions.

Establishing research questions, determining research methods and collecting data

The researchers and participants proceeded with the research following Freire's dialogical method to enable them to act as equally knowing subjects who jointly developed a group atmosphere that facilitated dialogue. Mutual dialogue between the women and researchers was an important part of collecting data in this evaluation and central to participatory approaches to research.

As the women expressed a preference for and felt more comfortable within their own groups in becoming co-participants in designing and conducting the evaluation, this evaluative research occurred within their own groups. The professional workers in each group conducted a session with the women where they introduced the concept of 'evaluation' and ensured that they understood what the research was about. Crucially, in this session the women began to think about research questions, including overarching questions and sub-questions they wanted to ask. Participation in setting the research questions was viewed as essential, given that a participatory methodological approach recognises that those affected, whether individuals or communities, are the 'experts' of their own experiences, 'local contexts, needs and understandings' (Gannon, 2013, p.343) and should revise and suggest changes (Gatenby and Humphries, 2000). Women asked for some questions in the staff schedule to be clarified and changed the wording of others. This flexibility in design and changes made upon participant recommendation and feedback is called 'construct validity' (Gouin *et al.*, 2011). This approach enriches experiential data collection.

The women were asked for their preferred method in undertaking the research. A visual summary of their decisions is indicated in Table 16.1.

Table 16.1: Summary of women's choice of research method (n=19)

Interviews/ face-to-face questions, one-to-one chats	Video for the group to record	Questionnaire	Speak to women in their own groups	Researcher-led but allow chatting freely
5	3	2	5	4

To reach their conclusions, women explored the strengths and weaknesses of various methods, including interviews and focus groups to make informed choices. The women completed worksheets in pairs and then discussed these as a group within a space that women considered their own comfort zone.

Twelve individual women were interviewed through semi-structured interviews across the women's groups and focus groups within their chosen location to enable women to express their stories and lived experiences and provide rich, in-depth data. This method allowed for the expression of emotions, thought and interpretations as well as describing 'what happened' – concerns that are particularly important in drawing out women's experiences of support groups (Chase, 2005, p.656). Staff members were similarly interviewed about the support and help they offered women. Giving voice to these narratives, women expressed strength and resilience (McKeown, 2001, McKeown *et al.*, 2010), identified positive changes made as a result of attending women's groups and highlighted 'distress, pain and failure' (Milner and Kelly, 2001, p.42). By enabling women to retell their stories in the women's groups in a 'common-sense' way, accepted narratives about their lives could be challenged within the group by the participants themselves, thereby facilitating a self-reflective understanding of personal situations.

The semi-conversational approach to interviews empowers participants to shape the interviews (Gouin *et al.*, 2011) and discuss matters relevant to them. Interviews typically included open-ended questions (Gouin *et al.*, 2011) to encourage detailed responses, which were followed up with probing questions. Following a FPAR approach, questions are designed and developed by participants and included the ways in which women talk about domestic violence, experiences of services and how parenting impacts on their experiences (Sullivan *et al.*, 2005).

Eleven professional workers and two neighbourhood managers were interviewed to triangulate data and explore the similarities and differences between the views of the women about the services utilised and those of the professional workers who provided them. Their data created a picture of the wider context and support offered to women experiencing domestic violence. Women service users were involved in the decisions about interviewing these workers and confirmed the range and roles covered.

Multiple methods are commonly used in feminist research (Gouin *et al.*, 2011). In the AWP, face-to-face questionnaires were conducted with women who attended the centre to ascertain why each woman attended, what support they received, and whether they had previously been aware of women's groups. As recommended by the women, questionnaires were a sent to staff members who had referred women to women's groups in the past. A separate paper will be written about these results. Their inclusion towards the end of the AWP exposed a difficulty in time-limited projects – insufficient time for follow-up actions.

Data analysis

The interviews were transcribed and NVivo software was used to code the data according to main themes and sub-categories. Trust overcame time limitations among both women and researchers, which restricted participants' involvement in compiling these beyond general themes. The women asked the researchers to pull together these tasks and submit their efforts on refined coding and summary of the main findings for validation in their women's groups (Gouin *et al.*, 2011) to affirm that both 'made sense' to them. The women's preferences were also utilised for the final report format and photographs for inclusion. Researchers were minded to follow the women's group ethos, and so 'the aim was to create space for women and anything then that developed was shaped by th[em]' (professional worker). Time and research skills are an issue in FPAR and can skew power relations between participants and researchers (Pain *et al.*, n.d.), thus making affirmation and validation of findings in ways that women feel comfortable crucial in the engagement process (Cousins and Whitmore, 1998). Women, with many demands on their time, may wish to curtail their involvement. This should be respected.

Despite our caution and attention to process, researcher interpretation of findings is another potential source of power that can exclude women, making checking and crosschecking results with them essential, as we did here. The satisfaction with the research was such that a proposal to roll out the project more widely had been agreed. This was lost when the research associate left for a more permanent post, and the women thought it was too complicated to begin establishing trust and confidence with a new researcher. At the end of project event, where the final report was presented and each woman received a copy, women expressed their sadness that the research had ended. Plans had previously been laid for a visit to women's groups linked to Durham University. Eventually, this was abandoned due to time and financial constraints. Field notes from that day contain the often repeated comments that, 'We [the women] valued the researchers for listening to us and making us feel included' and, despite the sadness that the evaluation had been completed, 'The day has ended on a very happy note', with many photographs taken.

Project findings: women's positive assessment of services

Professional workers set the scene and ambiance

The women were extremely positive in their evaluations of services. The women's groups followed a person-centred approach drawing upon relationship-based working and trust. This underpinned the good experiences that women had in their groups and they really valued the professional workers' personal approach. Workers were: friendly, welcoming, sensitive, accepting, open, honest, straightforward, non-judgemental, good listeners, someone women could share problems with, original thinkers with their own ideas, working on the same level as the women (not leading them), not approaching sessions like a 'teacher', sharing and communicating plans, helpful and patient, explaining information at an individual's own pace, providing one-to-one support when needed, and had a sense of humour. They set the scene: 'Just they are warm. They are good people. You want to be around them. That is why people go' (Woman 7).

Feeling accepted, being treated as an individual with strengths (while not ignoring weaknesses and needs), not being judged and being welcomed were central to how the women's groups were organised and run and set the ambiance in which women received and evaluated the services.

Women's voices portray resilience and engagement

Women participating in this research faced a range of challenges in their personal lives, families and communities. As service users, they came across as resilient and willing to engage with other women and seek solutions to their problems. This is a credit to them given the harsh realities many faced, including low incomes, poor housing, social isolation, domestic violence and lack of opportunities, especially in education, employment and leisure. The professional workers indicated that a number of women felt depressed and had other mental health problems when they first attended women's groups. The women also identified multiple reasons for their predicament including problematic personal relationships, parenting difficulties, experiences of bereavement or domestic violence. Physical illnesses and health conditions were discussed in relation to depression, feelings of isolation, debt, and financial difficulties. The women deemed these rooted in both individual and structural considerations including poor housing, low incomes, lack of employment opportunities and living in communities that made local social isolation worse. One manager reflecting on these conditions commented on the importance of linking these to developing women's self-confidence to ensure sustainable change in their behaviours:

> I am sure they are all multi-layered, but the more we get involved the more the underlying layer is the personal esteem and self-confidence and unless you deal with that, you can forget all the money skills and debt advice because they don't feel good about themselves. (Manager 2)

Several women shared difficulties in finding employment, particularly full-time jobs and having meaningful employment contracts. One woman commented on 'zero hour' contracts:

> At the moment I'm not doing anything...I've been working PT [part-time] for 13 years now. We have flexi-hours so it is up to them when they call you. Mine is fixed because I only do 4 hours... after that, it is just whatever they can give you, which is [usually] nothing. (Woman 1)

Women's evaluations revealed that they were aware of the social contexts that shaped their lives and how services were delivered, including benefit changes, low incomes, poverty, lack of opportunities, marginalisation, gendered relations, social isolation and personal difficulties. They also recognised that resources in the agencies were limited. They were more optimistic about improving existing provisions than future expansion and felt that the *services provided were worth it and well-used.*

The AWP findings focused on:

- personal growth in women's lives
- women's relationships within their families, communities and wider society
- women's relationships with professional workers in women's groups.

The women reported growth in all aspects of their lives, increased self-confidence in their families, communities, education and employment and gave positive evaluations of the services offered.

Personal growth in women's lives

Changing women's lives and lifestyles because these intensified marginalisation and feelings of disempowerment were important objectives for the women's groups. Positive changes in women's lives occurred through increased: self-care; self-esteem and confidence; capacity to be assertive including acquiring a sense of control over what happened to them; self-knowledge, especially essential to enhancing mental health and lifestyles; sense of achievement and recognition of this; capacity to accept past events and move on; educational capacities by obtaining qualifications, certificates and awards; occupational skills and employment opportunities; social networks; relationship-making skills; mediation; enjoyment of the company of other women;

knowledge about wider issues; personal safety including home safety, 'digital stalking' and internet security; first aid; food hygiene; DIY; awareness covering subjects like breast cancer (exploring risk factors) and alcohol misuse through talks by health visitors and others; and positive mental health and discussions of different mental health issues.

The illustrative quotes below cover these points and are indicative of the growth women achieved.

Building confidence and self-esteem

The majority of women revealed that prior to attending the women's groups, they lacked confidence and found it challenging to socialise with others or talk within the group. Some women related this to a fear of 'failure' often associated with negative experiences of school. One woman recalled: 'I remember when you first came. You sat in that corner and you wouldn't mix or talk!' (Woman B, Focus Group 6).

Attending a women's group, the first step in building confidence, led to other opportunities for growth. Confidence increased through small steps, for example completing short courses like first aid, gaining certificates, and building up a portfolio of work. These achievements encouraged women to attend courses outside the group and complete more formal educational qualifications.

Confidence building programmes strengthened women's capacities and self-belief. One initiative, a six-week programme, built up self-confidence from scratch. Looking to the past, present and future was an important part of this process because it relied upon critical self-reflection to identify strengths and weaknesses and utilised contributions from other group members to reformulate positive future possibilities for growth:

> At the book and paints [group] you make your own book and when you look back on it [there] is a profile of yourself. Negative ways in your life…[the] story of your life. It was starting from how low you are and then from that…build your confidence up. Have individual chat and a one-to-one and a group discussion…it is looking at things, how we see ourselves. (Woman, Focus Group 6)

Some group sessions focused directly on building confidence and self-esteem. Another programme encompassed building confidence, well-being and self-defence. Some of the lessons learnt were transferable to other settings. Women reflected that attending these groups had helped them.

Transformative changes required

The agency recognised that in an area with high levels of deprivation and unemployment, women required services that they would use and would meet their specific needs. Women and existing women's groups were involved in consultation exercises and assessments to respond to identified gaps in services revealed through research and interactions with women in the community (Ponic *et al.*, 2010). Women's concerns with daily routines in their homes and communities were common points of departure in identifying needs and responding to them. Over time, collaboration between agencies and researchers encompassed door-knocking consultations and completion of questionnaires that targeted new tenants on the estate. These indicated that many women had experienced or were experiencing domestic violence, depression and social isolation and lacking services that met their needs. Transformative change was necessary.

Three professionals, including the health development worker, conducted a health needs assessment, utilising a qualitative survey of approximately 200 people across the city to determine the reasons that people were not responding to messages from health service providers. This indicated that people were aware of key health messages concerning smoking, alcohol and exercise, but rarely followed the advice given. Women felt isolated, lacked support networks, had mental health problems and 'faced hardship'. Lone parents, especially lone mothers, were identified as a significant group requiring services.

Moreover, the area was one of serious disadvantage, particularly among black and minority ethnic (BME) groups. One women's group aimed to address and reduce violence against women and girls. Another study and a needs assessment revealed that women in this area were experiencing domestic violence, sexual exploitation of young people, female genital mutilation (FGM) and gaps in services for women living there that the agency sought to address:

> ...someone will say something that is a little bit worrying and you think we'll have to have a chat about that. Then you can refer to health service, to the counsellor, to the domestic violence services. (Professional worker 6)

The agency's formation of partnerships for group delivery reflected a needs-based transformative personal approach, as indicated:

> If people are coming in talking about sexual health or drug abuse...
> someone will come in and talk about that. So we react to what is
> coming up in general conversation. (Professional worker 2)

The agency also sought to enhance efficiency through strategic
coordination:

> It is really about having strategic coordinated services as well...It
> isn't about us doing everything, it is about people recognising they
> have their own skills to do things, and it is also about supporting
> other agencies to work more efficiently, about us all working
> efficiently, not duplicating services and maximising resources.
> (Professional worker 6)

The 'strategic' element of partnerships revolved around practical issues
such as meeting with agencies, discussing events and identifying gaps
in services, rather than strategic thinking. One professional worker was
involved in the 'domestic abuse and violence strategy' being developed
for the entire city and in the Marketing and Communication Working
Group. The latter explored how information is disseminated within
agencies and across communities. Other strategic developments included
the development of community interventions to prevent women
offenders from entering the criminal justice system and multiagency
training.

Managers highlighted the importance of multiagency work with
local education providers, including universities and schools at city-
wide level. Universities were significant in promoting collaboration
around specific projects and supporting student placements, particularly
those training in social work and education. Joint initiatives with
schools included the delivery of a project on healthy relationships. A
manager stressed that they sought to keep strategic partnerships 'as
local as possible. So that we develop a more personal relationship'
(Manager 1). The agency had strong links with the council, probation
and police. These could be problematic when workers advocated for
specific women, as occurred over housing repairs with the housing
department. Relationships with children's centres could become
difficult when workers supported parents whose children exhibited
difficult behaviour. Close working relationships also existed with the
voluntary and charitable sectors.

Challenges highlighted regarding partnership working included:
lack of time to establish partnerships; lack of equality between different

agencies in partnership; resource differentials between agencies; agencies being precious about their work; and agencies working to different timescales and objectives. Despite these problems, agencies were overwhelmingly considered 'open' and 'passionate' about what they do' (Professional worker 6).

Conclusions

Overall, the AWP evaluation was extremely positive and demonstrated that women could contribute fully to evaluative research and co-produce knowledge if supported in doing so. FPAR enabled women to retain control of research processes, usually proceed at their own pace and identify what worked and why. Converting experiential evidence and subjective interpretations of how services impacted upon their lives into evaluative outcomes used by the funders, a central part of AWP, was successfully achieved. Women-focused research processes controlled by women collected data that revealed these service users wanted more women's groups that followed women-centred, participative approaches and sought their expansion. The evidence provided through their narratives and analyses furnished guidance for future funding priorities and policies and identified themes for group activities to meet current and future needs. These were: prosperity; health and well-being; children and young people; clean and green environments; and safe and stronger communities.

Women service users also envisaged outcomes that would:

- establish supportive and positive friendships with other women to develop helpful social networks; reduce social isolation; and enhance well-being and mental health

- improve their aspirations, motivation, resilience, self-esteem, self-worth, self-awareness, confidence and self-reliance

- become part of a community, access services in their community and improve outcomes for themselves and their families and maximise community well-being, thereby narrowing the outcome gap between the least and most well-off people

- be empowered to make positive decisions and changes in their lives

- 'move on' to experience new opportunities and broaden their horizons and lives by encouraging progression through education, training and employment to achieve economic prosperity and/or housing

- participate in and influence decision making locally and realise that they have a voice individually and collectively

- engage with non-judgemental professionals who interact with them to improve existing skills and gain new ones, including social skills.

The women's stories provided evidence that their objectives and outcomes have been met. As a result, the *women service users are feeling more personally fulfilled, more successful and better integrated into their communities.* Funders can use this evidence to maintain, improve and transform their services. Also, PAR is a valuable method with transferable skills for researchers to use in engaging women to evaluate services and is recommended to other researchers interested in hearing and disseminating the insights of people whose voices have been marginalised or silenced.

Acknowledgements

Many thanks to the women and workers involved in the AWP and Beth Casey, its Research Associate.

References

Belenky, M. F., Clinchy, B. M., Goldberger, N. R. and Tarule, J. M. (1998) *Women's Ways of Knowing.* New York: Basic Books.

Chase, S. (2005). 'Narrative inquiry: Multiple lenses, approaches, voices', in Denzin, N.K. and Lincoln, Y.S. (eds.), *The SAGE Handbook of Qualitative Research* (3rd ed.), 651–679. Thousand Oaks, CA: Sage.

Chevalier, J. M. and Buckles, D. J. (2013) *Participatory Action Research: Theory and Methods for Engaged Inquiry.* London: Routledge.

Cousins, J. B. and Whitmore, E. (1998) 'Framing Participatory Evaluation.' In E. Whitmore (ed.) *New Directions for Evaluation.* San Francisco: Jossey-Bass.

Cullen, A. and Coryn, C. (2011) 'Forms and functions of participatory evaluation in international development: A review of the empirical and theoretical literature.' *Journal of Multi-Disciplinary Evaluation 7,* 16, 32–47.

Crotty, M. (1998) *The Foundations of Social Research: Meaning and Perspective in the Research Process.* Thousand Oaks, CA: Sage.

Dalrymple, J. and Burke, B. (1998) *Anti-Oppressive Practice: Social Work and the Law.* Maidenhead: Open University Press.

Davies, N., Browne, J., Gannon, S., Honan, E., and Somerville, M. (2005) 'Embodied Women at Work in Neoliberal Times and Places.' *Gender, Work and Organization, 12,* 4, 343–362.

Dominelli, L. (2005) 'Social Work Research: Contested Knowledge for Practice'. in R. Adams, L. Dominelli, and M. Payne, (eds.) *Social Work Futures*. London: Palgrave Macmillan, 223–236.

Freire, P. (1972) *Pedagogy of the Oppressed*. London: Basic Books.

Gannon, S. (2013) 'Sketching subjectivities', in S. L. Holman Jones, T. E. Adams, and C. Ellis (eds.), *Handbook of Autoethnography*. Walnut Creek, CA.: Left Coast Press, Chapter 10.

Gatenby, B., and Humphreys, M. (2000) 'Feminist Participatory Action Research: Methodological and Ethical Issues', *Women's Studies International Forum, 23*, 1, 89–105.

Gavey, N and McPhillips, K. (1999) 'Subject to Romance: Heterosexual Passivity to Women Initiating Condom Use.' *Psychology of Women Quarterly, 23(May)*, 349–367. DOI: 10.1111/j.1471-6402.

Genat, B. (2009) *Action Research*. London: Sage.

Gouin, R. R., Cocq, K., and McGavin, S. (2011) 'Feminist Participatory Research in a Social Justice Organisation.' *Action Research, 9*, 3, 261–281. DOI: 10.1177/1476750310396945.

Joyappa V. and Martin D., 1996 'Exploring alternative research epistemologies for adult education: Participatory research, feminist research and feminist participatory research.' *S*, 417, 1–14.

Kemmis, S. (2001) 'Exploring the Relevance of Critical Theory for Participatory Action Research: Emancipatory Action Research in the Footsteps of Jürgen Habermas', in Reason, P., and Bradbury, H. (eds.) *Handbook of Action Research: Participative Inquiry and Practice*. London: Sage. 84–113.

King, N., Henderson, G., and Stein, J. (eds.) (1999) *Beyond Regulations: Ethics in Human Subjects Research*. Chapel Hill, NC: University of North Carolina Press.

Langan, D. and Morton, M. (2009) 'Reflecting on Community/Academic 'Collaboration': The Challenge of 'Doing' Feminist Participatory Action Research.' *Action Research, 7*, 2, 165–184.

Lewin, K. (1946) 'Action research and minority problems.' *Journal of Social Issues 2*, 4, 34–46.

Lewin, K. (1948) *Resolving Social Conflicts: Selected Papers on Group Dynamics*. New York: Harper and Row.

McIntyre, A. (2008) *Participatory Action Research*. London: Sage.

McKeown, A (2001) *Chinese Migrant Networks and Cultural Change: Peru, Chicago and Hawaii*. Chicago: Chicago University Press.

McKeown, M, Malihi-Shoja, L., and Downe, S. (2010). *Service User and Carer Involvement in Education for Health and Social Care*. Oxford: Wiley-Blackwell.

Nilner, P. and Kelly, B. (2009) 'Community Participation and Inclusion: People with Disabilities Defining Their Place.' *Disability and Society, 24*, 1, 47–62, DOI: 10.1080/09687590802535410.

O'Connell Davidson, J. (2003) 'Sleeping with the Enemy'? Some Problems with Feminist Abolitionist Calls to Penalise Those Who Buy Commercial Sex', Social Policy and Society, 2(1): 55-63. DOI: 10.1017/S1474746403001076.

Ponic, P., Reid, C., and Frisby, W. (2010) 'Cultivating the Power of Partnerships in Feminist Participatory Action Research in Women's Health.' *Nursing Inquiry, 17*, 4, 324–335. DOI: 10.1111/j.1440-1800.2010.00506.

Pain, R., Whitman, G., Milledge, D. and Lune Rivers Trust (no date) *Participatory Action Research*. Durham: Durham University. Available at www.dur.ac.uk/resources/beacon/PARtoolkit.pdf, accessed on 9 April 2015.

Penuel, W. R., and Freeman, T. (1997) 'Participatory Action Research in YOUth Programming: A Theory in Use.' *Child and Youth Care Forum, 26*, 3, 175–186.

Reason, P. and Bradbury, H. (2008) (eds) *The Sage Handbook of Action Research: Participative Inquiry and Practice.* London: Sage.

Sullivan, M., Bhuyan, R., Senturia, K., Shiu,-Thornton, S., and Ciske, S. (2005) 'Participatory Action Research in Practice: A Case Study in Addressing Domestic Violence in Nine Cultural Communities.' *Journal of Interpersonal Violence, 20,* 8, 977–995.

Whyte, W. F. (1989) *Street Corner Society: The Social Structure of an Italian Slum.* Chicago: The University of Chicago Press. First published in 1943.

Williams, J. and Lykes, M. B. (2003) 'Bridging theory and practice: Using reflexive cycles in feminist participatory action research.' *Feminism and Psychology 13,* 3, 287–294.

Chapter 17

'A LITTLE BIT OF
WHAT I'M ABOUT'

Urban Photography for Social Work Research

NATALIE ROBINSON
University of Liverpool

Photography has been variously recognised as a valuable methodological tool for doing social work research (Molloy, 2007; Shaw and Holland, 2014; Wang and Burris, 1997; Wang, Cash and Powers, 2000). Photographs have typically been used in two key ways: in photo-elicitation work, which involves using images as stimulus for debate in qualitative interviews or focus groups, and through 'photovoice', where participants take and talk about their own pictures (Harper, 2012). In both cases, the photographs become the data discussed by researchers and participants, with the aim of opening up dialogue pertaining to particular social issues. Studies have covered wide-ranging themes – including family care (Angelo and Egan, 2015), homeless experiences (Fotheringham, Walsh and Burrowes, 2014), youth studies (Johansen and Le, 2014), addiction (Rosen, Goodkind and Smith, 2011) and even photography as a method to engage social work students themselves (Peabody, 2013).

Concentrating on photographs of places in the city, this chapter explores the urban image as a creative source for participatory data analysis. I suggest that this is particularly relevant for social work, described as a theoretically informed practice intervening 'at the point where people interact with their environments' (International Association of Schools of Social Work and the International Federation of Social Workers, 2001, cited in Hardwick and Worsley 2011, p.1). As Proshansky, Abbe Fabian and Robert Kaminoff (1983/2014, p.73) observe, '[e]xploring the relationship between place and identity deepens our understandings of identity formation and the role of place in social and psychological development'. Urban images have the potential to call this interaction into focus, inviting a discussion of identities, emotions and opinions that are situated in nature.

To locate and elucidate this argument, I invite the reader to return with me to Downtown Eastside Vancouver (DTES), British Columbia, the site for my Master's level fieldwork and a city neighbourhood in which the annual Hope in Shadows photography contest demonstrates how community photographs of the city might speak to individual and collective concerns.

This chapter focuses on a research project undertaken in the DTES, forming part of my postgraduate study in 'Cultural Inquiry' at the University of Birmingham and drawing on the interdisciplinary legacy of the Centre for Contemporary Cultural Studies, specifically pulling together the fields of visual sociology, cultural studies and environmental psychology. My thesis focused on the tenth annual Hope in Shadows contest, which took place in the summer of 2012 and formed a case study for an exploration of photography and identity. Each year the contest invites 200 low-income residents to take pictures of their local community, of people and of the urban environment. Through observational research and focus groups, I sought to develop an insight into the ways that people might use photography to talk about personal and collective issues. The aims of the research were as follows:

1. To explore how repeat representation can (re)create perceptions of individual and community identities.

2. To understand the impact of photographic practice on individuals and groups in an area with a high percentage of individuals labelled or self-identifying as socially excluded.

3. To make recommendations regarding the use of photography in social research.

I will explore two notable findings that came out of this work. First, how taking and talking about images of the DTES enabled participants to say something meaningful about personal and collective identities; second, and leading from this, how participants used images to speak to wider publics. I discuss the study in terms of its 'participatory' analysis and make some recommendations for future social work research projects.

Doing research in the DTES

The DTES neighbourhood lies just several city blocks from Vancouver's affluent centre yet sits apart – characterised by multiple social agencies variously oriented towards low-income individuals, drug users, those facing housing issues and sex-workers (Cooper, 2006; Robinson, 2013). Depictions of the DTES circulate relentlessly in local and national press, and more often than not emphasise poverty, drug abuse and violence, framing all of these in starkly negative terms. Wider city residents avoid the DTES streets, and tourists are warned against venturing too far into the neighbourhood, especially after dark (Robinson, 2013). The DTES is the site of ongoing gentrification; residents are divided from the low-income locals through a series of social, spatial and economic barriers (Robinson, 2013; Smith, 2000). Expensive new-build condos erase a once familiar landscape of affordable single room occupancy hotels (SROs), providing accommodation for a young consumer class, longstanding neighbourhood stores are replaced with chic coffee shops and bars, policing is stepped up in public spaces and local people are locked out of regeneration efforts. Such changes are nevertheless met with passionate community objection, with grassroots organising amplifying local voices.

As one such self-proclaimed response to negative stereotypes, media (mis)representation, and gentrification, the Hope in Shadows contest is described online as, 'a community-driven project that uses photography as a vehicle for people living in poverty to share their stories and to represent their community on their own terms' (Hope in Shadows, 2014, see also Cran and Jerome, 2008). Disposable cameras are distributed on a first-come, first-served basis, and participants have three days to capture their images. Photographs are developed in colour and in black and white, to be judged by a panel of local, professional photographers and artists, as well as by residents themselves. The top 13 pictures are chosen each year to form part of a calendar, sold by street vendors for profit, using a similar model to the UK's *Big Issue* magazine. Pictures are exhibited annually in the local neighbourhood as well as in other city venues, and are available to purchase online,[1] with 50 per cent of the proceeds after costs going directly to the photographers. For the project organisers, Hope in Shadows is about 'telling stories, creating connections, and changing lives' (Hope in Shadows, 2014).

The Hope in Shadows contest represents a community attempt to explore DTES lifeworlds in a non-academic context. The photography

---

1   www.hopeinshadows.com

contest was not conceived for research purposes; while participants were often explicitly speaking to the title theme and its connotations with their images, they were not doing so with a future focus group or interview in mind. In this way the work departs from studies such as Caroline Wang's (1999) research with women and with homeless individuals in Ann Arbor, MI, and Alun Radley, Darrin Hodgetts and Andrea Cullen's (2005) work with homeless individuals in Bristol – photovoice projects that were conceptualised and carried out by academics explicitly for research purposes. The DTES is an 'over-researched' community (Jerome, 2012; O'Neill and Seal, 2012; Walls, 2011) and I endeavoured to take this into account, basing my study on an event already happening, rather than attempting a more active intervention.

My research involved both participatory observation and focus groups: I volunteered for the Hope in Shadows camera hand-out and collection and spent time in the local area attending community events and meeting residents. I organised and facilitated two discussion groups on the theme of 'photography and identity' at Carnegie Community Centre – a popular neighbourhood hub providing daily classes such as art and IT, affordable food and other social support services. The focus groups were advertised widely in the community through posters and word of mouth and took place just a few days after the cameras had been collected from Hope in Shadows contest participants for development.

The first discussion group included Danny, Jack, Carl and Ron; the second included Sam, Sarah, David and Clare. Laura was interviewed independently. Six participants identified as male and three as female. Six participants identified as White Canadian and three as 'other', including First Nations and English (Commonwealth) origin. Participants were aged between 33 and 65. Danny identified as First Nations, and Sam identified in three ethnic groups (Chinese, First Nations and 'other'), with the rest of the participants as White Canadian or other (various). This is reflective of the diverse DTES demographic (Cooper, 2006; Lewis *et al.*, 2008) though due to the random selection process does not represent an entirely accurate population snapshot. Names have been changed to preserve anonymity as far as possible. All participants used Carnegie Community Centre's facilities on a regular basis and identified as DTES residents. Importantly, participants in this study were not asked to disclose any engagement with any additional social support. The study did not position participants as service users, but nevertheless makes a case for the project as a useful model for future social work research.

I introduced each group with an explanation of my research project and the themes of 'photography' and identity' that I was hoping to explore through facilitated discussion. A selection of images from the Hope in Shadows contest printed from the online archive was placed over the table. Photographs were selected to represent the variety of pictures in the contest – a representative sample including pictures from each year, some depicting people and some with no people in the frame at all. I invited participants to talk about these photographs, as well as the photographs that they themselves may have taken as part of the recent or past contests. The use of images in this way encouraged a conversation that went in its own direction as participants moved at their own pace and in their chosen order. Each group lasted approximately two hours.

In May 2013, one year after my fieldwork visit, I returned to Vancouver to present my findings to the community involved. I wanted to discuss the work with those whose voices I had included, and to attempt to 'check' the representations that formed my final analysis with participants and interested members of the community, prior to publication (Robinson, 2013). I was mindful that my research must avoid repeating the mistakes of journalists – explicitly criticised by participants for 'parachuting' in and out of the DTES without reengaging or following up with those involved.

Observations

My research in the DTES points to how individuals and communities can use images of meaningful places in their neighbourhood to explore concepts transcending immediate environmental observations, speaking to more personal perceptions of self and collective identity. Photographs provoked a recognition of environmental, social and psychological interconnections – informing insights into individual lifeworlds. As recognised by Ian Shaw and Suzanne Holland (2014, p.126), images can 'prompt the participant to consider instances that may depart from their generalised perceptions of life'. In a social work research context, the act of photography and the analysis of images invites both service users and practitioners to move away from routinised qualitative interview structures, which often mirror the conversations that form social work needs assessments and develop related support plans. The visual text encourages an inversion of hierarchical assumptions surrounding professional researcher or practitioner knowledge, positioning the participant as expert (Saleeby 1996) and inviting reflection and reflexivity.

My work emphasised the situated nature of social research – the stories that were unique to the DTES and to individuals living in the neighbourhood. At the same time, the research pointed to the entanglements of the local and the general, connecting what C. Wright Mills (1959) describes as 'personal troubles' to the level of 'public issues'. Focus group participants noted the importance of their stories being made visible through the Hope in Shadows photography, actively seeking engagement beyond their neighbourhood to catalyse change. Using photography in this way promotes participatory creation and analysis of key data, going at least some way to democratising the research process.

Key innovative elements
1. Using urban images to talk about personal and collective issues
In his discussion of visual methods in sociology, Douglas Harper (2012, p.202) asserts: 'photographs are not important by themselves, but they are important for their role in the lives of those who make them'. In my study, participants indicated that using images to talk about personal and collective issues enabled them to:

1. move away from a normative linear accounts of life experiences

2. articulate difficult concepts through visual metaphor

3. explore the importance of place as part of ongoing identity construction

4. participate in meaningful interpretations and analysis of community-generated data.

I will consider each of these in the context of DTES discussion groups.

1. Using images of the DTES neighbourhood to talk about their everyday lives encouraged participants to **move away from a normative linear account**, exploring their lifeworlds as 'snapshots', using the themes that came out of the images to

direct group discussions. During each two-hour discussion group, our conversations moved in multiple directions as participants linked images to everyday perceptions of and experiences in their community. In this way, the images enabled participants to lead the conversation themselves. The semi-structured interview questions that I brought to the table were rendered somewhat redundant as each group talked through themes of photography and identity quite naturally. The images represented an entry point into the discussion of personal stories, highlighting the 'entanglements of the city and the self' (Lancione, 2011).

2.   Discussion group participant Danny professed: 'In the Hope in Shadows I did use the photography to define, kinda to define what…a little bit of what I'm about.' Danny explained that he used his camera to capture positive images of the Downtown Eastside – for example of children playing and of colourful street scenes. In doing so, he was actively and consciously connecting positive framing of his locale with a positive sense of self. He was able to **use visual metaphors to articulate difficult concepts**, both in terms of the emotional demands and the intellectual complexities of identity politics:

Danny: I'll tell you what I did, I made some angel wings and I wore them around the Downtown Eastside for a couple of days and I just asked people if they would like to have a picture taken with the angel wings on and I got a really good response, everybody was…everybody liked it, everybody wanted to wear the wings. And so…and so I was trying to say like in this bad area there…there are angels and there could be angels, and there's good…where, where everybody thinks is maybe not so good, you know?

Danny used angel wings as props to suggest something 'good' about the people in his neighbourhood, actively casting the community in a positive light. Danny's approach works in contrast to the media-made images of the neighbourhood due to his insider status. Danny used his photographs to enter into a discussion about his own experiences of media (mis) representation, specifically involving his mother who was interviewed by a national Canadian newspaper and portrayed, in Danny's opinion, extremely badly. Through his own practice he attempted to interrogate and offer an alternative to this negative framing.

Homemade angel wings (made using hanger wire and white paper) were used to create an imaginative visual metaphor, challenging a presumed perception of the DTES as 'hell' (Robinson, 2013). Through a staged enactment of the angelic, Danny (re)creates identities within his community. These identities may be transient – dependent on and constructed for a contrived contest scenario. However, when understood as part of the much larger Hope in Shadows archive, Danny's approach contributes to a legacy of affirmative repeat-representation. At the core of Proshansky *et al.*'s theory of place-identity is the concept of our 'environmental past…consisting of places, spaces and their properties which have served instrumentally in the satisfaction of the person's biological, psychological, social and cultural needs' (Proshansky *et al.*, 1983/2014, p.73). The online archive of images goes some way to constructing, and (re)presenting the 'environmental past' of the DTES, enabling a collective reference point for understandings of the city and the self.

3. Participants explored **the importance of place as part of their ongoing identity construction**. Discussing hypothetical photographs that they would take to represent their personal identities, Jack, Carl and Sam chose pictures of places in the DTES, without any people in the frame:

Jack: I would take a picture downstairs in the kitchen – but empty, you know, I – just so because, that's what I do, you know – I'm one of the chefs here…it's my community.

Carl: I'd think more about an aerial photo from 100 feet above, probably using…probably Carrall and the centre up to Gore from one edge and the Victory Square at another edge and just Hastings and that alleyway… Just a long panoramic shot of just everything going on.

Sam: I'd take a picture of Chinatown looking out Main Street past the Carnegie and the mountains. Because that's where I came from. It's part of my blood.

There was a sense articulated by participants that urban photography is intrinsically and emotionally associated with individuals and groups regardless of whether people are included in the picture. Photographs of the neighbourhood were discussed in terms of psychological well-being, aspirations and identities; participants demonstrated just how we might picture meaningful places, and in so doing, say something about ourselves. For Jack, Carl and Sam these started at the scale of the kitchen, zoomed out to a bird's eye street view and, further still, tracing the city to the scenery beyond. These choices of pictures without people were described as a protest of sorts – a response to media images that explicitly depict people often in a negative light and often at their most vulnerable.

As Jeff Ferrell (2001, p.224) posits, '[q]uestions of meaning, beauty and emotion can of course be answered theologically or epistemically. But, especially in the shared experience of the city, they must also be answered spatially.' In their discussion group, Ron and Danny used geographic metaphor to position the socio-economic status of the DTES community:

Ron: We've all gotta be helping each other because this is the last stop.

Danny: Yeah. There's only ocean now.

Ron invokes an urgent spirit of solidarity that is rooted in a shared sense of 'place' – both on the urban map and identified through common struggles. Ron and Danny's positioning of the DTES as the 'last stop' provoked a number of comments about 'outsider' perceptions of the neighbourhood; the ways that wider city residents would drive through in a hurry, would actively avoid being in the area after dark and made value judgements about drug users and sex workers in the area. Proshansky *et al.* (1983/2014, p.77) state, '[w]e not only experience the physical realities, for example, of the particular neighbourhood we grew up in, but also the social meanings and beliefs attached to it'. For Ron and Danny, identity and spatiality are always already enmeshed and influenced by 'those who live outside of it as well as residents' (Proshansky *et al.*, 1983/2014, p.77).

4.   Through my research DTES residents were invited to **participate meaningfully in the analysis of community photographs**, in a way that would be difficult – or at least very different –

for those unfamiliar with the ever-changing neighbourhood landscape. A feeling of being increasingly abandoned by wider city services is emphasised through Carl's photograph, which is reliant on 'insider knowledge':

Carl: It was just of a police station – the sign was gone. On Main Street I'm so used to sitting at the Wave [coffee shop] looking over Vancouver Police Department and…it disappeared! I don't know how, because I'm there every day and I said to these people 'Where'd the sign go?' and they said 'What do you mean?' and I said 'Well they're finally gone.' The Vancouver police had been leaving there for over a year…I said 'Their sign's gone' and started taking pictures of this sign being gone.

Picturing the disappeared enables community photography to establish itself as an 'insider' practice. The need for accompanying explanation as to why an image is significant, and what it means, can be empowering for the photographer. The discussion of symbolic urban landscape images seems to imply that DTES residents share a visual language at a community level. As Stuart Hall (2007) observes:

> What signifies is not the photographic text in isolation but the way it is caught up in a network of chains of signification that 'overprint' it, its inscription into the currency of other discourses, which bring out different meanings. Its meaning can only be completed by the ways we interrogate it.

In the case of this study, the impact of a photograph became contingent on and controlled by those with local knowledge.

In her work on urban landscape history, Dolores Hayden (1995/2014, p.85) reminds us that, '[p]eople's experiences of the urban landscape intertwine the sense of place and the politics of space'. Photographic practice and related discussions around the Hope in Shadows contest represent a lived example of just how place and identity 'are co-produced as people come to identify with where they live, shape it, however modestly, and are in turn shared by their environments, creating distinctive environmental autobiographies' (Proshansky *et al.*, 1983/2014, p.73).

2. Using urban images to speak to wider publics

This section of the chapter will focus on how using urban images in social research might enable participants to elevate 'personal troubles' to the status of 'public issues' (Mills, 1959, p.8). I argue that photography is a medium that can enable 'experiences which are lived through as thoroughly personal and subjective' and 'problems fit to be inscribed into the public agenda and become matters of public policy' to reconnect (Bauman, 2000, p.78–79 cited in Robinson 2013, p.37–38). Participants in my study expressed their understandings of the camera as a powerful tool for representation and related advocacy; gentrification, policing and service provision were key themes, raised repeatedly. Proshansky *et al.* (1983/2014, p.73) assert, 'a sense of place-identity derives from the multiple ways in which place functions to provide a sense of belonging, construct meaning, foster attachments and mediate change'. The Hope in Shadows contest was seen by participants as a platform for increased visibility, on DTES residents' terms. This coalesces with Caroline Wang and Mary Ann Burris' (1997, p.369) definition of photovoice research aims:

> (1) To enable people to record and reflect their community's strengths and concerns, (2) to promote critical dialogue and knowledge about important issues through large and small group discussions of photographs and (3) to reach policy makers and people who can be mobilised for change.

For discussion group participant David, urban photography can be used to represent the DTES on resident terms to wider publics, specifically Vancouver residents outside of the neighbourhood. He explains that photography might be used:

David: [T]o educate people who don't know about this neighbourhood – maybe never been in an SRO, maybe never been in Carnegie, never been to the UGM [Union Gospel Mission] or Salvation Army, educate them a little bit as to… the vast majority of people here are ordinary human beings with fears, hopes, desires, pain…they suffer, they feel…The kind of people who know the Downtown Eastside know that it's a mix of good and bad, it's a mix of healthy and unhealthy, like everywhere in life, it's in every other geographic location on this planet, it's a mix of things. And that's what we are. I'm not…I'm not saying we're super special, that we're all saints down here but we're just a mix of good and bad and healthy and unhealthy, and that's what photography can maybe help with.

David suggested that the Hope in Shadows contest offered a platform to resist actively negative perceptions of his community. For David, photography as a medium might help to bridge the divide between insider/outsider communities, resisting negative media portrayal with nuanced representations. He emphasised the importance of resident-led visibility, organised and disseminated at a grassroots level through the online archive and associated print materials, calling attention to the manifold experiences that make up the DTES.

Sam spoke of a specific way to increase understandings of community needs, emphasising the importance of First Nations spaces in the neighbourhood to nurture important social relationships:

Sam: I'd take pictures of children interacting with Elders you know – outdoors and indoors – like storytelling and then, then playful activity, nature walks...

He suggested that such a photograph would capture the community in action and make demands for much-needed service provision in the area.

Carl spoke about a project run by DTES residents, involving using photography to record questionable policing:

Carl: I worked on 'Cop Watch' – taking photos of cops jacking people up and just...we don't get in their way we just take their pictures. We don't ask – we don't care. It's happening on the sidewalk, this man's getting himself busted for something. I mean we just want to make sure he's not getting his arm twisted up around his ass and not getting hauled off to jail for something that's unwarranted...I try not to get his picture, I try to get a picture of the cops that are...dealing with, right?

Carl emphasises the importance of making issues within the community visible, questioning normative power structures and sharing knowledge through photographic practice.

The importance of visibility was echoed by Laura. Discussing a picture of graffiti in the DTES (that was later removed due to construction work), she observes: '[the photograph] saved the graffiti piece forever. They started tearing down the building but we had already captured it.' The photograph enabled a symbolic reclamation of lost sites, preserving memories of everyday places in the midst of gentrification. Laura goes on to talk about a portrait of herself, taken by a Hope in Shadows contest participant, a picture that she has a framed copy of: 'I was called beautiful in the photograph in the Downtown Eastside amongst rubble and drugs and grief – but they see beauty, they see me.' This photograph preserves a similarly affirmative memory for Laura, emphasising Harper's (2012, p.202) position that in many projects, 'photographs are not important by themselves, but they are important for their role in the lives of those who make them'. As the human subject of the photograph, Laura was invited to the Hope in Shadows exhibition and related community events. She explained that this afforded her the space to tell her personal story and the interwoven narrative of her neighbourhood on her own terms, in various forums: '[t]he click of the camera, it changed my life – it got me into places I would never, ever be otherwise. I've met politicians'.

The Hope in Shadows contest does not simply invite participants to document spaces and places, but also to (re)claim representations of space, place and self in personal and political ways. The contest provides a platform for community access to public representation, bolstered by its reputation as a high profile event. Photography can offer a visual language to talk about community issues and aspirations that can be far more accessible and interpretatively open than the formalised rhetoric of social agencies. Indeed, in this way, photography can enable individuals to (re)imagine, reshape, redefine or reclaim their social reality (Chatman, 1996), removing barriers that expectations for certain kinds of 'expert' knowledge can create.

Strengths and challenges

As with much social research, all of the strengths identified in my project simultaneously present various challenges. These fall into four broad categories – interdisciplinarity, reflexivity, participatory research and the idea of doing 'empowering' work.

My study presents an example of *interdisciplinary research*, synthesising cultural studies with visual methods in social sciences and aspects of environmental psychology. Such an interdisciplinary approach might be perceived as a strength of the project, incorporating multiple viewpoints and retaining a transferability to various intellectual projects

– in this case, social work research (Shaw, 2007). While the study was not conceived as a social work research project, the orientation of the work towards 'social justice' through community inclusion arguably situates the work as a relevant model for future social work research. Working across disciplines for a common aim must be approached as a continuous challenge, to ensure clarity of insight from multiple perspectives.

Through this study I strove to provide an example of *reflexive research,* or at least an attempt to consider my own social, economic and cultural position, to talk openly about the 'decisions and dilemmas' in my fieldwork (Finlay, 2002, p.210) and to approach the work as a dialogue, moving away from notions of 'expert' knowledge that prevail in much social scientific work today. Incorporating an interrogation of my own position as researcher from outside the community – and even from outside Canada itself – into my thesis was a start point in grounding the study reflexively. I endeavoured to present a transparent account of research methods, both in the field and in my written analysis. I recognised participants as co-researchers, involved in the generation and subsequent discussion of visual data. It is important to ensure that interrogations of power and positionality are not simply written into research after the fact but are considered in practice, informing ways of working on the ground; reflexivity must be approached as an ongoing challenge.

There are multiple examples of *participatory research* in which the community members in focus are involved from the very start in conceptualising research questions and planning the project itself (Petrie, Fiorelli and O'Donnell, 2006; Jacobson and Rugeley, 2007; Bagnoli and Clark, 2010). While I defined my research aims prior to entering the field, I relied solely on the meanings attributed by participants as 'codes' for the various images discussed, facilitating a participatory analysis of community images in small discussion groups. Several limitations, typically attributed to focus group research, applied to the study, including the potentiality for bias due to conversational dominance by one or two participants, researcher influence and the politics of representing subjective participant responses (Oates, 2000). In my DTES discussion groups, I found that male participants seemed more confident imparting their opinions and ideas and made several interventions to mediate this; at times asking participants to avoid talking over one another and on occasion asking direct questions to members of the group who were less vocal. Conscious of my personal influence, I made every effort to avoid leading questions, using a diverse selection of images to stimulate spontaneous dialogue. As previously discussed, the photographs encouraged participants to lead discussions mutually and analyse images from their own point of view I transcribed and analysed these discussions in further depth after leaving the field, connecting the conversations that we had in Carnegie Community Centre to theory and to broader themes. I organised the stories that were told in four hours in Vancouver into three chapters, creating a cohesive narrative; I attached personal interpretations and drew my own conclusions. I was concerned that the next step was to involve participants themselves in some way at the final stage of analysis, prior to publication. I wanted to reconnect with participants, to ask their opinions about how I had interpreted what they themselves had contributed to the project and to check if the themes that I had identified felt appropriate to them. Without this, the project did not entirely depart from the journalistic 'parachuting' approach.

The overseas nature of the research coupled with the time limitations of a postgraduate project afforded just over one month in the field, and I was restricted with regards to opportunities for meaningful reengagement. While I was ultimately able to return to Vancouver to follow up with participants, I would have ideally liked to do this at more regular intervals and to revisit sooner than was feasible here. If the scope for a larger-scale project had been available to me, I feel that the study would have also benefited from an increased participant sample, opening up space for as many DTES residents as possible to engage with the research. Notwithstanding, I maintain that the potential of the Hope in Shadows project as a case study to explore photography and identity outweighed the issues presented by my relatively limited resources.

In May 2013, one year after my fieldwork visit, and thanks to funding from the Economic and Social Research Council, I was able to go back to present (and check) my findings in a community context. I hoped that returning would represent a gesture of appreciation for participant involvement – setting the research apart in some small way from the widely criticised journalistic approach of certain local and national press. All but two participants attended the presentation, along with interested DTES residents, local photographers and a photojournalist from a national newspaper, who was interested in the ethics of working with the community, generating a fruitful discussion. Participants expressed their understanding and satisfaction with my write-up and were particularly keen to talk to me about transferring the ideas behind the Hope in Shadows contest to understand social phenomena in new research projects. A copy of the final thesis was made available in the community centre library, and the community newsletter published an article on my work, including my contact details for anyone who wanted to ask any questions or make any comments. I received several emails from readers who wanted to discuss the ideas further and happily engaged with these. What became increasingly apparent as I shared my findings in the community, however, was a need to generate tangible outcomes from research itself, beyond the written work – something that, if we are to use the Hope in Shadows contest as a model for future research, is arguably essential. The dissemination of the photographic work through exhibition and archive is the point that, as I have suggested in this chapter, has the potential to raise 'personal troubles' to the level of 'public issues'. This would eventually influence my ongoing PhD work at the University of Liverpool.

Ian Shaw (2007, p.660) argues that a 'knowledge of and sensitivity to conducting research in emancipatory ways' constitutes a distinct aspect of social work research. The Hope in Shadows contest is positioned by community organisers as a liberating project – opening up a much needed dialogue with the wider community and enabling DTES residents to (re)claim ownership of individual and community representations. Contest images encourage a kind of 'citizen social science', promoting critical evaluation of community circumstances.

Jennifer K. Molloy (2007, p.50) describes taking and talking about images as a technique that enables social workers to 'share the power' and engage 'in mutual learning experiences', which might be described as '*empowering*'. The images discussed in this study were created by participants or by self-identifying members of the DTES community. Through individual and group meaning making, participants were involved at the initial stage of data analysis, analysing archival material and present-day community photographs and connecting these images to their everyday lifeworlds. Harper (2002, p.23) avers, 'when two or more people discuss the meaning of photographs they are trying to figure something out together. This is, I believe, the ideal model for research'. Using images taken by community members in social work research can add an interesting layer of meaning to the traditional focus group – as a space 'in which [participants] can define their own categories and labels, and unmask ideas and opinions through dialogue and debate with others' and which 'can potentially provide opportunity for marginalized groups to discuss issues relevant to their lives and share experiences with others from a similar social position in order to produce a collective testimony' (Bagnoli and Clark, 2010, p.104). It is nonetheless imperative that we continue to problematise notions of 'empowerment' in research, always asking for and by whom, how and for what ends any claims are being made. Foregrounding the contextually specific aspects of every new project should eternally disrupt dangerous assumptions of straightforward relationships between methods and outcomes.

The Hope in Shadows contest demonstrates how taking and talking about community images can enable participants to reclaim ownership of their representations and where appropriate to share these images in community forums, speaking to their peers, to wider publics and to policy makers. This chapter makes a case for the use of urban images in social work research as a tentative but nonetheless valuable move towards increasingly interdisciplinary, reflexive, participatory and empowering work. Social researchers must critique these objectives even as they work towards them, considering and continuously (re)evaluating the issues that can arise both epistemologically and methodologically with each claim.

References

Angelo, J. and Egan, R. (2015) 'Family caregivers voice their needs: A Photovoice study.' *Palliative and Supportive Care, 13,* 3, 701–712.

Bagnoli, A. and Clark, A. (2010) 'Focus groups with young people: A participatory approach to research planning.' *Journal of Youth Studies 13,* 1, 101–109.

Bauman, Z. (2000) 'Sociological enlightenment – For whom, about what?' *Theory, Culture and Society 12,* 4, 71–82.

Chatman, E. A. (1996) 'The impoverished world of outsiders.' *Journal of the American Society for Information Science 47,* 3, 193–206.

Cooper, M. (2006) *Social Sustainability in Vancouver.* Vancouver: Canadian Policy Research Networks.

Cran, B. and Jerome, G. (2008) *Hope in Shadows: Stories and Photographs of Vancouver's Downtown Eastside.* Vancouver: Arsenal Pulp Press and Pivot Legal Society.

Ferrell, J. (2001) *Tearing Down the Streets: Adventures in Urban Anarchy.* New York: Palgrave.

Finlay, L. (2002) 'Negotiating the swamp: The opportunity and challenge of reflexivity in research practice.' *Qualitative Research 2,* 209–230.

Fotherngham, S., Walsh, C. A. and Burrowes, A. (2014) '"A place to rest": The role of transitional housing in ending homelessness for women in Calgary, Canada.' *Gender, Place and Culture 21*, 834–853.

Hall, S. (2007) 'Lives on film.' *The Guardian,* 15 October. Available at www.guardian.co.uk/ uk/2007/oct/15/britishidentity.race, accessed on 9 April 2015.

Hardwick, L. and Worsley, A. (2011) *Doing Social Work Research.* London: Sage.

Harper, D. (2002) 'Talking about pictures: A case for photo elicitation.' *Visual Studies 17*, 1, 13-26. Harper, D. (2012) *Visual Sociology.* Oxford: Routledge.

Hayden, D. (1995/2014) 'Urban Landscape History: The Sense of Place and the Politics of Space.' In J.J. Gieseking and W. Mangold (eds) *The People, Place and Space Reader.* Oxford: Routledge.

Hope in Shadows (2014) *Our Story.* Vancouver: Hope in Shadows. Available at www. hopeinshadows.com, accessed on 9 April 2015.

Jacobson, M. and Rugeley, C. (2007) 'Community-based participatory research: Group work for social justice and community change.' *Social Work with Groups 30*, 4, 21–39.

Jerome, G. (2012) *Interview with Author* (personal communication, 31 May 2012). Vancouver.

Johansen, S. and Le, T. N. (2014) 'Youth perspective on multiculturalism using photovoice methodology.' *Youth and Society 46*, 4, 548–565.

Lancione, M. (2011) *Homeless Subjects and the Chance of Space: A More-than-human-geography of Homelessness in Turin* (PhD thesis). Durham: University of Durham.

Lewis, M., Boyes, K., McClanaghan, D. and Copas, J. (2008) *Downtown Eastside Demographic Study of SRO and Social Housing Tenants.* Vancouver: BC Housing, The Vancouver Agreement.

Mills, C. W. (1959) *The Sociological Imagination.* New York: Oxford University Press.

Molloy, J.K. (2007) 'Photovoice as a tool for social justice workers.' *Journal of Progressive Human Services 18*, 2, 39-55.

Oates, C. (2000) 'The Use of Focus Groups in Social Science Research.' In D. Burton (ed.) *Research Training for Social Scientists.* London: Sage Publications.

O'Neill, M. and Seal, L. (2012) 'Crime, Poverty and Resistance on Skid Row' (proof copy). In M. O'Neill and L. Seal *Transgressive Imaginations: Crime, Deviance and Culture (Critical Criminological Perspectives).* London: Palgrave MacMillan.

Peabody, C. G. (2013) 'Using Photovoice as a Tool to Engage Social Work Students in Social Justice.' *Journal of Teaching in Social Work 33*, 251–265.

Petrie, S., Fiorelli, L. and O'Donnell, K. (2006) '"If we help you what will change?" Participatory research with young people.' *Journal of Social Welfare and Family Law 28*, 1, 31-45.

Proshansky, H. M., Fabian, A. K. and Kaminoff, R. (1983/2014) 'Place-identity: Physical World Socialisation of the Self.' In J. J. Gieseking and W. Mangold (eds) *The People, Place and Space Reader.* Oxford: Routledge.

Radley, A., Hodgetts, D. and Cullen, A. (2005) 'Visualizing homelessness: A study in photography and estrangement.' *Journal of Community and Applied Social Psychology 15*, 1, 273–295.

Robinson, N. (2013) 'Picturing social inclusion: Photography and identity in Downtown Eastside Vancouver. *Graduate Journal of Social Science 10*, 2.

Rosen, D., Goodkind, S. and Smith, M. L. (2011) 'Using photovoice to identify service needs of older African American methadone clients.' *Journal of Social Service Research 37*, 5.

Saleeby, D. (1996) 'The strengths perspective in social work practice: Extensions and cautions.' *Social Work 41*, 3, 296–305.

Shaw, I. (2007) 'Is social work research distinctive?' *Social Work Education 26*, 7, 659–669.

Shaw, I. and Holland, S. (2014) *Doing Qualitative Research in Social Work.* London: Sage.

Smith, H. A. (2000) *Where Worlds Collide: A Social Polarisation at the Community Level in Vancouver's Gastown/Downtown Eastside* (PhD thesis). Vancouver: University of British Columbia.

Walls, R. (2011) *Visibility in Vancouver: Screen Stories and Surveillance of the Downtown Eastside* (PhD thesis). Nottingham: University of Nottingham.

Wang, C. (1999) 'Photovoice: A participatory action research strategy applied to women's health.' *Journal of Women's Health 8*, 2, 185–192.

Wang, C. and Burris, M. A. (1997) 'Photovoice: Concept, methodology, and use for participatory needs assessment.' *Health, Education and Behaviour 24*, 1, 369–387.

Wang, C., Cash, J. L. and Powers, L. S. (2000) 'Who knows the streets as well as the homeless? Promoting personal and community action through photovoice.' *Health Promotion Practice 1*, 1, 81–89.

Chapter 18

INCORPORATING 'KNOWLEDGE EXCHANGE' INTO RESEARCH DESIGN AND DISSEMINATION STRATEGIES

AISHA HUTCHINSON AND CHERILYN DANCE
University of Bedfordshire

Introduction

This chapter focuses on how knowledge exchange was incorporated into the dissemination strategy of a series of three linked, survey-based, research studies. Dissemination is defined as 'spreading' or 'scattering' and in the research context is associated with researchers ensuring that their research findings reach relevant audiences. Knowledge exchange is usually defined or understood as a two-way, or multi-way, process where social scientists, users of research and wider groups and communities share learning, ideas, evidence, expertise and experiences (ESRC, 2014). It therefore offers a forum to create a dialogue between these communities. Knowledge exchange helps research influence policy and practice and thus offers increased potential for research impact (HEFCE, 2015). However, it also aims to ensure that knowledge from policy and practice is included in the research process by taking account of policy and practice perspectives when constructing, sorting and organising knowledge.

The studies outlined below set out to build an 'evidence base' concerning social work and social care practitioners' experiences of, response to and preparedness for working with people affected by problematic use of alcohol or other drugs (AOD). The misuse of alcohol and other drugs is a factor that features in the lives of many people needing to access social work and social care services. The extent to which the workforce feels prepared to work with these problems, and the ways in which practice and policy can be developed to support front-line workers, are therefore pertinent issues.

Accordingly, our studies focused on both developing our understanding of the challenges faced by front-line practitioners when responding to problems associated with problematic AOD use and how these difficulties might be overcome by investigating the training opportunities available to practitioners. Increasingly social work research has embedded the perspectives of practitioners and policy makers within the process of knowledge generation, application and implementation. It has recognised the added value of their unique knowledge of constraints and enablers in the practice field. Within this context we discuss our experience of using 'knowledge exchange' as an integral part of the research process and its role in disseminating the research findings to practitioners, policy makers, social work educators and training leads.

Our use of the knowledge exchange platform was planned to occur towards the end of our work on the three linked surveys, each of which we summarise here. The first study in the series, completed in 2011, used a study-specific online survey complemented by focus groups and interviews with key informants across ten children's and seven adults' social care directorates in England (Galvani, Dance and Hutchinson, 2011). This project was focused on:

- identifying the extent and nature of practitioners' experiences with AOD problems across the range of local authority provided social work and social care services

- exploring practitioners' knowledge of and attitudes towards working with AOD problems (using an adapted version of The Alcohol and Alcohol Problems Perceptions Questionnaire (AAPPQ), see Hutchinson, Galvani and Dance, 2013)

- appraising the nature and extent of joint working with specialist substance misuse professionals

- examining practitioners' experience of and desire for training in working with service users whose AOD use is problematic.

Invitations to participate in the online survey were delivered to front-line social work and social care practitioners via contacts in each directorate. A total of 597 responses were received (excluding those working in specialist substance use roles at the time). The overall response rate was

21 per cent, with rates ranging from 12 per cent to 56 per cent across individual directorates.

The findings of this study pointed to variation in the extent to which participants encountered AOD problems depending on their area of service. The highest rates of encounters with AOD problems were reported by those working in children and families teams in relation to child protection or children in need or in care, those working with young people, and those working with adults with mental health problems. Practitioners working with older people and people with learning difficulties reported the lowest rates, although they still encountered people affected by AOD use on a regular basis. For the most part, problems with alcohol or, less often, a mix of alcohol and illicit drugs were most commonly encountered – although misuse of prescription medicines was also noted fairly often by those working with people who had physical disabilities.

An adapted version of AAPPQ standardised measure (Cartwright, 1980; Gorman and Cartwright, 1991) was embedded in the online questionnaire. Analysis based on the data returned in this study revealed differences between practitioner groups, with average scale scores for workers in adults' services indicating lower levels of confidence in their knowledge about AOD, in their access to support and in their sense of legitimacy or entitlement to intervene than was the case for workers in children's services (see Hutchinson *et al.*, 2013 for a detailed discussion of the measure, analysis and findings). Both the quantitative and qualitative data also indicated significant challenges for practitioners in working with AOD problems, particularly in managing risk and encouraging engagement with treatment services.

Despite the issues faced by practitioners when working with service users who had AOD problems, 49 per cent reported receiving no training in this area of practice on their qualifying courses and a fifth had not received it as part of Continuing Professional Development (CPD). Again children's services workers fared better that those working in adults' services and those employed as social workers fared better than practitioners from other service backgrounds. These findings provided the rationale for further analysis of these data and a further two surveys that focused on provision of AOD training in qualifying education for social workers and AOD training opportunities provided by local authorities for their social work and social care workforce.

The second study in the series built on research completed by Harrison in 1992, which examined the extent to which substance use was covered in social work education. With this survey we sought to gauge the degree to which qualifying social work programmes in England were delivering and/or integrating substance use learning into their curriculums some 20 years later. A full sampling frame of all social work qualifying programmes, and their programme leads, was constructed (157 courses in 79 universities in England). In total, responses were received from 41 universities, representing 63 qualifying programmes, which equates to a 52 per cent response rate for universities and 40 per cent response rate for programmes. There were no significant differences between responders and non-responders to the survey in terms of region, university type or faculty/department of programme, which increases confidence in the generalisability of the findings.

Initial findings suggested that 94 per cent of responding qualifying programmes provided some teaching and learning on AODs. However, further analysis revealed significant variation in what is taught and the depth of coverage. Only a few specialist modules on AOD were reported (n=13), although there were a higher number of specialist sessions (n=53). The majority reported that AOD teaching was integrated into other modules. Overall, the research highlighted a lack of consistency across programmes and possible over-reporting. The priority given to AOD teaching was considered to be too low by almost three-quarters of the respondents. No respondents thought it was too high.

The AOD-related topics most commonly included in teaching were the impact of AODs on physical/mental health, attitudes and values, and risk assessment. Gender and ethnic differences in AOD use, prescribed drug use and identifying problematic drug use were the AOD-related topics least covered. As with Harrison's (1992) research, there was a concerning degree of mismatch between the reported topic coverage and the hours in which it was taught. In a significant minority of specialist AOD modules and in half of all AOD specialist sessions far too many topics were reported as being covered in the time available. This suggests either that the coverage of topics was brief or that reporting was inaccurate.

The third survey comprised an online survey of local authority training provision, examining the extent and nature of AOD training within statutory children's services (CS) and adults' services (AS) in

England. A sampling frame was developed, which included almost all of the workforce development departments linked with every CS and AS in England. In total, 200 invitations to participate in the survey were sent to contacts in workforce learning development (WLD) departments in 94 per cent of all Local Authorities. A total of 98 surveys were returned from respondents, representing 94 workforce development departments (46% response rate) and 80 LAs (56% response rate). Data was collected on the broad characteristics of these departments and respondents; information on how substance use training is developed; and characteristics of individual substance use training courses. Comparisons of survey responders and non-responders suggest the responding departments were broadly representative of all workforce development departments in the sampling frame by region and type.

Findings indicated that between 2011 and 2012, AOD training was provided by 77 WLD departments (83%); on average, 4.56 courses on AOD were delivered per department, although AOD training was mandatory in less than one quarter (n=15, 23%). Just over one quarter of WLD departments (n=22, 28%) said there was a dedicated training strategy or a series of programmes on working with AOD use for social work and social care practitioners; slightly more reported awareness of policies and practice guidelines for working with AOD concerns (n=30, 40%). Almost 60 per cent (n=44) of WLD departments said they provided tools or resources for assessing and identifying AOD use to support social care professionals in their work.

Mirroring the reports of the practitioners surveyed in the first study, more training was aimed at social care professionals in CS than in AS, and social workers were the target of more training opportunities than other social care practitioners. Most AOD courses lasted a day at most and were considered basic (n=83, 50%) or intermediate (n=68, 41%). Three-quarters (75%) of AOD training courses were externally commissioned (n=64, 39%) or provided jointly with others (n=59, 36%). Most common topics covered in training were alcohol and its effects, illegal drugs and their effects, identifying problematic alcohol use, treatments and interventions available and impact on physical and mental health. This reflects some overlap with topics covered in qualifying education.

Taken together, the findings from all three surveys suggest practitioners face challenges in working with people affected by problematic AOD use but that training to work with these issues is far from embedded into qualifying training or CPD. Therefore, towards the end of the research a knowledge exchange event was held to discuss these findings with research users. This occurred after data collection and initial analysis of the second and third surveys. The event allowed us to present initial findings on all three surveys to potential users of the research to discuss our interpretation of the results and the implications of findings so far and to help us decide on further analysis. The way in which we incorporated this into our research process, the reasons why we did so and the role of knowledge exchange in dissemination are the focus of the remainder of this chapter.

Key innovative elements

Exploring the origins of knowledge exchange in social work research we searched the SocINDEX bibliographic database using the terms 'social work' and 'knowledge exchange' or 'knowledge transfer'. The results suggested that this terminology began to be used in late 1970s. At this point the references tended to point to 'knowledge transfer' implying that the exchange of knowledge might be in one direction with the focus being on empirical research knowledge being absorbed and utilised by policy and practice. Although the notion of exchange, rather than transfer, has become increasingly popular, the legacy of previous thinking remains strong in some areas and many dissemination strategies are based on a transfer model of knowledge sharing. The potential value of exchange of information and ideas between researchers and practitioners seems to have been first noted in relation to evaluation of planned organisational change.

These discussions about the transfer or exchange of knowledge in the literature are not confined to consideration of social work, rather ideas about facilitating change through sharing of knowledge and experience between research practice and service users span the range of activities in all human endeavour, especially in relation to health care research (e.g. Allen *et al.*, 2007).

The aim of applied social, or social work, research is, and should be, to inform policy and practice and thus contribute to changes that might lead to improvements in people's lives or their experience of using services (JUCSWEC Joint University Council Social Work Education Committee, 2006). However, there have long been tensions in this field in terms of what is to be considered knowledge, who can legitimately claim to hold knowledge, what the source of the knowledge is and what its worth is. These considerations are intrinsically bound to the debate that has raged in social work in relation to 'evidence-based practice' (Fisher, 2005, 2012; Fook, 2005).

Over the years there has been increasing critique regarding the concept of knowledge transfer or knowledge transition, which is associated with a one-way flow of 'knowledge' from researchers to policy makers and practitioners (Chew, Armstrong and Martin, 2013; Davis, Nutley and Walter, 2008; Oborn, Barrett and Racko, 2010; Murdock, Shariff and Wilding, 2013).

Knowledge 'exchange', which aims to enhance interaction between researchers and research users, can help to facilitate the conditions and circumstances that support the use of research evidence in policy and practice (Cherney *et al.*, 2012). Our experience suggests that incorporating 'knowledge exchange' as an integral part of any social work research project has huge potential to validate and ground that research activity in terms of research user involvement. Social work research is generally anxious to involve the perspectives or participation of those using services as well as policy makers and practitioners. It is worth noting at this point, that while our research was ultimately intended to inform changes that might benefit users of social work or social care services, the immediate focus was in understanding the practitioner and education provider experience. Therefore, our 'research users' were providers of social work education and workforce-based training services and the practitioners who received this training, rather than those using the services provided by social workers and social work agencies. However, knowledge exchange is conducive to a participatory and inclusive model of working with service users and their voices might be included as research users in projects with a different focus.

Our engagement with knowledge exchange reflects our recognition that the process by which research relates to policy and practice is complex, multi-way, non-linear and interactive, usually requiring behaviour change (Davies *et al.*, 2008; Knight and Lyall, 2013; Ward, House and Hamer, 2009). Clavier and colleagues (2012) write about the co-construction of knowledge by researchers and participants as research partners, suggesting that new knowledge is produced at the interface between 'academic and experiential' exchange rather than transferred from one sector to another.

This is encapsulated in the words of Davies and colleagues (2008), where they state:

we suggest that 'knowledge interaction' might more appropriately describe the messy engagement of multiple players with diverse sources of knowledge, and that 'knowledge intermediation' begins to articulate some of the managed processes by which knowledge interaction can be promoted. (p190)

Knowledge exchange can also be understood as an interactive process of learning together. Through collaboration, partners learn about each other's expertise, share knowledge and gain an appreciation of different professional cultures. As a collaborative activity, knowledge exchange can lead to a better understanding of the ways in which academic research can add value and offer insights to key issues of concern for policy and practice and can result in researchers having an improved understanding of practice and policy experience, concerns and constraints.

A variety of models of knowledge exchange have been discussed in the literature, some involving formal, long-term partnerships between universities and organisations in the form of knowledge transfer partnerships and sometimes including academic mentoring of practitioner research (Murdock *et al.*, 2013). Such activities have examined the issue of engaging involuntary service users for example (Smith *et al.*, 2012). However, these approaches can have significant cost implications (Murdock *et al.*, 2013). The model of knowledge exchange that we used was less elaborate and is illustrated in Figure 18.1. In total, 40 people took an active part in a one-off event discussing not only the findings from the three surveys, but also possible solutions to some of the challenges and barriers identified. We felt it was important not just to focus on the challenges of providing substance use education to social workers, but also to use joint and different knowledge to think about solutions and ways forward. Therefore, participants in the knowledge exchange included:

- research team members representing each strand of the research (4)
- practitioners from children's and adults services in England (20)
- social work academics/educators in England (9)
- workforce development leads (WDLs) from different LAs across England (7)

The knowledge exchange was structured as follows:

- On arrival, participants were allocated to tables for the morning session. Different types of professionals (i.e. social work educators, practitioners and WDLs) were seated together to facilitate a mixed professional discussion in the morning.

- Each study was introduced in terms of the objectives and an overview of the methodology used, but not findings. Key questions were highlighted and groups were asked to discuss what they thought the findings would be and why. Each table was asked to focus on a specific topic (issues for practitioners, issues for educators, issues for workforce development).

- Responses were sought from tables of mixed professionals on their allocated strand. Professionals were asked to predict some of the research findings and discuss reasons why they thought the research would find certain things (e.g. percentage of LAs providing training on AOD).

- Actual research findings were then presented with further invited responses from participants.

- The afternoon brought professional groups together (practitioners, educators and WDLs) and they were asked to discuss solutions to identified problems and give examples of best practice in relation to the findings relating to their professional interest area.

- The day concluded with a plenary session and final update.

- Participants were aware at the point of invitation that we would want to draw on the day's discussions when writing up our report. They therefore agreed that notes may be taken of the content of the discussions throughout the day.

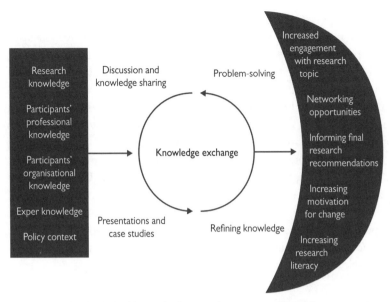

Figure 18.1: Model of knowledge exchange used in this research

Our approach, as illustrated in Figure 18.1, was to bring together research knowledge, professional knowledge/expertise and an understanding of the policy and practice context in order to facilitate discussion, mutual understanding and new learning in relation to the subject matter. We hope that participants experienced an increased understanding of the researcher perspective, found opportunities to create new networks and felt validated in their desire for change. As researchers we certainly appreciated understanding their professional and practice perspectives in helping us to draw realistic conclusions and recommendations from our studies.

Qualitative analysis was used to examine the notes written up from the day and this fed into the overall discussion for each of the studies. There was a range of reflections raised on the availability, nature and extent of training on alcohol and drugs for social work practitioners from different perspectives. Most participants assumed a poor engagement from university qualifying courses and LAs, especially regarding the strategic priority afforded to practitioner training for working with AOD. Particular attention was paid to organisational barriers that limit either training availability or the time that practitioners have to attend such events. Social work/care practitioners, social work educators and WDLs also shared their own experiences about what they do to overcome some of the challenges and barriers, which helped bring life and realism to the research recommendations. WDLs, for example, spoke about how they ensured practitioners turned up for training and how they measured the impact of the training they provided, and practitioners discussed the potential of establishing special interest study groups within their own practice context. These insights and discussions fed directly into the final research recommendations made and the nature of outputs that were developed specifically for research users. Our final report and the discussion of our findings was therefore informed by the contextual and experiential knowledge of participants. Other outcomes, as indicated in Figure 18.1, included networking opportunities, increased engagement with the research topic and increased motivation for change for all involved as well as an increased awareness of the perspectives of and constraints on other professional roles.

Strengths and challenges

When exploring the factors that facilitate the use of research in both health and social care practice, many researchers have found that opportunities for interaction between researchers, policy makers and practitioners were central to this process (Buckley *et al.*, 2014, Cherney *et al.*, 2012; McEwen *et al.*, 2008; Morton, 2014; Reimer, Sawka and James, 2005). Such interactions allow for research ideas to be communicated to researchers, research findings to be shared and discussed and new research projects to be developed. Interactions between researchers and research users also help to build 'trusting relationships' of mutual respect, which contributes to developing the 'motivation' needed to invest in the process of knowledge exchange (Allen *et al.*, 2007; Contandriopoulos *et al.*, 2010; Lencucha, Kothari and Hamel, 2010; Wilkinson, Gallagher and Smith, 2012).

Research users are more likely to invest in the process of knowledge exchange if they are confident that their contribution will be recognised, valued and used in some way. It is also thought that 'tacit' knowledge held by experienced practitioners and policy makers is best shared from interpersonal social practices (Rashman and Hartley, 2002). However, 54 per cent of respondents in a study by Cherney *et al.* (2012) said that there were a lack of networks and forums for bringing together researchers and non-academic research users. Setting up a knowledge exchange event that brings different knowledge stakeholders together in one place is one way of facilitating such interactions. In an age of competing priorities, researchers now need to invest in relationships with policy makers and practitioners to increase participation and to help research users justify valuable time spent in knowledge exchange, which may have few immediate tangible outputs.

A further factor important for ensuring research is accessible for research users is ensuring that research evidence is synthesised and disseminated in user friendly forms (Buckley *et al.*, 2014; Kouri, 2009; McEwen *et al.*, 2008). A key strength of our knowledge exchange event was that it played an important role in the final analysis of each research strand, the suggested 'solutions' or 'ways forward' and the nature of the research outputs produced. Ensuring all outputs were available at no cost and through electronic means via various networks was highlighted by the knowledge exchange participants, for example.

The programme of research described above was effective at identifying the nature and extent of substance use training provided to social workers and other social care practitioners in England, along with the barriers of providing such training and the need for it. The research was less effective at identifying the ways in which training could be improved or increased, with few examples of best practice being available. Without such data, it becomes difficult for researchers who are not part of a particular organisational context to make specific recommendations for change, often resulting in generic and sometimes unhelpful sweeping recommendations from research. Jacobson, Butterill and Goering (2003) and Kouri (2009) argue that researchers need to know more about the end user context to increase more effective use of research in practice, as end users often have to adapt research findings to create impact. Specific contexts for research use have huge implications for how research is understood, interpreted, integrated and used, and researchers often have limited scope in understanding the influence of research and how this can change over time (Morton, 2014). Our knowledge exchange invited those who would be using the research to facilitate change in their organisations and to highlight some of the policy and organisational factors impacting on this process. Findings can be open to multiple interpretations, particularly when taking into account different contexts and perspectives (Goering *et al.*, 2003; Rashman and Hartley, 2002). Inviting users of research to comment on the findings at an early stage resulted in the development of recommendations and outputs that had already received input from a wide range of research users.

Therefore, we suggest that to be most effective, knowledge exchange (whether it occurs during the research or as a dissemination strategy) should not be treated as an 'add-on' at the end of a research project. Such exchanges work best when considered at the research proposal stage and built into a project with sufficient funds allocated to the planned activities (Goering *et al.*, 2010). Holding a knowledge exchange event, which might be best considered a form of dissemination, during the research process highlights a shift in mentality about the nature of dissemination and 'application' of knowledge. A knowledge 'exchange' recognises that research findings or recommendations are not interpreted and implemented in a vacuum, but within a particular organisational, economic and political context (Buckley *et al.*, 2014; Gredig and Sommerfeld, 2008; Brownson *et al.*, 2006; Waddell *et al.*, 2005). Voices from social work education, policy and practice are not only a source from which to gather rich research data, but also partners in problem-solving ways to implement and integrate 'best practice' evidence-based research recommendations.

While knowledge exchange can occur in many formats, bringing many participants together for a specific event helped policy makers, educators and practitioners create space to engage in knowledge exchange in a tangible way, while also contributing to their own professional development. Knowledge exchange that involves structured activities with clear aims, objectives and outputs is more likely to appeal to busy research users who have to justify time spent on such activities, especially when there are funding implications.

Another reason why our knowledge exchange event was particularly successful was the relevance of the research to the participants invited to attend (as suggested by Kouri, 2009). The research gave social work educators and WDLs, in particular, straightforward and rigorous evidence about the training needs of social work practitioners in relation to substance use. Using the focus of workforce development to facilitate research transfer at an organisational level, as recommended by Reimer *et al.* (2005), was therefore easy to do. The research findings in themselves act as a resource for those meeting the training and development needs of social workers and provide evidence and justification for increased spending or prioritisation in this area. Participants were able to use the research findings shared with them at the knowledge exchange event to give substance to practical ideas about how they might go about using the research in their own specific organisational and professional contexts.

The knowledge exchange model therefore offers an alternative to a more traditional 'dissemination' style event and is one that recognises the complex process of implementing and integrating research knowledge into practice. The event allowed those who would be using the research to ask questions before they were presented with the final research recommendations, holding the research team accountable for taking into consideration the organisational, political and economic contexts of practice within which 'best' and 'evidenced-based' practice needs to function. Importantly then, our knowledge exchange took place at a point in the research that enabled the responses and participation of the beneficiaries to be reflected in the project outputs, and the event was conducted in the spirit of discussion and debate about the data already collected (and sometimes the methodology!).

It also has to be recognised that clear and targeted knowledge exchange activities are extremely attractive to research funders at this time, who have come under increased pressure from the UK government and research councils to ensure more effective use of research evidence in policy making (Holmes and Harris, 2010; Knight and Lyall, 2013). The UK government, the ESRC and the Academy of Social Sciences have played a particular role in advancing knowledge exchange activities in the social sciences, with the ESRC providing specific funding streams for programmes of knowledge exchange (Benyon, 2009; Hardill and Baines, 2009). Budgeting and planning in knowledge exchange activities was also a priority for our funder who expected outputs to be communicated to those in a policy and practice context. Commitment at a systematic level from research funders is likely to encourage researchers to think about more creative ways of interaction with research users in the future (Reimer *et al.*, 2005). Knowledge exchange activities are also increasingly being used to evidence 'impact' as defined by the Research Excellence Framework (Murdock *et al.*, 2013; Wilkinson *et al.*, 2012), shifting some of the responsibility of ensuring the use of research in practice from practitioners themselves to researchers (Brownson *et al.*, 2006).

For a multi-strand piece of research, the knowledge exchange event was also key in bringing each strand of the research together to examine the connections and relevance across different providers and receivers of social work education and training. The knowledge exchange event therefore provided the opportunity for social work practitioners, social work educators and WDLs to discuss the training they receive and provide on alcohol and drugs and how they might better share resources and reduce duplication.

One of the main challenges when designing our knowledge exchange event was how to include as many participants and knowledge bases as possible while ensuring exchanges were productive, within budget and meaningful. While the temptation might be to open up a knowledge exchange event to a large number of participants or different groups (such as service users), this needs to be balanced with the logistics of ensuring meaningful contributions and sharing. In our event the inclusion of service users might have offered a valuable perspective but would have changed the focus and the dynamic of the group. Events that become too large risk losing learning from the exchanges that take place and increase the logistical elements of facilitating meaningful and purposeful exchanges. Because our knowledge exchange event was held as part of the research process rather than as a specific form of dissemination, the event was 'invitation only' to ensure that only those professionals with relevant experience in relation to the three strands of the project were present. This allowed us to manage numbers and organise activities that would maximise both participation and exchange, ensuring that all contributions and exchanges were fed back into the research. Invitations were made based on relationships the researchers had built with relevant practice, policy and education networks. However, Cherney *et al.* (2012) warn that the partnerships built through such networks can be undermined by the high turnover of staff in public agencies or frequent reorganisations that change the nature of roles and responsibilities. This is a very real issue when working with LAs in particular.

A further challenge we encountered when developing our knowledge exchange event was ensuring the exchange was beneficial for all participants/stakeholders/attendees rather than just the research team. While we had budgeted for the venue and refreshments at the proposal stage, we were unable to pay travel costs for the attendees. This meant that in most cases participants had to apply for organisational funding (predominantly from LAs) by providing a clear justification of what they would get out of the event in terms of both professional and organisational development. This contributed to the lower than anticipated numbers of social work educators and WDLs, and inadequate agency resources for engaging with research has been cited as a significant barrier to implementing evidenced-based practice (Gray and Schubert, 2012). We were also only able to hold one event (in London), which led to a bias in the regional distribution of attendees. Nevertheless, feedback from attendees suggested they valued highly the interactive nature of the day and that it had enabled attendees to develop their own networks. We also provided access to a range of resources on alcohol and other drugs to maximise the benefit to participants.

How a knowledge exchange event is structured is likely to reflect the aims, objectives, value base and resources of the organisers (Murdock *et al.*, 2013), with decisions having to be made regarding whom to invite (such as service users, social care practitioners, qualified social workers, policy makers, managers or educators), how to share knowledge (such as through presentations, case studies, discussion groups, question and answer sessions or roundtables) and how much time to give various participants to share and exchange knowledge. Such decisions will be based on the resources available to facilitate the process and will also reflect the values and priorities of the organisers, such as whether they are willing to power share and change agendas based on the needs of various stakeholders (Kouri, 2009). While as researchers we had a specific agenda for the event, we were also aware that we had to ensure the event was valuable and meaningful for all participants.

One further consideration that needs to be borne in mind when designing 'exchange' events is the danger of research independence being diluted or agendas being dominated by practice or policy imperatives. While increased understanding of different perspectives is important, it is critical that both research and practice are able to retain their distinct value bases and perspectives. Research must retain the ability to challenge policy and practice – and vice versa.

Conclusion

Across social care, approaches to knowledge exchange and knowledge exchange events are held under various names and in various formats (Murdock *et al.*, 2013). Such exchanges might happen as 'roundtables', 'policy forums', 'professional advisory groups', 'knowledge transfer partnerships' or 'knowledge brokering events', for example. The common strengths appear to be the interactive nature of exchange that values contributions from a range of research users and seriously takes forward knowledge that is developed through these interfaces within different practice, organisational and political contexts. While there has been an increased engagement by organisations with 'knowledge brokering' activities (Chew *et al.*, 2013; Knight and Lyall, 2013), this chapter has aimed to highlight the action that can be taken by individual research teams to ensure they do all that is possible to create the environment and circumstances that facilitate rather than hinder the use of research in practice and policy contexts in social work.

Our experience of knowledge exchange as part of the research process has been a positive one and one that has highlighted for us both the opportunities it presents and the considerations for conducting future events of this kind. In our discussion of the implications of our research findings we were able to incorporate perspectives from the front-line and we hope that those who participated returned to their agencies more aware of the importance of research in the development of the services they provide. The challenges that are faced by social care today are complex, and very often daunting, and cannot be solved by researchers alone. 'Exchange' events provide an opportunity to bring various stakeholders together to identify best ways forward based on different types of knowledge. In an era of austerity and competing priorities, it is not enough to passively disseminate research and hope it will be useful – research agendas and findings need to be located in specific organisational, political and practice contexts. Applied researchers in the social sciences therefore have a responsibility to take such 'exchange' events seriously at the beginning of the research process rather than leave it as an afterthought at the end.

References

Allen, P., Peckham, S., Anderson, S. and Goodwin, N. (2007) 'Commissioning research that is used: The experience of the NHS Service Delivery and Organisation Research and Development Programme.' *Evidence and Policy: A Journal of Research, Debate and Practice* 3, 1, 119–134.

Benyon, J. (2009) 'Developing greater dialogue: Knowledge transfer, public engagement and learned societies in the social sciences.' *Twenty- First Century Society 4*, 1, 97–113.

Brownson, R., Royer, C. Reid, B. and McBride, T. (2006) 'Researchers and policymakers, travelers in parallel universes.' *American Journal of Preventive Medicine 30*, 2, 164–172.

Buckley, H., Tonmyr, L., Lewig, K. and Jack, S. (2014) 'Factors influencing the uptake of research evidence in child welfare: A synthesis of findings from Australia, Canada and Ireland.' *Child Abuse Review 23*, 1, 5–16.

Cartwright, A. K. J. (1980) 'The attitudes of helping agents towards the alcoholic client: The influence of experience, support, training and self-esteem.' *British Journal of Addiction 75*, 413–431.

Cherney, A., Head, B., Boreham, P., Povey, J. and Ferguson, M. (2012) 'Perspectives of academic social scientists on knowledge transfer and research collaborations: A cross-sectional survey of Australian academics.' *Evidence and Policy: A Journal of Research, Debate and Practice 8*, 4, 433–453.

Chew, S., Armstrong, N. and Martin, G. (2013) 'Institutionalising knowledge brokering as a sustainable knowledge translation solution in healthcare: How can it work in practice?' *Evidence and Policy: A Journal of Research, Debate and Practice 9*, 3, 335–351.

Clavier, C., Sénéchal, Y., Vibert, S. and Potvin, L. (2012) 'A theory-based model of translation practices in public health participatory research.' *Sociology of Health and Illness 34*, 5, 791–805.

Contandriopoulos, D., Lemire, M., Denis, J. and Tremblay, E. (2010) 'Knowledge exchange processes in organizations and policy arenas: A narrative systematic review of the literature.' *Milbank Quarterly 88*, 4, 444–83. doi: 10.1111/j.1468-0009.2010.00608.x.

Davies, H., Nutley, S. and Walter, I. (2008) 'Why "knowledge transfer" is misconceived for applied social research.' *Journal of Health Services Research and Policy 13*, 3, 188–190.

ESRC (2014) *Knowledge Exchange*, Online. Swindon: ESRC. Available at www.esrc.ac.uk/collaboration/knowledge-exchange/, accessed on 9 April 2015.

Fisher, M. (2005) 'Knowledge Production for Social Welfare: Enbancing the Evidence Base.' In P. Sommerfeld (ed.) *Evidence-Based Social Work: Towards a New professionalism?* Bern: Peter Lang.

Fisher, M. (2012) 'Beyond evidence-based policy and practice: Reshaping the relationship between research and practice.' *Social Work and Social Sciences Review 16*, 2, 20–36.

Fook, J. (2005) 'What Professionals Need From Research: Beyond Evidence-based Practice.' In D. Smith (ed) *Social Work and Evidence Based Practice, Research Highlights in Social Work 45*. London: Jessica Kingsley Publishers.

Galvani, S., Dance, C. and Hutchinson, A. (2011) *From the Front Line: Alcohol, Drugs and Social Care Practice: A National Study*. Luton: University of Bedfordshire.

Goering, P., Butterill, D., Jacobson, N. and Sturtevant, D. (2003) 'Linkage and exchange at the organizational level: A model of collaboration between research and policy.' *Journal of Health Services Research and Policy 8*, 14–19.

Goering, P., Ross, S., Jacobson, N. and Butterill, D. (2010) 'Developing a guide to support the knowledge translation component of the grant application process.' *Evidence and Policy: A Journal of Research, Debate and Practice 6*, 1, 91–102.

Gorman, D. M. and Cartwright, A. K. J. (1991) 'Implications of using the composite and short versions of the Alcohol and Alcohol Problems Perception Questionnaire (AAPPQ).' *British Journal of Addiction 86*, 327–334.

Gray, M. and Schubert, L. (2012) 'Sustainable social work: Modelling knowledge production, transfer, and evidence-based practice.' *International Journal of Social Welfare 21*, 2, 203–214.

Gredig, D. and Sommerfeld, P. (2008) 'New proposals for generating and exploiting solution-oriented knowledge.' *Research on Social Work Practice 18*, 4, 292–300.

Hardill, I. and Baines, S. (2009) 'Personal reflections on knowledge transfer and changing UK research priorities.' *21st Century Society: Journal of the Academy of Social Sciences 4*, 1, 83–96.

Harrison, L. (1992) 'Substance misuse and social work qualifying training in the British Isles: A survey of CQSW courses.' *British Journal of Addiction 87*, 635–642.

Higher Education Council for England (HEFCE) (2015) *REF Impact*. Available at: www. hefce.ac.uk/rsrch/REFimpact/. Accessed on 2 August 2015.

Holmes, J. and Harris, B. (2010) 'Enhancing the contribution of research councils to the generation of evidence to inform policy making.' *Evidence and Policy: A Journal of Research, Debate and Practice 6*, 3, 391–409.

Hutchinson, A., Galvani, S. and Dance, C. (2013) 'Working with substance use: Levels and predictors of positive therapeutic attitudes across social care practitioners in England.' *Drugs, Education, Prevention and Policy 20*, 4, 312–321.

Jacobson, N., Butterill, D. and Goering, P. (2003) 'Development of a framework for knowledge translation: Understanding user context.' *Journal of Health Services Research and Policy 8*, 2, 94–99.

JUCSWEC Joint University Council Social Work Education Committee (2006) *A Social Work Research Strategy in Higher Education 2006–2020*. London: Social Care Workforce Research Unit.

Knight, C. and Lyall, C. (2013) 'Knowledge brokers: The role of intermediaries in producing research impact.' *Evidence and Policy: A Journal of Research, Debate and Practice 9*, 3, 309–316.

Kouri, D. (2009) 'Knowledge exchange strategies for interventions and policy in public health.' *Evidence and Policy: A Journal of Research, Debate and Practice 5*, 1, 71–83.

Lencucha, R., Kothari, A. and Hamel, N. (2010) 'Extending collaborations for knowledge translation: Lessons from the community-based participatory research literature.' *Evidence and Policy: A Journal of Research, Debate and Practice 6*, 1, 61–75.

McEwen, J., Crawshaw, M., Liversedge, A. and Bradley, G. (2008) 'Promoting change through research and evidence-informed practice: A knowledge transfer partnership project between a university and a local authority.' *Evidence and Policy: A Journal of Research, Debate and Practice 4*, 4, 391–403.

Morton, S. (2014) 'Creating research impact: the roles of research users in interactive research mobilization.' *Evidence and Policy*. Available at http://dx.doi.org/10.1332/17 4426514X13976529631798, accessed on 9 April 2015.

Murdock, A., Shariff, R. and Wilding, K. (2013) 'Knowledge exchange between academia and the third sector.' *Evidence and Policy: A Journal of Research, Debate and Practice 9*, 3, 419–430.

Oborn, E., Barrett, M. and Racko, G. (2010) *Knowledge Transaction in Healthcare: A Review of the Literature. Cambridge Judge Business School Working Paper Series (No 5/2010)*. Cambridge: Cambridge Judge Business School. Available at www.jbs.cam.ac.uk/fileadmin/user_upload/research/workingpapers/wp1005.pdf, accessed on 9 April 2015.

Rashman, L. and Hartley, J. (2002) 'Leading and learning? Knowledge transfer in the Beacon Council Scheme.' *Public Administration 80*, 3, 523–542.

Reimer, B., Sawka, E. and James, D. (2005) 'Improving research transfer in the addictions field: A perspective from Canada.' *Substance Use and Misuse 40*, 11, 1707–1720.

Smith, M., Gallagher, M., Wosu, H., Stewart, J., Cree, V., Hunter, S., Evans, S., Montgomery, C., Holiday, S. and Wilkinson, H. (2012) 'Engaging with Involuntary Service Users in Social Work: Findings from a Knowledge Exchange Project.' *British Journal of Social Work 42, 1460–1477 doi:10.1093/bjsw/bcr162*.

Waddell, C., Lavis, J. N., Abelson, J., Lomas, J. *et al.* (2005) 'Research use in children's mental health policy in Canada: Maintaining vigilance amid ambiguity.' *Social Science and Medicine 61*, 8, 1649–1657.

Ward, V., House, A. and Hamer, S. (2009) 'Developing a framework for transferring knowledge into action: A thematic analysis of the literature.' *Journal of Health Services Research and Policy 14*, 3, 156–164.

Wilkinson, H., Gallagher, M., and Smith, M. (2012) 'A collaborative approach to defining the usefulness of impact: Lessons from a knowledge exchange project involving academics and social work practitioners.' *Evidence and Policy: A Journal of Research, Debate and Practice 8*, 3, 311–327.

Chapter 19

YOU'RE NOT IN THE PICTURE

Service Users, Research, Involvement and Change

JENNIFER TAYLOR, GINA BARRETT, VIC FORREST,
PETER BERESFORD AND BECKI MEAKIN
People First Lambeth, Shaping Our Lives and Brunel University

Introduction

Let's start at the beginning. Aidan Worsley, one of the editors of this book, contacted me (Peter) at Shaping Our Lives and asked if we would like to write a chapter for this book. He said he'd particularly like us to write about 'dissemination' (we'll come back to that word!) and 'how broader approaches to an understanding of that word might be' helpful. Five of us have been involved in writing this chapter: Peter, who Aidan was originally in touch with – who is Co-Chair of Shaping Our Lives; Becki, the General Manager of Shaping Our Lives, who has said some things about our organisation; and last and certainly not least, Jennifer, Gina and Vic, who have written most of what's here. First let me (Peter) explain how we went about this. I let people know about the contact from Aidan at a Shaping Our Lives Management Board meeting. Some of us who were interested signed up to get the work done. We had a meeting of all five of us to work out how we would go ahead with it and then Gina, Vic and Jennifer got together to write their bit. They have worked this way before, so it was something they knew they could do okay.

We have wanted to be clear about how we have written this chapter so that other service users and people with learning difficulties can have a clear picture of how we did it. Sometimes we have read things that are supposed to be written by people with learning difficulties and it is not really clear how they did it or what part supporters or non-disabled people played in writing it. That can mean people don't really believe people with learning difficulties did it themselves, or what is written may be as difficult to understand as anything else. So we wanted to be clear. We should also explain that Vic is an experienced and skilled supporter who has done a lot of work to support people with learning difficulties. And I (Peter) would want to say that I have often seen him working like this and he is great because he never speaks for them, but is very good at making it possible for them to say what they want to say. We can also hear from him here in his role as a supporter.

So, in this chapter, next we will tell you something about Shaping Our Lives (that will be in Becki's words), then you will hear what Vic, Jennifer and Gina want to say about 'dissemination' and finally we will make some general points from this, which we hope are helpful.

Shaping Our Lives

Shaping Our Lives[1] is a national organisation and network of user-led organisations, service users and disabled people. We are a non-profit making organisation. We are a user-led organisation (ULO) committed to inclusive involvement and we specialise in the research and practice of involving diverse communities in policy, planning and delivery of services. This is reflected in both our own ways of work and governance as well as our focus. We are run by a management board, all of whom are disabled people and other service users and also a larger National User Group, again made up entirely of service users, all of whom are strongly networked and actively involved in supporting service users. We facilitate service user involvement at local and national level and use lived experiences to influence and inform regulators and statutory providers.

Our vision

Our vision is of a society where all people have the same rights, responsibilities, choices and opportunities; a society where people have choice and control over the services they use and how they live their lives. Shaping Our Lives has 12 years' experience of undertaking research with and consulting with service users and representing their views. Our inclusive approach enables people from all communities to have an equal say, including people with physical, sensory and cognitive impairments, older people, people in care, homeless people, mental health service users, people with alcohol or drug use issues,

1   www.shapingourlives.org.uk

people from black and minority ethnic (BME) communities and people from the lesbian, gay, bisexual and transgender (LGBT) communities. We understand that people have complex identities and recognise that people often face multiple disadvantages and that there is interconnection between economic, social, cultural and environmental influences.

Our aims

Through our network of nearly 450 user-led organisations Shaping Our Lives aims to improve the quality of care and support services people receive by:

- involving service users in helpful consultation and research initiatives to demonstrate user-led outcomes and influence the planning and provision of services

- supporting the development of local user involvement so better outcomes are achieved for service users in their communities

- giving a shared voice to user controlled organisations and service users

- enabling service user involvement at a national and local level

- enabling groups to link to other user controlled groups

- working across all user groups in an equal and accessible manner.

Some of our projects

To give you an idea of the work we do, here are some of our current activities and projects.

Shaping Our Lives is a Strategic Partner for the Department of Health, NHS England and Public Health England representing service user voices. We have worked with the Joseph Rowntree Foundation, National Skills Academy for Social Care, Health and Care Professions Council and Social Care Institute for Excellence among many others, to involve service users in policy and regulatory consultations.

PowerUs[2] is a partnership between Lillehammer University Norway, Lund University Sweden and Shaping Our Lives National User Network in the UK. It has been funded by the EU Education and Culture Learning Programme. The project focuses on social work education

---

2   http://powerus.se

and practice. For the last two years the partnership has pioneered a model for service user involvement in social work education – 'mending the gap'. It brings service users into the classroom to study alongside social work students for a module of the course. The outcomes in all the test sites have been extremely positive and by learning together it has been possible to break down many barriers between service users and future social workers. As part of this project we have developed a UK and international charter.

Shaping Our Age – Involving Older Age: The
Route to Twenty First Century Well-being
We recently conducted an evaluation of the Shaping Our Age three-year research study funded by the Big Lottery Fund and led by the Royal Voluntary Service in partnership with De Montfort and Brunel University London.[3] The evaluation examined the views of older people from diverse communities (who may not have been represented in the initial study) and asked them to share their views on well-being and involvement in the services they use. The groups included older people in residential nursing care, older disabled people, older LGBT people, older people from BME communities and older men.

Beyond the Usual Suspects: Towards Inclusive User Involvement
Beyond the Usual Suspects has produced a range of resources resulting from four years of research conducted by Shaping Our Lives, funded by the Department of Health, into the continued exclusion of diverse communities in involvement activities, the factors that contribute to this and ways to overcome it. This includes a research report, findings and practical guide supplemented with a DVD of case studies, a poster and eight electronic resources for putting theory into practice.[4]

'Dissemination' and 'impact' – from a service user perspective
Having put what we do and who we are in context, here is the heart of our contribution – a discussion from people with learning difficulties, offering their thoughts and perspectives on the issues we were asked to consider.

---

3   www.royalvoluntaryservice.org.uk/our-impact/involving-older-people
4   www.shapingourlives.org.uk/ourpubs.html#Beyond

Gina: I'm kinda stuck with research 'dissemination'. I've never heard that phrase. So that's just kind of thrown me … Even though you explained, it's getting your head around the long word and I don't think it's a good word for people with learning difficulties. People won't understand it.

Jennifer: And it's not easy reading.

Gina: It's a jargon word to us and we've always said we don't understand jargon words.

Vic: Research books and papers often have lots of words like that in them…

Gina: The world we live in and the world they live in is two different worlds. We live in the real society and they live in – I don't know what society they live in.

Vic: Research about social work and the best ways for social workers to work goes on all the time in different universities. Do you get to see and understand much of it?

Jennifer: No. I don't think so Vic. The only person who sees it is them, the social workers…and the universities. …They should work better.

Gina: And show us what they do.

Jen: They should work in partnership with us.

Gina: …I think they should show it to us, or read it to us, what they put down on paper. So we will have an opinion about it and we could say if it was good or bad.

Jen: …For me I think that's bad for them not showing us what they put down on paper.

Gina: They can write anything and we wouldn't know. They could say horrible stuff about us and we still wouldn't know.

Jen: They should put it in a book or a magazine.

Vic: They do. They put it in academic journals and some social work magazines and in books and on websites.

Jen: Then we won't get to see it.

Gina: We definitely won't be hearing about it either.

Jen: They might put it in a film then everyone could see it. I don't know?

Vic: Well, some people do that but not a lot of researchers do, I don't think they do... How do you think things should work? What should happen in your opinion?

Gina: Basically, what I think they should do is consult with us. Tell exactly what they are going to say so that we will have an opinion and say if it's good, or bad, or okay, what they are writing.

Jennifer: They should show us what they are writing about... Because we have got every right to see what they are writing about us and other service users.

Vic: ...They also write about how social workers should behave.

Jen: In the workforce ... We should know about it because we are service users and we need to see what's going on in the workforce... We know what we want and how to work with us.

Gina: Cause we know what we want and we know what we would like to do, and we would like them to work in a way that we can relate to them – so they know where we are coming from and how we can get support to do the things that we want to do in our lives. ...We would like to see the finished research because then we could read it and...say what our views are.

Vic: The research journals cost money, sometimes quite a lot. It would take a long time for supporters to explain much of the research in Plain English, if we could afford the journals and magazines. ...Some supporters might not understand the academic language themselves, and I've never heard of a job where a supporter was asked to keep up with social work research and explain it in ways that are more accessible to more people, including people with learning difficulties. Some research is on the internet in short versions that are easier to understand, but I don't think many people are spending time keeping service users, who need support to access the information, up with the latest social work research. I don't think many funders are paying for that to happen. Do you think people should be trying to get over these problems?

Jennifer: Yes, Vic. It's about time we did see the research and see it for ourselves as service users. I would be very interested to see it ... I am a researcher and I would to find out who the researchers are and what they do. I would like to find out more what they've written about people with learning difficulties.

Gina: ...I would be very interested to see it, to see if they have said what we've said. To see if they've wrote what we've been saying all along ... For years we've been saying we're not included, that they haven't involved us in what they say about us and about how they work with us ... We know about us and what we want from them...the social workers.

Jen: And what we go through, as people with learning difficulties. We get bullied and called nasty names. We know what we want in our lives and exactly what's going on in our lives ... We've got every right to have a say, and get our rights met and be ourselves like everybody else and just live our lives to the full. Social workers need to know what we go through as people with learning difficulties.

Gina: ...We need to know if they are moving in the right direction, because they could be moving in the wrong direction ... I think the social workers need to tell us more because the way they work, I don't think they include service users, [in] the way they work and I think they should ... They can have all these books but I'm sure that half of the service users don't see the books. So what's the point of having the books if the service users don't get to see them, unless they want to hide it ... I think it's wrong, absolutely wrong ... We don't know what they're thinking and we don't know how they're researching everything. So, I think it's very difficult ... You're not involved so that's why you're out of the picture.

Vic: You have done quite lot of research here and been involved in other research projects ... Didn't you make one [a research report] accessible for Shaping Our Lives?

Gina: Yeah we did. We made the writing accessible with pictures and easy reading... We got to understand the research and we got a book as well, with the research in ... It was good because I understood it, when I did it.[5]

Jennifer: I was involved in the book We Are Not Stupid with Raymond, Vanessa, Maggie and Ian [People First Lambeth members]. After we done the book we had a launch about the book and we gave copies to everybody that was interested to read the book – to service users and carers and their families. And I did another book for Jessica Kingsley. It was called *Service User Involvement* ... They were very interesting books. I gave a copy of *We Are Not Stupid* to my mum to take back to the United States, as a present really.[6]

Vic: How do you feel about people reading *We Are Not Stupid?*

Jennifer: I feel really proud of myself. My mum's proud of me for doing the book and I gave one to everyone I know where I live because they wanted a copy ...[The book explains] what people with learning difficulties go through in life and what they want to achieve in life.

Vic: I've never seen any jobs in universities that would allow me to work in a way where service users with learning difficulties are fully involved in research. None of the jobs I've seen advertised so far seem to be anything like how we work in People First Lambeth.

Gina: They won't be like that because they don't work like that, the way we work. So, there's not going to be a job like that – that works the way we work.

Vic: Perhaps we should explain how we work?

Gina: We work in a way that everybody, the service users, can understand...and relate [to] and we have a say in everything we do in People First [Lambeth] and...organisations should follow us because we do things in a way that people with learning difficulties can understand.

---

5   www.shapingourlives.org.uk/documents/person-centred-support_summary.pdf
6   www.shapingourlives.org.uk/documents/wansweb.pdf

Vic: …Day in day out we've worked on every little bit of the [latest People First Lambeth research] project with a group of people with learning difficulties.

Jennifer: Before it even started Vic, before we even done it.

Vic: And I don't think universities work like that really, not really. And we struggle so much for money.

Jen: Funding as well, Vic.

Vic: We have to work really hard for people to take us seriously. I agree that people with learning difficulties should be right in the middle of research that's anything to do with your lives.

Jennifer: …Because we know what's best for us and we know what we want and I've said this in *We Are Not Stupid* as well. It's like they're trying to hide things away from us and they shouldn't be doing that… We've been through it since we were kids. We've been bullied and called names and we know what's best for us and we know what we want in our lives.

Vic: Peter Beresford wrote a book about how first-hand experience is not always valued in research and about how people who've lived something know so much more than someone who's only read about it. I never feel like I'm an expert on what you want or what you should have. You understand more about that because it's your life and experience. You are the ones who can say what you want and whether it works.

Jennifer: Or not.

Vic: It's like a lot of research is removed from the people who it's about or for – and it can't be as good for helping people as research that really involves service users at a deep level, all the way through.

Gina: …With this research we're doing, with our research, we want to know what service users think about what we're doing… whether it works or whether it don't work we want to hear, and if they understand it or they don't understand it we still want to hear – if we're doing something good or something bad. …I hope people can use it and understand it.

Vic: What people?

Gina: Service users, social workers, mums and dads – all the people that need to use it – maybe even doctors or nurses, dentists, even police.

Jennifer: …What about carers they need to hear about it as well and know what's going on around them. The research needs to be spread around to everybody in a way that they can understand it properly.

Discussion

What is good about what's happened here, is that, for once, the editors of a social work research book have actively involved people as service users and given them the chance to say what they think about something important in research – dissemination. The first thing this highlights, of course, is how far away service users can feel from this discussion. But it also provides the opportunity to start a conversation about it and to let people in social work know how it might feel and that there is an issue to think about. It's also important to remember that the people with learning difficulties here are people who have been involved in research and carried out some of their own. So there may be even bigger barriers to overcome for many others, if social work researchers really want to reach and engage them. This seems very important if research is to be something that empowers people rather than disempowers them (Beresford, 2003).

One thing we have learned in Shaping Our Lives, is that dissemination or information sharing or knowledge exchange – call it what you will – can have different meanings. Often people think it just means telling politicians and policy makers what you find out from research, so that they may act or think differently. Sadly, in modern times, often they don't take much notice, since they have their own ideas of what they want to do, which tend to be different to what service users say they want.

All the evidence highlights that service users get involved because they want to make things better for other service users (Beresford and Carr, 2012). For us the key point of dissemination is bringing about positive change. Getting that from politicians and policy makers can be very difficult, especially when the emphasis is on funding and spending cuts. But dissemination can be geared much more to reaching service users themselves and their families. And this is very important, because if service users find out about things, then it can help them have new hopes, higher expectations and more positive feelings about themselves. And when we gain more confidence and feel stronger about ourselves, for example by learning from research what might be possible for our lives, from the experience of other people, then we become a stronger force for change. We are part of a movement – working from the bottom up – trying to make improvements happen. We can call for things to change and, as there are more of us, our voices get louder and more powerful. So researchers planning dissemination should also work to spread the word to disabled people, service users and our organisations.

This is why what Gina and Jennifer have said in this chapter is so important. People with learning difficulties and other service users need to be involved. Researchers should reach out to include them in dissemination. They should get in touch with service users and their user-led organisations to advise them on how to have more accessible and inclusive dissemination policies. They should do more to use simple English and easyread – providing information clearly, accessibly and without jargon – when they write up their research and findings. It is also important to involve as diverse a range of service users as possible to avoid mirroring the way many groups tend to get left out of things generally in society (Beresford, 2013). Then more and more people with learning difficulties and other service users will be calling for the results of research to be put into practice – and that research will have more positive effects. This will be helpful for social workers, researchers and, most importantly, service users and their families. Also, I hope social work researchers will increasingly support the direct involvement of service users as researchers, helping them gain skills and qualifications to carry out research themselves, leading to the kind of change they want to see.

References

Beresford, P. (2003) *It's Our Lives: A Short Theory of Knowledge, Distance and Experience.* London: Citizen Press in association with Shaping Our Lives.

Beresford, P. (2013) *Beyond the Usual Suspects: Towards inclusive User Involvement – Research Report.* London: Shaping Our Lives.

Beresford, P. and Carr, S. (eds) (2012) *Service Users, Social Care And User Involvement, Research Highlights Series.* London: Jessica Kingsley Publishers.

CONCLUSION

| LOUISE HARDWICK AND AIDAN WORSLEY
| *University of Liverpool and University of Central Lancashire*

The chapters in this book highlight how, at differing stages of the research process, contributors have stepped into diverse territories demanded by the social work endeavour (excellence in research and practice). In this way the accounts are intended to provide inspiration and guidance, and lead to the confident engagement with a wide range of methodological approaches appropriate to social work.

As Thompson argues in Chapter 12, social work research should both inform, and be informed by social work practice, and should be viewed as ' inextricably linked' to the social work endeavour. This is important given the present difficult context practitioners work in. The recent parliamentary inquiry into the state of social work in the UK (British Association of Social Workers (BASW), 2013, p.8) revealed that the recommendations from the Munro Review (2011) were 'already old news', and had failed to effect the change needed for the profession. Unfortunately, social workers continue to experience endemic low morale, high caseloads and unacceptable levels of bureaucracy. Inevitably, this impacts on practitioners' ability to address the needs of social groups at the extreme end of social inequality. This has been compounded by the Comprehensive Spending Review of 2010, leading as it has to draconian responses from the Conservative-led Coalition government who have chosen, amongst other policies, welfare reform and major cuts to public sector funding as a means to tackle the fiscal shortfall of the economic downturn of 2008. These factors have contributed to social work practice becoming curtailed when attempting to address the increasing levels of social injustice faced by service users, and this is exemplified by the tighter threshold criteria for preventative intervention with children and stricter eligibility criteria for social care for adults (BASW, 2013). Social work research can play a vital part in supporting social work practice, providing a complementary way of giving voice to service users' perspectives – voices that might otherwise remain unheard. It can also propose and develop new ways of working, as well as highlighting unintended consequences of social policies. It offers 'another approach for achieving social work objectives' (D'Cruz and Jones, 2004, p.58).

Although the approaches taken in these chapters are highly diverse they have a common 'identity and purpose', in ways that mark them out as part of the social work endeavour (Smith, 2012, p.433). They demonstrate a 'commitment to service users and social justice' (Smith 2012, p.434) by connecting the personal troubles of participants to wider public issues (Mills, 1959, p.8) and adopting ethical and emancipatory approaches attuned to the Joint University Council of Social Work Education Committee (JUCSWEC) Code of Ethics for social work research (2008). Taken together, these approaches have the potential to effect change for the better by unmasking structural inequalities that have conditioned the lives of service users and the policies and legislative frameworks that social workers practice within.

Although social work research can incorporate both social statistics and quantitative methods, the bias in this book and in social work research more generally, is towards qualitative and participatory approaches because they lend themselves more readily, although not exclusively as will be evidenced in the next section, to allowing the voices of the marginalised to be heard. Any social work research project will, of course, be influenced by numerous practical considerations such as the experience of the researcher, the agenda of the sponsor, the context of the study and the wishes of other stakeholders. But, despite these considerations, social work research has an explicit value base that permeates through with its critical and reflexive mindset, whatever the methods adopted. There is an awareness of the researcher's own position in the research process both ethically and politically, alongside an awareness of the participant's position and that of other stakeholders. There is acknowledgement of the differing social and political positions held and consequent subjectivities that make any claims to value-free objectivity highly problematic (Stanley and Wise, 1993). This is inevitable given that social workers are trained to be critically reflexive and aware of the impact of self on practice and in the research process.

Quantitative methods, secondary data and new technologies

The chosen epistemological and methodological approaches of social work research are becoming increasingly eclectic, including moving into territories traditionally seen as the domain of the natural sciences. As Elliott points out in his account of using logistic regression analysis to test the hypothesis that there is a link in the UK between certain socio-economic factors and child welfare concerns (Chapter 15), there is nothing in itself pioneering about using quantitative methods, but in the arena of social work research they remain underutilised. Similarly, another method uncommon for social work research is explored in Jessiman, Carpenter and O'Donnell's exploration of the challenges of undertaking a randomised controlled trial (RCT) when investigating an intervention for children affected by sexual abuse in Chapter 2. Westlake (Chapter 3) also adopts an RCT in his account of two naturalistic observational studies designed to facilitate 'practice-near' insights into the encounters of social workers and service users (parents/guardians and children). And in Chapter 6 Wade and Fisher use a systematic review, usually associated with the medical sciences, to understand the views of people living with dementia. The review is enhanced by gathering additional data on the views of a small group of people with the condition, thereby enabling some people with dementia to 'have a say' on what the systematic review revealed as their views.

In Hackett *et al.*'s account (Chapter 5) we are encouraged to be adventurous and try new technologies to track down groups considered to be hard-to-reach participants. The research team in this account wanted to trace adults who, as children, were subject to professional interventions because of their sexually abusive behaviours. It was thought they would be difficult to find and that, because of sensitive biographical histories, they would want to remain hidden and/or be reluctant to engage in the research. The research team used the internet and social media to locate the sample and invite individuals to participate, and, perhaps even more innovatively, used this medium for some interviews. Prescinding the ethical considerations implicit in this approach, the readers are directed to the chapter where these are thoroughly covered. The authors conclude by highlighting the usefulness of the internet for social work research when looking into historical documents and for tracing individuals and social groups using social media. In Chapter 4 this theme is taken up from a different perspective by Starkey with her guide to how to use archive material to research the history of social work. Although she acknowledges that there is a substantial amount of material available on-line, and that internet searching is a key aspect of this type of research, she offers a cautionary note regarding what constitutes a reliable site and emphasises the need for interrogation of when a document was written and why and by whom and for whom?

Shifting engagements and 'insider knowledge'

Many of the accounts in the preceding chapters can be characterised by the nature of the relationship between the researcher and participants. They are very different from research in which the expert is strongly distinguished from and 'acts/experiments upon' their (often unwitting) 'subjects' – a process whereby researchers engage in 'othering' research participants (Eikeland, 2006, p.37). From the value perspective of social work, it unjustly distinguishes the researcher from participants by allowing the research to take the role of the expert doing research *on* and *for* the participant(s). By way of contrast, many of the participants in the studies documented are treated as experts, informing the researcher(s) about what they should treat as relevant, helping to balance structural power differentials. Researchers have engaged in research *with* participants often involving the social work practitioners, service users, community groups and/or other representatives who can at different times and in different permutations actively contribute to the research process, not just as participants but as co-designers, gatekeepers, recruiters and beneficiaries. These shifting engagements (Simon and Mosavel, 2010, p.8) can help significantly overcome trust barriers and facilitate 'insider knowledge'.

This is particularly evident in Banks' account of a community action research project on debt in low-income households in Teeside (Chapter 1). The project brought together a university, local community organisation and national charity. It was action orientated through three activities: a mentoring scheme, campaigning and community action. Those who might have been considered 'subjects' within a differently designed study instead played a part in contributing to its design and contributing to the research process, thus embedding insider knowledge at the heart of the project. The impact of the research was targeted towards local campaigning, policy makers and politicians with the aim of 'making life better for people experiencing indebtedness in the local and national area'.

Similarly, in Chapter 16 Dominelli describes an evaluation undertaken with a women's organisation where a Feminist Participatory Action Research (FPAR) approach is taken. FPAR involves interested parties engaging in a cyclical process of action and reflection leading to the co-production of knowledge and solutions and facilitating the possibility of participants seeing their social situation in new ways that identify their social, economic and political position (Friere, 1972).

Jackie Robinson's account explores a Participatory Action Research (PAR) project with three co-researchers with Asperger's syndrome (Chapter 14). She focuses in particular on understanding the data from the perspective of the co-researchers and together they develop the 'Triad of Understanding' (me understanding myself, me understanding others and others understanding me). She comments on how despite her previous experience of working with people with this condition she still miscalculated that one of the three co-researchers would be willing to chair meetings and reflects how easy it is to unintentionally undermine participation.

Challenging our taken-for-granted assumptions is a central theme in Temple's detailed account of a study that explores research participants who speak another language and whose voice is heard through use of an interpreter (Chapter 13). She evidences how these voices are too easily assumed to have a similar world view to the researcher, and how this can contribute to these voices being less valued or even wiped out of the research data.

In Chapter 12, Thompson explores the importance of reciprocity for dependent older people through a phenomenological lens that provides a 'sensitising framework' and a tool for analysis. This helps reveal the constraints of the wider political and social forces on dependent older people and their unique perspective and ways of understanding the world.

Awareness of shifting engagements between the individual researcher and collaborators is also evident in Smith's account of exploring the elements involved in a maintaining a good relationship between himself, as the invited professional consultant, and a 'training for trainers' project for people with learning difficulties (Chapter 7). He found that certain tasks, like collation, recording and analysis of responses, were reserved for him because of his 'assumed expertise', reinforcing existing power relations that were not necessarily explicitly discussed at the outset. Readjusting the power dynamics involved Smith actively reflecting and renegotiating tasks in an inclusive way that drew on the organisation's expertise and encouraged dialogue and trust between parties. He observes that this study led him to conclude that in such collaborations it is the *quality of the relationship* between the parties that ultimately determines how well the project works and that leads to more rigorous research.

Ethnographic approach and mobile and visual methods

Ferguson's study (Chapter 8) uses an ethnographic approach that combines with mobile methods as a means to getting closer to practice. This comes alive in his account of a home visit with the social worker who is tasked with assessing how well a father is coping after the mother has been charged with assault on her stepson (now removed to extended family) and with caring for the remaining three young children. Significant data on the anxieties of the social worker, the physicality of the home environment and the process before, during and after the encounter are elicited through shadowing the social worker.

Natalie Robinson's account of the annual 'Hope in Shadows' photography contest in a low-income inner-city neighbourhood in Canada explores how photography can facilitate a discussion about personal and collective identities (Chapter 17). The methods adopted are participatory observation and focus groups, and the visual data is analysed through means of an open dialogue with participants. She actively retreats from taking on the role as 'expert', allowing participants to give accounts that move beyond the 'normative' and that reveal the significance of self and place.

Similarly, in Chapter 10 Leigh recalls how her comparative ethnography study uses photography to help reveal hidden cultural aspects of two differing practice settings, and how these in turn influence the construction of the professional identities of the two differing groups of social workers. In Chapter 9 Roy *et al.* adopt a mobile method (walking while listening and watching), and allowing the participant to take the researcher on a guided tour of significant places of their choosing. The physical activity helps relax the walkers, allowing disclosures regarding the significance of self and space/environment. Manley, Roy and Froggett (Chapter 11) use a 'visual matrix' as a means of facilitating getting close or 'practice-near' to participants in recovery. This approach, like the others discussed above, does not rely solely on language but encourages 'visual thinking' and new ways of understanding complex and embodied emotions.

Sharing knowledge with the people who matter

As has already been noted, social work researchers are concerned with working for social justice and often have a long-term commitment to the participants and communities they research with, including sharing knowledge, expertise and recommendations for future practice and policy strategies. This is focus of the account given by Hutchinson and Dance in Chapter 18 that involved practitioners who used a knowledge exchange platform to discuss the findings of the three online surveys that had explored the nature and extent of substance use training. They found bringing together practitioners, researchers, policy makers and educators was a constructive way of disseminating the findings and including all the relevant stakeholders in discussion on future strategies for training and practice.

But lest we become too buoyant about the potential of social work research to effect change for the better, Taylor *et al.* acknowledge that this can sometimes be more wishful thinking than reality (Chapter 19). Taylor *et al.*'s chapter is collated by Peter Beresford on behalf of key members of a user-led organisation for people with learning difficulties and it explains the range of strategic forums and funded research initiatives the organisation has been involved with and their mission to give voice to services users and ensure they are properly represented in policy, education and practice. Taylor *et al.* evidence useful dissemination strategies they themselves have used, but, more generally, they warn that social work research does not always get properly fed back to or discussed with service users. Getting it published in an academic journal or book or attempting to influence the policy-making process is seen as disingenuous if the people directly involved and affected are not also part of the feedback and discussion and if this was not done in an 'accessible and inclusive' way.

Moving forward

These authors are striving in different ways to develop and inform practice and policy in the social work sector – during turbulent and challenging times. The context in which this research community currently operates poses significant questions as to how best it ought to respond and in which contested areas it ought to engage. We present here, in effect, a snapshot of social work research in the UK in 2015 affording a glimpse of the range and variety of research that our community engages in through their work. But the emphasis in this book has been on innovation, as we strongly believe that the mere delivery of social work research is insufficient of itself to affect such change – both in terms of impact on the ground and the standing of our knowledge base as a discipline in its own right. It is innovation at the boundaries, at the edges, in the places that others seldom look and in new and creative forms – that offers us the most opportunities to move forward.

And so, as we make our way towards the end of this book, the time arrives for some more general reflections on the state of innovation in social work research. The social and political environment that it inhabits is, as ever, a changing and potent influence on the experience of research for the researcher. There were two significant events in 2014 that merit our attention. The first is the publication of not one, but two reviews into social work education. For the majority of social work researchers, the educative base in taught qualifying programmes is usually the platform from which they are able to research. The fates of professional education and research are intertwined.

Both reports came as something of a surprise, not least because the work of the Social Work Reform Board (2010) had led to a significant redrawing of qualifying professional education in social work that had only commenced in September 2013. Yet at the same time, the Department of Health and Department for Education separately commissioned these two substantial reviews – indicating both a fracture and competitive element mirrored in the appointment of two inaugural Chief Social Workers in 2013. Narey's (2014) report was published early in February and Croisdale-Appleby's (2014) later that month, and they largely represent a battle between genericism and specialism. Both reports recognise the need to develop research-minded practitioners who are able to practice in an evidence-based way. Indeed, Croisdale-Appleby makes a strong bid to develop the social worker as a 'practitioner, professional and a social scientist'. However, neither report offers any indication of a real awareness or sympathy towards the need to generate new social work knowledge, the time needed to do so and the opportunity to deliver this to qualifying students in an effective manner (Moriarty *et al.*, 2014). One danger in this scenario is that we develop the practitioner as a passive recipient of centrally determined, officially sanctioned, 'evidence-based practice' that affords limited opportunity for dissent, reflection, imagination or innovation.

Another danger is that we magically think that research into social work practice and policy will continue regardless of the strength of its link to qualifying education. With such a volatile environment in qualifying training, the concern is that Higher Education Institutions see social work programmes as time consuming and expensive delivery models and look, where possible, to maintaining the discipline in the institution's portfolio in different ways – perhaps through emphasising research endeavour and grant capture. But this is a poor step to take – pushing researchers into social science partnerships without the anchor of professional education. Furthermore, elements of the research infrastructure – such as Quality Related, funding and Research Council awards – arguably already institutionalise research gaps between certain types of institutions and, in so doing, reinforce gaps in the experience of education and professional development in the profession (Bywaters, 2008). The path we must not go down is one where research and qualifying training are seen as unnecessary bedfellows. The growth of immersion training models dominated by technical, employer-led curricula whilst significantly reducing academic input add to this concern.

Of course, the other major event of 2014 was the outcome of the Research Excellence Framework (REF). At the time of writing, the dust had barely settled on the findings published in December of that year. One of the major changes compared with the previous Research Assessment Exercise 2008 (Higher Education Funding Council for England 2006) was the introduction of an 'impact' factor that was assessed through case studies in terms of reach and significance. Impact accounted for 20 per cent of the overall assessment (with outputs at 65% and environment at 15%). Interestingly, one early indication is the different levels of concern researchers have felt dependent on their role. Professors have been more exercised about the REF's effect on intellectual freedom, whilst more junior researchers have been worried about impact. Perhaps unsurprisingly, concerns about institutional inequality were more prevalent in the more teaching-intensive institutions (Murphy and Sage, 2014).

Imogen Taylor (2015) recently presented to the Association of Professors of Social Work conference some initial thoughts on what the REF 2014 means for social work research. She noted the pleasing increase in collaborations in a number of dimensions: between disciplines, between universities and between international partners. However, a note of concern was expressed about the dangers of an emerging link between REF success and a disconnect from teaching. Taylor also noted evidence that methodologically our research community is maturing – with more large-scale, multi-method work, greater rigour in qualitative approaches and an increase in the use of quantitative methods. Imagination and innovation also had a strong showing in the collective submission from social work.

What these developments point towards is the problematic issue of capacity, infrastructure and growth in social work research. Thinking broadly about our comparative strength to other subject areas, we perhaps remain on the early steps of our journey to disciplinary strength and our struggle to emerge within the social science and broader research community has been a constant theme. Indeed, it is only in relatively recent years that the Economic and Social Research Council acknowledged social work as a separate discipline (Bywaters, 2008). But strides are being made and some evidence is emerging of social work's ability to fight its corner. For example, Barner, Holosko and Thyer (2014) compared the citations of US leading academics in social work and psychology and found that overall levels of impact (in its broader sense) did not differ between the two groups. They point to the development of greater rigour in research and the 'professional maturation' of the subject and suggest that this is: '…due to faculty responding to an increased emphasis on scholarship within academic social work, rather than any decline in scholarly influence within psychology' (Barner *et al.*, 2014, p.2457).

Whilst Moriarty *et al.*'s (2014) overview of research explored survey data from 2008 on the tensions between education and research in social work, its messages still resonate. Having surveyed 249 social work academics they found that key issues for researchers included relief from teaching, access to funding and the comparatively limited infrastructure for social work research in many institutions. Inequality was visible between Russell Group researchers, whose typical workload pattern included a third of a week on research and a quarter on teaching, and others, for whom the proportions were reversed. Furthermore, their survey suggested that in terms of specific access to research council funding, the two key success factors appeared to be time and whether one worked within a pre-1992 institution – and not whether one had a PhD or significant experience, perhaps depressingly: '…suggesting that ultimately it is the research culture of the institution that is more important in attracting funding than an individual's own personal resources' (Moriarty *et al.*, 2014, p.13).

A further aspect of this issue is the thorny subject of what it is that social work academics are researching. On broad levels, the role of the Social Care Institute for Excellence (SCIE) has been helpful in grappling with some of the challenges of evidence-based practice. Its inclusive approach to evidence for practice has helped mitigate against some of the hegemony that supports RCTs – supporting, for example, the value of personal testimony and professional opinion. Similarly, systematic review's undoubted merits can also create huge time lags of over ten years between practice developments and the review's conclusions becoming available. Authors such as Fisher (2014) helpfully argue that without an awareness of the reality of implementation, the artifice of RCTs can produce ultimately unhelpful results:

> We began to understand that national policy requires more than evidence of effectiveness: we also need to know whether the intervention can be provided in ordinary services (not just under experimental conditions), whether it is acceptable to the people it was designed to assist and whether it is affordable. (p.5)

The solution is the enhancement of the relationship between practitioners, service users and researchers and the strengthening of the reputational validity of practice research (Fisher, 2014). A question mark remains over the social work research community's engagement here – not helped by a research and funding infrastructure that doesn't always value such approaches. And yet, for most social work researchers, their orientation remains policy driven. Moriarty *et al.* (2014) found that the majority (53%) of social work academics were engaged in some form of service evaluation. Interestingly, relatively few (24%) had been involved in any form of pedagogic research in their previous two years. This chimes with the lack of informed debates on effective professional education in social work and the growth of immersion (fast-track) training. As a profession we have relatively little information about what works best for the professional development of social workers. However, there are some signs in the REF that this deficit is being corrected and the sector should encourage more pedagogical research (Taylor, 2015).

But throughout this challenging journey, and adverse context, the contents of this book reveal that innovative social work research is very much alive and well – reports of its death, as they say, are greatly exaggerated. Indeed, it appears the insistent calls for innovative research with service users, for more research relevant to practice and for transformative research are being met. However, it's clearly important, as Phillips and Shaw (2011) note, that we don't fall into an uncritical, romanticised notion of innovation – beguiled by its novelty or technological prowess. Indeed, innovation is as susceptible to poor practice as any other form. *How* we do our research matters: 'Methodological choices, indeed all aspects of research practices, are not innocent and can rupture or contribute to the negative effects of societal changes' (Phillips and Shaw, 2011, p.610).

Each chapter in this book has managed to explore an example of high-quality, innovative yet practical, applied research that seeks to make that all important difference in practice, in understanding and in the diverse communities in which we live. This is not innovation for the sake of it. In applauding the work of the authors – and acknowledging the contributions of all the people who have, in many different ways, shared of themselves to enable us to understand more – we must particularly praise their commitment to innovative research. It is to be hoped that these examples of innovation will inspire other researchers to think more broadly and creatively about their approach and to make the case for their inclusion in the projects they propose and manage. J. K. Rowling (2008), speaking at Harvard University, also reminds us that behind the innovative lies the imaginative, and it is there – in that space – that we will understand others best:

> Imagination is not only the uniquely human capacity to envision that which is not, and therefore the fount of all invention and innovation. In its arguably most transformative and revelatory capacity, it is the power that enables us to empathise with humans whose experiences we have never shared.

References

Barner, J. R., Holosko, M. J. and Thyer, B. A. (2014) 'American social work and psychology faculty members' scholarly productivity: A controlled comparison of citation impact using the h-index.' *British Journal of Social Work 44*, 2448–2458.

British Association of Social Workers (2013) *Inquiry into the State of Social Work Report. For the All Party Parliamentary Group of Social Work.* Birmingham: British Association of Social Workers. Available at http://cdn.basw.co.uk/upload/basw_90352-5.pdf, accessed on 10 April 2015.

Bywaters, P. (2008) 'Learning from experience: Developing a research strategy for social work in the UK.' *British Journal of Social Work 38*, 936–952.

Croisdale-Appleby, D. (2014) *Re-Visioning Social Work Education: An Independent Review.* London: Department of Health.

D'Cruz, H. and Jones, M. (2004) *Social Work Research.* London: Sage.

Eikeland, O. (2006) 'Condescending ethics and action research.' *Action Research 4*, 1, 37–47.

Fisher, M. (2014) 'The Social Care Institute for Excellence and evidence-based policy and practice.' *British Journal of Social Work*, DOI: 10.1093/bjsw/bcu143.

Freire, P. (1972) *Pedagogy of the Oppressed*. London: Basic Books.

Higher Education Funding Council for England (HEFCE) (2006) *RAE 2008 Panel Criteria and Working Methods, ref RAE 01/2006*. Available at www.rae.ac.uk/pubs/2006/01/, accessed on 9 July 2015.

Joint University Council of Social Work Education Committee (2008) *JUCSWEC's Code of Ethics for Social Work and Social Care Research*. Nottingham/Aix-en-Provence: Joint University Council of Social Work Education Committee. Available at: www.juc.ac.uk/swec-research-code.html, accessed on 10 April 2015.

Mills, C. W. (1959) *The Sociological Imagination*. New York: Oxford University Press.

Moriarty, J., Manthorpe, J., Stevens, M. and Hussein, S., (2014) 'Educators or researchers? Barriers and facilitators to undertaking research among UK social work academics.' *British Journal of Social Work*, DOI: 10.1093/bjsw/bcu077.

Munro, E. (2011) *The Munro Review of Child Protection: Final Report - A Child Centred System*. London: Department of Education.

Murphy, T. and Sage, D. (2014) 'Perceptions of the UK's Research Excellence Framework 2014: A media analysis.' *Journal of Higher Education Policy and Management 36*, 603–615.

Narey, M. (2014) 'Making the education of social workers consistently effective.' Available at www.gov.uk/government/uploads/system/uploads/attachment_data/file/278741/Social_worker_education_report.pdf, accessed on 9 July 2015.

Phillips, C. and Shaw, I. (2011) 'Innovation and the practice of social work research.' *British Journal of Social Work 41*, 609–624.

Rowling, J. K. (2008) 'The fringe benefits of failure and the importance of imagination.' *Harvard Magazine,* 6 May. Available at http://harvardmagazine.com/2008/06/the-fringe-benefits-failure-the-importance-imagination, accessed on 10 April 2015.

Simon, C. and Mosavel, M. (2010) 'Community members as recruiter of human subjects: Ethical considerations. *American Journal of Bioethics 73*, 3, 3–11.

Smith, R. (2012) 'Values, practice and meaning in social work research.' *European Journal of Social Work 15*, 4, 433–448.

Social Work Reform Board (2010) *Building a Safe and Confident Future: One Year On*. London: Department of Education.

Stanley, L. and Wise, S. (1993) *Breaking Out Again: Feminist Ontology and Epistemology*. London: Routledge.

Taylor, I. (2015) 'What the REF tells us about social work research.' *Association of Professors of Social Work Annual Conference*, Aston, 22 January 2015. Available at www.apsw.org.uk/wp-content/uploads/2015/02/APSW-REF-presentation-Imogen-Taylor-22-1-15-Slides-only.pdf, accessed on 10 April 2015.

About the Editors and Contributors

Editors

LOUISE HARDWICK lectures in the Department of Sociology, Social Policy and Criminology at the University of Liverpool. She originally practised as a social worker before moving into academia. As well as research interests in critical pedagogical approaches and the impact of welfare reform on differing social groups, she is also Chair of the registered charity Interchange that links student researchers and voluntary organisations in Participatory Action Research projects.

ROGER SMITH BA, MA, MPhil, PhD is Deputy Head of School (Research) and Professor of Social Work in the School of Applied Social Sciences at Durham University. He qualified as a social worker and practised as a probation officer, specialising in youth justice. He was head of policy with The Children's Society, before taking up an academic role as a social work educator and researcher. During his academic career he has developed an interest in research methods in social work, particularly participatory approaches.

AIDAN WORSLEY BA, MA, MPhil, FRSA is a Professor of Social Work and Executive Dean of the College of Business, Law and Social Sciences at the University of Central Lancashire. He is a qualified, registered social worker, with a background in criminal justice work and wide experience as an academic manager, external examiner and active researcher in areas of social work education, social work and service user led research, practice learning and interprofessional learning and teaching. He has provided training and consultancy to a wide range of organisations across the health and social care sectors.

Contributors

DR MYLES BALFE completed his Ph.D. at the University of Sheffield in 2006. Previously Research Associate at the University of Huddersfield, he is now Lecturer in Medical Sociology at University College Cork, Ireland. Myles has published a number of articles on long-term outcomes of children with sexual behaviour problems.

SARAH BANKS is Professor in the School of Applied Social Sciences and Co-director of the Centre for Social Justice and Community Action at Durham University. She teaches and researches in the fields of professional ethics, community development and community-based participatory research. She has published a range of books on these topics, as author and editor/ co-editor, including: *Ethics and Values in Social Work* (4th edition, 2012 Palgrave Macmillan); *Ethical Issues in Youth Work* (2nd edition, 2010, Routledge); *Critical Community Practice* (2007, The Policy Press); and *Managing Community Practice* (2nd edition, 2013, The Policy Press).

GINA BARRETT works for People First Lambeth where she runs groups and takes part in managing the organisation. She is also part of Shaping Our Lives' Management Committee and gives advice and support to other organisations. Gina aims to change the way that services work with people with learning difficulties. She wants to see people with learning difficulties, like herself, have a better life where they are in control.

PETER BERESFORD OBE is Professor of Social Policy at Brunel University London and Co-Chair of Shaping Our Lives, the national independent disabled people's and service users' organisation and network. He is a Visiting Professor at the Universities of East Anglia and Edgehill. He has a longstanding involvement in issues of participation as educator, activist, researcher and writer. He is author of *A Straight Talking Guide To Being A Mental Health Service User* (2010, PCCS Books).

JOHN CARPENTER is Professor of Social Work and Applied Social Science at Bristol University. He was previously Professor and Director of The Centre for Applied Social and Community Studies at Durham University (1997-2005), Senior Lecturer in Applied Psychology at Kent University (1987-1996) and Lecturer in Social Work and Mental Health at Bristol (1979-1987). He is a registered social worker and chartered psychologist. He has directed research on the outcomes of social work and interprofessional education, adult mental health services and therapeutic services for children and families using quasi-experimental and experimental research designs. His research has been funded by the National Institute of Health Research, ERSC, the Joseph Rowntree Foundation, SCIE and the Departments of Health and Education.

JENNIFER CHRISTENSEN is a KTP Substance Misuse Research Associate with the Psychosocial Research Unit at the University of Central Lancashire. Research interests include the use of mobile methods, recovery orientated practice and service delivery. Her latest project 'Examining Recovery Journeys in East Lancashire using Mobile Methods' focuses on individual recovery journeys.

DR CHERILYN DANCE is a member of the Tilda Goldberg Centre for Social Work and Social Care at the University of Bedfordshire's Institute for Applied Social Research. She has been involved in a range of research studies, many focused on children's services. She has also worked with colleagues Aisha Hutchinson, Sarah Galvani and Debra Allnock on a series of studies exploring practitioners' preparedness for working with alcohol and drug use in social work and social care practice. This work involved the use of a range of research methodologies and had a significant focus on ensuring practitioners, educators, workforce development leads and policy makers could access, use and develop the research findings.

PROFESSOR LENA DOMINELLI holds a Chair in Applied Social Sciences in the School of Applied Social Sciences and is Co-Director at the Institute of Hazards, Risk and Resilience at Durham University where she heads the Programme on Vulnerability and Resilience. She is currently working on a significant NERC funded project (as CoI) called Earthquakes without Frontiers, and another as CoI funded by the Wellcome Trust and DfID on Volcanoes (HIVE). Alongside the wealth of experience she has had as a university educator and researcher, Lena has worked in social services, probation and community development. She has published widely in social work, social policy and sociology. She has also been the recipient of various honours for her contributions to social work including a Medal in 2002 by the Social Affairs Committee of the French Senate, an honorary doctorate in 2008 from the University of KwaZulu-Natal in Durban, South Africa, and the Katherine A Kendall Memorial Award in 2012.

MARTIN ELLIOTT is a social worker with 17 years' statutory children's services experience including: front-line management and practice; contracting and commissioning; and strategic development work. He is an ESRC-funded PhD student at Cardiff University (Wales Doctoral Training Centre). The focus of his current research is a quantitative analysis of 'looked-after' children's numbers in Wales, exploring differences in rates and characteristics in looked-after children populations both between different local authority areas in Wales and between Wales and England.

HARRY FERGUSON is Professor of Social Work at the University of Nottingham. His books include *Child Protection Practice* (2011, Palgrave) and *Understanding Research for Social Policy and Social Work* (2012, Policy Press, with Saul Becker and Alan Bryman).

MIKE FISHER is Director of the Institute of Applied Social Research at the University of Bedfordshire. He was Director of Research at the National Institute for Social Work (1996–2001) and at the Social Care Institute for Excellence (2001–12) before joining the Tilda Goldberg Centre for Research in Social Work and Social Care at the University of Bedfordshire in 2012 as

Professor of Evidence-Based Social Work. He is a registered social worker and a Fellow of the Academy of Social Sciences.

VIC FORREST PhD specialises in collaborative support for people with learning difficulties who are working to bring about social change. He also researches into the processes involved in supporting the self-empowerment of people with learning difficulties. Vic is a community activist and service user. He has worked with a number of different groups of service users and organisations, including the Joseph Rowntree Foundation, Shaping Our Lives and the University of Exeter.

LYNN FROGGETT is Professor of Psychosocial Welfare, with academic background in both the Humanities (History and Philosophy) and Social Sciences (Sociology and Social Policy). She pursued a career in social work practice and management before joining the University of Central Lancashire. The distinctive profile of the Psychosocial Research Unit reflects her interests in trans-disciplinary approaches to the arts and humanities, psychoanalytic studies and the applied social sciences. She has led research projects in a range of fields: health, welfare, education, communities, socially engaged arts and youth justice. Current research interests include a particular focus on practice-near and creative methodologies.

PROFESSOR SIMON HACKETT is Professor of Applied Social Sciences and Principal of St Mary's College at Durham University. His research focuses on child maltreatment and the nature and impact of professional responses to children and families. With Professor Helen Masson, Myles Balfe and Josie Phillips he has recently completed an ESRC-funded study of long-term outcomes for children between 10 and 20 years after the initial identification of their harmful sexual behaviours, which forms the basis of his chapter in this book. Simon was previously Programme Director of G-MAP, a leading UK community-based specialist service for young people. Simon is the author of five books and a wide variety of other book chapters and journal articles relating to children and young people, including *Children and Young People with Harmful Sexual Behaviours* (2014, Research in Practice).

JENNY HUGHES is Senior Lecturer in Drama at the University of Manchester (UK). Her research explores the intersections of theatre, performance and poverty, and she has also conducted research on protest performance, theatre and war, and applied theatre, especially theatre practices with young people living with risk. Publications include a monograph, Performance in a time of terror (Manchester University Press, 2011), which was joint winner of the Theatre and Performance Research Association (TaPRA) New Career Research prize, and a co-authored book (with James Thompson and Michael Balfour), *Performance in place of war* (2009, Seagull/Chicago). At the time of writing, she is working on a research project called 'Poor theatres: a critical exploration of theatre, performance and economic precarity', funded by an Arts and Humanities Research Council Early Career Research Fellowship (www.manchester.ac.uk/poortheatres).

DR AISHA HUTCHINSON works with the Tilda Goldberg Centre for Social Work and Social Care at the University of Bedfordshire. She has post-doctoral experience in a range of research projects in social work and social care, nationally and internationally. Of note, Aisha Hutchinson has been working together with Cherilyn Dance, Professor Sarah Galvani and Dr Debra Allnock on a series of research projects exploring the experiences of social work and social care practitioners of working with people affected by alcohol and drug use. This work has facilitated the development of a body of knowledge on how social work and social care practitioners are equipped to work with alcohol and drug use, and ways to increase confidence and skills for work in this area.

TRICIA JESSIMAN joined the School for Policy Studies as a Research Associate in 2011. She is a qualitative researcher with substantial expertise in service evaluation, commissioning and managing programmes of research as well as participative methodologies with children and young people. She has been the project manager of an RCT of a therapeutic service for children affected by sexual abuse and their safe carers, funded by the NSPCC, since 2012. Prior to that she was a research director in the Families and Children group at NatCen where she led the qualitative aspects of a range of studies and evaluations involving children, young people and families. These included an evaluation of the Public Law Outline in child protection cases, the Disabled Children's Access to Childcare Pilot, Teens and Toddlers (a teenage pregnancy intervention), and The Youth of Today leadership programme for young people. Between 2003 and 2008, Tricia coordinated the research programme at The National Youth Agency.

JADWIGA LEIGH is a qualified social worker and a Lecturer in Social Work at the Sociological Studies Department in Sheffield University. Prior to taking up her post at Sheffield, Jadwiga worked as a social worker for eight years in the field of child protection. Her current research focuses on using visual methods to explore professional identity and organisational culture in social work by employing different psycho-social theories to explore the notion of affect, blame and power. She is currently in the process of turning her PhD thesis into a monograph, which will be called *Blame, Culture and Child Protection*.

DR JULIAN MANLEY researches and teaches at the Psychosocial Research Unit, School of Social Work, University of Central Lancashire. His PhD was a study of social dreaming and his research interests centre on the development of visual thinking and ways of registering affect in the research process within the field of the psychosocial. He is Trustee of the Gordon Lawrence Foundation for the Promotion of Social Dreaming and Chair of its Academic Research

Committee. Other areas of interest include community and cooperation, reactions to climate and environmental change, the socially engaged arts, understanding recovery from substance misuse and group relations in the Tavistock tradition.

PROFESSOR HELEN MASSON is Emerita Professor of Social Work at the University of Huddersfield. Having originally qualified and practised as a social worker in children and family work, she has been an academic for many years involved in qualifying and post-qualifying social work training, research and consultancy and journal editing. Completing her Ph.D. in 2000, Helen has published extensively, most recently in relation to children and young people with harmful sexual behaviours.

BECKI MEAKIN (General Manager at Shaping Our Lives) has worked in the voluntary and community sector for 20 years as a researcher, involvement facilitator and project manager. Prior to this she worked for several marketing agencies. In her spare time, she has a personal interest in teaching English to isolated communities such as refugees and asylum seekers. Becki has broad experience of researching service user experiences of health and social care services and has co-authored a number of reports for Shaping Our Lives. She is a disabled person who has a wealth of knowledge in disability policy and is actively involved in establishing a user-led organisation of disabled people in her area, with the aim of positively influencing policy makers to give people more control over the services they use.

TRISH O'DONNELL is a Development Manager for sexual abuse at the NSPCC. After specialising as a child protection social worker she moved to the NSPCC to set up a specialist centre for working therapeutically with children who had been abused including their carers. As an NSPCC Assistant Director she has been a chair of and member of LSCBs, also chairing and authoring Serious Case Reviews. Since 2010 in her current role she had been responsible for the development and commissioning of research and evaluation of evidence informed services in NSPCCs portfolio of sexual abuse services. Trish led the development of NSPCC's 'Letting the Future In'. Other services include an assessment and intervention service, for men who pose a risk of sexual harm, set in the child protection system and including the voice of the child as a component in assessing risk; a group work programme for women developed by Circles South East but extended in the NSPCC to include work with children in the family. She is currently working on an intervention based on 'Letting the Future In' which will include the forthcoming research findings, a trauma focused approach to notice and listen to troubled children where sexual abuse may be an undisclosed concern.

JOSIE PHILLIPS worked as a social worker and trainer in the local authority for a number of years before moving to the NSPCC to work with children and young people with problematic or harmful sexual behaviour. She completed her MSc in Child Forensic Studies from Leeds University in 2009, and came to Durham University as a Research Associate in School of Applied Social Sciences in the same year. She is currently undertaking her Ph.D. at Durham.

DR JACKIE ROBINSON is a Principal Lecturer in Social Work at De Montfort University, Leicester. Prior to working as a lecturer, Jackie was a social work practitioner and manager working with children and adults with a learning disability, including adults, children and young people with autism and Asperger's syndrome. Jackie's PhD thesis involved participatory research with adults with Asperger's syndrome. Jackie and a small group of adults with Asperger's syndrome designed the study and research tools, analysed the data and disseminated the findings jointly.

NATALIE ROBINSON is an ESRC-funded PhD candidate supervised across sociology and geography at the University of Liverpool, with research interests including visual methodologies, place identity, social in/exclusion and homelessness. She holds a BA in Sociology as well as a Master of Philosophy in Cultural Inquiry from the University of Birmingham. Natalie has previously worked in a support level role in Birmingham's Homeless Service.

DR ALASTAIR ROY is Reader in Psychosocial Research based at the Psychosocial Research Unit, School of Social Work, University of Central Lancashire. He has a particular interest in the development of psychosocial and psychosocietal approaches to research. Exploring the links between social responsibility and the social imagination has been central to work undertaken across the fields of social welfare, health and the cultural sector. Recent work has centred on substance use, contemporary masculinities and the role of cultural activity in health, welfare and justice. He is currently leading a three-year Knowledge Transfer Partnership (KTP) funded by the ESRC and the Technology Strategy Board, which uses mobile methods to explore the evidence base around recovery-oriented drug and alcohol treatment provision.

PAT STARKEY is an Honorary Research Fellow in the Department of History at the University of Liverpool. Her research interests include the history of voluntary social work agencies working with families and women's history. She is currently working on material in the archives of Liverpool Cathedral that relates to various forms of relief work undertaken during the Second World War and on aspects of local ecumenical relations.

JENNIFER TAYLOR is an author and researcher. She works at People First Lambeth and goes to a lot of meetings with other organisations, such as Shaping Our Lives and the Social Care Institute for Excellence. She speaks out for people with learning difficulties to help them stand up for themselves and take control of their own lives. Jennifer is a woman with learning difficulties.

PROFESSOR EMERITA BOGUSIA TEMPLE is Professor Emerita at the University of Central Lancashire. She has had an interest in cross-disciplinary methodology, both quantitative and qualitative, for most of her career. Her research has been funded by statutory and voluntary organisations as well as research councils. She has published and presented in a range of areas, including the use of narrative, research with disabled people and refugees but she is particularly interested in cross-language research. Her latest book – *Approaches to Social Research: The Case of Deaf Studies* (Young and Temple, 2014, Oxford University Press) highlights the problems of current neglect of the significance of the actual language used in research.

DR SUE THOMPSON began her career as a nurse, but then went on to study sociology before becoming a qualified social worker in 1992. Being committed to informed and reflective practice, Sue combined practice with study and research, being awarded an MA in 1994 and a doctorate in 2012. Since leaving direct social work practice she has continued her own professional development, and facilitated that of others, through mentoring, practice teaching, tutoring and the writing or co-writing of books including *Age Discrimination* (2005, Russell House Publishing), *Reciprocity and Dependency in Old Age: Indian and UK Perspectives* (2013, Springer), *The Critically Reflective Practitioner* (2008, Palgrave Macmillan) and *The Social Work Companion* (2008, Palgrave Macmillan). As a director of Avenue Media Solutions[1] she is currently involved in the production of e-learning and v-learning resources and continues to facilitate continuous professional development as part of the team that hosts the Avenue Professional Development Programme.[2]

NICOLETTE WADE is a Principal Lecturer in Social Work at the University of Bedfordshire. She is a qualified social worker and whilst in practice had responsibility for developing a range of services for people with dementia living in a semi-rural area.

DAVID WESTLAKE is a Senior Research Fellow at the Tilda Goldberg Centre, University of Bedfordshire. His research has incorporated a wide range of topics and methods within child and family social work. His methodological interests lie in using experimental and quasi-experimental methods in 'real world' settings, and the challenges and opportunities this entails. David is currently leading an action research project which aims to use embedded evaluation to change organisational culture in a local authority and improve practice and outcomes for children and families.

---

1   www.avenuemediasolutions.com

2   www.apdp.org.uk

Subject Index

Author Index